The Church

Sacrament of Salvation

The Didache Series

— SEMESTER EDITION —

The Didache

[DID-uh-kay]

The *Didache* is the first known Christian catechesis. Written in the first century, the *Didache* is the earliest known Christian writing outside of Scripture. The name of the work, "*Didache*," is indeed appropriate for such a catechesis because it comes from the Greek word for "teaching," and indicates that this writing contains the teaching of the Apostles.

The *Didache* is a catechetical summary of Christian Sacraments, practices, and morality. Though written in the first century, its teaching is timeless. The *Didache* was probably written by the disciples of the Twelve Apostles, and it presents the Apostolic Faith as taught by those closest to Jesus Christ. This series of books takes the name of this early catechesis because it shares in the Church's mission of passing on that same Faith, in its rich entirety, to new generations.

Below is an excerpt from the *Didache* in which we see a clear example of its lasting message, a message that speaks to Christians of today as much as it did to the first generations of the Church. The world is different, but the struggle for holiness is the same. In the *Didache*, we are instructed to embrace virtue, to avoid sin, and to live the Beatitudes of our Lord.

My child, flee from everything that is evil and everything that is like it. Do not be wrathful, for wrath leads to murder, nor jealous nor contentious nor quarrelsome, for from all these murder ensues.

My child, do not be lustful, for lust leads to fornication, nor a filthy-talker nor a lewd-looker, for from all these adulteries ensue.

My child, do not be an interpreter of omens, since it leads to idolatry, nor an enchanter nor an astrologer nor a magical purifier, nor wish to see them, for from all these idolatry arises.

My child, do not be a liar, for lying leads to theft, nor avaricious nor conceited, for from all these thefts are produced.

My child, do not be a complainer, since it leads to blasphemy, nor self-willed nor evil-minded, for from all these blasphemies are produced.

Be meek, for the meek will inherit the earth.

Be long-suffering and merciful and guileless and peaceable and good, and revere always the words you have heard.[1]

The *Didache* is the teaching of the Apostles and, as such, it is the teaching of the Church. Accordingly, this book series makes extensive use of the most recent comprehensive catechesis provided to us, the *Catechism of the Catholic Church*. The *Didache* series also relies heavily on Sacred Scripture, the lives of the saints, the Fathers of the Church, and the teaching of Vatican II as witnessed by the pontificates of Bl. John Paul II and Benedict XVI.

1. Swett, Ben H. " The Didache (The Teaching)." © January 30, 1998. http://bswett.com/1998-01Didache.html

The Church

Sacrament of Salvation

Author: Dr. Scott Hahn
General Editor: Rev. James Socias

MIDWEST THEOLOGICAL FORUM
Woodridge, Illinois

Published in the United States of America by

Midwest Theological Forum
1420 Davey Road
Woodridge, IL 60517

Tel: 630-739-9750
Fax: 630-739-9758
mail@mwtf.org
www.theologicalforum.org

Author: Dr. Scott Hahn

General Editor: Rev. James Socias

Editor in Chief: Jeffrey Cole

Editorial Board: Rev. James Socias, Rev. Peter V. Armenio, Dr. Scott Hahn, Jeffrey Cole

Contributing Editors: Michael Hahn, Gerald Korson

Design and Production: Marlene Burrell, Jane Heineman of April Graphics, Highland Park, Illinois

Acknowledgements

Excerpts from the English translation of the *Catechism of the Catholic Church* for the United States of America, copyright ©1994, United States Catholic Conference, Inc.—Libreria Editrice Vaticana. Used with permission.

Excerpts from the English translation of the *Catechism of the Catholic Church: Modifications from the Editio Typica*, copyright ©1997, United States Catholic Conference, Inc.—Libreria Editrice Vaticana. Used with permission.

Scripture quotations are adapted from the *Revised Standard Version of the Bible*, copyright ©1946, 1952, 1971, and the *New Revised Standard Version of the Bible*, copyright ©1989, by the Division of Christian Education of the National Council of the Churches of Christ in the United States of America, and are used by permission. All rights reserved.

Excerpts from the *Code of Canon Law, Latin/English Edition*, are used with permission, copyright ©1983 Canon Law Society of America, Washington, DC.

Citations of official Church documents from Neuner, Josef, SJ and Dupuis, Jacques, SJ, eds., *The Christian Faith: Doctrinal Documents of the Catholic Church*, 5th ed. (New York: Alba House, 1992). Used with permission.

Excerpts from *Vatican II: The Conciliar and Post Conciliar Documents, New Revised Edition* edited by Austin Flannery, OP, copyright ©1992, Costello Publishing Company, Inc., Northport, NY, are used with permission of the publisher, all rights reserved. No part of these excerpts may be reproduced, stored in a retrieval system, or transmitted in any form or by any means—electronic, mechanical, photocopying, recording or otherwise, without express written permission of Costello Publishing Company.

Disclaimer: The editor of this book has attempted to give proper credit to all sources used in the text and illustrations. Any miscredit or lack of credit is unintended and will be corrected in the next edition.

Library of Congress Cataloging-in-Publication Data

Hahn, Scott.
    The church : sacrament of salvation / author, Scott Hahn ; general editor, James Socias. – 1st ed.
       p. cm. – (The Didache series)
    Includes index.
    ISBN 978-1-936045-09-9 (hardcover : alk. paper)
    1. Church – Textbooks. 2. Salvation – Christianity – Textbooks. I. Socias, James. II. Title.
  BV600.3.H34 2010
  262 – dc22
                                               2009036076

Printed in Canada

TABLE OF CONTENTS

TABLE OF CONTENTS

TABLE OF CONTENTS

TABLE OF CONTENTS

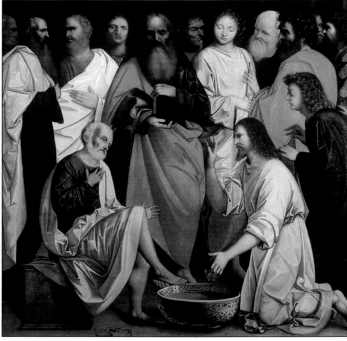

Washing of the Feet by Agostino da Lodi.

ABBREVIATIONS USED FOR THE BOOKS OF THE BIBLE

OLD TESTAMENT

Genesis	Gn	Tobit	Tb	Ezekiel	Ez
Exodus	Ex	Judith	Jdt	Daniel	Dn
Leviticus	Lv	Esther	Est	Hosea	Hos
Numbers	Nm	1 Maccabees	1 Mc	Joel	Jl
Deuteronomy	Dt	2 Maccabees	2 Mc	Amos	Am
Joshua	Jos	Job	Jb	Obadiah	Ob
Judges	Jgs	Psalms	Ps	Jonah	Jon
Ruth	Ru	Proverbs	Prv	Micah	Mi
1 Samuel	1 Sm	Ecclesiastes	Eccl	Nahum	Na
2 Samuel	2 Sm	Song of Songs	Sg	Habakkuk	Hb
1 Kings	1 Kgs	Wisdom	Wis	Zephaniah	Zep
2 Kings	2 Kgs	Sirach	Sir	Haggai	Hg
1 Chronicles	1 Chr	Isaiah	Is	Zechariah	Zec
2 Chronicles	2 Chr	Jeremiah	Jer	Malachi	Mal
Ezra	Ezr	Lamentations	Lam		
Nehemiah	Neh	Baruch	Bar		

NEW TESTAMENT

Matthew	Mt	Ephesians	Eph	Hebrews	Heb
Mark	Mk	Philippians	Phil	James	Jas
Luke	Lk	Colossians	Col	1 Peter	1 Pt
John	Jn	1 Thessalonians	1 Thes	2 Peter	2 Pt
Acts of the Apostles	Acts	2 Thessalonians	2 Thes	1 John	1 Jn
Romans	Rom	1 Timothy	1 Tm	2 John	2 Jn
1 Corinthians	1 Cor	2 Timothy	2 Tm	3 John	3 Jn
2 Corinthians	2 Cor	Titus	Ti	Jude	Jude
Galatians	Gal	Philemon	Phlm	Revelation	Rev

GENERAL ABBREVIATIONS

AG — *Ad Gentes Divinitus* (Decree on the Church's Missionary Activity)

CA — *Centesimus Annus* (On the Hundredth Anniversary)

CCC — *Catechism of the Catholic Church*

CDF — Congregation for the Doctrine of the Faith

CIC — *Code of Canon Law* (*Codex Iuris Canonici*)

CPG — *Solemn Profession of Faith*: Credo of the People of God

CT — *Catechesi Tradendæ* (On Catechesis in our Time)

DCE — *Deus Caritas Est* (God is Love)

DD — *Dies Domini* (The Lord's Day)

DH — *Dignitatis Humanæ* (Declaration on Religious Freedom)

DoV — *Donum Vitæ* (Respect for Human Life)

DV — *Dei Verbum* (Dogmatic Constitution on Divine Revelation)

DS — Denzinger-Schonmetzer, *Enchiridion Symbolorum, definitionum et declarationum de rebus fidei et morum* (1985)

EV — *Evangelium Vitæ* (The Gospel of Life)

FC — *Familiaris Consortio* (On the Family)

GS — *Gaudium et Spes* (Pastoral Constitution on the Church in the Modern World)

HV — *Humanæ Vitæ* (On Human Life)

IOE — *Iura et Bona* (Declaration on Euthanasia)

LE — *Laborem Exercens* (On Human Work)

LG — *Lumen Gentium* (Dogmatic Constitution on the Church)

MF — *Mysterium Fidei* (The Mystery of Faith)

PH — *Persona Humana* (Declaration on Sexual Ethics)

PL — J.P. Migne, ed., *Patrologia Latina* (Paris: 1841-1855)

PT — *Pacem in Terris* (On Establishing Universal Peace)

QA — *Quadragesimo Anno* (The Fortieth Year)

RP — *Reconciliatio et Pænitentia* (On Reconciliation and Penance)

RH — *Redemptor Hominis* (The Redeemer of Man)

SC — *Sacrosanctum Concilium* (The Constitution on the Sacred Liturgy)

SRS — *Solicitudo Rei Socialis* (On Social Concerns)

SS — *Spe Salvi* (In Hope We Are Saved)

USCCB — United States Conference of Catholic Bishops

VS — *Veritatis Splendor* (Splendor of the Truth)

Introduction

he eternal Father, by a free and hidden plan of His own wisdom and goodness, created the whole world. His plan was to raise men to a participation of the divine life. Fallen in Adam, God the Father did not leave men to themselves, but ceaselessly offered helps to salvation, in view of Christ, the Redeemer "who is the image of the invisible God, the firstborn of every creature" (Col 1:15). All the elect, before time began, the Father "foreknew and pre-destined to become conformed to the image of His Son, that he should be the firstborn among many brethren" (Rom 8:29). He planned to assemble in the holy Church all those who would believe in Christ. Already from the beginning of the world the foreshadowing of the Church took place. It was prepared in a remarkable way throughout the history of the people of Israel and by means of the Old Covenant.[1] In the present era of time the Church was constituted and, by the outpouring of the Spirit, was made manifest. At the end of time it will gloriously achieve completion, when, as is read in the Fathers, all the just, from Adam and "from Abel, the just one, to the last of the elect,"[2] will be gathered together with the Father in the universal Church....

All men are called to belong to the new people of God. Wherefore this people, while remaining one and only one, is to be spread throughout the whole world and must exist in all ages, so that the decree of God's will may be fulfilled. In the beginning God made human nature one and decreed that all His children, scattered as they were, would finally be gathered together as one (cf. Heb 1:2). It was for this purpose that God sent His Son, whom He appointed heir of all things, that He might be teacher, king and priest of all, the head of the new and universal people of the sons of God. For this too God sent the Spirit of His Son as Lord and Life-giver. He it is who brings together the whole Church and each and every one of those who believe, and who is the well-spring of their unity in the teaching of the apostles and in fellowship, in the breaking of bread and in prayers.

(*Lumen Gentium*, 2, 13)

---

1. Cf. S. Cyprianus, *Epist.* 64, 4: PL 3, 1017. CSEL (Hartel), III B, p. 720. S. Hilarius Pict., *In Mt.* 23, 6: PL 9, 1047. S. Augustinus, passim. S. Cyrillus Alex., *Glaph. in Gen.* 2, 10: PG 69, 110 A.
2. Cf. S. Gregorius M., *Hom. in Evang.* 19, 1: PL 76, 1154 B. S. Augustinus, *Serm.* 341, 9, 11: PL 39, 1499 s. S. Io. Damascenus, *Adv. Iconocl.* 11: PG 96, 1357.

God Prepares the Way for His Church in the Old Testament

Beginning with Adam and Eve, God gradually unfolded his plan of salvation to the world.

The Church
CHAPTER 1

God Prepares the Way for His Church in the Old Testament

Christians of the first centuries said, "The world was created for the sake of the Church."[1] God created the world for the sake of communion with his divine life, a communion brought about by the "convocation" of men in Christ, and this "convocation" is the Church. The Church is the goal of all things...[2]

Just as God's will is creation and is called "the world," so his intention is the salvation of men, and it is called "the Church."[3] (CCC 760)

rom all eternity, God had a plan to draw all people into *communion* with himself—a plan that was put into effect at the dawn of *creation*. Even after the Original Sin committed by Adam and Eve, God did not abandon his people, but provided a plan for their *redemption*. He promised to send them a *Redeemer*, who would restore mankind to his friendship.[4] In this manner, God foresaw Christ and the Church from the very dawn of creation. Thus, "we begin our investigation of the Church's mystery by meditating on her origin in the Holy Trinity's plan and her progressive realization in history."[5]

Beginning with Adam and Eve, God gradually unfolded his plan of salvation to the world. He established covenants with his people and revealed his moral law to prepare mankind for the coming of his Son.

The stories in the *Old Testament* relate the gradual *Revelation* of God to the world. In the fullness of time, God fulfilled his promise of a Redeemer, sending his Son, Jesus Christ, who was born of the Virgin Mary. Jesus would reveal the fullness of truth, including the Revelation of God as a communion of divine Persons—Father, Son, and Holy Spirit—which is the central mystery of our faith. His sacrifice on the Cross would reconcile God and man, restoring the communion that had been lost in Original Sin. Thus, the Incarnation of Jesus Christ is the pivotal event in human history.

Through his Death on the Cross, Jesus offered the perfect sacrifice for our sins. The salvation won by Christ on Calvary continues today through the ministry of the Church, and it is through the Church that God reconciles his people with himself.

The Church is both the means and the goal of God's plan: prefigured in creation, prepared for in the Old Covenant, founded by the words and actions of Jesus Christ, fulfilled by his redeeming cross and his Resurrection, the Church has been manifested as the mystery of salvation by the outpouring of the Holy Spirit. She will be perfected in the glory of heaven as the assembly of all the redeemed of the earth.[6] (CCC 778)

The Church founded by Christ is known as the Family of God, the People of God, the Mystical Body of Christ, the Kingdom of Heaven, the Temple of the Holy Spirit, the Bride of Christ, the Sacrament of Salvation, and by many more names, each of which illuminates specific aspects of the Church's nature. However, the common thread linking each of these names is the Church's relation to God. Apart from its communion in Christ and intimate sharing in the Divine Life of the Blessed Trinity, the Church has no life. This means that the Church is entirely "Christ-centered."

Holy Trinity (detail) by Balen. The Church founded by Christ is known as the Family of God, the People of God, the Mystical Body of Christ, the Kingdom of Heaven, the Temple of the Holy Spirit, the Bride of Christ, the Sacrament of Salvation, and by many more names, each of which illuminates specific aspects of the Church's nature.

Like the dual nature of Christ himself—true God and true man—the Church has two distinct natures. As the Mystical Body of Christ, the Church is a divine institution. As a community, into which individuals are incorporated through Baptism, the Church also has a human dimension. In order to better understand the nature of the Church, therefore, we need to go back to the very beginning of the human story to see how God prepared his people for the coming of Christ and the establishment of his Church.

IN THIS CHAPTER, WE WILL ADDRESS SEVERAL QUESTIONS:

✤ Why were we created?

✤ How did God prepare his people for the Church?

✤ How was the Church foreshadowed in the Old Testament?

✤ What is the meaning of *covenant*?

✤ What covenants did God establish with the Israelites?

✤ What were the primary features of the Old Testament Covenant, and how did these features point the way to the New Covenant?

God Creating the Sun, the Moon and the Stars by Brueghel. Created in communion with him, Adam and Eve would enjoy an intimate friendship with God in the paradise that he had created for them.

CREATION IS MADE FOR MAN

In the beginning God created the heavens and the earth. (Gn 1: 1)

These opening verses from the Book of Genesis relate God's great work of creation. We see that the universe was formless and void in the beginning, that God brought all creation into being by the power of his Word.

The six days that follow are divided into two corresponding groups of three days. Throughout Scripture, the number three is used to denote perfection or completeness. Here, the Sacred Author uses the number three to signify the perfection of God's creation.

In the first set of three days, God gave shape to the world, overcoming its formlessness and creating the forms that would sustain life.

- ✤ On the first day, God created light and separated it from the darkness, calling one "day" and the other "night." (Gn 1: 3-5)

- ✤ On the second day, he separated the waters, forming the "sky" and the "sea." (Gn 1: 6-8)

- ✤ On the third day, he created "dry land" and gave life to the "plants and vegetation." (Gn 1: 9-13)

During the next set of three days, God filled the world with the life that will rule over the forms that he has created.

- ✤ On the fourth day, God created the "sun and moon" to rule over the "day and night." (Gn 1:14-19)

- ✤ On the fifth day, he called forth "birds and fish" to rule over "sky and sea." (Gn 1: 20-23)

- ✤ On the sixth day, he created "animals" to rule over the "dry land." (Gn 1: 24-25)

By dividing the act of creation into these two corresponding groups of three-day periods, the creation story is telling us that the act of creation was complete and perfect. However, at this point in Scripture, the purpose of God's creation had not yet been revealed. Finally, God added one last creature to his new world.

> God said, "Let us make man in our image, after our likeness; and let them have dominion over the fish of the sea, and over the birds of the air, and over the cattle, and over all the earth, and over every creeping thing that creeps upon the earth." So God created man in his own image, in the image of God he created him; male and female he created them. (Gn 1:26-27)

By creating Adam and Eve, and placing them over his creation, God was not only creating caretakers or stewards for his new world. Instead, God made man and woman in his "own image," endowing them with the ability to understand, to make choices, and to love. Created in communion with him, Adam and Eve would enjoy an intimate friendship with God in the paradise that he had created for them. The world had been created for mankind, and mankind had been created for God.

> The *imago Dei* consists in man's fundamental orientation to God, which is the basis of human dignity and of the inalienable rights of the human person. Because every human being is an image of God, he cannot be made subservient to any this-worldly system or finality. His sovereignty within the cosmos, his capacity for social existence, and his knowledge and love of the Creator—all are rooted in man's being made in the image of God.[7]

WE WERE MADE FOR COMMUNION WITH GOD

> God, infinitely perfect and blessed in himself, in a plan of sheer goodness freely created man to make him share in his own blessed life. (CCC 1)

What does Scripture mean when it says that we were made in the "image and likeness" of God? When reading Scripture, it is often best to understand the meaning of a particular word or phrase by looking to

Paradise by Cranach the Elder.
As descendants of Adam and Eve, we, too, are children of God made in his "image and likeness."

other instances of its use in the text. In this case, we next see the term "image and likeness" used to describe Adam becoming the father of Seth "in his own likeness, after his image."[8]

Just as Seth had received his biological nature from his father, Adam shared in the nature of his heavenly Father. As human beings, we are unique in possessing intelligence, free will, and the capacity to love. Above all, we possess the ability to know God and to understand the purpose of our existence. These gifts enable us to love God and to follow his plan for our lives, and thus fulfill our purpose of entering into communion with him. Moreover, through the Church, people are predestined to conform to and reproduce the image of the Son of God, who took on human nature.

There is a second significance in the use of the term "image and likeness." It denotes the relationship between a father and a son. Unlike the birds of the air or the fish of the sea, Adam was a beloved son of the Father. As descendants of Adam and Eve, we, too, are children of God made in his "image and likeness."

> Created in the image of God, human beings are by nature bodily and spiritual, men and women made for one another, persons oriented towards communion with God and with one another, wounded by sin and in need of salvation, and destined to be conformed to Christ, the perfect image of the Father, in the power of the Holy Spirit.[9]

GOD PREPARES HIS PEOPLE FOR THE CHURCH

> This "family of God" is gradually formed and takes shape during the stages of human history, in keeping with the Father's plan. In fact, "already present in figure at the beginning of the world, this Church was prepared in marvelous fashion in the history of the people of Israel and the old Advance."[10] (CCC 759)

From the beginning of creation, God desired to gather all mankind into communion with himself. Adam and Eve had been created in communion with God, but they lost this gift when they disobeyed God and ate from the Tree of the Knowledge of Good and Evil. What follows this infamous act in Scripture is the story of God's efforts to restore the original communion for which mankind had been created. The biblical record of how God's plan of redemption in Christ unfolded is called *salvation history*.

God Presents Eve to Adam (detail from *Garden of Earthly Delights*) by Bosch. As originally designed by God, creation was a setting where man and woman could know God and live in his presence.

Beginning in the first books of the Old Testament, we read how God established covenants with his people and revealed his *moral law*, preparing the world for the sending of his Son, Jesus Christ. In the New Testament, we see how these preparations come to fruition in the Person and life of Christ and in the Church he established.

One way of following the events of salvation history is to see it as a series of covenants between God and man. In fact, the idea of *covenant* is a central theme throughout the entire Bible. But what exactly is a covenant? A covenant is a solemn agreement between God and people—an agreement that involves mutual commitments and promises.

Throughout salvation history, God made use of covenants to unite himself to his people. By examining God's covenants with Adam, Abraham, Moses, and David, we will see how God prepared his people for the New and Everlasting Covenant in Christ Jesus.

> Fallen in Adam, God the Father did not leave men to themselves, but ceaselessly offered helps to salvation, in view of Christ, the Redeemer "who is the image of the invisible God, the firstborn of every creature." All the elect, before time began, the Father "foreknew and predestined to become conformed to the image of His Son, that he should be the firstborn among many brethren." He planned to assemble in the holy Church all those who would believe in Christ. (*Lumen Gentium* 2)

The Saints
PILLARS OF THE CHURCH

St. Irenæus of Lyons
EXPLAINING GOD'S COVENANT PLAN

St. Irenæus of Lyons is generally regarded as the father of Christian theology. He was born around AD 125 in Smyrna (located in modern-day Turkey) and was raised in a devoutly Christian home. At that time, Smyrna was home to a number of Christians who had known the Apostles personally, and it was from one of these men—the future martyr St. Polycarp, a disciple of the Apostle John—that he received his education and Christian formation.

St. Irenæus was ordained a priest and was sent to the missionary territory of what is now Lyons, in France. Christianity had only recently arrived in this area, and in addition to the challenges of evangelization and combating heresy, the faithful of Lyons had to contend with fierce persecution from the Roman emperor, Marcus Aurelius. After the first bishop of Lyons was martyred AD 178, St. Irenæus was named as his successor. He immediately set about the task of being both a shepherd to his new flock and a missionary to those who had yet to hear about Christ.

One of St. Irenæus' great contributions to the Church is that he spoke of the "old" and "new" covenants of Scripture. He taught that the covenants of the Old Testament and the New Covenant of Jesus were related, and he interpreted all of salvation history as a series of covenants in which God revealed his plan to humanity in stages as his people became ready to receive it. God's covenants with Adam, Noah, Abraham, Moses, and David expressed God's love for creation, his forgiveness, and his desire for the redemption of humanity.

St. Irenæus taught that the same God was there within each covenant, and that each of the covenants God made with humanity represented a progression from the previous covenant. Finally, when Jesus came as the Messiah, humanity was reunited with the image of God, thus restoring what had been lost by Original Sin.

The tradition of the Church relates that St. Irenæus was martyred in Lyons around AD 202 during a persecution by the emperor Septimius Severus.

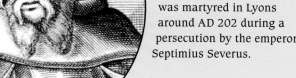

St. Irenæus of Lyons, pray for us.

THE COVENANT OF CREATION

> Already from the beginning of the world the foreshadowing of the Church took place. It was prepared in a remarkable way throughout the history of the people of Israel and by means of the Old Covenant. (*Lumen Gentium* 2)

The story of creation tells us how God, after creating the Heavens and the earth, saw all that he had made and declared that it was good. Finally, he rested on the seventh day, blessing this day and making it holy. This day of rest was the first *Sabbath*, intended by God to be the sign of his covenant with creation.

> The Lord said…"The people of Israel shall keep the sabbath, observing the sabbath throughout their generations, a perpetual covenant. It is a sign for ever between me and the people of Israel that in six days the Lord made heaven and earth, and on the seventh day he rested." (Ex 31: 12, 16-17)

In making the seventh day his day of rest, God made a covenant with all of creation and specifically with mankind: God gives himself as a Father to Adam, and Adam in turn is made to give of himself, through his obedience as a son, back to God.

The Sabbath was created in order to remind us that we are created out of God's love so that we may enter into communion with him. For us, this communion is expressed in the way we live our lives and especially in our prayer and worship of God on the Lord's Day.

These very same tasks—work and worship—were what God gave to Adam when he created him. After placing him in the garden, God told Adam to till it and to keep it. Adam was to have dominion over every plant and tree, and over the birds of the air, the fish of the sea, and every living thing that moved upon the earth.[11] We can see that human work is something that has had special value from the very beginning of creation. Work is not a curse, even though it was eventually made harder because of Adam's sin. Just as God labored to bring creation into existence, we are called to work in imitation of God.

God Resting After Creation, Byzantine Mosaic.
This day of rest was the first Sabbath, intended by God to be the sign of his covenant with creation.

It is important to note, however, that in the Bible the words "till" and "keep" do not refer to manual labor alone. In fact, the only other time these words are found together in the first five books of the Bible, called the *Pentateuch*, is in reference to the ministry of the priests in the sanctuary of the Temple.[12] Adam's responsibility as a son of God was, therefore, not just to exercise dominion over creation, but to strive for holiness as well.

ADAM'S DISOBEDIENCE

As originally designed by God, creation was a setting where man and woman could know God and live in his presence. Everything was "good," as God had pronounced. However, in the third chapter of Genesis, something went wrong. An intruder had entered the garden.

> The serpent was more subtle than any other wild creature that the Lord God had made. He said to the woman, "Did God say, 'You shall not eat of any tree of the garden?'" And the woman said to the serpent, "We may eat of the fruit of the trees of the garden, but God said, 'You shall not eat of the fruit of the tree which is in the midst of the garden, neither shall you touch it, lest you die.'" But the serpent said to the woman, "You will not die. For God knows that when you eat of it your

Adam and Eve's Life of Toil by Master Bertram. "therefore the LORD God sent him forth from the garden of Eden, to till the ground from which he was taken." (Gn 3: 23)

eyes will be opened, and you will be like God, knowing good and evil." So...she took of its fruit and ate; and she also gave some to her husband, and he ate. (Gn 3: 1-6)

When God placed Adam and Eve in the Garden of Eden, he gave them a command. They could eat the fruit from every tree in the garden except one, the Tree of the Knowledge of Good and Evil. This command also came with an ominous warning: "In the day that you eat of it, you shall die."[13]

But the serpent told Eve that she and Adam would *not* die, and from all appearances it would seem that he was right. On the day they ate of the fruit, Adam and Eve did not die a *physical* death. However, the serpent deceived Adam and Eve, neglecting to point out that they would die a *spiritual* death when they ate the fruit. This is why the serpent is typically identified as the *Devil*, whom Jesus calls "the father of lies" and "a murderer from the beginning."[14]

When Adam and Eve disobeyed God, they lost something greater than natural life. They lost supernatural life and their original communion with God. Losing this life is true death— a death much worse than mere physical death. By their sin, Adam and Eve forfeited their own communion with God, as well as the inheritance of that communion, which they would not be able to hand down to their children. As a result, the entire human race after Adam and Eve would be burdened with Original Sin and would be born into a state of lost *grace*—a world fallen from the original design with which it was created.

A PLAN FOR RESTORATION

Although the Original Sin committed by our first parents ruptured their relationship with God and introduced sin and suffering into the world, it did not destroy the plan that God had for his people. God already knew that Adam and Eve would fall to sin, and he had a plan through which he could bring their descendants back to him. In fact, not only would this plan restore mankind to its original communion, it would also raise God's people to an even greater communion.

After confronting Adam and Eve about their sin, God turned to Satan and told him, "I will put enmity between you and the woman, and between your seed and her seed; he shall bruise your head, and you shall bruise his heel."[15]

> After his fall, man was not abandoned by God. On the contrary, God calls him and in a mysterious way heralds the coming victory over evil and his restoration from his fall.[16] This passage in Genesis is called the *Protoevangelium* ("first gospel"): the first announcement of the Messiah and Redeemer, of a battle between the serpent and the Woman, and of the final victory of a descendant of hers. (CCC 410)

Sin and death had entered the world to stay, but sin and death would not have the final say. With his first announcement of the *Messiah*, God promised mankind's eventual redemption in Christ and began unfolding his plan to draw man back to himself.

This plan, however, would neither be easy nor quick to accomplish. Once evil had entered the world, it firmly took root. Adam and Eve had two sons, Cain and Abel. The next thing that we read in Genesis is the story of how Cain killed Abel. The story of Cain and Abel shows how all future generations would be affected by Original Sin. Deprived of intimate knowledge of God's love and his moral law, the descendants of Adam and Eve are blind to their own wicked ways and ruled by their passions.

The Dove Returns to Noah by Tissot.
God established his second covenant with Noah.
"I establish my covenant with you, that never again shall all
flesh be cut off by the waters of a flood, and never again
shall there be a flood to destroy the earth." (Gn 9:11)

Adam and Eve had a third son, Seth, after Cain had killed Abel. These two sons' descendants would fill the earth. Cain's descendants were notoriously wicked, but Seth's offspring were more faithful to God. From the family of Seth, God would call Noah, who delivered the human race from the great Flood.[17]

God established his second covenant with Noah, after destroying the earth to recreate it from the lineage of this righteous man. However, just as God's family had been torn apart by sin after the *Fall*, man once again fell into sin after the Flood. As we have seen, sin always causes more sin. Yet, God continued his task of regathering his family. God blessed Noah's firstborn son, Shem, for his obedience and faithfulness, and it is in Shem's family line that we find one of the most important people in the Old Testament. His name was Abram, and through him God would reunite his family.

GOD CALLS ABRAM

The remote *preparation* for this gathering together of the People of God begins when he calls Abraham and promises that he will become the father of a great people. (CCC 762)

Abram was the great-great-great-great-great-great-great-grandson of Shem, and he lived in Ur, a prosperous center of trade that was located in modern-day Iraq. Abram was the firstborn son of his family and had inherited great power and wealth. He was the leader of a large tribe consisting of possibly 3,000 people.

Most of Abram's life is not recorded in the Bible. We can imagine he lived a normal life for the time, running his family estate and maintaining the relationships necessary for survival. If there was unhappiness in Abram's life, it was that he never had children and that there was no one to whom he could pass on his inheritance. By the time God spoke to him, Abram was already seventy-five years old.

> The LORD said to Abram, "Go forth from your country and your kindred and your father's house to the land that I will show you. And I will make of you a great nation, and I will bless you, and make your name great, so that you will be a blessing. I will bless those who bless you, and him who curses you I will curse; and in you all the families of the earth shall bless themselves" (Gn 12:1-3)

In speaking to Abram, God made three distinct promises:

✤ **Land and Nation.** Any people who did not possess land could not be a nation, great or otherwise. God promised that Abram's descendants would have a vast amount of land where they would live and serve the one true God.

✤ **Kingship and a Name.** The Hebrew word for "name" also refers to a kingdom or dynasty, which carries the idea of political power. God was essentially saying, "I will give my humble and faithful servant Abram a lasting legacy by raising the nation of his family to royal power. I will make them a kingdom that rules other nations."

✤ **Blessing for All Nations.** God did not explain what he meant by this, but as we will see, this promise refers to how God would use Abram and his descendants to bring salvation to the entire world.

The Departure of Abraham by Molnar. Abram believed what God had promised, and so he left his homeland with his wife, his nephew, their servants, and all their possessions.

These promises would be reemphasized in the covenant that God would make with Abram, which would in turn be fulfilled in later covenants with Moses and David and, finally, with the New Covenant in Jesus.

ABRAHAM, OUR FATHER IN FAITH

God's promises to Abram were difficult to believe. Abram was an old man, and his wife had never been able to conceive a child. How were his descendants to become a great nation when he had no descendants? Nevertheless, Abram believed what God had promised, and so he left his homeland with his wife, his nephew, their servants, and all their possessions.

But when Abram came to the land that God had promised, he found that it was already inhabited by another nation, the *Canaanites*. God returned to Abram and again promised that he would give the land to Abram's descendants. This time, Abram replied by asking how this could be possible, since he did not have any children. So God swore a covenant oath to Abram.

> **Know of a surety that your descendants will be sojourners in a land that is not theirs, and will be slaves there, and they will be oppressed for four hundred years; but I will bring judgment on the nation which they serve, and afterward they shall come out with great possessions....To your descendants I give this land. (Gn 15: 13-14, 18)**

This was probably not the answer that Abram had been hoping for. Although his descendants would eventually inherit the land that was promised, this would only happen after they had spent hundreds of years in slavery. But Abram continued to trust in God, and he and his family set up a home in *Canaan*.

It was almost twenty-five years later that God appeared to Abram again, telling him that Abram and his wife at last would have a son, and that his name would be Isaac. God then made another covenant with Abram.

> Behold, my covenant is with you, and you shall be the father of a multitude of nations. No longer shall your name be Abram, but your name shall be Abraham; for I have made you the father of a multitude of nations. I will make you exceedingly fruitful; and I will make nations of you, and kings shall come forth from you. And I will establish my covenant between me and you and your descendants after you throughout their generations for an everlasting covenant. (Gn 17: 4-7)

Just as God had instituted the Sabbath as the sign of his covenant with Adam, he also gave a sign of his covenant with Abraham. The sign of *circumcision* was meant to distinguish those who kept God's covenant from those who did not. From that point on, the People of God would be identified by their faithfulness to the two covenant signs of the Sabbath and circumcision.

ABRAHAM'S OBEDIENCE

For Abraham and his wife, Sarah, the promise of a son seemed impossible to believe. They were nearing a hundred years old, and Sarah was long past the years of childbearing. But Abraham maintained his *faith* in God's promise, and in a few years, just as God had said, Abraham and his wife had a son whom they named Isaac.

After so many years of steadfast faithfulness to God's Word, Abraham and his wife now had evidence that God's promises would be fulfilled through their son Isaac. But God's greatest test of Abraham's faith was still ahead.

When Isaac had grown into a young man, God came again to Abraham and said, "Take your son, your only son Isaac, whom you love, and go to the land of *Moriah*, and offer him there as a burnt offering upon one of the mountains of which I shall tell you."[19]

God was asking Abraham to sacrifice his only son—an inconceivable request. But Abraham did not turn away from God in disobedience. He trusted in God completely.

The Sacrifice of Isaac by Caravaggio.
Isaac could have resisted, but instead, he was obedient, trusting in God, just like Abraham.

> Abraham took the wood of the burnt offering and laid it on Isaac his son; and he took in his hand the fire and the knife. So they went both of them together. And Isaac said to his father Abraham... "Behold, the fire and the wood; but where is the lamb for a burnt offering?" Abraham said, "God will provide himself the lamb." (Gn 22: 6-8)

When Abraham and Isaac reached the place where God had told him to go, Abraham built an altar and tied up his son, placing him on the altar. Abraham's faith and obedience are remarkable, but it is important to note that Abraham was not the only one who was faithful and obedient. Isaac was strong enough to carry the wood for the sacrifice, and Abraham was a very old man. Isaac could have resisted, but instead, he was obedient, trusting in God, just like Abraham.

Their trust was well placed, for when the time came for Abraham to complete his sacrifice of Isaac, an angel called to him, saying, "Do not lay your hand on the lad or do anything to him; for now I know that you fear God, seeing you have not withheld your son, your only son." (Gn 22: 12) As soon as the angel had finished speaking, Abraham saw a ram that was caught by its horns in the bushes, so he took it and offered it to God. Just as Abraham had said, God indeed had provided the sacrifice.

A BLESSING FOR ALL NATIONS

Christians from the earliest times have understood the sacrifice of Isaac as a foreshadowing of (or a "type" for) the sacrifice of Christ, and we can see a number of parallels between this story and the story of Jesus' Crucifixion.

Even the location of Abraham's sacrifice offers us a preview of a greater sacrifice yet to come. *Mount Moriah* was located in what would later become Jerusalem. It would be here that Jesus would suffer death, making a perfect and final sacrifice on our behalf.

God made his final covenant with Abraham immediately following the sacrifice of Isaac. Because of Abraham's unconditional faith and obedience, God promised that he would bless Abraham, and that all the nations of the earth would be blessed through Abraham's descendants.

"On the mount of the Lord it shall be provided."
(Gn 22:14)

Isaac Bears the Wood for His Sacrifice by Tissot.

The Ascent to Calvary (detail) by Tintoretto.

ISAAC	CHRIST
A father offers his beloved son.	The Father offers his beloved Son.
The son submits to the father's will.	The Son submits to the Father's Will.
Isaac carries the wood for his own sacrifice.	Jesus carries the wood of his own Cross.
God himself provides the sacrifice.	God provides himself as the perfect sacrifice.

This covenant was partially fulfilled by the people of Israel, who were called by God to be a light to the nations. But it was only with the coming of Jesus Christ, himself a descendant of Abraham, that God's covenant would reach its complete fulfillment, for it is in Christ and through his Church that the entire world is called back into communion with God.

The Book of Genesis shows us the early stages of the long process by which God the Father re-gathered his family. What had begun with just two people, Adam and Eve, had expanded to the entire family of Abraham. Through Abraham's obedience, the chaos created by Adam and Eve's disobedience had begun to be reversed. It is because of his obedience and faith that Abraham is called "the father of all who believe."

As the family of Abraham continued to grow, so too did the need for God to remind them of his covenant. For just as Adam had sinned, so too would the descendants of Abraham. But God would not forget his covenant. Despite their sins and failings, God used the descendants of Abraham to prepare the world for Christ and his Church.

GOD CALLS MOSES

By the time of Moses, much had changed for the descendants of Abraham. They had moved from the *Promised Land* of Canaan to the land of *Egypt*, where, initially at least, they had prospered. But as the

Moses Before the Burning Bush by Feti.
God now began preparing Moses for a new covenant, one that would involve the entire people of Israel.

families of the sons of Israel began to grow into large and powerful tribes, the *Egyptians* became resentful of them and worried that they might eventually rise up against them. With this in mind, the *pharaoh* (the Egyptian king) decreed that the *Israelites* would now be slaves, and that all the male children of the Israelites would be killed. It was a hopeless time, and the descendants of Abraham—called the Israelites after Abraham's grandson Israel, or Jacob—seemingly were doomed to complete annihilation through genocide. But God had not forgotten his people or his promises.

Moses was born during the time when the pharaoh had ordered the death of all male Israelite children. In an attempt to save his life, Moses' mother hid him in a reed basket and set him afloat in the *River Nile*, where he was found by the pharaoh's daughter. The Pharaoh's daughter had pity on the small child and took Moses into the royal household to rear as her own child. Not being a mother herself, pharaoh's daughter needed a slave to be the child's wet nurse, and she was led to Moses' own mother, who nurtured him and secretly instructed him in the faith of his Israelite ancestors.

One day, after Moses had grown into a young man, he saw an Egyptian taskmaster beating a Hebrew slave. In anger, Moses struck the Egyptian and killed him. Fearing pharaoh's punishment, Moses fled Egypt, finding refuge in the land of *Midian*, with Jethro, a priest. There, Moses settled into his new life of tending the flocks and eventually married Jethro's daughter, Zipporah.

Moses probably thought that this was how he would spend the rest of his days. God, however, had other plans for him. When Moses was eighty years old, God appeared to him in a burning bush, saying:

> **The cry of the people of Israel has come to me, and I have seen the oppression with which the Egyptians oppress them. Come, I will send you to Pharaoh that you may bring forth my people, the sons of Israel, out of Egypt. (Ex 3: 9-10)**

Moses was hesitant to fulfill his mission.

"If I come to the people of Israel and say to them, 'The God of your fathers has sent me to you,' and they ask me, 'What is his name?' what shall I say to them?" So God revealed his name to Moses: "I AM WHO I AM." (Ex 3: 13-14)

In the *Hebrew* culture, names were typically used to communicate something about a person, not just what they were called, but who they were. By revealing his name to Moses, God was revealing something about himself. God is not an "anonymous force," but a God who desires a relationship with man. This desire had previously been revealed in God's covenants with Adam and with Abraham, but God now began preparing Moses for a new covenant, one that would involve the entire people of Israel.

In revealing his name, "I AM WHO I AM," God was also highlighting the fact that he is unchanging, that he has no beginning and no end—God simply is, and he is for all eternity. He will always desire communion with his people, and he will always be faithful to the covenants he has made with them, even when man himself is not faithful. In the New Testament, God explicitly revealed himself—and only he could reveal this—to be a communion of three Persons: Father, Son, and Holy Spirit. This is central mystery of the Christian Faith and affects every aspect of the Christian life.

THE EXODUS FROM EGYPT

Following God's instructions, Moses went back to Egypt and told the pharaoh what God had said: "Thus says the LORD, Israel is my firstborn son, and I say to you, 'Let my son go that he may serve me'; if you refuse to let him go, behold, I will slay your firstborn son."[20]

The Signs on the Door by Tissot.
The angel of death would pass over all the houses that were marked with the blood of the lamb.

God knew that the pharaoh would not obey, so he directed Moses to unleash one plague after another, all designed to change the pharaoh's mind. God sent ten plagues in all, the last one being the worst. The angel of death would go throughout Egypt, killing every firstborn son.

The Israelites would be spared from this plague only if they followed God's instructions. They were to take a young lamb, without any blemish or broken bones, and sacrifice it, eating the flesh and brushing its blood on their lintels and doorposts. The angel of death would then pass over all the houses that were marked with the blood of the lamb, allowing the firstborn of the house to live. This was the first *Passover* feast, and it was to be celebrated every year as a remembrance of how God had saved his people.

God followed through on his warning to slay the firstborn sons of Egypt if Israel, his firstborn son, was not permitted to leave. This final plague was enough for pharaoh to let God's people go. Frightened by this terrible manifestation of the God of Israel, the Egyptians bade the Israelites to leave as soon as possible, returning all their gold and fine clothing. Just as God had warned Abraham that his descendants would be enslaved for four hundred years, God was now fulfilling the second part of that prophecy, that after the enslavement, "I will bring judgment on the nation which they serve, and afterward they shall come out with great possessions."[21]

TEN PLAGUES OF EGYPT

After the pharaoh refused to let the Hebrews leave as Moses had requested, God sent a series of ten plagues upon all of Egypt.

First: **River Turned To Blood**
(Ex 7: 14-24)

Second: **Frogs** (Ex 8: 1-15)

Third: **Lice** (Ex 8: 16-19)

Fourth: **Flies** (Ex 8: 20-32)

Fifth: **Sickness of Animals** (Ex 9: 1-7)

Sixth: **Boils** (Ex 9: 8-12)

Seventh: **Hail** (Ex 9: 13-35)

Eighth: **Locusts** (Ex 10: 1-20)

Ninth: **Darkness** (Ex 10: 21-28)

Tenth: **Death of Every Firstborn Male**
(Ex 12: 29-30)

The Plague of Lice, the Plague of Frogs, the Plague on Livestock, the Plague of Flies. Illustration from *The Golden Haggadah*, ca. 1320. The *Haggadah* is the Hebrew service book used in Jewish households on Passover Eve at the festive meal to commemorate the Israelites' Exodus from Egypt.

Departure of the Israelites by Roberts.
"And Moses said to the people, 'Remember this day, in which you came out from Egypt, out of the house of bondage, for by strength of hand the LORD brought you out from this place;...'" (Ex 13: 3)

As soon as Israel fled Egypt, in what we still today call the *Exodus*, pharaoh had a change of mind. He summoned his army, and they pursued the Israelites all the way to the *Red Sea*. God said to Moses, "Stretch out your hand over the sea and divide it, that the people of Israel may go on dry ground through the sea."22 Moses did as God had commanded, and the Israelites walked through the sea on dry ground. When pharaoh and his men saw this, they resumed their pursuit. But God again spoke to Moses and told him to stretch out his hand once more. He did so, and the waters returned, destroying the Egyptian army.

Freed from the danger of the Egyptians, the Israelites continued on their journey toward *Mount Sinai*, the mountain where God had first spoken to Moses. God had shown his faithfulness to Israel in delivering them from Egypt, and he would continue to provide for his people on their trek through the wilderness: When the Israelites grew thirsty, he gave them water from a dry rock; when they became hungry, God sent them *manna*, a wafer-like bread from the sky. All of this was done in preparation for his covenant with them at Mount Sinai, where he would establish Israel as a great nation in fulfillment of his promise to Abraham.

GOD'S COVENANT WITH ISRAEL

After more than a month of traveling through the desert, the Israelites arrived at the foot of Mount Sinai, where God spoke to Moses, telling him what to say to his people.

> **You shall say to the house of Jacob, and tell the people of Israel: You have seen what I did to the Egyptians, and how I bore you on eagles' wings and brought you to myself. Now therefore, if you will obey my voice and keep my covenant, you shall be my own possession among all peoples; for all the earth is mine, and you shall be to me a kingdom of priests and a holy nation. (Ex 19: 3-6)**

Israel, God's firstborn son among the nations, was given the task of bringing all the other nations into the Family of God. God's covenant plan to reunite mankind was at last taking shape.

So God gave Moses the conditions of the covenant—the laws we know as the *Ten Commandments*—which were to govern his holy nation. Moses read aloud all of the laws that Israel was to follow, and the Israelites gave a resounding "yes" to what God was asking of them. "All that the LORD has spoken we will do, and we will be obedient."[23]

> In the promise to Abraham and the oath that accompanied it,[24] God commits himself but without disclosing his name. He begins to reveal it to Moses and makes it known clearly before the eyes of the whole people when he saves them from the Egyptians: "he has triumphed gloriously."[25] From the covenant of Sinai onwards, this people is "his own" and it is to be a "holy (or "consecrated": the same word is used for both in Hebrew) nation,"[26] because the name of God dwells in it. (CCC 2810)

The Israelites' Camp and Wilderness Temple at Mount Sinai.
God gave Moses detailed instructions for building the tabernacle, a moveable tent that would be used as a temple for the Israelites as they journeyed to the Promised Land.

Immediately after the covenant was made, God called Moses and asked him to climb to the top of Mount Sinai. There he gave Moses the stone tablets on which he had written the Commandments, as a reminder to Israel of the permanence of the covenant. God also gave Moses detailed instructions for building the *tabernacle*, a moveable tent that would be used as a temple for the Israelites as they journeyed to the Promised Land. At the center of the tabernacle was to be placed the *Ark of the Covenant*—an ornate box covered in gold containing the stone tablets—which would serve as God's throne. Not only would God's name dwell in the nation of Israel, but God himself would dwell among them as well.

Sanctified by the presence of God in the tabernacle, the entire assembly of Israelites—who were called the *qahal* in Hebrew or *ekklesia* in Greek, which is translated *church*—was to serve God as a kingdom of priests, with God as their king. Israel was "God's possession among the peoples," called out of Egypt to assist him in bringing salvation to all the nations. This was a unique and glorious calling, but it depended on Israel's continuing obedience. As we will see, it did not take long for the Israelites to break their covenant with God.

ISRAEL'S DISOBEDIENCE

After Moses revealed God's Law to the Israelites, he returned to the top of Mount Sinai, where he remained for forty days and nights speaking with God. While he was on the mountain, God presented Moses with stone tablets inscribed with the Law and the instructions for the construction of the tabernacle. While Moses was away, the Israelites in their camp at the base of the mountain grew restless and impatient. They approached Aaron, Moses' older brother, who had been left in charge while Moses was gone.

> **When the people saw that Moses delayed to come down from the mountain, the people gathered themselves together to Aaron, and said to him, "Up, make us gods, who shall go before us; as for this Moses, the man who brought us up out of the land of Egypt, we do not know what has become of him." And Aaron said to them, "Take off the rings of gold which are in the ears of your wives, your sons, and your daughters, and bring them to me." (Ex 32: 1-2)**

Moses finally returned from the top of Mount Sinai and was enraged by what he saw. The prophet took the stone tablets and hurled them to the ground, shattering them.

We can see parallels between the effects of Israel's disobedience and the effects of the disobedience of Adam and Eve. In each case, the communion established by God's covenant with man was lost. God had intended Israel to be a kingdom of priests that would be a light to the nations to bring all into God's family. However, after Israel showed its disloyalty by committing idolatry, God had to establish a different order of priests— the *Levites*. And because Israel had shown that it could not overcome the temptation of worshiping the gods of other nations, they were given a second set of laws—found in the Book of *Deuteronomy*—intended to keep Israel separate from the other nations.

Even though the Israelites had abandoned their covenant with God, God would not abandon his people, nor would he abandon his plan to establish a holy nation and a kingdom of priests, a plan that would reach its partial fulfillment in God's covenant with David. The Israelites had sinned, but through God's faithfulness and mercy they would still be God's instrument in reuniting all mankind to himself.

Joshua Passing the River Jordan with the Ark of the Covenant by West. Joshua leads the Israelites into the Promised Land.
"the LORD said to Joshua, 'Take twelve men from the people, from each tribe a man, and command them, "Take twelve stones from here out of the midst of the Jordan, from the very place where the priests' feet stood, and carry them over with you, and lay them down in the place where you lodge tonight."'" (Jos 4: 1-3)

ISRAEL DEMANDS A KING

As punishment for their disobedience, the Israelites were forced to wander in the wilderness for forty years before they could enter the Promised Land. Moses was told by God that he could not enter it, so he chose a successor. "Joshua...was full of the spirit of wisdom, for Moses had laid his hands upon him; so the people of Israel obeyed him."[27] Under Joshua's leadership, the Israelites were faithful to God's commands, and he led them in conquering much of the Promised Land.

Almost immediately after Joshua's death, however, Israel began to turn away from God. The Book of Judges recounts how Israel turned to idolatry and anarchy time and again, only to be saved by a series of *judges*—men and women sent by God to return his people to righteousness. But as soon as order and prosperity were restored, the Israelites would grow forgetful of God and turn once more to worshiping idols—and the vicious cycle was repeated.

The Israelites continued to fall away from the Law of God because they were attracted to the customs and idols of neighboring nations. Israel had been chosen by God to be a people set apart, but after years of wandering in the wilderness and many more years of wandering during their conquest of the Promised Land, they longed for the power, wealth, and stability that other nations enjoyed. The Israelites asked for a king so that they could be ruled like other nations and build a kingdom in their homeland, thus ending their centuries of wandering. Fortunately, Israel's second set of laws given in Deuteronomy provided for the selection of a king.

> **When you come to the land which the LORD your God gives you, and you possess it and dwell in it, and then say, "I will set a king over me, like all the nations that are round about me"; you may indeed set as king over you him whom the LORD your God will choose. One from among your brethren you shall set as king over you. (Dt 17: 14-15)**

The role of the king in Israel was unique to that of other nations. God was always the king of Israel, and the ability to establish a monarchical government was seen to originate from God's kingship. Seeing that the provision for selecting a king is contained in Deuteronomy, it can also be interpreted that a temporal king of Israel was part of God's plan for the nation. Nonetheless, the Israelites wanted a king to enforce their moral order. The establishment of a king would also fulfill God's promise to Abraham that kings would be among his descendants.

Saul Is Anointed King By Samuel by Michiel van der Borch. "And Samuel said to all the people, 'Do you see him whom the LORD has chosen? There is none like him among all the people.' And all the people shouted, 'Long live the king!'" (1 Sm 10: 24)

God would choose the Israelite king, and he wanted a "man after his own heart"—someone who would recognize his fatherly plan of salvation and would respond in obedience and love.

God led his prophet Samuel to a man from the tribe of Benjamin named Saul. Samuel anointed Saul's head with oil—an action previously reserved for the ordination of priests—and declared him to be God's chosen. The anointing with oil was a visible sign of Saul's *consecration*. It is also significant because "anointed one" is "messiah" in Hebrew and "christ" in Greek. The messiah was to be the one chosen by God to be the leader and savior of his people.

At first, things went well for Saul, and he led the Israelites to military victory. However, in time, Saul's power corrupted him and he lost God's favor. God would then remove the kingdom from Saul and give it to a man who was truly "after his own heart."

Anointing of David by Barrias. Because David was just a young man when Samuel anointed him King of Israel, he would not ascend to the throne until he was thirty years old.

KING DAVID

God told his prophet Samuel to go to the house of a man named Jesse, where he found Jesse's youngest son, David, tending a flock of sheep. Although he was only a young man, David was God's choice to serve Israel as its king. Samuel anointed David with oil and "the spirit of the LORD came mightily upon David from that day forward."[28]

At the time David was anointed king, there were two major difficulties facing the people of Israel. First, the twelve tribes were constantly getting into disputes, some of which blew up into full-scale civil wars. The new king would have to find a way to maintain the unity of the kingdom. The second major difficulty that David faced was how best to deal with the nations around Israel. Here David faced a two-front battle presented by these neighboring nations, defending against both political threats and moral threats as he tried to keep his people from adopting these nations' customs and religions of *idolatry*.

Because David was just a young man when Samuel anointed him King of Israel, he would not ascend to the throne until he was thirty years old. As king, David made immediate decisions to help preserve Israel. In order to preserve the kingdom's fragile unity—as well as to prove that he was not playing favorites among the tribes—he moved his capital to Jerusalem, a city near the center of Israel that none of the tribes had claimed as its own.

King David Playing the Zither by Celesti. "And David danced before the LORD with all his might;...So David and all the house of Israel brought up the ark of the LORD with shouting, and with the sound of the horn. As the ark of the LORD came into the city of David, Michal the daughter of Saul looked out of the window, and saw King David leaping and dancing before the LORD; and she despised him in her heart." (2 Sm 6:14-16)

David understood that it was not enough for this new capital city to be a political center; it also needed to serve as a central place of worship as well. So David began preparations for bringing the Ark of the Covenant into Jerusalem and establishing the tabernacle there permanently. Wearing the robes of a priest, David himself led the procession of the Levites carrying the Ark into the city. When it was put in its resting place, it was David who offered the sacrifices. He also established the *thank offering*, a sacrifice that included unleavened bread and wine and was made in gratitude for God's deliverance, as the primary worship in the Temple. Previously, the Israelites had offered only animal sacrifices to God.

Where Israel had failed in the past, David succeeded. He did not succumb to the idolatrous ways of Israel's neighbors; he subdued them and brought them under his rule. The ultimate reason for this was not to increase the wealth or power of his kingdom, but rather to share with all the nations the wisdom, truth, and righteousness that God had generously given to Israel. Being a man after God's own heart, David did not destroy or oppress the people surrounding the Israelites; instead, he worked to incorporate them into God's covenant family.

GOD'S COVENANT WITH DAVID

God was pleased with David's faithfulness, and he continued to bless him and the entire Kingdom of Israel. But God had something even greater in store for David, and he sent his prophet to give David a message.

> **I will raise up your offspring after you, who shall come forth from your body, and I will establish his kingdom. He shall build a house for my name, and I will establish the throne of his kingdom for ever. I will be his father, and he shall be my son.... And your house and your kingdom shall be made sure for ever before me; your throne shall be established for ever. (2 Sm 7:12-14, 16)**

God was renewing his covenant with Israel through David. Once again, we can see the language of family being used. Just as Israel was to be God's firstborn son, so too would God be a Father to David's offspring. There is an important difference here, however: While Israel's future depended on their obedience ("if you obey..."), God's covenant with David was unconditional and permanent.

THE SEVEN PRIMARY FEATURES OF THE DAVIDIC COVENANT

The covenant that God made with King David included several promises:

✤ David's line would have a KINGDOM. David and his descendants would be not just kings, but *great* kings.

✤ The covenant established a royal DYNASTY. David had already been chosen by God to be king, but God was telling David that his kingship would continue even after he died, for it would be passed on to his descendants.

✤ The king of Israel would not only be the son of David, but the SON OF GOD as well. God was promising to be a Father to David's descendants and was reestablishing the family relationship that was offered to both Adam and to Israel.

✤ The covenant would be UNLIMITED AND EVERLASTING. God's covenant with David was permanent, and he promised that David's dynasty would last forever. The king of Israel was to rule not only over the twelve tribes, but also over all the nations. David's line was intended to lead Israel and all the other nations in worship of and obedience to God.

✤ Jerusalem, and particularly MOUNT ZION, would be Israel's spiritual center. In the Book of *Psalms*, God said, "I have set my king on Zion, my holy hill,"[29] and it was here that David's son Solomon would build the *Temple*—the "house for God's name"—which would be the place of *pilgrimage* for both the Israelites and all the nations.

✤ The TEMPLE was the visible sign of the covenant and of God's kingdom. The construction of the Temple was central to the terms of the covenant, for it would be God's permanent dwelling place and a "house of prayer for all peoples."

✤ WISDOM would be the new law of the Davidic Covenant. Solomon, David's son, would be given wisdom to govern, and Wisdom literature would guide the people.

THE REIGN OF SOLOMON AND THE COLLAPSE OF THE KINGDOM

After David's death, his son Solomon became king, and the kingdom flourished more than ever. In the course of two generations—those of David and Solomon—Israel had become a vast empire. All the neighboring nations sought out Solomon to make alliances with him and to worship the God of Israel. Solomon built the Temple on Mount Zion, just as God had requested, and he designed it to accommodate the pilgrims from other nations who came to Jerusalem to worship the one true God.

Although Solomon sustained and even added to the glory of his father's kingdom, his faithfulness to God began to waver. His desire for wealth and power caused him to impose high taxes on the twelve tribes, thus disobeying the Law of Moses that governed his kingship. Further, he took hundreds of wives and concubines from other nations for himself, and instead of leading them to worship God, he allowed them to turn him toward their foreign idols.

Because of Solomon's disobedience, God told him that his kingdom would be taken away from him. But God added, "For the sake of David your father I will not do it in your days, but I will tear it out of the hand of your son."[30] Just as God had said, when Solomon's son became king after his death, ten of the twelve tribes rebelled, splitting off to form a *Northern Kingdom*. The collapsing kingdom fell easily to Israel's neighboring

The Idolatry of Solomon by Conca.
"And so he did for all his foreign wives, who burned incense and sacrificed to their gods. And the Lord was angry with Solomon, because his heart had turned away from the Lord, the God of Israel, who had appeared to him twice, and had commanded him concerning this thing, that he should not go after other gods; but he did not keep what the Lord commanded. Therefore the Lord said to Solomon, 'Since this has been your mind and you have not kept my covenant and my statutes which I have commanded you, I will surely tear the kingdom from you and will give it to your servant.'" (1 Kgs 11:8-11)

THREE ADDITIONAL FEATURES OR SECONDARY CHARACTERISTICS OF THE DAVIDIC COVENANT

✚ The QUEEN MOTHER became an important part of the royal government. Beginning with the reign of Solomon, the king's mother takes on a key role of interceding to him on behalf on his subjects.[31]

✚ The PRIME MINISTER became a distinct office in the royal government. The king had many important ministers (in 1 Kings 4:7 there are twelve), but one man was chief among them and stood between the king and his other ministers. The prime minister had the authority of the king, and was second only to the king and the queen mother. Everyone in the kingdom could identify the prime minister by the sign of his office: the keys of the kingdom.

✚ The THANK OFFERING became the primary sacrifice offered in the Temple. Previously, the Israelites had offered animal sacrifices to God; the thank offering included unleavened bread and wine, which were offered to God in gratitude for his deliverance.

nations. The Northern Kingdom was attacked and destroyed by the *Assyrians* in 722 BC. In 597 BC, Babylon sacked Jerusalem and destroyed the Temple, slaughtering the royal family and sending the remaining citizens into exile.

Both the kingdom and the royal line of David were all but destroyed. Despite the seeming fulfillment of the promises of God to Israel through the reign of David and the Kingdom of Israel, the restoration of Israel as a priestly nation and the fulfillment of the promise to Abraham of a worldwide blessing through his descendants seemed further away from realization than ever. As a result of the fall of the Kingdom of Israel, the gathering of God's family, as promised in God's covenant with Adam and Eve, had fallen apart.

The challenge for the Israelites in the coming centuries would be maintaining their faith, despite the seeming hopelessness of their situation. Through a series of prophets, who appeared both while Israel was in exile and when the Hebrew people finally returned to Canaan, the Israelites were repeatedly called back to the ways of God. This exile helped deepen the faith of the nation and solidified their hope in God's promise of an everlasting kingdom—one that would be truly universal, ruled by the son of David, the Messiah. God's people continued to trust in God and eagerly awaited the coming of the promised *Christ*.

CONCLUSION

When we study God's plan of salvation as it unfolds throughout the Old Testament, we see a God of great love and mercy. It tells the story of humanity's repeated infidelity to God and of his unending forgiveness. Although the Chosen People continued to break their covenants with God, God remained faithful. Whenever humanity failed to live up to the terms of their covenant, God offered a new covenant time and time again.

What God had in mind all along was the redemption to be completed by the Incarnation of his Son, Jesus Christ, and Christ's ultimate triumph over sin and death. Humanity had to be brought along gradually to the realization of this plan, however. The law given to Moses gave the Hebrews standards by which to live; the priesthood of Aaron's family and of the Levites provided humanity with a means of approaching God in prayer and sacrifice. The development of a system of kings and judges placed the People of God under human authority, and the Ark of the Covenant—which for the Israelites was the very presence of God—gave a material sign that God dwelled among his people.

Moses by Schile. The law given to Moses gave the Hebrews standards by which to live. The development of a system of kings and judges placed the People of God under human authority.

Examined in light of salvation history and the covenants between God and man, we can see that God always forgives, loves, and heals his people. He is a God who greets every failure with a promise of hope. He is a God who never tires of drawing his people to himself, even when their stubbornness or weakness causes them to drift from him. He is a God who, from the moment of the Original Sin of Adam and Eve, set into motion his plan for the redemption of the world, a plan that included a long period of preparing his people for the coming of his Son, Jesus Christ, and the establishment of the Church, its Sacraments, and its teaching authority that would continue Christ's mission of salvation until the end of time. Christ and his Church in the New Covenant would become the ultimate fulfillment of all that God had promised Israel in the covenants of the Old Testament.

SUPPLEMENTARY READING

1. Prophecies Regarding the People of God and Their Fulfillment in Christ

✤ I [the LORD] will make of you [Abram] a great nation, and I will bless you, and make your name great, so that you will be a blessing. (Gn 12:2)

✤ [The LORD] brought [Abram] outside and said, "Look toward heaven, and number the stars, if you are able to number them." Then he said to him, "So shall your descendants be." And he believed the LORD; and he reckoned it to him as righteousness. (Gn 15:5-6)

✤ If you will obey my [the LORD's] voice and keep my covenant, you shall be my own possession among all peoples; for all the earth is mine, and you shall be to me a kingdom of priests and a holy nation. These are the words which you shall speak to the children of Israel. (Ex 19:5-6)

✤ You are a people holy to the LORD your God; the LORD your God has chosen you to be a people for his own possession, out of all the peoples that are on the face of the earth. (Dt 7:6)

✤ It shall come to pass in the latter days that the mountain of the house of the LORD shall be established as the highest of the mountains, and shall be raised above the hills; and all the nations shall flow to it, and many peoples shall come, and say: "Come, let us go up to the mountain of the LORD, to the house of the God of Jacob; that he may teach us his ways and that we may walk in his paths." For out of Zion shall go forth the law, and the word of the LORD from Jerusalem. He shall judge between the nations, and shall decide for many peoples; and they shall beat their swords into plowshares, and their spears into pruning hooks; nation shall not lift up sword against nation, neither shall they learn war any more. O house of Jacob, come, let us walk in the light of the LORD. (Is 2:2-5)

✤ Incline your ear, and come to me [the LORD]; hear, that your soul may live; and I will make with you an everlasting covenant, my steadfast, sure love for David. (Is 55:3)

✤ Jesus said to them, "Truly, I say to you, in the new world, when the Son of man shall sit on his glorious throne, you who have followed me will also sit on twelve thrones, judging the twelve tribes of Israel." (Mt 19:28)

✤ [Jesus said,] "As my father assigned to me a kingdom, that you may eat and drink at my table in my kingdom, and sit on thrones judging the twelve tribes of Israel." (Lk 22:29-30)

✤ Like living stones be yourselves built into a spiritual house, to be a holy priesthood, to offer spiritual sacrifices acceptable to God through Jesus Christ. (1 Pt 2:5)

✤ [The holy city Jerusalem] had a great, high wall, with twelve gates, and at the gates twelve angels, and on the gates the names of the twelve tribes of the sons of Israel were inscribed; on the east three gates, on the north three gates, on the south three gates, and on the west three gates. And the wall of the city had twelve foundations, and on them the twelve names of the twelve apostles of the Lamb. (Rev 21:14)

The First Commandment by Cranach the Elder.
"You shall have no other gods before me. You shall not make for yourself a graven image, or any likeness of anything that is in heaven above, or that is in the earth beneath, or that is in the water under the earth." (Ex 20:3-4)

SUPPLEMENTARY READING Continued

2. The New People of God

Israel according to the flesh, which wandered as an exile in the desert, was already called the Church of God. So likewise the new Israel which while living in this present age goes in search of a future and abiding city is called the Church of Christ. For He has bought it for Himself with His blood, has filled it with His Spirit and provided it with those means which befit it as a visible and social union.

God gathered together as one all those who in faith look upon Jesus as the author of salvation and the source of unity and peace, and established them as the Church that for each and all it may be the visible sacrament of this saving unity. While it transcends all limits of time and confines of race, the Church is destined to extend to all regions of the earth and so enters into the history of mankind.

Moving forward through trial and tribulation, the Church is strengthened by the power of God's grace, which was promised to her by the Lord, so that in the weakness of the flesh she may not waver from perfect fidelity, but remain a bride worthy of her Lord, and moved by the Holy Spirit may never cease to renew herself, until through the Cross she arrives at the light which knows no setting.

—*Lumen Gentium*, 9

3. The Old Testament in God's Plan of Salvation

In carefully planning and preparing the salvation of the whole human race the God of infinite love, by a special dispensation, chose for Himself a people to whom He would entrust His promises. First He entered into a covenant with Abraham (see Gn. 15:18) and, through Moses, with the people of Israel (see Ex. 24:8). To this people which He had acquired for Himself, He so manifested Himself through words and deeds as the one true and living God that Israel came to know by experience the ways of God with men. Then too, when God Himself spoke to them through the mouth of the prophets, Israel daily gained a deeper and clearer understanding of His ways and made them more widely known among the nations (see Ps. 21:29; 95:1-3; Is. 2:1-5; Jer. 3:17).

The plan of salvation foretold by the Sacred Authors, recounted and explained by them, is found as the true word of God in the books of the Old Testament: these books, therefore, written under Divine Inspiration, remain permanently valuable. "For all that was written for our instruction, so that by steadfastness and the encouragement of the Scriptures we might have hope" (Rom 15:4).

—*Dei Verbum*, 14

The Water Rushing From the Rock by Raphael.
'"Behold, I will stand before you there on the rock at Horeb; and you shall strike the rock, and water shall come out of it, that the people may drink.' And Moses did so, in the sight of the elders of Israel." (Ex 17:6)

VOCABULARY

ARK OF THE COVENANT
An ornate box that held the tablets of the Law (Ten Commandments), the rod of Aaron, and some manna; it represented God's throne on earth.

ASSYRIANS
The people of Assyria who destroyed Israel's Northern Kingdom in 722 BC.

CANAAN
The land of the Canaanites, which was to become the Promised Land for the Israelites.

CHRIST
Greek for "anointed." This is used in reference to Jesus because he accomplished perfectly the divine mission of priest, prophet, and king, signified by his being "anointed" as Christ.

CIRCUMCISION
The sign of God's covenant with Abraham. Circumcision set the People of God apart from other nations.

COMMUNION
The unity of the faithful as one Body in Christ; also refers to the reception of the Eucharist at Holy Mass.

CONSECRATION
The act of separating someone or something apart as holy and devoted for a particular purpose. Israelite kings of the Old Testament were consecrated by being anointed with sacred oil. Today, we refer to the Consecration of individuals to the priesthood, the religious life, or to ministry as a bishop; in the context of the Mass, we also refer to the Consecration of the bread and wine by which it becomes the Body and Blood of Christ.

COVENANT
A solemn agreement between people or between God and man made by swearing an oath before God and involving mutual commitments and promises.

CREATION
God's bringing forth the universe and all its inhabitants into being out of nothing. Creation is good, yet it has been corrupted by sin.

DEVIL
A fallen angel, who sinned against God by refusing to accept his reign; also called Satan or the Evil One.

DEUTERONOMY
The fifth book of the Bible. It contains the second set of laws given by God to the Israelites.

EXODUS
Greek for "going out." Liberation of the Hebrew people from slavery in Egypt into the Promised Land by the saving acts of God; the Book of Exodus, the second book of the Bible, recounts these acts. This also describes the liberation from slavery to sin into eternal life by the saving act of Jesus Christ.

FAITH
The theological virtue by which one believes, because of God's authority, in all that God has revealed and that the Church proposes for belief.

FALL
Biblical Revelation about the Original Sin which introduced sin into human history, as narrated in the Book of Genesis.

GENESIS
The first book of the Bible. It begins with the story of creation and ends with the death of Joseph in Egypt.

HEBREWS
The name given to the People of God, later known as the Israelites, Israel, or the Jews.

IDOLATRY
The worship of idols.

IMAGO DEI
Latin for "image of God," which refers to the fact that God created man in his own image and likeness.

VOCABULARY Continued

ISRAEL
The Israelites, the people chosen by God to be his people and inherit the promises of Abraham. This people is named after Israel (Jacob), from whose twelve sons the tribes of Israel descend. During the time of the divided nation, this refers to the northern ten tribes.

JUDGES
Men and women appointed by God to govern the Israelites and return them to righteousness after they had fallen into sin and idolatry after the death of Joshua; also, the Old Testament book describing this period in Israel's history.

LEVITES
The priestly class of Israel, members of the tribe of Levi.

LEVITICUS
The third book of the Bible, primarily an enumeration of the laws given to the Hebrews by God.

MANNA
A kind of bread "from Heaven" given by God to the Hebrews as their daily food to sustain them during their years of wandering in the desert.

MARRIAGE
The Sacrament by which a man and a woman, in accordance with God's design from the beginning, are joined in an intimate union of life and love, "so they are no longer two but one" (Mt 19: 6). This union is ordered to the mutual benefit of the spouses and the procreation and education of children ("Be fruitful and multiply" [Gn 1: 28]).

MESSIAH
Hebrew for "anointed." This is used in reference to Jesus because he accomplished perfectly the divine mission of priest, prophet, and king, signified by his being anointed as Christ.

MORAL LAW
For the Israelites, the Ten Commandments and other laws given by God revealing how he wants his people to conduct themselves.

MORIAH
The mountains around Jerusalem where Abraham offered his son Isaac as a sacrifice.

MOUNT SINAI
The mountain where Moses received the Ten Commandments from God.

MOUNT ZION
The hill on which the oldest part of Jerusalem was built. A poetic name for the city of Jerusalem.

MYSTICAL BODY OF CHRIST
The faithful People of God, who in a supernatural way become one body, with Christ as its head. The faithful are united together in Christ's Mystical Body; that is, we are brought into communion with one another through our communion with Christ. For this reason, St. Paul refers to Jesus as the head of the Mystical Body: "He is before all things, and in him all things hold together. He is the head of the body, the church."[32] As the Mystical Body of Christ, the Church extends throughout time Christ's work of salvation.

NORTHERN KINGDOM
The term used to refer to the ten tribes of Israel that split from Jerusalem during the reign of King Solomon's son Rehoboam.

NUMBERS
The fourth book of the Bible, it tells about two censuses taken at the beginning and end of the Hebrews' time in the desert and more of the laws under which the Hebrews lived.

OATH
A promise transformed into a sacred commitment by calling on God's name.

OLD TESTAMENT
That part of the Bible, containing forty-six books, that tells the story of salvation history through God's covenant with Israel in preparation for the coming of Jesus Christ.

VOCABULARY Continued

ORIGINAL SIN
Adam and Eve's abuse of their human freedom in disobeying God's command. As a consequence they lost the grace of original holiness and justice, and became subject to the law of death; sin became universally present in the world; every person is born into this state of Original Sin. This sin separated mankind from God, darkened the human intellect, weakened the human will, and introduced into human nature an inclination toward sin.

PASSOVER (*Pasch*; *Pascha*)
A Jewish feast commemorating the deliverance of their firstborn males from death by the blood of the lamb sprinkled on the doorposts while in bondage in Egypt; the angel of death passed over their homes, allowing them to leave Egypt for the Promised Land. This was a type of the sacrificial Passion and Death of Jesus Christ, saving men from bondage to sin. The Eucharist celebrates Christ's Passover.

PENTATEUCH
The first five books of the Bible; it comprises Genesis, Exodus, Leviticus, Numbers, and Deuteronomy.

PHARAOH
A king or ruler of Egypt.

PLAGUE
Any of the ten signs God sent upon the people of Egypt in an effort to convince Pharaoh to let the Israelites go free. The plagues were: river turned to blood; frogs; lice; flies; sick animals; boils; hail; locusts; darkness; and the death of every firstborn male, both of man and of beast.

PROMISED LAND
The area to which God led the Israelites to live after their wanderings in the desert.

PROTOEVANGELIUM
From the Greek meaning "first gospel." The first message of Good News—the first Gospel—is Genesis 3:15, in which the promise of the Messiah and Redeemer is foretold.

PSALMS
A book of the Old Testament filled with hymns and poetry, much of which was written about the Israelites' captivity and some of which are credited to King David. The Psalms are rich in prophecy.

RED SEA
Sea through which Moses and the Hebrews passed in their flight from Egypt after God miraculously parted the waters for them.

REDEEMER
The expected Messiah (Jesus Christ), the one whom God promised would come and save his people from their sins.

REDEMPTION
The act of redeeming, used to refer to God's saving act of sending his Son, Jesus, to suffer and die on the cross for the sins of humanity and then rise from the dead in triumph, thus making possible our salvation, our hopes for being reunited with God in Heaven.

REVELATION
God's free decision to make himself known to us in a way that is beyond our natural capacity to learn of him by the use of human reason alone. God fully revealed himself through his Son, Jesus Christ. God's Revelation is transmitted through Sacred Scripture and Sacred Tradition.

RIVER NILE
Or the Nile River; waterway in Egypt upon which the infant Moses' mother placed him in a reed basket, hoping to save him from the pharaoh's order to kill all male Israelite children; the pharaoh's own daughter found him and raised him as her own child.

SABBATH
The Sabbath—or seventh—day on which God rested after the work of the six days of creation was completed. In honor of Christ's Resurrection, Sunday, the new Sabbath, must include rest from servile labor and the worship of God as required by the Third Commandment.

VOCABULARY Continued

SALVATION HISTORY
The story of God's plan to save men from the consequences of sin. This plan begins with the Fall after creation, is unfolding now, and will continue until the end of time.

TABERNACLE
In Israelite history, the tent containing the Ark of the Covenant and other sacred items; this portable sanctuary was taken through their wandering in the wilderness until the building of the Temple. An ornamented receptacle in the church in which the consecrated Eucharist is reserved for Communion for the sick and dying as well as for adoration.

TEMPLE
The house of God in Jerusalem that contained the Ark of the Covenant. When the Temple was dedicated, God's glory overshadowed it just as it had done in the tabernacle. The Temple became the center of worship for Israel.

TEN COMMANDMENTS
Decalogue. The fundamental laws given by God at Sinai that govern divine and human relationships.

THANK OFFERING
A sacrifice made in thanksgiving for God's deliverance. Under David and his successors, it became the primary liturgy of the Temple.

Madonna and Child with the Lamb of God by Cesare da Sesto.
The blood of the Passover lamb was a type of the Blood of Christ, who by his Blood saved us from eternal death. The Eucharist celebrates Christ's Passover.

STUDY QUESTIONS

1. What was the crowning achievement of God's creation?

2. Why did God create mankind?

3. What is the significance of *seven* days of creation?

4. What is the meaning of *image and likeness*? How is man created in the image and likeness of God?

5. What is *salvation history*?

6. What is a *covenant*?

7. What does it mean that God rested on the seventh day?

8. What happened when Adam and Eve ate from the fruit of the Tree of Knowledge of Good and Evil?

9. What did God promise in the *Protoevangelium*?

10. How did Original Sin have dire consequences for the family of Adam and Eve?

11. What were the three promises that God made to Abram?

12. In what ways was the near-sacrifice of Isaac a foreshadowing of the sacrifice of Christ?

13. What other sacrifice would occur on Mount Moriah?

14. Why did Moses flee Egypt? Why did he return?

15. What is the significance of God revealing his name to Moses?

16. What were the ten plagues of Egypt?

17. How were the faithful Israelites spared the horror of the death of every firstborn son?

18. Why did God have to establish a different order of priests to ensure that Israel stayed faithful to him in the future?

19. What is the meaning of the Hebrew *qahal*, and how is it translated into English?

20. Why were the Israelites given a second set of laws? Where are they found in the Bible?

21. Why did the Israelites need a king?

22. How would the king of Israel be chosen?

23. What is the meaning of the word *messiah* or *christ*?

24. What were the seven primary features of the Davidic Covenant?

25. What do the three additional features or secondary characteristics of the Davidic Covenant foreshadow in the New Testament?

26. What new Temple sacrifice did David establish as the primary form of worship?

27. What terrible things happened because of Solomon's disobedience to God?

28. How did St. Irenæus advance the Church's understanding of the covenants of the Old Testament and the New Testament?

PRACTICAL EXERCISES

1. God did not create man to fall, yet he knew Adam and Eve would sin. In God's Creation and his promises to Adam, there is a foreshadowing of the coming of Christ, who would restore the Eden with which Adam was originally entrusted. How is Christ present in Creation and in the covenant with Adam? How do the subsequent covenants with Noah, Abraham, Moses, and David shed light on what Christ's role would be in the New Covenant?

2. The great tension in the history of the nation of Israel is between Israel becoming a nation of priests or a nation of princes. Often this balance between the sociopolitical and the religious plays out in each individual's life. Describe the conflicts posed in your own life between being a member of society and a member of Christ's Church. In what ways are the Church's expectations and teachings contrary to society's? In what ways do they coincide? Looking at your own experience, do you think the aim of Israel to be a nation of priests was an impossible dream or something that could have come to pass?

3. Compare and contrast each of these leader's (a) faithfulness to God and (b) leadership capabilities: Abraham, Moses, Saul, David, and Solomon. Produce a chart with four columns for each person, listing each one's manifestations of faithfulness, faithlessness, positive leadership capabilities, and negative leadership capabilities. Be prepared to discuss your choices.

4. Research a *seder* meal and describe the traditions used to memorialize the Passover and what some of the food items and other elements symbolize.

5. Catholics have always venerated the Blessed Virgin Mary and other saints, addressing them in prayer. How do these acts differ from practices such as divination or polytheism?

6. Read the following Scripture passages about the punishment that befalls blasphemers: 1 Kings 21:13-16; 2 Kings 19:4-7. Why do you think God severely punished those Israelites who blasphemed his name?

Abraham and the Three Angels by Tissot. The three visitors are considered by some to represent the Holy Trinity. "And the LORD appeared to him by the oaks of Mamre, as he sat at the door of his tent in the heat of the day. He lifted up his eyes and looked, and behold, three men stood in front of him. When he saw them, he ran from the tent door to meet them, and bowed himself to the earth, and said, 'My lord, if I have found favor in your sight, do not pass by your servant.'" (Gn 18:1-3)

FROM THE CATECHISM

759 "The eternal Father, in accordance with the utterly gratuitous and mysterious design of his wisdom and goodness, created the whole universe and chose to raise up men to share in his own divine life,"[33] to which he calls all men in his Son. "The Father...determined to call together in a holy Church those who should believe in Christ."[34] This "family of God" is gradually formed and takes shape during the stages of human history, in keeping with the Father's plan. In fact, "already present in figure at the beginning of the world, this Church was prepared in marvelous fashion in the history of the people of Israel and the old Alliance. Established in this last age of the world and made manifest in the outpouring of the Spirit, it will be brought to glorious completion at the end of time."[35]

760 Christians of the first centuries said, "The world was created for the sake of the Church."[36] God created the world for the sake of communion with his divine life, a communion brought about by the "convocation" of men in Christ, and this "convocation" is the Church. The Church is the goal of all things,[37] and God permitted such painful upheavals as the angels' fall and man's sin only as occasions and means for displaying all the power of his arm and the whole measure of the love he wanted to give the world:

> Just as God's will is creation and is called "the world," so his intention is the salvation of men, and it is called "the Church."[38]

761 The gathering together of the People of God began at the moment when sin destroyed the communion of men with God, and that of men among themselves. The gathering together of the Church is, as it were, God's reaction to the chaos provoked by sin. This reunification is achieved secretly in the heart of all peoples: "In every nation anyone who fears him and does what is right is acceptable" to God.[39]

762 The remote *preparation* for this gathering together of the People of God begins when he calls Abraham and promises that he will become the father of a great people.[40] Its immediate preparation begins with Israel's election as the People of God. By this election, Israel is to be the sign of the future gathering of all nations.[41] But the prophets accuse Israel of breaking the covenant and behaving like a prostitute. They announce a new and eternal covenant. "Christ instituted this New Covenant."[42]

ENDNOTES - CHAPTER ONE

1. *Pastor Hermæ*, Vision 2, 4,1: PG 2, 899; cf. Aristides, *Apol.* 16, 6; St. Justin, *Apol.* 2, 7: PG 6, 456; Tertullian, *Apol.* 31, 3; 32, 1: PL 1, 508-509.
2. Cf. St. Epiphanius, *Panarion* 1, 1, 5: PG 41, 181C.
3. Clement of Alex. *Pæd.* 1, 6, 27: PG 8, 281.
4. Cf. Gn 3: 15.
5. CCC 758.
6. Cf. Rev 14: 4.
7. International Theological Commission, *Communion and Stewardship*, 22.
8. Gn 5: 3.
9. International Theological Commission, *Communion and Stewardship*, 25.
10. *LG* 2.
11. Cf. Gn 1: 28; 2: 15.
12. Cf. Nm 3: 7-8; 8: 26; 18: 5-6.
13. Gn 2: 17.
14. Jn 8: 44.
15. Gn 3: 15.
16. Cf. Gn 3: 9, 15.
17. Cf. Gn 6: 11–9: 17.
18. Cf. Gn 12: 2; 15: 5-6.
19. Gn 22: 2.
20. Ex 4: 22-23.
21. Gn 15: 14.
22. Ex 14: 16.
23. Ex 24: 7.
24. Cf. Heb 6: 13.
25. Ex 15: 1; cf. 3: 14.
26. Cf. Ex 19: 5-6.
27. Dt 34: 9.
28. 1 Sm 16: 13.
29. Ps 2: 6.
30. 1 Kgs 11: 12.
31. Cf. 1 Kgs 2: 19.
32. Col 1: 17-18.
33. *LG* 2.
34. *LG* 2.
35. *LG* 2.
36. *Pastor Hermæ*, Vision 2, 4, 1: PG 2, 899; cf. Aristides, *Apol.* 16, 6; St. Justin, *Apol.* 2, 7: PG 6, 456; Tertullian, *Apol.* 31, 3; 32, 1: PL 1, 508-509.
37. Cf. St. Epiphanius, *Panarion* 1, 1, 5: PG 41, 181C.
38. Clement of Alex., *Pæd.* 1, 6, 27: PG 8, 281.
39. Acts 10: 35; cf. *LG* 9; 13; 16.
40. Cf. Gn 12: 2; 15: 5-6.
41. Cf. Ex 19: 5-6; Dt 7: 6; Is 2: 2-5; Mi 4: 1-4.
42. *LG* 9; cf. Hos 1; Is 1: 2-4; Jer 2; 31: 31-34; Is 55: 3.

Jesus Christ Instituted the Church

Each of the covenants made with Adam, Noah, Abraham, Moses, and David were brought to completion in the Person of Jesus Christ and his Church.

The Church

CHAPTER 2

Jesus Christ Instituted the Church

od has willed to make men holy and save them, not as individuals without any bond or link between them, but rather to make them into a people who might acknowledge him and serve him in holiness" (*Lumen Gentium,* n. 9). This plan of God began to be revealed in the history of Abraham by the first words God spoke to him: "The Lord said to Abram: 'Go forth from the land of your kinsfolk...to a land that I will show you. I will make of you a great nation and I will bless you'" (Gn 12:1-2). The promise was then confirmed by a covenant (Gn 15:18; 17:1-4) and solemnly proclaimed after the sacrifice of Isaac.

Moses was called to lead that people out of Egypt. However, Moses was only God's agent in fulfilling his plan, the instrument of his power, for according to the Bible God himself led Israel out of slavery in Egypt. The divine initiative, the Lord's sovereign choice, assumes the form of a covenant. This occurred in regard to Abraham. It occurred after the deliverance of Israel from slavery in Egypt. The mediator of this covenant at the foot of Mt. Sinai is Moses. "All these things, however, happened as a preparation and figure of that new and perfect covenant which was to be ratified in Christ, and of the fuller revelation which was to be given through the Word of God made flesh" (*Lumen Gentium,* n. 9).

In the Old Testament Israel already owed its existence as the People of God to God's choice and initiative. However, this people was limited to a single nation. The new People of God goes beyond this limitation. It includes people of all nations, languages and races. It has a universal character, i.e., it is catholic.

"Those who believe in Christ, who are reborn, not from a corruptible seed, but from an incorruptible one through the word of the living God (cf. 1 Pt 1:23), not from flesh, but from water and the Holy Spirit (cf. Jn 3:5-6), are finally established as a 'chosen race, a royal priesthood, a holy nation...who in times past were not a people, but now are the People of God.'" (*Lumen Gentium,* n. 9)

— Pope Bl. John Paul II, *L'Osservatore Romano*, n. 44, November 4, 1991, and n. 45, November 11, 1991.

PART I: GOD PREPARES HIS PEOPLE FOR THE CHURCH

Up to this point, our examination of salvation history has been focused on the Old Testament covenants between God and man. With each covenant, God continued to expand the boundaries of his family—beginning with Adam and Eve, it grew to include the descendants of Abraham, then the nation of Israel, and finally the entire kingdom of David. The aim of each of these covenants is clear. God wanted to restore the communion between man and himself that he had intended from the very beginning.

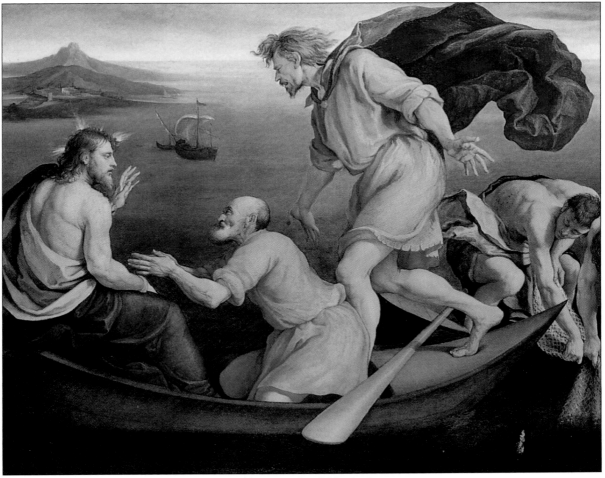

The Miraculous Draught of Fishes by Bassano.
"But when Simon Peter saw it, he fell down at Jesus' knees, saying, 'Depart from me, for I am a sinful man, O Lord.'
For he was astonished, and all that were with him, at the catch of fish which they had taken; and so also were James and John,
sons of Zebedee, who were partners with Simon. And Jesus said to Simon, 'Do not be afraid; henceforth
you will be catching men.'" (Lk 5: 8-10)

IN THIS CHAPTER, WE WILL ADDRESS SEVERAL QUESTIONS:

✤ What is the significance of the Incarnation?

✤ What are the two natures of Christ?

✤ What did Christ teach about the Kingdom of Heaven?

✤ What is our source of salvation?

✤ How is the Old Covenant fulfilled in the Church?

✤ What are some of the metaphorical images used to describe the Church?

✤ How is the Church the *Family of God*?

✤ How is the Church the *People of God*?

✤ What does it mean to say that the Church is the *Mystical Body of Christ*?

Each of these stages in God's plan to reunite his family reveal an important aspect of the reality of the Church, which is the place of God's final and perfect re-gathering of his people. Taken together, the series of covenants between God and man were God's way of preparing the world for the *Incarnation*—the coming of God himself as man in the Person of Jesus Christ—and for Jesus' institution of the Church.

From the very first words of the New Testament, Jesus is presented as the culmination and fulfillment of the Old Testament covenants. St. John calls to mind God's covenant with creation by opening his Gospel with the same words found in the opening verses of the Book of Genesis, "*In the beginning* was the Word."[1] St. Matthew begins his Gospel by identifying Jesus as "the son of David" and "the son of Abraham." Later, in the Sermon on the Mount, St. Matthew highlighted Jesus' role as a second Moses who gave the people a New Law of love from the top of a mountain.

The Sermon of the Beatitudes (detail) by Tissot.
St. Matthew highlighted Jesus' role as a second Moses who gave the people a New Law of love from the top of a mountain.

Such connections between the Old and New Testaments involve *typology*. When a character, event, or thing in the New Testament can be seen as having been allegorically foreshadowed in the Old Testament, we say that the Old Testament reference was an archetype, or simply a *type*, of the New Testament reference. In the latter example of the preceding paragraph, we can say that Moses as the instrument of the Old Law was a type of Jesus as the giver of the New Law.

We also saw how Isaac, the beloved son of Abraham, was a type of Jesus, the Son of God. When Abraham, acting on God's command, took his son Isaac to be sacrificed on the mountain, Isaac submitted to his father's will and carried the wood for his own sacrifice. He was a type of Jesus in that God was willing to sacrifice Jesus, the beloved Son of God, who was in turn obedient to the will of his Father and carried the wood (his cross) for his own sacrifice. In the end, in both instances, God provided the sacrifice; for Isaac, he provided a ram, while he provided Christ himself as the perfect sacrifice.

Many other types can be found between the Old and New Testament. Here are just a few:

OLD TESTAMENT TYPE	NEW TESTAMENT
Adam	Christ, the "New Adam"
Eve	Mary, the "New Eve"
Noah's Ark, which saved God's people	The Church, which saves God's people
Pharaoh's slaying of the firstborn children	Herod's slaying of the Holy Innocents
Israel saved by crossing through the Red Sea	Faithful saved today by waters of Baptism
Israel wanders in desert for forty years	Jesus fasts in desert forty days and nights
Manna in the desert, from God	The Eucharist, which is God himself
Ark of the Covenant	Mary as the new "Ark of the Covenant"
Passover meal	The Holy Mass
Passover shedding of spotless lamb's blood for sacrifice and deliverance from slavery	Jesus, the perfect Lamb of God, sacrifices his own life to deliver us from slavery to sin

The Saints
PILLARS OF THE CHURCH

St. Augustine
"THE OLD TESTAMENT IS REVEALED IN THE NEW"

Of all the saints and theologians throughout the two-thousand-year history of the Catholic Church, few could be considered as influential as St. Augustine. His thought permeates many of the doctrines developed since his time, and aside from the Bible, he is among the most frequently cited sources within official Church documents.

St. Augustine's contributions to the study of Scripture are especially important, for he sought to understand the inner unity of God's plan of salvation. He was a master of *typology*, the discernment of the Old Testament foreshadowing of New Testament realities.[2] As he once stated, "The New Testament is concealed in the Old, and the Old Testament is revealed in the New."

Augustine was born AD 354 in North Africa. His mother, St. Monica, was a devout Christian. In the North African city of Carthage, Augustine excelled in the study of law, literature, and philosophy. Nevertheless, whatever Christian beliefs and practices he had learned as a child, he soon ignored or forgot. For the next seventeen years, he lived an immoral life and soon began to follow the heretical teachings of Manichæism.

By the age of thirty, Augustine had firmly established himself as a brilliant teacher of rhetoric. Even so, he became increasingly restless. In AD 383, he took a position at the rhetorical school in Italy. In Milan, he met St. Ambrose, a bishop who would later be declared a Doctor of the Church. Like Augustine, St. Ambrose possessed a powerful intellect and a love for truth; but unlike Augustine, he also had found peace.

Through the example and patient instruction of Ambrose, Augustine gradually came to see the truth of Scripture, and, AD 387, to the great joy of his mother, he at last became a Christian. Upon his return to North Africa, Augustine was ordained a priest, and AD 395, he became the Bishop of Hippo (in modern-day Algeria). Over the next three and a half decades, Augustine dedicated himself to the pastoral care of his diocese, preaching thousands of homilies and fighting heresies within the Church.

St. Augustine died AD 430, at the age of seventy-five, and was soon thereafter proclaimed a saint. In AD 1298, Pope Boniface VIII named St. Augustine a Doctor of the Church in recognition of his innumerable contributions to Christian thought.

St. Augustine of Hippo, pray for us.

THE INCARNATION

For generations, mankind had awaited the Savior that had been promised in the *Protoevangelium* after the sin of Adam and Eve, the worldwide blessing that had been promised to Abraham, and the coming of the everlasting kingdom that had been promised to David. Now at last, "in the fullness of time," God sent his Son, who was the eternal Word and substantial Image of the Father, to accomplish all that he had promised. In the Incarnation, Christ assumed human nature without losing his divine nature. "Jesus Christ is true God and true man, in the unity of his divine person; for this reason he is the one and only mediator between God and men" (CCC 480).

Incarnation of Jesus by Piero di Cosimo.
Now at last, "in the fullness of time," God sent his Son, who was the eternal Word and substantial Image of the Father, to accomplish all that he had promised.

Describing the significance of the Incarnation, St. Paul says: "When the time had fully come, God sent forth his Son, born of woman...so that we might receive adoption as sons."[3] There are four key elements to this verse to which we should pay close attention.

✤ The Incarnation takes place "when the time had fully come," translated elsewhere as "in the fullness of time." The Incarnation did not occur randomly at some otherwise forgotten moment of history. God's plan was perfect, and he chose a specific time and place to enter the world and truly dwell with us. Additionally, the entrance of Christ into the world brought time itself to its fullness. The Incarnation is the single most important event in history, so much so that we measure all time in relation to it—BC means "Before Christ" and AD means "In the year of Our Lord" (in Latin, *"Anno Domini"*).

✤ Jesus is fully divine; he is called God's Son.

✤ Jesus is also fully human, being "born of woman."

✤ Our redemption in Christ is accomplished through our "adoption as sons," that is, by being made part of the Family of God through the redemption of Jesus Christ.

In the story of the *Annunciation*, when the angel Gabriel was sent to Nazareth to announce to Mary that she would be the Mother of the Messiah, he speaks of Jesus as the fulfillment of God's covenant with David.

[The angel Gabriel] came to [Mary] and said, "Hail, full of grace, the Lord is with you!...Behold, you will conceive in your womb and bear a son, and you shall call his name Jesus. He will be great, and will be called the Son of the Most High; and the Lord God will give to him the throne of his father David, and he will reign over the house of Jacob for ever; and of his kingdom there will be no end." (Lk 1: 28; 31-33)

This same theme is found again and again in the events surrounding Jesus' Birth. The angel who appeared to the shepherds outside of *Bethlehem* says, "I bring you good news of a great joy which will come to all the people; for to you is born this day in the city of David a Savior, who is Christ the Lord."[4] And later, when the infant Jesus is brought by his parents to the Temple, an elderly man named Simeon sees him and begins to praise God: "Lord...mine eyes have seen thy salvation which thou hast prepared in the presence of all peoples, a light for revelation to the Gentiles, and for glory to thy people Israel."[5]

Even as a newborn baby, Jesus was identified as the Messiah who had been sent by God the Father to redeem Israel—and through Israel, the entire world. We can see the beginning of God's Revelation to the *Gentiles* in the Epiphany, when the *magi* came and worshiped the child Jesus.

The Adoration of the Magi by Massys.
We can see the beginning of God's Revelation to the Gentiles in the Epiphany, when the magi came and worshiped the child Jesus.

In the magi, representatives of the neighboring pagan religions, the Gospel sees the first-fruits of the nations, who welcome the good news of salvation through the Incarnation. The magi's coming to Jerusalem in order to pay homage to the king of the Jews shows that they seek in Israel, in the messianic light of the star of David, the one who will be king of the nations.[6] (CCC 528)

Jesus, the eternal Son of God, now also the son of Mary, had come to take up the throne of David and establish the everlasting kingdom promised in the Old Testament and offering salvation to all the nations.

THE PROCLAMATION OF THE KINGDOM OF GOD

The Gospels do not contain much information about Jesus' life between his birth and the beginning of his public ministry, a period that is called the *hidden life* of Christ. We can assume that during this time he lived a normal life with his parents in Nazareth—learning the trade of his father, enjoying his friends, and studying at the local *synagogue*. The normality of Jesus' life during this time is also emphasized in the *synoptic Gospels*, when Jesus preached to his home town and is rejected by those who knew him and could not accept him as the promised Messiah.

Jesus' public ministry—the period of his preaching and healing of the sick—began when he was around thirty years old. At that time, "Jesus came into Galilee, preaching the gospel of God, and saying, 'The time is fulfilled, and the Kingdom of God is at hand; repent, and believe in the gospel.'"[7] The proclamation of the kingdom was the central theme of Jesus' preaching. All of his teaching was focused on what the Kingdom of Heaven is like, and how we are to live in it.

> It was the Son's task to accomplish the Father's plan of salvation in the fullness of time. Its accomplishment was the reason for his being sent.[8] "The Lord Jesus inaugurated his Church by preaching the Good News, that is, the coming of the Reign of God, promised over the ages in the scriptures."[9] To fulfill the Father's will, Christ ushered in the Kingdom of Heaven on earth. The Church "is the Reign of Christ already present in mystery."[10] (CCC 763)

So what is the Kingdom of Heaven? Jesus spent much time trying to teach his followers about the kingdom, often using *parables* to capture in simple language this difficult concept. We know from these parables, as well as from Jesus' dialogue with Pontius Pilate before his Death, that the Kingdom of Heaven was not to be a *temporal* kingdom like that of David's. Simply put, it is the state of communion between God and man that was intended from the very beginning and reinstituted on earth through the Incarnation of Christ.

Although the kingdom is ultimately made perfect only in Heaven, it is also present in the here and now. It is present both invisibly and visibly—invisibly within the spiritual reality of the Mystical Body of Christ and in the hearts of all the faithful who welcome God's reign in their lives, and visibly within the communion of human members of the *pilgrim Church* on earth that was established by Christ and built on the rock of St. Peter.

WHAT IS THE KINGDOM OF GOD LIKE?

Jesus frequently employed comparisons in the form of similes and metaphors to describe the Kingdom of Heaven.

The Kingdom of Heaven is like a grain of mustard seed which a man took and sowed in his field; it is the smallest of all seeds, but when it has grown it is the greatest of shrubs and becomes a tree, so that the birds of the air come and make nests in its branches. (Mt 13:31-32)

The Kingdom of Heaven is like leaven which a woman took and hid in three measures of flour, till it was all leavened. (Mt 13:33)

The Kingdom of Heaven is like treasure hidden in a field, which a man found and covered up; then in his joy he goes and sells all that he has and buys that field. (Mt 13:44)

The Kingdom of Heaven is like a merchant in search of fine pearls, who, on finding one pearl of great value, went and sold all that he had and bought it. (Mt 13:45-46)

The Kingdom of Heaven is like a net which was thrown into the sea and gathered fish of every kind; when it was full, men drew it ashore and sat down and sorted the good into vessels but threw away the bad. So it will be at the close of the age. The angels will come out and separate the evil from the righteous, and throw them into the furnace of fire; there men will weep and gnash their teeth. (Mt 13:47-50)

Jesus was aware of Israel's expectations of an earthly, political kingdom, so he used *parables*—stories or allegories based on familiar experiences that illustrate deeper, less familiar ideas—in an attempt to bring them to an understanding of the heavenly kingdom that he had come to establish, namely, the Church. The stories recounted in Jesus' parables are simple and accessible to everyone and contain profound truths about Jesus and the Church.

For example, in the Parable of the Sower,[11] Jesus revealed his mission of proclaiming the kingdom to all mankind—he is the sower who sows the Word. All men are called by Jesus to be part of the Church, but as Jesus explained in the Parable of the Treasure[12] and the Parable of the Pearl,[13] we have to be willing to give up everything to follow him.

The Parable of the Wheat and the Weeds[14] gives us an explanation of why, even in the Church, there is a "mixed composition" of good and evil. Although Jesus has sown good seed, the Devil has planted seed of his own—weeds that are meant to ruin the work of Christ the sower. But for the sake of the good seed (the wheat that represents the faithful followers of Christ), Jesus allows both to grow side by side until the time of judgment at the end of the world.

In the Parable of the Mustard Seed[15] and the Parable of the Leaven,[16] Jesus highlights the way that Christ's heavenly kingdom is present in the world. Although she will start out small in appearance, the Church will

THE PARABLE OF THE SOWER
(Mt 13: 3-8, 19-23)

"A sower went out to sow. And as he sowed, some seeds fell along the path, and the birds came and devoured them. Other seeds fell on rocky ground, where they had not much soil, and immediately they sprang up, since they had no depth of soil, but when the sun rose they were scorched; and since they had no root they withered away. Other seeds fell upon thorns, and the thorns grew up and choked them. Other seeds fell on good soil and brought forth grain, some a hundredfold, some sixty, some thirty."

"When any one hears the word of the kingdom and does not understand it, the evil one comes and snatches away what is sown in his heart; this is what was sown along the path. As for what was sown on rocky ground, this is he who hears the word and immediately receives it with joy; yet he has no root in himself, but endures for a while, and when tribulation or persecution arises on account of the word, immediately he falls away. As for what was sown among thorns, this is he who hears the word, but the cares of the world and the delight in riches choke the word, and it proves unfruitful. As for what was sown on good soil, this is

The Sower by Tissot.

he who hears the word and understands it; he indeed bears fruit, and yields, in one case a hundredfold, in another sixty, and in another thirty."

grow on earth until she has spread throughout the world and brought the Gospel to all men. The Church is present in the world like leaven, sanctifying it from within by continuing the work of Christ.

The Parable of the Mustard Seed also helps us to understand why so many of Jesus' listeners did not grasp the deeper meaning of his parables.[17] Like the seed, the Church during Jesus' public ministry is present but hidden. It is already present in the Person of Christ, but it has not yet been fully revealed. The revealing of the Church will take place after Jesus' *Resurrection* and *Ascension*, at *Pentecost*. Until that time, Jesus would explain the meanings of his parables only to the Twelve Apostles. And as we will see, this private instruction served as a preparation for the Apostles' foundational role as teachers and shepherds of the Church.

> **"This Kingdom shines out before men in the word, in the works and in the presence of Christ."[18] To welcome Jesus' word is to welcome "the Kingdom itself."[19] The seed and beginning of the Kingdom are the "little flock" of those whom Jesus came to gather around him, the flock whose shepherd he is.[20] They form Jesus' true family.[21] To those whom he thus gathered around him, he taught a new "way of acting" and a prayer of their own.[22] (CCC 764)**

Christ Healing the Sick by Brée. By giving the Apostles the task of assisting him in his public ministry, Jesus established them as leaders within the community of disciples.

JESUS CALLS THE TWELVE APOSTLES

From the start of his public ministry, Jesus' preaching and healing of the sick attracted great crowds of people. Some of these people were simply curious about this new teacher; some were looking for miraculous cures. Many others, however, were sincerely attracted to Jesus' message, and they came to believe in him. The Gospels refer to these people as Jesus' *disciples*. These disciples—hundreds of men and women of all ages and backgrounds—often followed Jesus, traveling with him as he went from town to town.

This growing community of disciples offers the first glimpses at the Church taking shape. We can observe both the invisible spiritual communion between the disciples and Christ as well as the visible form of the community itself.

Although the community of believers who surrounded Christ during his lifetime was rather formless and unorganized, Jesus did call forth from this group Twelve Apostles, whom he appointed "to be with him, and to be sent out to preach and have authority to cast out demons."[23]

By giving the Apostles the task of assisting him in his public ministry, Jesus established them as leaders within the community of disciples. After Christ's Resurrection and Ascension into Heaven, they began to exercise their responsibilities as shepherds of the Church, leading the faithful in continuing Christ's work. We can also see that in the Acts of the Apostles, even at this early stage in her development, the Church possessed a hierarchical structure that was established by Christ himself.

> The Lord Jesus endowed his community with a structure that will remain until the Kingdom is fully achieved. Before all else there is the choice of the Twelve with Peter as their head.[24] Representing the twelve tribes of Israel, they are the foundation stones of the new Jerusalem.[25] The Twelve and the other disciples share in Christ's mission and his power, but also in his lot.[26] By all his actions, Christ prepares and builds his Church. (CCC 765)

It was only to the Apostles that Jesus explained the deeper meanings of his parables, and much of his teaching in the Gospels was given to the Apostles alone. In doing this, Jesus was equipping these twelve men to provide the foundation of his Church. At the *Last Supper*, Jesus revealed more explicitly the role that his Apostles would play in the kingdom.

> You are those who have continued with me in my trials; as my Father assigned to me a kingdom, that you may eat and drink at my table in my kingdom, and sit on thrones judging the twelve tribes of Israel. (Lk 22:28-30)

In this passage, Jesus clearly connected the kingdom of the Church with the restoration of the kingdom of Israel, which he entrusted to the Twelve Apostles. This task of leading the Church would last until the end of time, and so, in time, the Apostles would appoint successors, called bishops, to fulfill their responsibilities as shepherds after the Apostles died. Jesus told the Apostles—and thus bishops and priests of every age— that they were to lead the Church by living lives of service to the faithful.[27] The hierarchy of the Church was established by Jesus so that his flock could be shepherded in holiness, being led in the communion with God that he had desired from the very beginning.

The Last Supper by Sassetta.
At the Last Supper, Jesus revealed more explicitly the role that his Apostles would play in the kingdom. Jesus clearly connected the kingdom of the Church with the restoration of the kingdom of Israel.

SALVATION THROUGH THE CROSS

Jesus' Last Supper could be defined as the event that founded the Church. Jesus gave His followers this Liturgy of Death and Resurrection and at the same time He gave them the Feast of Life. In the Last Supper he repeats the covenant of Sinai—or rather what at Sinai was a simple sign or prototype, that becomes now a complete reality: the communion in blood and life between God and man.

Clearly the Last Supper anticipates the Cross and the Resurrection and presupposes them, otherwise it would be an empty gesture. This is why the Fathers of the Church could use a beautiful image and say that the Church was born from the pierced side of the Lord, from which flowed blood and water.[28]

Each time we recite the *Nicene Creed* at Mass, we say that Jesus came down from Heaven "for us men and for our salvation." The purpose of the Incarnation is the restoration of man's communion with God. This communion, which was lost through the disobedience of our first parents, is offered to man once more through Christ, who was "obedient unto death, even death on a cross."[29]

At the very start of his public ministry, Jesus was proclaimed by St. John the Baptist to be "the Lamb of God, who takes away the sin of the world."[30] The image would not have been lost on those who heard St. John's proclamation at the time. This image of the lamb was intimately tied to the Passover lamb, the symbol of Israel's salvation from slavery. In order for mankind to be led out of its slavery to sin, a new lamb would have to be offered in sacrifice. Christ would be that sacrifice—the new lamb, the *Lamb of God*.

Christ's whole life was an offering to the Father for the sake of our salvation, but it was specifically in the sacrifice of his Crucifixion that our redemption was won. Another image that Jesus used to describe this sacrifice was that of the Good Shepherd, who lays down his life for his sheep. On the Cross, Jesus freely gave up his own life, and in doing so, he gave life to his flock, the Church.

> **The Church is born primarily of Christ's total self-giving for our salvation, anticipated in the institution of the Eucharist and fulfilled on the cross. "The origin and growth of the Church are symbolized by the blood and water which flowed from the open side of the crucified Jesus."[31] "For it was from the side of Christ as he slept the sleep of death upon the cross that there came forth the 'wondrous sacrament of the whole Church.'"[32] As Eve was formed from the sleeping Adam's side, so the Church was born from the pierced heart of Christ hanging dead on the cross.[33] (CCC 766)**

After his Resurrection, Jesus explained to the Apostles that it was necessary that he should suffer death in order to fulfill the plan of his Father:

> **He opened their minds to understand the scriptures, and said to them, "Thus it is written, that the Christ should suffer and on the third day rise from the dead, and that repentance and forgiveness of sins should be preached in his name to all nations." (Lk 24: 44-47)**

WHAT DOES IT MEAN TO BE SAVED?

"We are God's children now."[34] When St. John spoke about this reality, he could not hide his astonishment: "See what love the Father has given us, that we should be called children of God; and so we are!"[35] More than saving us *from* our sins, Jesus has saved us for sonship, to be sons and daughters of God. To be "saved" means to be accepted into God's family.

Natural birth, wonderful as it is, pales in comparison to supernatural birth—called *divine filiation*—that Christians receive in Baptism. There, the Christian becomes identified with Christ and united to him. Incorporated into Christ's Mystical Body, the person becomes a son or daughter of God and is raised up to share in the life of the eternal Son of God in the Blessed Trinity. We become, like Jesus, children of the Almighty and Eternal God.

Christ is the *Only*-Begotten Son of God. Our sonship is not the same as his, but a participation in the Sonship of Christ. His Sonship is uncreated and eternal. Ours is a grace; it is created and adoptive, but real. Through Baptism, we are as much a child of God as we are children of our earthly parents. We are truly at home in Heaven. We have joined what St. Paul called "the assembly of the firstborn,"[36] and therefore we are the heirs[37] of Christ. "All are yours," said St. Paul, "and you are Christ's, and Christ is God's."[38]

This task given to the Apostles—to preach repentance and forgiveness of sins—was a continuation of Christ's proclamation of the kingdom ("repent, and believe the gospel"), and was closely bound to the reconciliation of God and man accomplished by Christ on the Cross. As the kingdom of Christ present in the world, the pilgrim Church imitates her founder by calling mankind to conversion and repentance. And just as Christ not only preached about the forgiveness of sins but also forgave sins himself, so too does the Church—through the Apostles and their successors—continue to exercise Christ's divine authority to forgive sins.[39] Through the ministry of the Church, Christ continually offers the salvation and reconciliation of the Cross to men and women in every age.

The Emmaus Disciples by Bloemaert.
The Emmaus disciples recognized Christ's presence in the breaking of the bread.

MADE KNOWN IN THE BREAKING OF THE BREAD

Many of Jesus teachings and parables contained in the Gospels teach about the mystery of God and his kingdom through the images of food and drink. "The Kingdom of Heaven may be compared to...a marriage feast."[40] This relationship is especially noticeable in the three meals hosted by Jesus that are recounted in the Gospel of St. Luke, the only instances where Jesus is said to "break bread."

- ✤ **The Feeding of the Five Thousand.**[41] Jesus was preaching about the kingdom, and when the people got hungry, he multiplied five loaves of bread to feed them. All five thousand were satisfied, and there were twelve baskets of leftovers, signifying the twelve tribes of the kingdom of Israel.

- ✤ **The Last Supper.**[42] Jesus said that he would not eat or drink until the kingdom had come, and he promised his disciples that they would eat and drink in his kingdom. It was here that Christ instituted the priesthood and instructed his Apostles to celebrate the Eucharist.

- ✤ **The Meal at Emmaus.**[43] Before they realized they were speaking with Jesus, two of his disciples explained that they had hoped Jesus would "redeem Israel" and restore the kingdom of David. They recognized Christ's Presence in the breaking of the bread.

Jesus' association of the kingdom with eating and drinking can only be understood in light of the Eucharist. After he fed the five thousand, Jesus revealed the deeper meaning behind the miracle of the loaves:

> **Do not labor for the food which perishes, but for the food which endures to eternal life, which the Son of man will give to you....I am the living bread which came down from heaven; if any one eats of this bread, he will live for ever; and the bread which I shall give for the life of the world is my flesh. (Jn 6: 27, 51)**

The bread that Jesus would give was his own flesh, which is exactly what he offered to the Apostles at the Last Supper: "This is my body," Jesus said, "This cup...is the new covenant in my blood."[44] By telling them to "do this in remembrance of me," Christ instituted the Sacrament of the Eucharist so that he could be present in his Church even after his Ascension into Heaven.

Communion of the Apostles (detail) by Signorelli. Christ instituted the Sacrament of the Eucharist so that he could be present in his Church even after his Ascension into Heaven.

> **Since Christ was about to take his departure from his own in his visible form, he wanted to give us his sacramental presence; since he was about to offer himself on the cross to save us, he wanted us to have the memorial of the love with which he loved us "to the end,"[45] even to the giving of his life. (CCC 1380)**

Jesus' sacramental presence in the Eucharist—often called simply the *Real Presence*—is so tangible and complete that, when he broke the bread and gave it to his disciples during the Meal at Emmaus, he then vanished from their sight. The disappearance of the risen Christ in this context emphasizes the fact that Jesus' visible and physical presence had given way to his sacramental presence in the Eucharist.

As we have already seen, the restoration of the kingdom that took place with the Incarnation is first and foremost a restoration of the communion between God and man. In the Mass, which is the "marriage feast" between Christ and his Bride, the Church, the Kingdom of Heaven is revealed in the Eucharistic presence of Jesus. Each and every time we receive Holy Communion, we receive the resurrected Christ, the son of David and King of Heaven and earth. The king and his kingdom are made known in the breaking of the bread.

THE FULFILLMENT OF THE OLD COVENANT IN THE CHURCH

The restoration of man's communion with God, accomplished through Christ's Death and Resurrection, marked the fulfillment of his promise to Adam and Eve after the Fall. The *Protoevangelium*[46] in the Book of Genesis was the first prophecy of mankind's salvation. It announced the future victory of the Messiah, when the sin and death brought into the world by Adam would be reversed by Christ.

> **As by one man's disobedience many were made sinners, so by one man's obedience many will be made righteous. (Rom 5: 19)**

In reversing the sin of Adam and conquering sin and death, Jesus became the New Adam. The *Protoevangelium* indicates that Jesus, the son of "the woman," would become the new man of the new creation. The Blood and water spilled from Christ's side—representing the Sacraments of Baptism and the Eucharist—also show us that the Church, the Bride of Christ, is created from his side, just as Eve was

Lamentation by Solario.
The Blood and water spilled from Christ's side—representing the Sacraments of Baptism and the Eucharist—also show us that the Church, the Bride of Christ, is created from his side, just as Eve was created from Adam's rib.

created from Adam's rib. As Eve was the mother of all the living, the Church would be a mother to all God's children in his new creation.

Likewise, God promised Abraham that through his descendants all people would be blessed through him. This promise of a universal blessing is fulfilled in Jesus Christ, "the son of Abraham."[47] Jesus blessed the world by instituting the Church, a new and perfect family of Abraham, which is also the Family of God. As faithful followers of Christ, we imitate the faith and obedience of Abraham, who himself imitated God the Father by willingly offering up his own only beloved son.

Some of the promises to Abraham were already fulfilled in the Old Testament. Abraham's descendants did become a great nation, and kings did come from his family line. As God's "firstborn son" among the nations, the nation of Israel was given the task of bringing the Word of God to all the other peoples of the world. The assembly of the Israelites at Mount Sinai—where God established his covenant with Israel—foreshadowed the assembly of the Church. Just like Moses led God's Chosen People out of slavery in the Exodus and gave

The Resurrection of Christ by Veronese.
The Church is the new kingdom of Israel, and Jesus is its king.

them the Ten Commandments as their moral law, so too does Jesus lead the new People of God out of bondage to sin, giving us a new commandment—that we love one another as Christ has loved us.

This commandment, given at the Last Supper, was directed first of all to the Apostles, to whom Christ appointed his kingdom. The Church is the new kingdom of Israel, and Jesus is its king. This kingdom is *catholic* (from the Greek word for "universal"), and it is meant to include all of humanity.

Jesus fulfilled God's covenant promise to David of an everlasting kingdom. Although it is ultimately "not of this world,"[48] the kingdom was still established *in* this world. Therefore, it is a pilgrim Church journeying toward its final end in Heaven.

"To carry out the will of the Father Christ inaugurated the kingdom of heaven on earth."[49] Now the Father's will is "to raise up men to share in his own divine life."[50] He does this by gathering men around his Son Jesus Christ. This gathering is the Church, "on earth the seed and beginning of that kingdom."[51] (CCC 541)

THE COVENANTS OF SALVATION HISTORY

The Church is the fulfillment of God's covenant plan for our salvation.

	ADAM	NOAH	ABRAHAM	MOSES	DAVID	JESUS
Covenant Mediator	ADAM	NOAH	ABRAHAM	MOSES	DAVID	JESUS
Covenant Role	Husband	Father	Father	Judge	King	Royal High Priest
Covenant Form	Marriage	Household	Family	Nation	Kingdom	Universal Church
Covenant Sign	Sabbath	Rainbow	Circumcision	Passover	Temple	Eucharist

A NEW AND EVERLASTING TEMPLE

In addition to the promise of an everlasting kingdom, an essential component of God's covenant with David was that the son of David must build the Temple:

> **He shall build a house for my name, and I will establish the throne of his kingdom for ever.**
> **(2 Sm 7:13)**

This is precisely what Solomon did by building a "house of prayer" for all the nations, and what Herod tried to imitate in order to be accepted as the heir to David's throne. In the Old Testament, the Temple in Jerusalem signified God's abiding presence with his people; it was his dwelling place amid all of Israel.

The Ascension by Tissot.
In John 2:19, Jesus spoke of the "temple of his body."

With the coming of Jesus, God's presence among his people reaches perfection: "And the Word became flesh and dwelt among us."[52] Christ's bodily presence in the world is the new and everlasting temple, for Jesus is *Emmanuel*, meaning "God with us."

Throughout his life and ministry, Jesus always showed reverence toward the Temple in Jerusalem. At the same time, he prepared his listeners for entering the new "temple" that he had come to build. Jesus identified this new temple with his own Body. When the Jews asked Jesus for a sign, he said, "Destroy this temple, and in three days I will raise it up."[53] Jesus was not only foretelling the raising of his physical body from the dead, but he was also speaking of how he would raise up his Mystical Body, the Church, which is the continuation of his presence on earth. At the time, Jesus' listeners did not understand what he was saying—as in the case with his parables and teachings about the kingdom, the Apostles understood the meaning of Jesus' remarks concerning "the temple of his body" in their fullness only after he sent his Holy Spirit to the Apostles at Pentecost.

This Holy Spirit, who has dwelled within the Church since Pentecost, is the source of the life of the Church. "What the soul is to the human body, the Holy Spirit is to the Body of Christ."[54] St. Paul saw this indwelling of the Holy Spirit as the fulfillment of God's Old Testament promise.

> **We are the temple of the living God; as God said**
> **"I will live in them and move among them, and I**
> **will be their God, and they shall be my people."**
> **(2 Cor 6:16)**

Like Solomon before him, Jesus, the son of David, had made a temple. Jesus' temple, however, was not one made of bricks and mortar, but rather one composed of "living stones" and built upon St. Peter, the rock. This new temple is Christ's Body, the Church, and Christ himself is both its builder and its foundation.

> **You are...members of the household of God, built upon the foundation of the apostles and prophets, Christ Jesus himself being the cornerstone, in whom the whole structure is joined together and grows into a holy temple in the Lord; in whom you also are built into it for a dwelling place of God in the Spirit. (Eph 2:20-22)**

The Church is the new and everlasting temple, the Temple of the Holy Spirit, built by Christ as a sign of his presence, a house of prayer for all the nations.

PART II: NAMES AND IMAGES OF THE CHURCH

In Scripture, we find a host of interrelated images and figures through which Revelation speaks of the inexhaustible mystery of the Church. (CCC 753)

The Church at various times is compared to a body, a temple, or a flock of sheep, to list only a few. These images, many of which surfaced very early in Christianity, help reveal her invisible, supernatural reality, present but hidden in the pilgrim Church on earth.

The Church has a dual reality; it is both a human and a divine institution, planned by the Father, established by the Son, and revealed at Pentecost by the Holy Spirit. As a human institution, it is a visible community of faith comprised of her members. As the Mystical Body of Christ, the Church is also a divine institution. It is only with the eyes of faith that we can recognize the action of the Blessed Trinity in the life of the Church, for she is at one and the same time the Family of the Father, the Kingdom of the Son, and the Temple of the Holy Spirit.

St. Paul describes the union of Christ and the Church as "a great mystery." We can see that this mystery extends to the Church herself: "Because she is united to Christ as her bridegroom, she becomes a mystery in her turn."[55] The fact that the Church is a mystery does not mean that we cannot come to an understanding of what she is, however. A *mystery* is not something incomprehensible, but rather something inexhaustible. And because she is a divine mystery, our understanding of the Church depends upon God's Revelation of her in Sacred Scripture and Sacred Tradition.

For the Apostles and the rest of the early Church, this meant interpreting the Old Testament in light of the Revelation of Christ. With the help of the Holy Spirit, they studied the Scriptures and reflected upon the persons, events, and institutions through which God had prepared the world for the Incarnation and Christ's establishing of the Church. We can see the fruit of this study and reflection throughout the New Testament, which is filled with quotations and images from the Old Testament that are given new significance when illuminated by the teaching of Christ.

Christ's Charge to Peter by Raphael.
"When they had finished breakfast, Jesus said to Simon Peter, 'Simon, son of John, do you love me more than these?' He said to him, 'Yes, Lord; you know that I love you.' He said to him, 'Feed my lambs.' A second time he said to him, 'Simon, son of John, do you love me?' He said to him, 'Yes, Lord; you know that I love you.' He said to him, 'Tend my sheep.' He said to him the third time, 'Simon, son of John, do you love me?' Peter was grieved because he said to him the third time, 'Do you love me?' And he said to him, 'Lord, you know everything; you know that I love you.' Jesus said to him, 'Feed my sheep.' (Jn 21:15-17)

Pentecost (detail) by Vivarini.
The Church is a divine institution, planned by the Father, established by the Son, and revealed at Pentecost by the Holy Spirit.

Pope Benedict XVI celebrates an outdoor Mass at the Basilica of the National Shrine of Our Lady of Aparecida, São Paulo, Brazil. The National Shrine of Aparecida (Apparition) is the second-largest Catholic place of worship in the world, second only to St. Peter's Basilica in Vatican City. In 1984 it was officially declared the largest Marian Temple in the world by the National Conference of Bishops of Brazil.

IMAGES OF THE CHURCH

The Church is revealed in the Sacred Scripture as the mystery of the communion between God and men, and among men, through Christ in the Holy Spirit.

As the mystery of the Church is very rich in content, different names are used in Holy Scripture to cast a light on this mystery, thus making it easy for us to understand its nature and aim. These names and figures have something in common. They all refer to a *visible* or human element, and to an *invisible* or divine element.

The following concepts or images are often used to explain the Church's nature:

- ✤ **Mystical Body of Christ**
- ✤ **The Bride of Christ**
- ✤ **The Family of God**
- ✤ **The People of God**
- ✤ **Kingdom of God**
- ✤ **Sheepfold, the Flock**
- ✤ **Branches of the Vine**
- ✤ **Temple or Building**

THE MYSTICAL BODY OF CHRIST

Within the New Testament, the image of the Church as the Body of Christ is found mainly in the letters of St. Paul, who uses this image to describe the relation of the Church to Christ. St. Paul's intimate understanding of the relationship comes directly from his conversion experience on the road to Damascus. When Christ revealed himself to St. Paul, he did not ask why Saul (as St. Paul was known at that time) was persecuting his followers. Instead, Christ said, "Saul, Saul, why do you persecute *me*?...I am Jesus, whom you are persecuting."[56] This intimate relationship between Christ and the Church, where the two are spoken of as one, was also expressed by Jesus during his time on earth.

> From the beginning, Jesus associated his disciples with his own life...and he proclaimed a mysterious and real communion between his own body and ours: "He who eats my body and drinks my blood abides in me, and I in him."[57] (CCC 787)

The image of the Church as the Body of Christ is significant because it indicates that the Church is not simply a community of members gathered around Christ, but that the Church is united in him, in his Body.[58] This reality is made explicit in our reception of Christ's Body and Blood in Holy Communion. Through the Sacrament of the Eucharist, the faithful are united together in Christ's Mystical Body; that is, brought into communion with one another through communion with Christ. For this reason, St. Paul refers to Jesus as the head of the Mystical Body.

> He is before all things, and in him all things hold together. He is the head of the body, the church. (Col 1:17-18)

As the *Mystical Body of Christ*, the Church extends throughout time Christ's work of salvation.

> If we should define and describe this true Church of Jesus Christ—which is the holy, Catholic, apostolic Roman Church—we shall find no expression more noble, more sublime or more divine than..."the mystical body of Jesus Christ."...Sacred Scripture frequently asserts that the Church is a body. "Christ," says the Apostle, "is the head of his body, the Church" (Col 1:18). If the Church is a body, it must be an unbroken unity according to those words of Paul: "We, though many, are one body in Christ" (Rom 12:5).[59]

Through the Sacrament of the Eucharist, the faithful are united together in Christ's Mystical Body.

The faithful play diverse roles in the Church, just as in the natural body the eyes, ears, and feet have diverse functions. "As all the members of the human body, though they are many, form one body, so also are the faithful in Christ. Also, in the building up of Christ's Body there is engaged a diversity of members and functions. There is only one Spirit who, according to his own richness and the needs of the ministries, gives his different gifts for the welfare of the Church."[60] The diversity of roles does not harm the body, but rather serves its unity.

The Church receives its life and growth from Christ, who is the Head of this Body. The Holy Spirit acts in the Church, the Mystical Body of Christ; by giving us grace, he gives life to, unifies, and moves the whole body. His work could be compared to the function that the soul fulfills in the human body. The Holy Spirit is also the source of unity in the Body of Christ, both between the faithful and Christ and among the faithful themselves.[61]

The life of Christ is communicated to the faithful by means of the Sacraments;[62] through the Sacraments, the faithful are united to the risen Christ. Baptism, Confirmation, and the Eucharist are the three Sacraments of initiation, which incorporate the faithful into the Body of Christ. "Christ and his Church thus together make up the 'whole Christ' (*Christus totus*)."[63]

THE BRIDE OF CHRIST

In his Letter to the Ephesians, St. Paul explains Christ's headship of the Mystical Body in an unexpected way. Making use of a different image of the Church—the Church as the *Bride of Christ*—St. Paul says that Christ is the head of his Body, the Church, in the same way that a husband is the "head" of his wife.[64]

Now at first glance it might seem that St. Paul has mixed his metaphors, confusing these two images of the Church with one another. Just a few verses later, however, he quotes a passage from Genesis that helps draw together these two seemingly unrelated images: "For this reason a man shall leave his father and mother and be joined to his wife, and the two shall become one flesh."[65]

> The comparison of the Church with the body casts light on the intimate bond between Christ and his Church. Not only is she gathered *around him*; she is united *in him*, in his body. Three aspects of the Church as the Body of Christ are to be more specifically noted: the unity of all her members with each other as a result of their union with Christ; Christ as head of the Body; and the Church as bride of Christ. (CCC 789)

Sts. Peter and Paul Present God's Temple, (detail) Byzantine Icon.
St. Paul recognized that it is specifically as Christ's Bride that the Church is made "one flesh" with him and is therefore truly his Body.

When Adam first saw Eve, the bride that God had taken from his side, he exclaimed, "This at last is bone of my bones and flesh of my flesh."[66] For Adam, then, Eve is both his bride and a part of himself. In interpreting this Old Testament passage in light of the teaching of Christ, St. Paul recognizes that it is specifically as Christ's Bride that the Church is made "one flesh" with him and is therefore truly his Body.

The marriage covenant between Adam and Eve took place alongside another covenant, the covenant of creation. Marriage was thus intended by God to reflect the union of God and man intended from the beginning. This original union, lost in the Fall, is restored and perfected in Christ, who reunites mankind to God through his Church. Together they form one flesh.

THE CHURCH IS A "SHE"

From the time of the Apostles onward, Christians have used the words "she" and "her" when referring to the Church. This is because of the Church's relationship to Jesus Christ, which is described by St. Paul in terms of marriage—the Church is the Bride of Christ. And just as we use feminine pronouns to describe brides, so too do we use these pronouns to describe the Bride that Jesus Christ has taken for himself.

Creation of Eve, Byzantine Mosaic. For Adam, Eve is both his bride and flesh of his flesh. The Church is the Bride of Christ and together they form one flesh.

THE FAMILY OF GOD

Among the many images that Jesus utilized for the new people—flock, wedding guests, plantation, God's building, God's city—one stands out as his favorite, that of the family of God. God is the father of the family, Jesus the master of the house, and it therefore stands to reason that he addresses the members of this people as children, even though they are adults, and that to gain true understanding of themselves, those who belong to this people must first lay down their grown-up autonomy and acknowledge themselves as children before God.[67]

The image of the Church as the Family of God is found throughout Jesus' teaching. In the Gospels, he makes frequent use of family terminology to define his mission, his Person, his commands, his relationship both with God and with his disciples, and the Church's own relationship with God. And although Jesus also uses other images—both primary and secondary—when speaking of his Church, the image of Family remains dominant. Christ is the eternal Son, sent to re-gather in himself those whom the Father has called to be his beloved sons and daughters.[68] For this reason, the *Catechism of the Catholic Church* tells us that "the Church is nothing other than 'the family of God.'"[69]

> Becoming a disciple of Jesus means accepting the invitation to belong to *God's family*, to live in conformity with His way of life: "For whoever does the will of my Father in heaven is my brother, and sister, and mother."[70] (CCC 2233)

The Fatherhood of God is not simply a metaphor. Christ has revealed that God is an eternal and perfect Father—our *Abba*, meaning "Father" or, still closer, "Daddy"—beside whom even the best of earthly fathers pales in comparison.

As Christ reveals to us in the Incarnation, God is not simply *like* a father because he is our Creator. Rather, independently of his creation, he is the eternal Father, just as Jesus is the eternal Son. St. Paul reminds us that God's Fatherhood is the origin and standard of human fatherhood. "For this reason I bow my knees before the Father, from whom every family in heaven and on earth is named."[71]

Although Christ alone is the eternal Son of the Father, he nonetheless teaches all of his disciples to approach God as "Our Father," for through his Cross and Resurrection he has extended the grace of divine sonship. United to Christ, the Son, in Baptism, we too become sons and daughters of the Father.

The heavenly Father desires us to experience his fatherly love in a deeply personal way. By sending his Son into the world, God invites us to know him as Our Father, for "no one knows the Father except the Son and anyone to whom the Son chooses to reveal him."[72]

THE CHURCH AS THE FAMILY OF GOD

In most ancient cultures, the large, extended family defined an individual's world. Your family included all the descendants of your patriarch—usually a man who had lived centuries before. Each tribe was a distinct family whose members shared the same faith and called one another "brothers" and "sisters," children of a common father. In fact, most ancient Semitic languages had no word for "cousin," since "brother" or "sister" served the purpose.

Jesus himself belonged to such a family: the nation of Israel and the Tribe of Judah. His large extended family lived together and was so closely knit that the twelve-year-old Jesus could disappear for an entire day without Mary and Joseph worrying about him, assuming instead that he was somewhere safe in the family's large caravan.

Yet Jesus' idea of family—based on God's fatherhood—seemed to run contrary to the old tribal notion. Jesus spoke of God as not merely the "God of our fathers," but as the universal Father. God's family transcended all national, tribal, and familial divisions.

It was a religion free of class distinctions in which all are siblings and equals. "For in Christ Jesus, you are all sons of God through

faith....There is neither Jew nor Greek, there is neither slave nor free, there is neither male nor female; for you are all one in Christ Jesus."[73]

God became a man in order to draw men and women away from their primal families, their tribes, and toward *his* family. Indeed, he described our initiation as being "born anew."[74] He spoke of our bond with God as a "new covenant."[75] He spoke of our ultimate destiny as a "marriage supper."[76] Birth, covenant, and marriage all share one thing in common: they incorporate an individual into a family—in this case, a supernatural family, the Catholic Church.

THE FAMILY OF GOD CELEBRATES TOGETHER
Pope Benedict XVI lovingly greeted by the Family of God during a visit to Brazil in 2007.

As our heavenly Father, God gives us many ways of knowing that we are his children and members of his Family.

✤ **We live in his house.** Jesus referred to the Temple as "my Father's house," and as members of the Church, we too live in Our Father's house, built by Christ upon the Rock of Peter.

✤ **We are called by his name.** When we were baptized, it was in the name of the Father and of the Son and of the Holy Spirit. Through Baptism, we become adopted sons and daughters of the Father, and are called Christians, because of our union with Christ.

✤ **We eat at his table.** In the Eucharist, we "partake of the table of the Lord." [77]

✤ **We share his Flesh and Blood.** When we receive the Eucharist, having eaten his Body and drunk his Blood, we mystically become "one flesh" with Christ.

✤ **His Bride is our Mother.** As we saw earlier, the Church is the Bride of Christ. But she is also our Mother, for through water and the Spirit in Baptism, the Church gives birth to new sons and daughters of God. "No one can have God as Father who does not have the Church as Mother." [78]

✤ **We celebrate together.** Just as families gather together to celebrate anniversaries, birthdays, and other important events, in the Mass the pilgrim Church on earth joins with those in Heaven to commemorate our redemption in Christ. Additionally, throughout the year, we celebrate the feast days of our Blessed Mother, Mary, as well as the saints, who are our brothers and sisters in Christ.

✤ **We receive instruction and discipline from him.** Through Scripture and Tradition, as taught by the Church, God reveals to us how we are to live as members of his Family. Further, he allows us to undergo hardships and trials so that we might be strengthened in holiness and love: "For the Lord disciplines him whom he loves.... He disciplines us for our good, that we may share his holiness." [79]

As beloved children of God, we can be confident that our almighty Father will lead us to our heavenly home: "I am sure that he who began a good work in you will bring it to completion at the day of Jesus Christ." [80]

THE PEOPLE OF GOD

"At all times and in every race, anyone who fears God and does what is right has been acceptable to him. He has, however, willed to make men holy and save them, not as individuals without any bond or link between them, but rather to make them into a people who might acknowledge him and serve him in holiness. He therefore chose the Israelite race to be his own people and established a covenant with it....All these things, however, happened as a preparation for and figure of that new and perfect covenant which was to be ratified in Christ."[81] (CCC 781)

The Church, the congregation of all those who believe in Christ, is the *People of God*, which he himself bought with his Blood. It is a people, which is brought into unity from the unity of the Blessed Trinity—Father, Son, and Holy Spirit. It was already prefigured in the people of Israel. Hence, the *Second Vatican Council* states: "As Israel according to the flesh, which wandered in the desert, was already called the Church of God, so too, the new Israel, which advances in this present age in search of a future and permanent city, is called also the Church of Christ."[82]

The image of the Church as the People of God is closely related to the assembly of Israel at Mount Sinai. God made his covenant with Moses and the Israelites at Mount Sinai, promising that if they kept the covenant, they would be his Chosen People, a kingdom of priests and a holy nation.

God's decision to form for himself a people—as opposed to a random assortment of individuals—reflects his understanding of and concern for the social nature of man. The human person always lives and functions in relation to others. We are drawn to live in communities. All that we have, we have received from

WORSHIPING AS THE NEW PEOPLE OF GOD

When Moses ascended Mount Sinai to speak with God, he received not only the Ten Commandments, but also instructions from God about how Israel was to worship. God knew that the only way that the Israelites were going to succeed in leading other nations to him was if they themselves remained in union with him, a union brought about and sustained through regular communal worship.

Here is how the Church, in celebrating the fulfillment of the Old Covenant, has retained key elements of its worship:

ELEMENT	OLD COVENANT	NEW COVENANT
Daily Sacrifice	The Israelites sacrificed a lamb as an offering to God every morning and evening.	At every Mass, the Church unites herself to the one sacrifice of Christ, the Lamb of God.
Weekly Rest and Worship	Rest from work on the Sabbath, the seventh day of the week. Worship given to God on the Sabbath.	Rest from work on Sunday, recalling Christ's Resurrection. Worship given to God on the Lord's Day.
Annual Feasts	The Israelites celebrated and recalled many special occasions of God's mercy and protection, such as Passover.	The Church celebrates Easter as the "Feast of feasts," along with many other Holy Days, feast days, and memorials.

Christ on the Cross (detail) by Velázquez.
Through the sacrifice of the new Passover Lamb, Jesus Christ, God once again sets his people free.

someone else, whether it is the gift of life, our knowledge and skills, or even the truth of the Gospel. All of these things ultimately come from God himself. "Every perfect gift is from above, coming down from the Father."[83]

Israel was the first People of God, chosen and commissioned by God to bring all the nations into the communion with him that he had desired from the beginning. In this way, the faith of the People of Israel was already a response to God's Revelation under the Old Covenant. It follows that neither all Jews at that time nor Jews today can be charged with the Death of Christ, and they cannot be spoken of as a rejected or accused People. Although the fulfillment of God's promises was not realized in the people of Israel, we know that God did not abandon his desire to unite them and all mankind to himself.

> **Behold, the days are coming, says the LORD, when I will make a new covenant with the house of Israel and the house of Judah....I will put my law within them, and I will write it upon their hearts; and I will be their God, and they shall be my people.** (Jer 31:31, 33)

God formed his people in the Old Covenant when he set his people free from slavery in Egypt by redeeming them through the blood of the Passover lamb, so that they might serve him through proclaiming his goodness to all mankind. But that covenant did not complete God's mission of reuniting all of mankind to himself. In the New Covenant in Jesus Christ, God once again sets his people free—this time from our slavery to sin—and he does so through the sacrifice of the new Passover lamb, the Lamb of God who takes away the sins of the world.

The Saints
PILLARS OF THE CHURCH

St. Francis of Assisi
"REPAIR MY HOUSE"

St. Francis of Assisi, the founder of the Franciscan religious order, was a friar who lived in the late twelfth and early thirteenth centuries. He was born in Italy around AD 1181 to a wealthy family and, from an early age, was expected to be a merchant like his father and to eventually take over the family business. Although he received a good education in preparation for this career, Francis showed little interest in business and was occupied instead with having fun and gaining fame as a soldier.

After being captured in battle and suffering from a serious illness, Francis gradually began to understand God's call in his life. Rather than riches or military fame, Francis realized that God was asking him to embrace a life of poverty and humility in imitation of Christ. The words that Jesus addressed to the rich young man in the Gospel seemed especially applicable to Francis: "If you would be perfect, go, sell what you possess and give to the poor, and you will have treasure in heaven; and come, follow me."[84]

One day, while he was praying in a small, rundown chapel outside of his hometown of Assisi, Francis heard the voice of Christ, saying, "Go, Francis, repair my house, which as you can see is falling into ruin." Thinking that Christ was referring to the church of San Damiano, where he was praying, Francis set about the task of repairing it by hand. But it was not simply the small church of San Damiano that Christ was calling Francis to repair, but rather the entire Church on earth.

For the remainder of his life, Francis did his best to imitate Christ in any way he could. He preached wherever he went; he embraced a life of poverty, giving what little he had to the poor; and he visited and served the sick and dying, especially those with leprosy. By his example and his preaching, Francis would serve as a reminder of the radical commitment to the Gospel that is entailed by being a follower of Christ.

In 1224, two years before his death at the age of forty-five, St. Francis received the *stigmata*, the visible marks of Christ's Passion and Death, which enabled him to imitate Christ even in his suffering. He died on October 3, 1226, and was canonized by Pope Gregory IX two years later.

St. Francis of Assisi, pray for us.

Jesus is the last and perfect son of David. The lineage of Jesus is illustrated in this
Tree of Jesse, an illuminated initial in a twelfth-century Bible.

THE KINGDOM OF GOD

One primary image that Jesus uses to describe the Church was the Church as the Kingdom of God. From the opening verses of the New Testament, Jesus' lineage firmly establishes him as the son of David, and therefore the true king of Israel, an heir to God's covenant with David. Jesus' new kingdom, however, would not be like the temporal empires established by David or Solomon. Jesus' kingship is not confined to Israel's geographical borders: "My kingship is not from the world."[85]

Christ makes it clear in his teaching that he is the king of the new Israel, the Church, which he frequently refers to simply as "the kingdom." This kingdom, Christ tells us, is the Kingdom of God. However, while Christ never set out to establish a temporal kingdom similar to that of David, the kingdom Christ preached can be seen as an inheritor of the primary characteristics of the kingdom of David.

Jesus himself is God's action, his coming, his reigning. In Jesus' mouth, "Kingdom of God" does not mean some thing or place but the present action of God. One may therefore translate the programmatic declaration of Mark 1:15, "the Kingdom of God is near at hand," as "God is near." We perceive once more the connection with Jesus, with his person; he himself is God's nearness. Wherever he is, is the Kingdom.[86]

By re-examining the seven main features of God's covenant with David, we can see how they take on new meaning in the kingdom established by Jesus Christ.

✤ **The covenant establishes a royal dynasty.** Jesus is the last and perfect son of David, "the highest of the kings of the earth."[87] At the Last Supper, he instituted the new covenant in his Blood, and speaks of the kingdom that the Father has appointed (literally, "covenanted") for him.[88]

✤ **The king of Israel will not only be the son of David, but the son of God as well.** Jesus is Son from all eternity, God's "only Begotten Son";[89] through Baptism, we are united to him as members of his Church and thus made adopted sons and daughters of the Father.

✤ **The king of Israel will be the "christ," that is, the "messiah,"** the Greek and Hebrew words for "the anointed one." As the Son, Jesus is eternally anointed with the Holy Spirit by the Father.[90] This anointing is manifested during Jesus' Baptism in the Jordan: "I saw the Spirit descend as a dove from heaven, and it remained on him."[91]

✤ **Jerusalem, and particularly Mount Zion, will be Israel's spiritual center.** In the Old Testament, the earthly Jerusalem was understood to be a sign of God's own heavenly dwelling place. But in the Mass, we are raised to participate in the worship of this heavenly city: "You have come to Mount Zion and to the city of the living God, the heavenly Jerusalem."[92]

✤ **The Temple is the visible sign of the covenant and of God's kingdom.** As the Temple of the Holy Spirit, the Church is the visible sign of God's New and Everlasting Covenant, built by Christ, the son of David, to be "a house of prayer for all peoples."

✤ **The king of Israel is to rule not only over the twelve tribes, but also over all the nations.** Christ is "a light for revelation to the Gentiles, and for glory to thy people Israel,"[93] and he commands his Apostles that "repentance and forgiveness of sins should be preached in his name to all nations."[94]

✤ **The kingship given to David and his descendants will be everlasting.** At the Annunciation, the angel Gabriel tells Mary that Jesus "will reign over the house of Jacob for ever; and of his kingdom there will be no end."[95]

OTHER IMAGES OF THE CHURCH

Here are a few other images used in Scripture to describe the Church:

The Church as a Sheepfold or Flock.
We are the flock, and Christ is the Good Shepherd who lays down his life for his sheep. Christ feeds us also through his human shepherds, who lead us and nourish us.

The Church as Fertile Land, Branches of the Vine.
The Church is a piece of land, a choice vineyard cultivated by God. The vine that grows is Christ. We are the branches, who are called to bear his good fruit.

The Church as a Temple or Building. The Church is the house built on solid ground. Jesus is the foundation, the cornerstone rejected by the builders. We are the living stones that also make up his building, his holy Temple.

The three additional features of the Davidic kingdom also find their fulfillment in the Church.

✤ **The queen mother became an important part of the royal government.** The Blessed Virgin Mary takes on the role of queen mother in Christ's kingdom, advising her son and interceding on behalf of his people.[96]

✤ **The prime minister became a distinct office in the royal government.** Of the Twelve Apostles whom Jesus chose as the ministers of his kingdom, it is to St. Peter and his successors that Christ gives special authority for leading the Kingdom of Heaven on earth. This authority is symbolized by the sign of his office: the keys of the kingdom (see Chapter Five).

✤ **The "thank offering" became the primary sacrifice offered in the Temple.** Christ transforms the Israelites' thank offering of unleavened bread and wine by instituting the Eucharist (from the Greek *eucharistia*, meaning "thanksgiving").

CONCLUSION

The Incarnation, the entrance of Jesus, the Son of God, into human history, marked the fulfillment of God's promise to reestablish communion with mankind. Each of the covenants made with Adam, Noah, Abraham, Moses, and David were brought to completion in the Person of Jesus Christ and his Church.

God's preparation of his people for the coming of Jesus Christ and the establishment of his Church becomes much more apparent in retrospect. The Holy Spirit who animates the Church and maintains it in truth has revealed the beautiful and intricate manner in which God led his people into a state of readiness for the promised Messiah. Christ and his teachings perfectly fulfill the Old Testament covenants in such a way that the old covenants were a foreshadowing of what was to come. The faithful today are the People of God, the Mystical Body of Christ, his Church, his Bride, his Sheepfold....These images of our communion with God, like the mystery itself, are inexhaustible and woefully inadequate to express the reality of the New Covenant, the new relationship with God that Jesus gained for us through his Cross and Resurrection.

Having reviewed in this chapter the prophecies and signs of the Old Testament covenants and how they were fulfilled in the Person of Christ, we will summarily examine their continued fulfillment after Christ's Ascension as the infant Church, guided by the Apostles led by St. Peter, developed and flourished under the inspiration of the Holy Spirit.

The Repentant Peter by El Greco.
"And I tell you, you are Peter, and on this rock I will build my church, and the powers of death shall not prevail against it."
(Mt 16: 18)

SUPPLEMENTARY READING

1. Christ the Good Shepherd (Jn 10: 1-10)

"Truly, truly, I say to you, he who does not enter the sheepfold by the door but climbs in by another way, that man is a thief and a robber; but he who enters by the door is the shepherd of the sheep. To him the gatekeeper opens; the sheep hear his voice, and he calls his own sheep by name and leads them out. When he has brought out all his own, he goes before them, and the sheep follow him, for they know his voice. A stranger they will not follow, but they will flee from him, for they do not know the voice of strangers." This figure Jesus used with them, but they did not understand what he was saying to them. So Jesus again said to them, "Truly, truly, I say to you, I am the door of the sheep. All who came before me are thieves and robbers; but the sheep did not heed them. I am the door; if any one enters by me, he will be saved, and will go in and out and find pasture. The thief comes only to steal and kill and destroy; I came that they may have life, and have it abundantly."

2. Why the Church Is Called *Ecclesia*

After this short survey of the acts by which Jesus founded the Church, we still have to turn our attention to the nascent Church of the apostolic period. In this context I would like to stick to two terms whose trail leads to the heart of the apostolic testimony and which follow from the structure we have just discovered in the activity of Jesus: the expression "People of God" and the Pauline idea of the "Body of Christ." By itself, however, the term "People of God" signifies almost without exception the people of Israel and not the Church, for which the vocable [*ecclesia*] is used instead; this word subsequently passed over into all the Romance languages and became the proper designation of the new communion that grew out of Jesus' activity.

Why was this word chosen? What is thereby expressed about his communion? Of all the abundant material that modern research has

The Good Shepherd (detail) by Tissot.
"When he has brought out all his own, he goes before them, and the sheep follow him, for they know his voice." (Jn 10: 4)

SUPPLEMENTARY READING Continued

accumulated on this question, I would like to take just one observation. The Greek term that lives on in the Latin loan word *ecclesia* derives from the Old Testament root *qahal*, which is ordinarily translated by "assembly of the people." Such "popular assemblies," in which the people [were] constituted as a cultic and, on that basis, as a juridical and political entity, existed both in the Greek and the Semitic world.

But there is a twofold distinction between the Old Testament *qahal* and the Greek plenary assembly of enfranchised citizens. Even women and children, who in Greece could not be active agents of political event, belonged to the *qahal*. A closely connected fact is that in Greece it is the males who determine by their decisions what is to be done, while the assembly of Israel gathers "to listen to what God proclaims and to assent to it." This typically biblical conception of the popular assembly is traceable to the fact that the convocation on Sinai was regarded as the normative image of all later such assemblies; it was solemnly reenacted after the Exile by Ezra as the refoundation of the people. But because the dispersion of Israel continued on and slavery was reimposed, a *qahal* coming from God himself, a new gathering and foundation of the people, increasingly became the center of Jewish hope. The supplication for this gathering—for the appearance of the *ecclesia*—is a fixed component of Jewish prayer.

It is thus clear what it means for the nascent Church to call herself *ecclesia*. By doing so, she says in effect: This petition is granted in us. Christ, who died and rose again, is the living Sinai; those who approach him are the chosen final gathering of God's people (cf., for example, Heb 12:18-24). In this light it becomes comprehensible why the common term "People of God" was not employed to designate the new communion and why the choice fell instead on that expression that stood for the spiritual and eschatological center of the concept of "people." This new communion is first brought into being in the dynamic movement of gathering.

Emanating from Christ and sustained by the Holy Spirit, this dynamism has its center in the Lord, who communicates himself in his very Body and Blood. The self-description of the new people as *ecclesia* defines it in terms both of the continuity of the covenant in saving history and of the newness of the mystery of Christ, which is open to what lies ahead. If we must say that now the "new law" becomes the decisive center whose ultimate criterion Christ has established in laying down his life on the Cross.

— Joseph Cardinal Ratzinger, *Called to Communion*[97]

3. Why the Church Is Called the "People of God"

The term "People of God" is a biblical one. The biblical use is thus also normative for how we might use it. It is first and essentially an Old Testament term; the term "people" comes long before the era of nations and is connected more with the clan, with the family.

Above all it is a relational term. More recent exegesis has made this very clear. Israel is not the People of God when it acts simply as a political nation. It becomes the People of God by turning to God. It is the People of God only in relation, in turning to God.

In the New Testament, the concept "People of God" (with perhaps one or two exceptions) refers only to Israel, that is, to the people of the Old Covenant. It is not a concept that applies directly to the Church. However, the Church is understood as the continuation of Israel, although Christians don't descend directly from Abraham and thus actually don't belong to this people. They enter into it, says the New Testament, by their descent from Christ and thereby also become children of Abraham. Thus, whoever belongs to Christ belongs to the People of God.

— Joseph Cardinal Ratzinger, *Salt of the Earth* (Ignatius Press: San Francisco), Part II: "We are the People of God."

VOCABULARY

ABBA
A name Jesus used for God the Father and invited us to use in our prayer as well. It is similar to "Daddy," indicating a close, familiar, and loving relationship.

ANNO DOMINI
Latin for "in the year of our Lord," usually abbreviated "AD" to reference a given year in history. The fact that today we count the years from the date of Jesus' Birth bears witness to his importance in the entire world.

ANNUNCIATION
The visit of the angel Gabriel to the Virgin Mary to inform her that she was to be the Mother of the Savior. After giving her consent to God's word, Mary became the Mother of Jesus by the power of the Holy Spirit.

APOSTLE
Literally, "one who is sent." Jesus selected Twelve Apostles to be his inner circle of companions and to carry out his mission after his Ascension. (*See* Twelve Apostles)

ASCENSION
Christ's return to Heaven from the Mount of Olives before his Apostles' very eyes, forty days after his Death and Resurrection.

BETHLEHEM
"Little town" where Jesus was born, in the land of Judea.

BODY OF CHRIST
A name of the Church used frequently by St. Paul; it highlights the unity of Christ and the Church.

BRIDE OF CHRIST
A name of the Church derived from the writings of St. Paul; it highlights the purity and holiness that Christ has bestowed upon the Church.

CATHOLIC
Literally, "universal." As used in the early Church, the term referred to the fact that the Gospel of Christ was for the entire world; today it is also the name for the Catholic Church, the universal Church established by Christ.

DISCIPLE
Literally, "one who follows." Sometimes in Scripture, the term is applied to the Twelve Apostles; at other times, and more generally, it refers to the entire crowd of Jesus' followers and believers.

DIVINE FILIATION
Refers to the fact that the Sacrament of Baptism makes us spiritual sons and daughters of God. While our divine filiation is not the same as that of Jesus, the Only-Begotten Son of God, it is a participation in the Sonship of Christ. Jesus' Sonship is uncreated and eternal. Ours is a grace that is created, adoptive, and real. It means that through Baptism, we are just as much a child of God as we are children of our earthly parents, and we are truly at home in Heaven.

EMMAUS
A small village a few hours' journey away from Jerusalem. After his Resurrection, two of Jesus' followers met him on the road to Emmaus, but did not recognize him until he broke bread with them.

EPIPHANY
From the Greek for "manifestation." The Feast of Epiphany celebrates the adoration of the Christ child by the Magi, the Baptism of Christ in the Jordan, and his first miracle at the wedding in Cana.

EUCHARIST
The Sacrament by which bread and wine are consecrated by a priest and become the true Body and Blood of Christ, which the faithful consume in Holy Communion; more broadly, Eucharist, which means "thanksgiving," refers to the Catholic Mass itself.

FAMILY OF GOD
A name of the Church derived from the teaching of Christ; it highlights the intimate communion that the Father offers to man in the Person of Jesus Christ, in whom we are made sons and daughters of God.

VOCABULARY Continued

GENTILE
Any non-Jew. Jesus himself preached to the Gentiles, and St. Paul's remarkable missionary journeys to non-Jewish communities showed how the Gospel message was meant to be preached not just to Jews, but to all of humanity.

INCARNATION
From the Latin meaning "to make flesh." The mystery of the hypostatic union of the divine and human natures in the one divine Person, the Word, Jesus Christ. To bring about man's salvation, the Son of God was made flesh (cf. Jn 1:14) and became truly man.

KINGDOM OF HEAVEN
A name of the Church used frequently by Jesus; it highlights the relationship between the Davidic kingdom and the Church.

LAMB OF GOD
The Passover sacrifice at the Exodus. This was a foreshadowing of Jesus Christ, the perfect sacrifice, "who takes away the sins of the world."

LAST SUPPER
The celebration of the final Passover meal of Jesus and his Apostles in the "upper room," just before his arrest, Passion, Crucifixion, and Death. It was during this meal that he instituted the Eucharist.

MAGI
The "wise men" who journeyed from the East to visit the Christ child at his Birth.

MYSTERY
An inexhaustible truth, something that can be known with certainty through faith but can never be fully understood by human reason.

MYSTICAL BODY OF CHRIST
The faithful People of God, who in a supernatural way become one body, with Christ as its head. The faithful are united together in Christ's Mystical Body; that is, we are brought into communion with one another through our communion with Christ. For this reason, St. Paul refers to Jesus as the head of the Mystical Body: "He is before all things, and in him all things hold together. He is the head of the body, the church."[98] As the Mystical Body of Christ, the Church extends throughout time Christ's work of salvation.

PARABLE
A brief narrative or allegory (usually of something that might naturally occur) used o illustrate and explain moral or spiritual principles.

PENTECOST
The descent of the Holy Spirit, in the form of a rushing wind and tongues of fire, upon the Apostles after Jesus' Ascension. This event fulfilled Jesus' promise to send his Spirit to teach, guide, and empower the Apostles in their mission.

PEOPLE OF GOD
Those born into the Church through faith in Christ and Baptism. The term is taken from the Old Testament, in which God chose Israel to be his people. Christ instituted the new and eternal covenant by which a new priestly, prophetic, and royal People of God, the Church, participates in the mission and service of Christ.

PILGRIM CHURCH
Name sometimes used to describe the Church because it is on a "journey" in this world; although the Church itself is perfect as created by Christ, its Faithful seek greater holiness and intimacy with Christ and thus are ever traveling toward the house of God the Father.

REAL PRESENCE
Term used to describe the Eucharist, in which Jesus is really and fully present—Body, Blood, Soul, and Divinity—under the species of bread and wine, which have been consecrated to become his Body and Blood.

RESURRECTION
Jesus' coming back to life on the third day after his Crucifixion, Death and burial, thus conquering both sin and death and making possible the redemption of humanity.

VOCABULARY Continued

SACRAMENT

An efficacious sign of grace, instituted by Christ and entrusted to the Church, by which divine life is dispensed to us through the work of the Holy Spirit. Specifically, any of the Seven Sacraments of the Catholic Church: Baptism, Eucharist, Penance (Reconciliation), Confirmation, Matrimony (marriage), Holy Orders, and Anointing of the Sick; more generally, any sign or means through which grace is received from God (for example, the Church as the "Sacrament of Salvation"). In the East, a Sacrament is often called a "mystery."

SYNAGOGUE

A local place for Jewish worship and study.

SYNOPTIC GOSPELS

The Gospels of Matthew, Mark, and Luke, given this name because they bear so much similarity of structure, with many stories appearing in all three books. The similarities have led scholars to speculate that the writers may have shared one another's recollections, or that all three may have used as a guide a previous Gospel account that is no longer in existence.

TEMPLE OF THE HOLY SPIRIT

A title of the Church used by St. Paul; it highlights the relationship between the Church and the Old Testament Temple in Jerusalem.

TEMPORAL

Related to time, being of this earth. A temporal king rules his kingdom on earth; an eternal or Everlasting King rules both Heaven and earth.

TOTUS CHRISTUS

Latin for "whole Christ," made up of Jesus, the head, and the Church, his Mystical Body.

TYPOLOGY

The study of how the New Testament is foreshadowed in the Old Testament. Certain figures and actions in the Old Testament are *types* that are reflected or fulfilled in the New Testament; for example, Christ as a type of the New Adam, or the Ark of Noah as a type for the saving role of the Church itself.

TWELVE APOSTLES

Also, "the Twelve" or "the Apostles," they assisted Jesus in his public ministry and are Christ's chosen witnesses of his Resurrection and the foundation on which the Church is built. The Apostles were the first bishops of the Church.

Appearance on Lake Tiberias by Duccio.
"Jesus said to them, 'Come and have breakfast.' Now none of the disciples dared ask him, 'Who are you?' They knew it was the Lord." (Jn 21: 12)

STUDY QUESTIONS

1. What is *typology*? Give a few examples of Old Testament persons or symbols that are *types* of New Testament figures.

2. Why are St. Augustine's contributions to the study of Scripture important?

3. What was prophesied in the Old Testament about the coming Messiah?

4. What does the Annunciation tell us about Jesus?

5. According to St. Paul, why did God send forth his Son?

6. Which Old Testament covenant does the angel Gabriel allude to at the Annunciation?

7. How is Jesus presented in the New Testament?

8. In what does the true restoration of the kingdom consist?

9. What is the central theme of Jesus' preaching?

10. What is the Kingdom of Heaven like?

11. When does Jesus entrust the kingdom of his Church to the Apostles?

12. What two images are used to describe Christ's sacrifice on the Cross?

13. What did St. John mean when he said, "We are God's children now"?

14. What is *divine filiation*, and how is it obtained?

15. What are the three meals recounted in St. Luke's Gospel where Jesus is said to "break bread"?

16. In light of which Sacrament are we able to understand Jesus' association of the kingdom with eating and drinking?

17. According to the *Catechism of the Catholic Church*, to what is the Holy Spirit comparable in relation to the Mystical Body of Christ?

18. What is the purpose of the various images of the Church?

19. Within Scripture, where do we find the image of the Church as the Body of Christ?

20. What book of the Bible does St. Paul quote in drawing together the images of the Church as Christ's Body and Bride?

21. What sort of terminology does Jesus frequently use to define his mission, his Person, and his relationship with both God and the disciples?

22. According to the *Catechism of the Catholic Church*, what does it mean to become a disciple of Jesus?

23. Through which Sacrament do we become adopted sons and daughters of the Father?

24. What concern is reflected in God's decision to form for himself a people, as opposed to a random assortment of individuals?

25. What similarities can be identified between the Church's worship and that of the people of Israel?

26. What special gift did St. Francis of Assisi receive two years before his death?

27. To which Old Testament covenant is the image of the Church as the Kingdom of God related?

PRACTICAL EXERCISES

1. The Incarnation is the central event in human history because through Jesus Christ man is brought back into communion with God. In order to accomplish this restoration of man's original state, Christ suffered on the Cross and died for our sins. Why was it necessary for Jesus to die in order to reestablish communion between God and man? What are some of the ways the Church communicates the fruits of Christ's sacrifice on the Cross?

2. When Christ preached the Kingdom of God, he disappointed many who had been waiting for a restoration of the temporal Kingdom of David. Imagine living during the time of Christ, and you have just heard him preach the Parables of the Sower and the Mustard Seed, both of which explain the Kingdom of Heaven. You are talking with some people who heard the same parables, and one is expressing his doubt that Christ is the Messiah because the Messiah, he says, is supposed to bring about the restoration of the Kingdom of David. How would you explain to him that what Christ says about the Kingdom of Heaven more completely fulfills the prophecies for the restoration of the Kingdom of Israel?

3. After the Resurrection, Christ's disciples did not recognize him when he joined them on the road to Emmaus, only later recognizing him when he broke bread with them. What does this story say about the Eucharist? How is this story supported by other instances in the Bible that point to the reality of the Eucharist as the Body and Blood of Christ?

4. Read again the section on the Church as the People of God. Why do you think God requires us to worship him not only individually but also as a community of faith? How would you respond to someone who thinks it is better for people to worship God in their own way, when and how they feel like it?

Christ and His Disciples on Their Way to Emmaus by Coecke Van Aelst.
"But their eyes were kept from recognizing him. And he said to them, 'What is this conversation which you are holding with each other as you walk?' And they stood still, looking sad. Then one of them, named Cleopas, answered him, 'Are you the only visitor to Jerusalem who does not know the things that have happened there in these days?' And he said to them, 'What things?' And they said to him, 'Concerning Jesus of Nazareth, who was a prophet mighty in deed and word before God and all the people, and how our chief priests and rulers delivered him up to be condemned to death, and crucified him.'" (Lk 24: 16-20)

FROM THE CATECHISM

790 Believers who respond to God's word and become members of Christ's Body, become intimately united with him: "In that body the life of Christ is communicated to those who believe, and who, through the sacraments, are united in a hidden and real way to Christ in his Passion and glorification."[99] This is especially true of Baptism, which unites us to Christ's death and Resurrection, and the Eucharist, by which "really sharing in the body of the Lord,... we are taken up into communion with him and with one another."[100]

791 The body's unity does not do away with the diversity of its members: "In the building up of Christ's Body there is engaged a diversity of members and functions. There is only one Spirit who, according to his own richness and the needs of the ministries, gives his different gifts for the welfare of the Church."[101] The unity of the Mystical Body produces and stimulates charity among the faithful: "From this it follows that if one member suffers anything, all the members suffer with him, and if one member is honored, all the members together rejoice."[102] Finally, the unity of the Mystical Body triumphs over all human divisions: "For as many of you as were baptized into Christ have put on Christ. There is neither Jew nor Greek, there is neither slave nor free, there is neither male nor female; for you are all one in Christ Jesus."[103]

792 Christ "is the head of the body, the Church."[104] He is the principle of creation and redemption. Raised to the Father's glory, "in everything he [is] preeminent,"[105] especially in the Church, through whom he extends his reign over all things.

793 *Christ unites us with his Passover*: all his members must strive to resemble him, "until Christ be formed" in them.[106] "For this reason we...are taken up into the mysteries of his life,...associated with his sufferings as the body with its head, suffering with him, that with him we may be glorified."[107]

794 *Christ provides for our growth*: to make us grow toward him, our head,[108] he provides in his Body, the Church, the gifts and assistance by which we help one another along the way of salvation.

795 Christ and his Church thus together make up the "whole Christ" (*Christus totus*). The Church is one with Christ. The saints are acutely aware of this unity:

> Let us rejoice then and give thanks that we have become not only Christians, but Christ himself. Do you understand and grasp, brethren, God's grace toward us? Marvel and rejoice: we have become Christ. For if he is the head, we are the members; he and we together are the whole man....The fullness of Christ then is the head and the members. But what does "head and members" mean? Christ and the Church.[109]

> Our redeemer has shown himself to be one person with the holy Church whom he has taken to himself.[110]

> Head and members form as it were one and the same mystical person.[111]

> A reply of St. Joan of Arc to her judges sums up the faith of the holy doctors and the good sense of the believer: "About Jesus Christ and the Church, I simply know they're just one thing, and we shouldn't complicate the matter."[112]

ENDNOTES - CHAPTER TWO

1. Jn 1:1.
2. CCC 128.
3. Gal 4:4-5.
4. Lk 2:10-11.
5. Lk 2:29-32.
6. Cf. Mt 2:2; Nm 24:17-19; Rev 22:16.
7. Mk 1:15.
8. Cf. *LG* 3; *AG* 3.
9. *LG* 5.
10. *LG* 3.
11. Mt 13:3-9.
12. Mt 13:44.
13. Mt 13:45.
14. Mt 13:24-30, 37-43.
15. Mt 13:31-32.
16. Mt 13:33.
17. Cf. Mt 13:13-15.
18. *LG* 5.
19. *LG* 5.
20. Lk 12:32; cf. Mt 10:16; 26:31; Jn 10:1-21.
21. Cf. Mt 12:49.
22. Cf. Mt 5-6.
23. Mk 3:14-15.
24. Cf. Mk 3:14-15.
25. Cf. Mt 19:28; Lk 22:30; Rev 21:12-14.
26. Cf. Mk 6:7; Lk 10:1-2; Mt 10:25; Jn 15:20.
27. Lk 22:25-27.
28. Ratzinger, Joseph, *The Ecclesiology of Vatican II*, 2.
29. Phil 2:8.
30. Jn 1:29.
31. *LG* 3; cf. Jn 19:34.
32. *SC* 5.
33. Cf. St. Ambrose, *In Luc.* 2, 85-89; PL 15, 1666-1668.
34. 1 Jn 3:2.
35. 1 Jn 3:1.
36. Heb 12:23.
37. Cf. Gal 4:7.
38. 1 Cor 3:22-23.

39. Jn 20:23.
40. Mt 22:2.
41. Lk 9:10-17.
42. Lk 22:7-38.
43. Lk 24:13-35.
44. Lk 22:19-20.
45. Jn 13:1.
46. Cf. Gn 3:15.
47. Mt 1:1.
48. Jn 18:36.
49. *LG* 3.
50. *LG* 2.
51. *LG* 5.
52. Jn 1:14.
53. Jn 2:19.
54. CCC 797.
55. CCC 772.
56. Acts 9:4-5.
57. Cf. Mk 1:16-20; 3:13-19; Mt 13:10-17; Lk 10:17-20; 22:28-30; Jn 6:56.
58. Cf. CCC 789.
59. Pius XII, Enc. *Mystici Corporis*, AAS 14 (1943), 199.
60. *LG* 7.
61. *LG* 7.
62. *LG* 7.
63. CCC 795.
64. Eph 5:23.
65. Eph 5:31, Gn 2:24.
66. Gn 2:23
67. Ratzinger, Joseph, *Called to Communion* (Ignatius Press: San Francisco, 1996), p. 24; cf. Mk 10:24; Mt 11:25; Jer 16:6.
68. Eph 1:5.
69. CCC 1655.
70. Mt 12:49.
71. Eph 3:14-15.
72. Mt 11:27.
73. Gal 3:26, 28.
74. Jn 3:3.
75. Lk 22:20.
76. Rev 19:9.

77. 1 Cor 10:21.
78. CCC 181.
79. Heb 12:6, 10.
80. Phil 1:6.
81. *LG* 9; cf. Acts 10:35; 1 Cor 11:25.
82. *LG* 9.
83. Jas 1:17.
84. Mt 19:21.
85. Jn 18:36.
86. Ratzinger, Joseph, *Called to Communion* (Ignatius Press: San Francisco, 1996), p. 22.
87. Ps 89:27.
88. Cf. Lk 22:29.
89. Jn 3:16.
90. CCC 438.
91. Jn 1:32.
92. Heb 12:22.
93. Lk 2:32.
94. Lk 24:47.
95. Lk 1:33.
96. Jn 2:3.
97. Ratzinger, Joseph, *Called to Communion* (Ignatius Press: San Francisco, 1996), p. 29.
98. Col 1:17-18.
99. *LG* 7.
100. *LG* 7; cf. Rom 6:4-5; 1 Cor 12:13.
101. *LG* 7 § 3.
102. *LG* 7 § 3; cf. 1 Cor 12:26.
103. Gal 3:27-28.
104. Col 1:18.
105. Ibid.
106. Gal 4:19.
107. *LG* 7 § 4; cf. Phil 3:21; Rom 8:17.
108. Cf. Col 2:19; Eph 4:11-16.
109. St. Augustine, *In Jo. Ev.* 21, 8: PL 35, 1568.
110. Pope St. Gregory the Great, *Moralia in Job, præf.*, 14: PL 75, 525A.
111. St. Thomas Aquinas, *STh* III, 48, 2.
112. Acts of the Trial of Joan of Arc.

The Church

The Story of the Early Church

*After the Ascension of Christ into Heaven, the Acts of the Apostles continues with the story
of the Church that he established to continue his work on earth.*

The Church

CHAPTER 3

The Story of the Early Church

he period following the Crucifixion was a time of confusion for the Apostles and the followers of Christ. Just a few days earlier, they had entered the city of Jerusalem in a scene of triumph. The crowd lined the path, laying down palm branches before him and honoring him with their cheers and prayers, "Hosanna! Blessed is he who comes in the name of the Lord, even the King of Israel!"[1] However, this period of joy was to be short-lived. A few hours after celebrating the Passover meal with his Apostles, Jesus would be betrayed and arrested, and on the following day, he would be tried, sentenced, scourged, and crucified.

Grief-stricken, remorseful for their lack of loyalty, and in hiding for fear that they would be arrested as well, the Apostles hid in the same Upper Room where they had shared Jesus' Last Supper. Then reports came from the women. They had seen Christ alive, and his tomb empty! Skeptical at first, they ran to investigate.

Finding the tomb indeed empty, they struggled to make sense of it. Then Christ appeared to them too, assuring them of his continued presence and support. He was risen from the dead, and with them again!

Forty days later, he would ascend into Heaven. Once again confused, they followed his instructions and returned to the Upper Room to await the coming of the Holy Spirit that he had promised to send.

Communion of the Apostles by Fra Angelico. After the Crucifixion, the Apostles hid in the same Upper Room where they had shared Jesus' Last Supper.

> **"When the work which the Father gave the Son to do on earth was accomplished, the Holy Spirit was sent on the day of Pentecost in order that he might continually sanctify the Church."[2] Then "the Church was openly displayed to the crowds and the spread of the Gospel among the nations, through preaching, was begun."[3] As the "convocation" of all men for salvation, the Church in her very nature is missionary, sent by Christ to all the nations to make disciples of them.[4] (CCC 767)**

After the Ascension of Christ into Heaven, the Acts of the Apostles continues with the story of the Church that he established to continue his work on earth. Through his presence and preaching, Christ instituted the Church as the Kingdom of Heaven on earth, but it was only with his gift of the Holy Spirit that this kingdom began to take definitive shape. Emboldened, the Apostles went forth from the room, proclaiming the Good News of Jesus Christ and the salvation he offers to all who believe in him. They were no longer fishermen, but were now fishers of men.

This chapter will trace the development of the early Church, from Christ's promise of the Holy Spirit at the time of his Ascension to the gradual spread of the Gospel to all the nations.

Pentecost by Van Der Werff.
The day of Pentecost marks the beginning of the Church's public ministry in the world.

IN THIS CHAPTER, WE WILL ADDRESS SEVERAL QUESTIONS:

✠ What instructions did Christ give to his Apostles before his Ascension?

✠ What is the role of the Holy Spirit in the Church?

✠ What was the role of St. Peter in the Church?

✠ How did the Church reach out to all nations?

✠ How did each of the Apostles fulfill the mission that Christ had given him?

Ministry of the Apostles by Zubov, Russian Icon. Jesus intended the Church to fulfill God's promise to David: that his kingdom would encompass the entire world.

"GO AND MAKE DISCIPLES OF ALL NATIONS"

Jesus remained on earth for forty days after his Resurrection, appearing to the Apostles and "speaking of the Kingdom of God." The Holy Spirit is the principal agent of the Church's mission; he guides the Church along her path. "The Church, urged on by the Spirit of Christ, must walk the road Christ himself walked, a way of poverty and obedience, of service and self-sacrifice" (*AG* 5). When the time came for his Ascension into Heaven, he gathered the Apostles together and told them to await the coming of the Holy Spirit:

> **You shall receive power when the Holy Spirit has come upon you; and you shall be my witnesses in Jerusalem and in all Judea and Samaria and to the end of the earth. (Acts 1: 8)**

The significance of the specific places listed by Jesus would not have been lost on the Apostles. Jesus was essentially drawing a verbal map of the ancient kingdom of David. Jerusalem was David's capital city. Judea was the tribal territory of David that surrounded Jerusalem. Samaria was the land to the north where the rest of the tribes of Israel were located. "The ends of the earth" represented all the Gentile nations that David had brought under his control. It also indicated that Jesus intended the Church to fulfill God's promise to David: that his kingdom would encompass the entire world.

The Apostles were being given the great command of Christ—to evangelize all the peoples who were once part of the old kingdom of David, reclaiming them for the restored kingdom, which is the Church.

> **Go therefore and make disciples of all nations, baptizing them in the name of the Father and of the Son and of the Holy Spirit, teaching them to observe all that I have commanded you.** (Mt 28: 19-20)

When Jesus established the Apostles as shepherds of the Church, he appointed them as symbolic rulers of the twelve tribes of Israel: "That you may…sit on thrones judging the twelve tribes of Israel."[6] For this reason, the number of Apostles—Twelve—is very important. However, one of the Apostles, Judas, had betrayed Jesus and taken his own life in despair.[7] If the Apostles were to be the foundation of the restored kingdom, they would need to find a replacement for Judas.

Appearance on the Mountain in Galilee (detail) by Duccio. "and lo, I am with you always, to the close of the age." (Mt 28: 20)

Immediately following Christ's Ascension, the Eleven remaining Apostles returned to Jerusalem, to the Upper Room, where the Last Supper had taken place. Together with Mary the Mother of Jesus and the rest of Jesus' disciples, the Apostles devoted themselves to prayer in preparation for the coming of the Holy Spirit that Christ had promised. St. Peter, the leader on earth now that Jesus had ascended into Heaven, stood up among the disciples and announced that the time had come to choose a twelfth Apostle.

> **One of the men who have accompanied us during all the time that the Lord Jesus went in and out among us, beginning from the baptism of John until the day he was taken up from us—one of these men must become with us a witness to his resurrection.** (Acts 1: 21-22)

A disciple named St. Matthias, who had been with Christ from the beginning, was selected as Judas' replacement. And with their number now complete, the Apostles continued in prayer, awaiting the descent of the Holy Spirit and the unveiling of the Church.

THE DAY OF PENTECOST

Ten days after Christ's Ascension into Heaven, the Apostles were again gathered together with Mary and the other disciples in the upper room; there were about 120 of them in all. At last, the time had come for them to receive the Holy Spirit.

> **When the day of Pentecost had come, they were all together in one place. And suddenly a sound came from heaven like the rush of a mighty wind, and it filled all the house where they were sitting. And there appeared to them tongues as of fire, distributed and resting on each one of them. And they were all filled with the Holy Spirit and began to speak in other tongues, as the Spirit gave them utterance.** (Acts 2: 1-4)

The transformation of the Apostles was immediate. They became like new men. Before the coming of the Spirit, they had remained hidden away in the upper room, afraid of the Roman soldiers and Jewish leaders. Now, they spoke out boldly, proclaiming the Gospel to all who would listen, unafraid of the consequences of bearing such bold witness.

> **So that she can fulfill her mission, the Holy Spirit "bestows upon [the Church] varied hierarchic and charismatic gifts, and in this way directs her."[8] "Henceforward the Church, endowed with the gifts of her founder and faithfully observing his precepts of charity, humility and self-denial, receives the mission of proclaiming and establishing among all peoples the Kingdom of Christ and of God, and she is on earth the seed and the beginning of that kingdom."[9]** (CCC 768)

At that time, Jerusalem was filled with faithful Jews from all over the world who had come to celebrate the Jewish feast of Pentecost. This feast was celebrated on the fiftieth day after the Passover (the word *Pentecost* is taken from the Greek word for "fifty") and commemorated the giving of the Law to Moses on Mount Sinai.

There were dwelling in Jerusalem Jews, devout men from every nation under heaven. And at this sound the multitude came together, and they were bewildered, because each one heard them speaking in his own language. And they were amazed and wondered, saying "Are not all these who are speaking Galileans? And how is it that we hear, each of us in his own native language?" (Acts 2: 5-8)

St. Peter Preaching (detail) by Masolino. "And fear came upon every soul; and many wonders and signs were done through the apostles. And all who believed were together and had all things in common." (Acts 2: 43-44)

St. Peter stood up and began to address the crowd, proclaiming to them that the long-awaited Messiah had come. It was Jesus, crucified and resurrected from the dead, who now sits at the right hand of God the Father in Heaven. Upon hearing this, the people asked St. Peter and the rest of the Apostles what they must do to be saved. St. Peter responded by telling them to repent and to be baptized.

From the very day of Pentecost the Church has celebrated and administered holy Baptism. Indeed St. Peter declares to the crowd astounded by his preaching: "Repent, and be baptized every one of you in the name of Jesus Christ for the forgiveness of your sins; and you shall receive the gift of the Holy Spirit."[10] (CCC 1226)

The day of Pentecost marks the beginning of the Church's public ministry in the world. The Apostles took up Christ's commission to be his witnesses and to baptize men and women from every nation. On the day of Pentecost alone, three thousand people were baptized and became Christians. But this was only the beginning of the mission. From Jerusalem, the Gospel message would go out to all the nations, to Jews and Gentiles alike. Filled with the power of the Holy Spirit, the Church on earth would continue to grow in number and in fervor.

THE DESCENT OF THE HOLY SPIRIT

When his visible presence was taken from them, Jesus did not leave his disciples orphans. He promised to remain with them until the end of time; he sent them his Spirit.[11] As a result communion with Jesus has become, in a way, more intense: "By communicating his Spirit, Christ mystically constitutes as his body those brothers of his who are called together from every nation."[12] (CCC 788)

Before his Ascension, Jesus had promised his Apostles that he would be with them always, and at Pentecost, he fulfilled his promise. Through the gift of the Holy Spirit, Christ gave life to the Church and united it to himself. It was the Holy Spirit who empowered the Apostles to preach the Gospel to the multitudes. It was the Holy Spirit who opened the hearts of those who heard the Good News, and it was the Holy Spirit who revealed the Church as Christ's instrument of salvation for the entire world. In fact, the Holy Spirit is the principal agent of the Church's mission, and it is through the Holy Spirit that the Church continues the redemptive mission of Christ in the world today.

"When the work which the Father gave the Son to do on earth was accomplished, the Holy Spirit was sent on the day of Pentecost in order that he might continually sanctify the Church."[13] Then "the Church was openly displayed to the crowds and the spread of the Gospel among the nations, through preaching, was begun."[14] As the "convocation" of all men for salvation, the Church in her very nature is missionary, sent by Christ to all the nations to make disciples of them.[15] (CCC 767)

As the "soul" of the Mystical Body of Christ, the Holy Spirit continues to work within the Church in many different ways.

✤ **Through the Pope and the Bishops.** The Holy Spirit assists the Pope and the bishops of the Church, in their role of governing, sanctifying, and proclaiming the Gospel in the Church.

✤ **In Sacred Scripture.** The Holy Spirit inspired the human authors of the Bible. Even though the Bible is made up of books written by different authors, the ultimate author of Scripture is the Holy Spirit. This is why we say that the Bible is inspired and without error. The Holy Spirit also guides the Church in infallibly interpreting the words of Sacred Scripture.

✤ **In the Sacraments.** The Holy Spirit gives life to new members of the Church through *Baptism*, incorporating them into the Mystical Body of Christ. In each of the *Sacraments*, the Holy Spirit works to give growth and healing to all the members of the Church.

✤ **In the Gifts of the Holy Spirit.** These supernatural gifts render us attentive to the will of God and to the actual graces that he sends us to follow his will.

St. Peter by Rubens. The authority given by Christ to St. Peter—and to his successors, the Popes—is referred to as the *primacy of Peter.*

✤ **In the Fruits of the Holy Spirit.** These are the supernatural works that a person is enabled to perform with the assistance of the Holy Spirit.

✤ **Through special graces.** The Holy Spirit also gives the faithful special graces, called *charisms*, so that they are able to contribute to the task of building up the Church.

ST. PETER'S AUTHORITY

While Christ was still on earth, he made it clear on a number of occasions that St. Peter would possess authority over the Church. St. Peter's role as leader of the Church on earth is evident in the stories of the early Church that have come down to us through the Sacred Scriptures. It was St. Peter who stood up among the disciples and announced the need to find a replacement for Judas, and it was St. Peter who spoke for the Apostles at Pentecost. Later, St. Peter performed the first miracle recounted in the Acts of the Apostles—the healing of a crippled man.[16] After some of the Apostles were arrested and questioned by the Jewish leaders, it was St. Peter, filled with the Holy Spirit, who spoke on their behalf.[17]

Christ himself proclaimed St. Peter as the rock on which he would build the Church.[18] The authority given by Christ to St. Peter—and to his successors, the Popes—is referred to as the *primacy of Peter.*

> Jesus entrusted a specific authority to Peter: "I will give you the keys of the Kingdom of Heaven, and whatever you bind on earth shall be bound in heaven, and whatever you loose on earth shall be loosed in heaven."[19] The "power of the keys" designates authority to govern the house of God, which is the Church. Jesus, the good Shepherd, confirmed this mandate after his Resurrection: "Feed my sheep."[20] The power to "bind and loose" connotes the authority to absolve sins, to pronounce doctrinal judgments, and to make disciplinary decisions in the Church. Jesus entrusted this authority to the Church through the ministry of the apostles[21] and in particular through the ministry of Peter, the only one to whom he specifically entrusted the keys of the kingdom. (CCC 553)

In the Old Testament kingdom of David, the king appointed a prime minister from among his twelve chief servants. Similarly, in the New Testament kingdom, Christ the king appointed one of the Twelve to have primacy over the others. In both cases, the prime minister is identified by the sign of his office—the *keys of the kingdom*.

> **I will place on his shoulder the key of the house of David; he shall open and none shall shut; and he shall shut and none shall open. (Is 22:22)**

As the one who has primacy in the Kingdom of Heaven on earth, St. Peter possesses the authority of the king himself. This is why we call the Pope the *Vicar of Christ* (from the Latin *vicarius*, meaning "in the person of"). St. Peter's authority over the Church is full, supreme, and universal, and it is given to him for the sake of the Church. Assisted by the Holy Spirit, he is to lead the Twelve in their ministry of shepherding the Church and proclaiming the Gospel to the world. In this way, St. Peter and his successors are the "visible source and foundation of the unity both of the bishops and of the whole company of the faithful."[22]

The role of the papacy has evolved through the centuries as the political and social circumstances surrounding the Church have changed. What has remained constant, however, is the role of the papacy as the Church's highest moral and doctrinal authority. When disagreement and conflict arise in the Church, it is the Pope who has the authority to resolve and clarify matters of faith and morals. It is the figure of the Pope who helps preserve the unity of the Church.

ST. PETER, THE VICAR OF CHRIST, THE GOOD SHEPHERD (Jn 21:15-17)

When they had finished breakfast, Jesus said to Simon Peter, "Simon, son of John, do you love me more than these?" He said to him, "Yes, Lord; you know that I love you." He said to him, "Feed my lambs." A second time he said to him, "Simon, son of John, do you love me?" He said to him, "Yes, Lord; you know that I love you." He said to him, "Tend my sheep." He said to him the third time, "Simon, son of John, do you love me?" Peter was grieved because he said to him the third time, "Do you love me?" And he said to him, "Lord, you know everything; you know that I love you." Jesus said to him, "Feed my sheep."

Feed My Lambs (detail) by Tissot.
Peter's Redemption:
Three times Peter had denied Jesus in front of a charcoal fire; now Jesus had given him a chance to undo that denial three times. Jesus in return gave Peter the care over his "lambs," all the believers everywhere. As he had declared before, Christ would build his Church on Peter.

TRIALS AND PERSECUTION

Through the work of the Apostles and disciples, the Gospel of Christ spread to many new believers in those early days of the Church. Nevertheless, there were many who sought to stop the spread of this new religion. Jewish authorities had assumed that Jesus' Death would scatter his followers and silence his message. After the events of Pentecost, however, it became clear that this was not the case. The Christian community was growing by the day, and the people of Jerusalem held the Apostles in higher and higher esteem. Even after they were imprisoned by the authorities and beaten, the Apostles refused to stop preaching about Jesus Christ.

A man named Stephen, a Christian convert and a deacon in the Church, was taken before the Jewish authorities and accused of blasphemy. Just as at the trial of Jesus, false witnesses were brought forward to testify against him. St. Stephen did not hold his tongue against these false accusations. Filled with the Holy Spirit, he began to preach, explaining how the Scriptures showed Jesus to be the promised Messiah. Those assembled immediately became enraged. Without even bothering to convict him, they took St. Stephen out of the city and stoned him to death. St. Stephen was the Church's first *martyr*, put to death because of his witness to faith in Jesus Christ.

The martyrdom of St. Stephen marked the beginning of a tremendous persecution of the Church in Jerusalem. Many of the Christians fled to the surrounding regions, where they continued to spread the Gospel. Those who did not leave were imprisoned. The persecution by the Jewish leaders was only the first of many similar persecutions during the first several centuries.

Later persecutions—particularly those initiated by the Roman emperors—would result in the martyrdoms of most of the Apostles, as well as the martyrdom of countless other Christian men and women of every age and social standing. Far from eliminating Christianity, these martyrs became the Church's greatest testimony to Jesus Christ, and, through their witness, Christianity soon spread throughout the entire Roman world.

Of all the *saints* honored and celebrated by the Church, martyrs hold a special place. Martyrs are the ultimate witnesses to the truth of the Faith, "bearing witness even unto death." All Christians are called to live in imitation of Christ. Those who are given the grace of martyrdom imitate Jesus in the fullest way possible, by dying like Christ died, out of love: "Greater love hath no man than this..."[23]

At the Last Supper, Jesus had warned the Apostles about the future suffering of the Church.

Martyrdom of St. Stephen, Church of St. Stephen. The early Christians were confident in the hope that the same Holy Spirit who empowered the Apostles at Pentecost would also strengthen them in the face of persecution and death.

> If the world hates you, know that it has hated me before it hated you.... If they persecuted me, they will persecute you...on my account, because they do not know him who sent me. (Jn 15:18, 20-21)

The early Christians were aware of the suffering that they would face for their faith. But they were confident in the hope that the same Holy Spirit who empowered the Apostles at Pentecost would also strengthen them in the face of persecution and death. In their lives, and especially in their deaths, the Church's martyrs gave witness to the resurrected Christ. And through their example, many more came to believe, for "the blood of martyrs is the seed of Christians."[24]

The Saints
PILLARS OF THE CHURCH

St. Polycarp
"A SECOND-CENTURY MARTYR"

St. Polycarp (d. ca. 155) was born sometime in the first century AD. Although not many details are known about him, it is believed that he was converted to Christianity by St. John the Apostle when St. John was the bishop of Smyrna. In about AD 80, St. John was exiled to Patmos, the island where he saw the vision recorded in the Book of Revelation. Before St. John's exile, he consecrated Polycarp, who was only in his late teens or early twenties, as bishop of Smyrna.

For decades, St. Polycarp loyally served as bishop during a very demanding time for Christianity. In this era, the Church was suffering great persecutions, her members being fed to wild animals or burned alive for the Faith. As bishop, it was St. Polycarp's duty to care for the faith of his flock throughout these persecutions, as well as to root out heresies that were springing up in the young religion. He was renowned for his piety.

When St. Polycarp was eighty-six, the persecution of Christians in his region became even more severe. Eventually St. Polycarp himself was singled out. Taken prisoner and brought in front of a vengeful crowd, St. Polycarp was told to renounce Christ or suffer greatly. He then gave the response that would lead to his martyrdom: "I have served him these eighty-six years, and he never did me any harm, but much good, and how can I blaspheme my King and my Savior?... Hear my free confession—I am a Christian."

Because he was unwilling to blaspheme Christ, St. Polycarp was killed and his body burned down to the bones. His example, though, lives on even now. Centuries later he is still providing an example of respect and love for God.

St. Polycarp, pray for us.

The Conversion of St. Paul by Murillo.
God had chosen Saul—thereafter known as Paul—for a specific mission: "I have set you to be a light for the Gentiles, that you may bring salvation to the uttermost parts of the earth." (Acts 13:47)

ST. PAUL, LIGHT FOR THE GENTILES

St. Paul is one of the most significant figures of the early Church. The author of several books of the New Testament, he was among the first Christians to preach the Gospel to the Gentiles. By the time of his death around AD 64, St. Paul, although not one of the Twelve, had also become the Church's most successful Apostle. In his three missionary journeys throughout the Roman Empire, he brought countless new believers to Christ, founded a number of new Christian churches, and provided vital guidance and encouragement to the churches that had been founded by the Twelve.

But St. Paul had not always been a faithful follower of Christ. For the first part of his life, he was a steadfast Pharisee, actively involved in persecuting the Christians in Jerusalem and the surrounding areas. Indeed, of all the conversions that took place in the Church's early years, none was more important—or more unlikely—than that of St. Paul.

Hearing that there were followers of Jesus in the Syrian city of Damascus, Saul decided to go and arrest them. On his way, however, he had an encounter with Christ that would forever change his life.

> As [Saul] journeyed he approached Damascus, and suddenly a light from heaven flashed about him. And he fell to the ground and heard a voice saying to him, "Saul, Saul, why do you persecute me?" And he said, "Who are you, Lord?" And he said, "I am Jesus, whom you are persecuting; but rise and enter the city, and you will be told what you are to do." (Acts 9:3-6)

ST. PAUL, THE MAN CHOSEN FOR THE CONVERSION OF THE GENTILES

Born around the year AD 5 in Tarsus (located in modern-day Turkey), a seaport on the Mediterranean and an important center of learning in the Roman Empire, St. Paul was raised as a devout Jew. As a Roman citizen, like many of the Jews who lived in the Roman Empire, he had both a Roman name (Paul) and a Jewish name (Saul). After completing his initial education in Tarsus, Saul (as he was then called) traveled to Jerusalem, where he studied under Gamaliel, one of the most learned Pharisees of the time. In Tarsus and Jerusalem, Saul had received the best of both Jewish and classical educations. He possessed an intimate knowledge of the Old Testament and was closely familiar with Greek literature and philosophies of his day.

Saul had a solid education and was devoted to the Law of Moses, which gained him the favorable attention of the Jewish authorities in Jerusalem. They gave him responsibility for carrying out the first major persecution of the Christians. We read in Acts that "Saul was ravaging the church, and entering house after house, he dragged off men and women and committed them to prison."[25]

With his conversion to Christianity, St. Paul was uniquely qualified to undertake his broad missionary efforts among the Gentiles:

✤ Because of his classical education, he could speak to the Greeks and Romans in language and concepts familiar to them.

✤ Because of his training in philosophy and logic, he was able to make important distinctions in explaining Christian doctrine.

✤ Because of his thorough knowledge of the Old Testament, he could counter the objections of the Jewish authorities that argued with him.

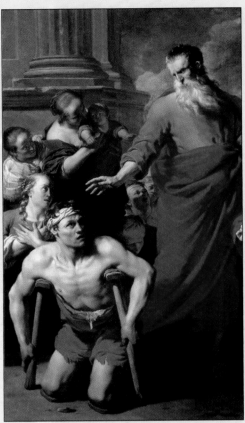

St. Paul Healing the Cripple at Lystra (detail) by Dujardin. "When they had preached the gospel to that city and had made many disciples, they returned to Lystra and to Iconium and to Antioch, strengthening the souls of the disciples, exhorting them to continue in the faith, and saying that through many tribulations we must enter the kingdom of God." (Acts 14: 21-22)

✤ Because of his Roman citizenship, he was kept safe from those who were conspiring to kill him.[26]

St. Paul's incredible success in fostering Christianity throughout the Mediterranean region proves that Christ's confidence in his abilities was well placed.

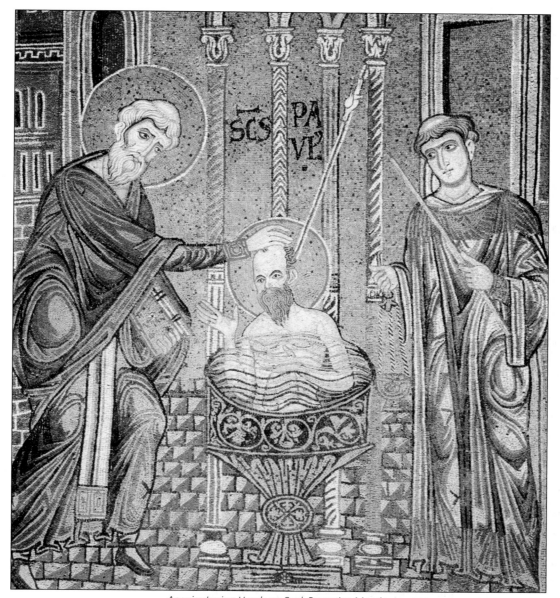

Ananias Laying Hands on Saul, Byzantine Mosaic.
"So Ananias departed and entered the house. And laying his hands on him he said, 'Brother Saul, the Lord Jesus who appeared to you on the road by which you came, has sent me that you may regain your sight and be filled with the Holy Spirit.' And immediately something like scales fell from his eyes and he regained his sight. Then he rose and was baptized, and took food and was strengthened." (Acts 9: 17-19)

Blinded, Saul was led by his companions into Damascus, where he was baptized by a man named Ananias and regained his sight. From that point on, the zeal for God that had led him to persecute Christians would now be employed in proclaiming the Gospel of Christ.

God had chosen Saul—thereafter known as Paul—for a specific mission: "I have set you to be a light for the Gentiles, that you may bring salvation to the uttermost parts of the earth."[27]

St. Paul's travels eventually took him through much of the Roman Empire, including what are now Turkey and Greece. After surviving many hardships and persecutions during his missionary journeys, St. Paul was finally arrested and taken to Rome, where he was imprisoned and put to death. Because he was a Roman citizen, however, St. Paul was spared the torture of crucifixion and was beheaded instead. In fact, many pictures of St. Paul show him holding a sword to remind us how he died for the Faith.

PREACHING TO ALL NATIONS

The Good News of Jesus Christ quickly spread throughout Jerusalem. From there, the Apostles brought the Gospel to the surrounding territories of Judea and Samaria, preaching and baptizing in the name of Christ.

Nearly all of the first believers were Jews living or traveling to Jerusalem. As the Apostles traveled out of the city, they came into contact with people who were not of the Jewish faith, called Gentiles, who were nonetheless equally attracted to their preaching. These Gentiles began to believe in Jesus, and soon the Apostles were faced with a dilemma. The Incarnation was the fulfillment of God's Old Testament promise to Israel, of which the Jews were the faithful remnant. All of the followers of Christ were also followers of the Mosaic Law, keeping both the Laws of the Old Testament and the teachings of Christ. Did this mean that the people of the whole world had to become Jews and follow the Mosaic Law before they could become Christians?

The early Christians were initially divided when it came to answering this question. After all, as Christ himself had explained to the Samaritan woman, "Salvation is from the Jews."[28] But in order for a person to become a Jew, the convert would have to adhere to the precepts of the Jewish law and give up some of the elements of his or her own culture and tradition.

St. Philip Baptizes the Ethiopian

So far the Apostles had put all of their effort into preaching the Gospel to the Jews and the Samaritans. But Jesus had sent them out to all nations.

> An angel of the Lord said to Philip, "Rise and go toward the south to the road that goes down from Jerusalem to Gaza." This is a desert road. And he rose and went. And behold, an Ethiopian, a eunuch, a minister of Candace, the queen of the Ethiopians, in charge of all her treasure, had come to Jerusalem to worship and was returning; seated in his chariot, he was reading the prophet Isaiah. (Acts 8: 26-28)

St. Philip Baptizing the Ethiopian (detail) by Rembrandt. This was the first time recorded in Scripture that a Gentile had been baptized as a Christian.

Ethiopia was governed by a line of queens (Candace seems to have been their title rather than their name), and those queens were capable enough leaders that even the Romans could never conquer Ethiopia.

There were many Jews among the Ethiopians, and the queen's treasurer must have heard about their religion from them. This *eunuch* was a man of very high position. He was important enough to ride in a chariot, more like a large carriage, on the long trip from Ethiopia to Jerusalem and back. Even so, because he was a eunuch he could never be a Jew.[29] He may have been a fan of Isaiah because he promised a place in the Kingdom even to eunuchs:

> Thus says the LORD: "To the eunuchs who keep my Sabbaths, who choose the things that please me and hold fast my covenant, I will give in my house and within my walls a monument and a name better than sons and daughters. I will give them an everlasting name which shall not be cut off." (Is 56: 4-5)

In those days, people often read aloud even when they were alone, so St. Philip could hear what the Ethiopian was reading.

> The Spirit said to Philip, "Go up and join this chariot." So Philip ran to him, and heard him reading Isaiah the prophet, and asked, "Do you understand what you are reading?" And he said, "How can I,

unless someone guides me?" And he invited Philip to come up and sit with him. Now the passage of the scripture which he was reading was this: As a sheep led to the slaughter or a lamb before its shearer is dumb, so he opens not his mouth. In his humiliation justice was denied him. Who can describe his generation? For his life is taken up from the earth. And the eunuch said to Philip, "About whom, pray, does the prophet say this, about himself or about some one else?" Then Philip opened his mouth, and beginning with this scripture he told him the good news of Jesus. (Acts 8: 29-35)

Showing how Jesus fulfilled the Scriptures was always the early Christians' most effective argument.

As they went along the road they came to some water, and the eunuch said, "See, here is water! What is to prevent my being baptized?" (Acts 8: 36)

Now St. Philip had a decision to make. Was there anything to prevent the Ethiopian from becoming a Christian? If being a Christian meant first being a Jew, then there was something to prevent it. A eunuch could not become a Jew. But St. Philip had been led by an angel and guided by the Spirit. Surely this must be the will of God.

He commanded the chariot to stop, and they both went down into the water, Philip and the eunuch, and he baptized him. (Acts 8: 38)

This was the first time recorded in Scripture that a Gentile had been baptized as a Christian, and it was symbolically appropriate that it was an Ethiopian. To the Romans, Ethiopia represented the farthest point of the known world—"the end of the earth." St. Philip had been led to the Ethiopian by the Holy Spirit. It was a sign the Apostles could hardly ignore. The Good News was not just for the Jews, but for all nations. The preaching of the Gospel to the whole world had begun.

The Vision of St. Peter

The question of the Gentiles would also arise in the context of other questions of the Mosaic Law. If they want to become Christians, then must Gentiles first be circumcised according to the Jewish law? Must they likewise observe all the Jewish dietary laws?

The solution to this latter dilemma was given to St. Peter in a vision.

Baptism of a Centurion by Corneille.
"And Peter opened his mouth and said: 'Truly I perceive that God shows no partiality, but in every nation any one who fears him and does what is right is acceptable to him.'" (Acts 10: 34-35)

He became hungry and desired something to eat; but while they were preparing it, he fell into a trance and saw the heaven opened, and something descending, like a great sheet, let down by four corners upon the earth. In it were all kinds of animals and reptiles and birds of the air. And there came a voice to him, "Rise, Peter; kill and eat." But Peter said, "No, Lord; for I have never eaten anything that is common or unclean." And the voice came to him again a second time, "What God has cleansed, you must not call common." This happened three times, and the thing was taken up at once to heaven. (Acts 10: 10-16)

Christ was calling together a new People of God, one that was united not by ethnicity or the Old Covenant, but rather by his Holy Spirit. Immediately after he received this vision, the Acts of the Apostles tells us that St. Peter went to meet St. Cornelius, a Roman centurion (and therefore a Gentile) who wanted to learn about Jesus. Now St. Peter fully understood Christ's command to "make disciples of all nations."

You yourselves know how unlawful it is for a Jew to associate with or to visit any one of another nation; but God has shown me that I should not call any man common or unclean. (Acts 10: 28)

The Council of Jerusalem

An assembly of the Apostles and the Church's elders (in Greek, *presbyteros*, from which we get the word "priest") was convoked in Jerusalem in order to decide the matter of circumcision once and for all. This assembly was the first council—and archetype for the later *Ecumenical Councils*—of the Church; today we refer to this as the *Council of Jerusalem* (AD 51). Here is found the first instance of a Pope officially defining a teaching of the Church.

After much heated discussion, St. Peter stood up among the Apostles and essentially put an end to the debate.

> **"Brethren, you know that in the early days God made choice among you, that by my mouth the Gentiles should hear the word of the gospel and believe....We believe that we shall be saved through the grace of the Lord Jesus, just as they will." And all the assembly kept silence. (Acts 15: 7, 11-12)**

The declaration of the Council—defined by St. Peter and later confirmed by St. James, the bishop of Jerusalem—was then sent out to Gentile Christians everywhere. With the controversy now settled, the Apostles returned to their task of evangelization, proclaiming the Gospel to the ends of the earth.

Ordaining of the Twelve Apostles by Tissot. (Mk 3: 13-19)

THE MEANING OF TWELVE

The Apostles represent the fundamental structure of the institutional Church on earth. By bestowing his divine authority on them, Christ established the means through which we are enabled to enter into the communion with God that had been planned for us from the beginning.

The number twelve was highly significant in the Hebrew tradition. Three was the perfect number; four represented the four corners of the earth. Multiply three and four, and you get twelve, symbolizing that the mission of the Apostles was to extend to the whole world. Twelve also referred to the twelve tribes of Israel, thus indicating that Christ was reestablishing the new People of God.

The gathering of God's people begun on Mount Sinai would be completed in his Church. The difference between that gathering and the new gathering was that the People of God would now be universal. The Apostles were to go out to "all nations,"[30] inviting the entire world into a communion with God.

This missionary aspect of Christ's calling has been apparent from the very beginning of the Church's ministry. When Christ first encountered Sts. Peter, Andrew, James, and John, they were simple fishermen tending their nets. Christ called out to them, inviting them to follow him. As Christ would later tell them, they would become "fishers of men."[31]

> **Jesus is the Father's Emissary.** From the beginning of his ministry, he "called to him those whom he desired...and he appointed twelve, whom also he named apostles, to be with him, and to be sent out to preach."[32] From then on, they would also be his "emissaries" (Greek *apostoloi*). In them, Christ continues his own mission: "As the Father has sent me, even so I send you."[33] The apostles' ministry is the continuation of his mission; Jesus said to the Twelve: "He who receives you receives me."[34] (CCC 858)

Indeed, the Twelve were to share fully in Christ's mission of announcing the promise of salvation to all people. After his Resurrection, Christ explicitly entrusted the Apostles with this task,[35] bestowing his divine authority on them, and promising that he would be with them always to the end of the age.[36]

ACTS OF THE APOSTLES

Like the faithful who make up the Mystical Body of Christ, each of the Apostles (along with St. Paul) had unique roles to play in carrying out Christ's mission of salvation. Using the available evidence from Scripture, history, and Tradition, we can follow the Apostles' lives from Jesus' invitation to follow him to their eventual deaths.

St. Peter

St. Peter was a fisherman who, along with Sts. James and John, ran a small fishing business on the Lake of Gennesaret. It was here, while tending his nets, that he received Christ's call to become a disciple. In the path he was to follow, Peter would no longer be a simple fisherman, but a fisher of men in the Church founded by Christ.

The defining moment for St. Peter came when Jesus asked his Apostles: "Who do men say that I am?"[37] The Twelve repeated many of the various opinions that they had heard from others in their travels with Jesus. However, Jesus insisted, "Who do *you* say that I am?"[38]

St. Peter, who at that time was called Simon, answered for the others: "You are the Christ"[39] It was then that Jesus gave Peter his new name. *Cephas*, an Aramaic word meaning "rock," comes to us in its Greek form, *Petros*, from which we get *Peter* in English. Along with his new name, St. Peter received a new mission:

> **You are Peter, and on this rock I will build my church....I will give you the keys of the kingdom of heaven, and whatever you bind on earth will be bound in heaven, and whatever you loose on earth will be loosed in heaven.** (Mt 16: 18-19)

Domine quo vadis? by Carracci.
Christ replied, "I am coming to be crucified again."

In this commissioning, Christ used three metaphors which help to define St. Peter's future role in the Church:

✤ **His new name, *Rock*,** signified that St. Peter would be the foundation of the Church that Christ would establish.

✤ **The keys** indicated that St. Peter would be both the leader in this Church and Christ's own representative.

✤ **The power of binding and loosing** granted St. Peter the authority to make decisions in Christ's Church.

Christ bestowed a position of leadership on St. Peter. He would be the final authority within the community of believers, an office that would later be known as the Holy See, the papacy.

St. Peter's position of leadership among the Apostles and in the Church can been seen in the events that followed the Ascension. St. Peter made vital decisions in the early Christian community and spoke for the Apostles. It was St. Peter who was given the task of guarding the Church of Christ for all time; and, as Christ's representative on earth, it was St. Peter who bore the responsibility of guaranteeing universal communion in the Church.

Eventually traveling to Rome, St. Peter helped to establish and nourish the Christian community in the very heart of the Roman Empire. There, he suffered martyrdom. That is why each Bishop of Rome becomes the successor of St. Peter, the Pope, the head of the Catholic Church.

Tradition has it that St. Peter was crucified around AD 64. By his own request, he was crucified upside-down, saying that he was not worthy to die in the same manner as Our Lord. A tradition says that during one of the persecutions under the Roman emperor Nero, St. Peter, while leaving Rome for his safety, met the Risen Christ along the road. When St. Peter asked him, *Domine quo vadis?* ("Lord, where are you going?"), Christ replied, "I am coming to be crucified again." St. Peter then understood that he must return to the city and suffer martyrdom.

Martyrdom of Peter by Giotto.
Tradition has it that by his own request, St. Peter was crucified upside-down.

St. James the Greater

The Bible lists two Apostles named James: James, son of Zebedee, and James, son of Alphaeus.[40] They are commonly distinguished as "James the Greater" and "James the Lesser," perhaps in reference to their height.

St. James the Greater by Crivelli.
St. James was the first of the Twelve Apostles to give his life for Christ.

St. James the Greater and his brother, St. John, were the Sons of Zebedee and Salome, and, like St. Peter, they were simple fishermen. Some traditions have it that their mother, Salome, was a sister of the Blessed Virgin Mary—which would make Sts. James and John cousins of Our Lord. This might explain the brothers' confidence with Jesus when asking him to make them the greatest in the kingdom;[41] it might also explain why Jesus gave his Mother over to the care of St. John at the Crucifixion.[42] Sts. James and John were also part of Jesus' inner circle of Apostles and were present with Christ at the Transfiguration and in the Garden of Gethsemane.

Certain verses in the Bible give us clues about the possible character of these brothers. Jesus called them *Boanerges* ("sons of thunder"), possibly in reference to their tempers. On one occasion, they wanted to send fire from Heaven down on a group of Samaritans who had refused to receive Christ. They certainly had evangelical zeal.

Jesus had assured Sts. James and John that they would drink from the same chalice of which he would drink,[43] meaning they would share in Christ's sufferings. St. James was beheaded AD 44 by Herod Agrippa, thus becoming the first of the Twelve to give his life for Christ.[44]

St. John

St. John, the son of Zebedee, was the brother of St. James the Greater. He also was a fisherman, and it was while mending his nets on the shore of Lake Tiberias with his brother that Jesus called him.[45]

St. John was an integral part of Jesus' inner circle. According to tradition and to the Gospel that bears his name, St. John was the "disciple whom Jesus loved." St. John sat beside our Lord at the Last Supper [46] and was the only disciple with the courage to stay with Jesus during the Crucifixion, where he stood at the foot of the Cross with Mary, the Mother of Jesus.[47] There, Jesus asked St. John to care for his mother and gave St. John to the Blessed Mother as her son.[48]

St. Paul lists St. John alongside Sts. James and Peter as pillars of the Church in Jerusalem,[49] and the Acts of the Apostles shows St. John present at some of the most important events in the life of the early Church.[50] St. John is sometimes called "the Theologian" because of the deep Christology permeating his Epistles and especially his Gospel; his Gospel begins by identifying Jesus Christ as the Word of God, whose Greek words ("*Logos*," Word; and "*Theos*," God) constitute the word *theologian*.

St. John has the distinction of being the last of the Apostles to die and the only Apostle not to suffer martyrdom, although he did endure much persecution. During the reign of the Roman Emperor Domitian, St. John was exiled to the isle of Patmos off the coast of modern-day Turkey. There he wrote the *Book of Revelation* (or *Apocalypse*), giving us a vision of the *heavenly liturgy* and the trials that would be suffered by the early Christians. In the Book of Revelation, St. John addressed the early Christian communities and encouraged them to be steadfast in their faith and not to identify with the pagan world that was personified by the Roman Empire.

A Latin legend held that Emperor Domitian attempted to kill St. John by placing him in a cauldron of boiling oil *ante portam Latinam* ("before the Latin Gate") leading out of Rome to the Roman province of Latium. Miraculously, St. John walked out of the oil unharmed. After his death, devotion to the Apostle John spread from the city of Ephesus where, according to an ancient tradition, he worked for many years and died during the reign of Emperor Trajan.

St. John the Evangelist by Tissot.
St. John has the distinction of being the last of the Apostles to die and the only Apostle not to suffer martyrdom.

The Martyrdom of St. Andrew by Murillo.
A devout Jew, Andrew was a disciple of St. John the Baptist and immediately recognized Jesus as the promised Messiah.

St. Andrew

St. Andrew was the brother of St. Peter and, like his brother, was a fisherman. A devout Jew, he was a disciple of St. John the Baptist and immediately recognized Jesus as the promised Messiah. Of the Apostles, it was St. Andrew who first met Christ and introduced him to Peter.[51]

While St. Andrew certainly had a close relationship with Jesus, he is not mentioned often in the New Testament and not much is known about his apostolic journeys. Eusebius, a historian of the early Church (AD 260-340), wrote that St. Andrew's missionary activities took him to Scythia (modern-day Ukraine and Russia). Other traditions consider St. Andrew as the Apostle to the Greeks. Indeed, his name, Andrew, comes from Greek, and the Bible does record him interceding on behalf of a group of Greeks who wished to see Christ.[52] Both of these traditions relate that his last journeys took him through Byzantium and Greece to Patras, where the governor of Patras crucified him on an X-shaped cross.

St. Philip

Like Sts. Peter and Andrew, St. Philip was from Bethsaida,[53] where he followed St. John the Baptist—which is why he was one of the first to encounter Christ. He immediately told Nathanael that he had found the promised Messiah. When Nathanael expressed his skepticism, St. Philip challenged him saying, "Come and see!"[54] Upon meeting Christ, Nathanael also believed and became a follower of Christ.

In the Gospels, St. Philip is generally listed fifth, after Sts. Peter, James, John, and Andrew. The New Testament does not say much about St. Philip or his missionary journeys, although it mentions that he was present throughout Christ's public ministry. Some of the Gospel scenes that mention St. Philip include the miracle of the multiplication of the bread and fish,[55] St. Philip presenting a group of Greeks to Jesus,[56] and the scene when St. Philip asked Jesus to show the Father to the Twelve.[57]

St. Bartholomew (Nathanael)

St. Bartholomew, whose name comes from the Aramaic *Bar-Talmai* (meaning "Son of Talmai/Ptolemy"), has traditionally been identified as Nathanael. We know that Nathanael came from Cana[58] and may have witnessed the first miracle that Jesus worked there.[59]

Nathanael met Jesus through the Apostle Philip, which perhaps is why he is usually placed after Philip in the New Testament lists of the Apostles. When St. Philip told Nathanael he had found the Messiah, Nathanael responded with native prejudice: "Can anything good come out of Nazareth?"[60] However, upon meeting Jesus, he immediately changed his mind.

> **Jesus saw Nathanael coming to him, and said of him, "Behold, an Israelite indeed, in whom is no guile!" Nathanael said to him, "How do you know me?" Jesus answered him, "Before Philip called you, when you were under the fig tree, I saw you." Nathanael answered him, "Rabbi, you are the Son of God! You are the King of Israel!" (Jn 1: 47-49)**

Although we do not know what the reference to the fig tree signified, it was enough for Nathanael. Jesus could read his heart, and he converted immediately, without reservation.

The Gospels do not indicate Nathanael's subsequent apostolic activity. Tradition holds that he preached the Gospel in and around Persia, an arduous journey from Palestine in the first century AD. Another tradition holds that he was martyred in Armenia, where he was flayed alive.

Apostle St. Bartholomew by El Greco.
"Philip found Nathanael, and said to him, 'We have found him of whom Moses in the law and also the prophets wrote, Jesus of Nazareth, the son of Joseph.'" (Jn 1: 45)

St. Matthew

The Gospels introduce St. Matthew simply as "the tax collector," and it was while on the job that he received his call from Christ. He may have practiced his profession in Capernaum. If so, he might have met Jesus and the other Apostles when they were visiting St. Peter's home.

At first glance, a tax collector seems like an unlikely choice for an Apostle. Tax collectors were generally hated by the Jews and were considered public sinners. Even the New Testament links their profession to that of sinners[61] and prostitutes.[62]

The choice of St. Matthew emphasizes the universality of Christ's call. No one was to be excluded from the Church. In addition, Jesus showed through his call of St. Matthew that the Church was to be a refuge for sinners, a means to repentance and forgiveness of sins.

> **Those who are well have no need of a physician, but those who are sick; I came, not to call the righteous, but sinners. (Mk 2: 17)**

The Gospel relates that St. Matthew, following the call of Christ, underwent a complete conversion, immediately leaving his profession and becoming his disciple.

According to the historian Eusebius, St. Matthew's apostolic mission was directed primarily to the Jews. His Gospel is the only one written in Aramaic, the common language spoken in Palestine during Jesus' time. Tradition holds that St. Matthew's Gospel was written to accommodate the Jewish people. It is interesting to note that he corroborates many details of Christ's life and words with Old Testament quotations.

St. Thomas

Doubting Thomas by Strozzi.
"Jesus said to him, 'Have you believed because you have seen me? Blessed are those who have not seen and yet believe.'" (Jn 20: 29)

St. Thomas' name comes from a Hebrew word meaning "paired" or "twin." The New Testament often refers to him by the Greek word for "twin," although the reason for this nickname is unclear.

The Gospel scene for which St. Thomas has become most associated occurred on the day of the Resurrection. St. Thomas, absent when Christ appeared to the Apostles, refused to believe in the Resurrection, saying, "Unless I see in his hands the print of the nails, and place my finger in the mark of the nails, and place my hand in his side, I will not believe,"[63] and it is from this episode that St. Thomas is often referred to as "Doubting Thomas."

When Jesus reappeared among his disciples eight days later, St. Thomas was present. Jesus came to him and said, "Put your finger here, and see my hands; and put out your hand, and place it in my side; do not be faithless, but believing."[64] St. Thomas then made a profession of faith in the Risen Lord, which has been often repeated throughout the history of the Church: "My Lord and my God!"[65]

Sources such as Eusebius[66] claim that St. Thomas evangelized the Parthians in present-day Iran and Turkmenistan; others, derived from the *apocryphal Gnostic* book *Acts of Thomas*, suggest that he established the Church in India and was martyred there. The Malabar Christians of India claim St. Thomas as their evangelizer. When Portuguese explorers arrived in India in the fifteenth century, they were amazed to find a very old Christian community there, traditionally tracing its founding to St. Thomas.

St. James the Lesser

The other Apostle named James, or James the Lesser, came from Nazareth and was the son of Alphaeus and Mary. This was possibly Mary, the wife of Clopas, who stood at the Cross with the Mother of Jesus.[67] St. James was most likely related to Jesus[68] as he was called a "brother" of Our Lord, which in the custom of the time was a title given to all close male relatives.[69]

After Pentecost, St. James became the head of the Church in Jerusalem. The Acts of the Apostles emphasizes the prominent role that James had in that Church. When the Apostles met in what has become known as the Council of Jerusalem to discuss whether Gentile converts should be required to follow Jewish law and customs, St. James presided over the gathering.

The epistle written by St. James shows us a very concrete and practical Christianity. The teachings of Christ must be put into practice, above all, in love of neighbor and in service to the needy. St. James teaches that works are the normal fruit of a living faith.

Apostle St. James the Less by El Greco.
St. James teaches that works are the normal fruit of a living faith.

A man is justified by works and not by faith alone....For as the body apart from the spirit is dead, so faith apart from works is dead. (Jas 2: 24, 26)

The Jewish historian and contemporary of Jesus, Flavius Josephus, wrote in his book *Jewish Antiquities* that St. James was handed over for death by stoning by the High Priest Ananias AD 62.

St. Jude (St. Judas)

St. Judas, not the betrayer, is also referred to as Thaddeus in Mark 3:18 and Matthew 10:3. It is believed that the Evangelists used this name to further distinguish him from Judas Iscariot. In tradition, he is sometimes called Judas Thaddeus; in English-speaking countries, he is typically known as St. Jude. He is the patron of lost causes, and he authored the Epistle of St. Jude.

Tradition holds that St. Jude traveled throughout Judea and Samaria as well as to Syria, Mesopotamia, and Libya in his apostolic journeys. He is a patron of the Armenian Church. One Armenian tradition relates that St. Jude suffered martyrdom about AD 65 in Beirut together with the Apostle Simon the Zealot. An apocryphal source, *The Passion of Simon and Jude*, describes the martyrdom of both of these men in Persia.

St. Simon

Bearing the same name as Simon Peter, the Gospels often refer to St. Simon as "Simon the Zealot" to distinguish him from Simon Peter. This distinction may indicate he used to belong to the Zealots, a violent group that desired a political messiah who would drive the Romans from Palestine and re-establish the earthly Kingdom of Israel; alternatively, it may simply indicate his zeal for the Jewish Law.

St. Simon is rarely mentioned in the New Testament, and very little is known of his missionary journeys. Some traditions have him preaching in Egypt and Northern Africa, or even as far away as Britain. However, nothing is certain, and even his place of burial is unknown. He is sometimes depicted with a saw, as one ancient tradition says he was martyred by being sawn in pieces. Tradition also holds that he was martyred with St. Jude, hence, their common feast day.

Judas Iscariot

Judas Iscariot betrayed Christ to the Jewish authorities. His motive was unclear, although financial gain may have played a role, as it did when Judas criticized the woman who anointed Jesus with ointment.[70]

Jesus harshly warned the man who would betray him: "Woe to that man by whom the Son of man is betrayed! It would have been better for that man if he had not been born."[71] Judas' fall serves as a warning that even the graces given to Christ's Apostles—and the familiar friendship of Jesus himself—may be of no avail if one is unfaithful and does not believe.

St. Judas Thaddeus by Leal.
Armenian tradition relates that St. Jude suffered martyrdom about AD 65 in Beirut.

St. Simon by Tissot.
Tradition holds that St. Simon was martyred with St. Jude, hence, their common feast day.

St. Paul

St. Paul by Castillo.
The New Testament records St. Paul's tremendous desire to spread the message of Christ in Spain and even to the ends of the earth.

St. Paul is not one of the Twelve; rather, he was called to apostleship by the ascended Christ. Originally named Saul, St. Paul was a dedicated and pious Jew who went to Jerusalem to study the Mosaic Law under the great rabbi Gamaliel.[72] He was also a tentmaker by profession,[73] a useful trade that permitted him to support himself during his apostolic travels.[74]

As a zealous Jew, Saul believed the Christian teachings were not only erroneous, but also blasphemous, and thus felt that he had the religious duty to prevent the spread of Christianity. He zealously persecuted the followers of Christ in Jerusalem and wherever else they might be found. As we read earlier in the chapter, while en route to Damascus to hunt down Christians, he had a remarkable encounter with Christ, a life-changing event that sparked his immediate conversion.

From that moment, St. Paul placed his life entirely at the service of Jesus Christ and his Gospel. St. Paul seemed to have an instinctive recognition of the universal message of the Gospel. He preached to the Gentiles throughout the Roman Empire and was known as the "Apostle to the Gentiles."

St. Paul is also known for the extent of his missionary journeys. Beginning with the Church of Antioch in Syria—where the name Christian was first used—he went to Cyprus and then throughout Asia Minor, preaching the Gospel in the cities of Ephesus, Philippi, Thessalonica, Corinth, Berea, Athens, and Miletus.

In his Second Letter to the Corinthians, St. Paul describes the hardships that he endured during his journeys:

Five times I have received at the hands of the Jews the forty lashes less one. Three times I have been beaten with rods; once I was stoned. Three times I have been shipwrecked; a night and a day I have been adrift at sea; on frequent journeys, in danger from rivers, danger from robbers, danger from my own people, danger from Gentiles, danger in the city, danger in the wilderness, danger at sea, danger from false brethren; in toil and hardship, through many a sleepless night, in hunger and thirst, often without food, in cold and exposure. (2 Cor 11:24-27)

The New Testament records St. Paul's tremendous desire to spread the message of Christ in Spain[75] and even to the ends of the earth, although it is unclear whether his dream of evangelizing Spain was ever realized. After working for many years in Palestine and Asia Minor, St. Paul was arrested in Jerusalem and sent to Rome for trial, where he spent his final days.

It is believed that St. Paul, like St. Peter, died in Rome between the years AD 62-65. Crucifixion, the cruelest form of execution, was reserved only for non-citizens and criminals. Because he was a Roman citizen, St. Paul was beheaded outside the walls of Rome.

CALLED TO BE APOSTLES

The stories of the Apostles offer amazing accounts of the power the grace of Jesus Christ offers to those called to the mission of evangelization. This mission, however, is not only for the Apostles or their successors—the bishops, priests, and deacons, who make up the hierarchical Church. All of the Church's members are called to build up the Body of Christ, each one in ways specific to his or her state of life.

> The whole Church is apostolic...in that she is "sent out" into the whole world. All members of the Church share in this mission, though in various ways. "The Christian vocation is, of its nature, a vocation to the apostolate as well." Indeed, we call an apostolate "every activity of the Mystical Body" that aims "to spread the Kingdom of Christ over all the earth."[76] (CCC 863)

Those of us who are incorporated into the Mystical Body of Christ have been given the task of proclaiming the Gospel to all mankind, both through our words and our witness of the Christian life. Through our communion with Christ, especially in the frequent reception of the Eucharist, Christ continues to work in us to draw those around us into the Catholic Church, in which alone subsists his One, Holy, Catholic, and Apostolic Church.

"THY KINGDOM COME"

The Last Supper (detail) by Holbein the Younger. With his institution of the Eucharist, Jesus gave the Church the means by which he remains with us to this day.

Jesus' proclamation of the kingdom was the central message of his public ministry: "The time is fulfilled, and the Kingdom of God is at hand; repent, and believe in the gospel."[77] As we have seen, this kingdom was not to be as many in Israel expected it to be.

The Jews of the day had various ideas of when and where the promised Messiah would arrive, and what he would do for the Jewish people. Some envisioned a great political or military leader, a literal king, one who would lead a revolution to end the Roman occupation of Israel. Probably few, if any, expected the Redeemer to be born in a stable in Bethlehem, or to preach a new commandment of love of God and neighbor, the need for repentance from sin, and the imminent arrival of a Kingdom of God that is not of this earth.

The Kingdom of God was made present in the Person of Jesus Christ in the Incarnation. Later, with his institution of the Eucharist, Jesus gave the Church the means by which he remains with us to this day. Through Christ's sacramental presence in the Eucharist, the Kingdom of Heaven is made present again and again on the altars and in the tabernacles of the Church throughout the world.

For us on earth, the presence of the King—and the kingdom—can only be seen with the eyes of faith. Even after Christ becomes present in the Eucharist, he still appears to our eyes as bread and wine. Likewise, even though the Kingdom of Heaven is present on earth in the visible pilgrim Church, she still looks to our eyes like just another human institution. There remains ahead a final unveiling of the kingdom, when the glory of Christ will be visible to the entire world.

> The Church is in history, but at the same time she transcends it. It is only "with the eyes of faith"[78] that one can see her in her visible reality and at the same time in her spiritual reality as bearer of divine life. (CCC 770)

It is no coincidence that, in the celebration of the Mass, the Lord's Prayer comes immediately after the Consecration of the Eucharist. When we pray, "Thy kingdom come," we are acknowledging his hidden presence in the Eucharist; but even more, we are asking him to hasten his final coming, when he will reveal the glory of that Presence now veiled under the appearance of bread and wine.

The entire Church longs for the time when Christ will come in glory, for it is only then, at the end of history, that all the faithful will be gathered together in *Heaven*. Far from distracting the Church from her earthly responsibilities, this desire for Heaven gives urgency to her task of bringing the light of Christ to all people.

As we have seen in this text several times already, the Church is sometimes called the *pilgrim Church*, because the Church on earth knows that her final destination has not yet been reached. She works constantly to remind the faithful that we too are on a pilgrimage, a pilgrimage filled with the dangers of temptation and sin, but one in which we are already united—really, but imperfectly—to Christ in Heaven. And so the Church continues the work of Christ by calling mankind to repentance and proclaiming the kingdom's presence as she awaits its glorious unveiling.

> **The Kingdom of God lies ahead of us. It is brought near in the Word incarnate, it is proclaimed throughout the whole Gospel, and it has come in Christ's death and Resurrection. The Kingdom of God has been coming since the Last Supper and, in the Eucharist, it is in our midst. The kingdom will come in glory when Christ hands it over to his Father. (CCC 2816)**

CONCLUSION

The Ascension by Copely.
Establishing the Kingdom of God on earth and causing it to reach its full potential is the work of all the faithful.

Before he ascended into Heaven, Christ instructed his Apostles to take his message to all the nations, baptizing them in the name of the Father, the Son, and the Holy Spirit. This must have seemed like an overwhelming directive at the time. Yet, empowered by the Holy Spirit, they went forward and, in the face of tremendous opposition, converted a significant proportion of the Jews and Gentiles of the known world to the Christian Faith. The fact that these simple fishermen and ordinary people whom Christ appointed as his Apostles were willing to risk their lives to the point of martyrdom for the Gospel is itself a strong witness to the truth they had heard from Christ and the gifts they had received through the Holy Spirit.

The Church that Christ founded is something of a paradox. As a Sacrament of Salvation, it is here with us humanly and visibly as well as mystically and invisibly. The Church is composed of fallible and sinful members. Yet, as the Body of Christ, it is supernatural and infallible.

Establishing the Kingdom of God on earth and causing it to reach its full potential is the work of all the faithful. Ever prone to sin and ever called to conversion, the faithful of the Church experience the coming Kingdom of Heaven at every Eucharist. As God calls us to re-gather as his people and to draw others toward faith in Christ, we look ultimately to that day when God's children will be united with him in Heaven. Until then, when we will achieve ultimate perfection in Heaven, we look to the Church on earth to guide us in our pilgrim journey.

SUPPLEMENTARY READING

1. Eucharistic Adoration

The worship of the Eucharist outside of the Mass is of inestimable value for the life of the Church. This worship is strictly linked to the celebration of the Eucharistic Sacrifice. The presence of Christ under the sacred species reserved after Mass—a presence which lasts as long as the species of bread and of wine remain—derives from the celebration of the sacrifice and is directed towards communion, both sacramental and spiritual. It is the responsibility of Pastors to encourage, also by their personal witness, the practice of Eucharistic adoration, and exposition of the Blessed Sacrament in particular, as well as prayer of adoration before Christ present under the Eucharistic species.

— Pope Bl. John Paul II, *Ecclesia de Eucharistia*, 25

2. Where Is the Catholic Church

And if ever you are sojourning in cities, inquire not...merely where the Church is, but where is the Catholic Church. For this is the peculiar name of this Holy Church, the mother of us all, which is the spouse of our Lord Jesus Christ, the Only-Begotten Son of God (for it is written, As Christ also loved the Church and gave Himself for it (Ephesians 5:25, and all the rest) and is a figure and copy of Jerusalem which is above, which is free, and the mother of us all (Galatians 4:26); which before was barren, but now has many children.

— St. Cyril of Jerusalem, *Catechetical Lectures*, 18.26

3. The Church Is Necessary for Salvation

Basing itself upon Sacred Scripture and Tradition, it teaches that the Church, now sojourning on earth as an exile, is necessary for salvation. Christ, present to us in His Body, which is the Church, is the one Mediator and the unique way of salvation. In explicit terms He Himself affirmed the necessity of faith and baptism (cf. Mc 16:16; Jn 3:5) and thereby affirmed also the necessity of the Church, for through baptism as through a door men enter the Church. Whosoever, therefore, knowing that the Catholic Church was made necessary by Christ, would refuse to enter or to remain in it, could not be saved.

— Second Vatican Council, *Lumen Gentium*, 14

Last Supper by Ribalta.
"The worship of the Eucharist outside of the Mass is of inestimable value for the life of the Church."
—Pope Bl. John Paul II

VOCABULARY

APOCALYPSE
Another name for the Book of Revelation, the final book of the Bible, which is attributed to St. John and written during his exile on the island of Patmos. This prophetic work in symbolic language was meant to encourage and strengthen persecuted Christians by foretelling the final victory of Christ and his Church over sin and evil.

APOCRYPHAL
Describes any book purporting to be inspired but ultimately not accepted by the Church as part of Sacred Scripture (the Bible).

BAPTISM
The first of the Seven Sacraments and the door that gives access to the other Sacraments; first and chief Sacrament of Forgiveness of Sins because the baptized Christian receives the remission of both personal and Original Sin. It incorporates a person into the Church, the Body of Christ (cf. CCC 977, 1213).

CHARISM
A specific gift or grace of the Holy Spirit that directly or indirectly benefits the Church. It is given in order to help a person live out the Christian life or serve the common good in building up the Church.

CHURCH
Generally, the entire assembly of the faithful People of God; more specifically, particularly when spelled with a capital C, it refers to the Catholic Church. The word comes from the Greek *ekklesia*, meaning assembly.

COUNCIL OF JERUSALEM
Recounted in Acts 15, this synod of the Apostles AD 49 or 50 spoke with the authority of Christ in deciding that Gentile converts to Christianity did not have to be circumcised according to the Law of Moses.

ECUMENICAL COUNCIL
From the Greek *oikoumene*, meaning "the whole inhabited world." A formal synod of bishops (sometimes with other ecclesiastics) from the whole inhabited world convened to define doctrine, regulate the Christian life, or apply discipline in the Church. The First Ecumenical Council was held in Nicæa AD 325.

GNOSTIC
An ancient heretical sect that believed, among other things, that salvation came from obtaining secret experiential knowledge.

HEAVEN
The eternal state of supreme and definitive happiness with God; communion of life and love with the Trinity and all the blessed.

HEAVENLY LITURGY
The worship of God in Heaven by the angels and saints, led by Christ the High Priest, who re-presents the sacrificial offering of himself to the Father, thus renewing the work of our redemption.

KEYS OF THE KINGDOM
In the Old Testament, the sign of the office of prime minister, who is appointed by the king to have primacy over all his other servants; in the New Testament, Jesus gives the "keys to the kingdom" to St. Peter, indicating that he would be both the leader in this Church and Christ's own representative on earth—in other words, the first Pope.

MARTYR
Greek for "witness." A witness to the truth of the Faith in which a Christian endures suffering and even death for Christ.

MASS
The principal sacramental celebration and worship of the Catholic Church, established by Jesus at the Last Supper, in which the mystery of salvation through participation in the sacrificial Death and glorious Resurrection of Christ is renewed and accomplished; also called the Eucharist or Lord's Supper. This name is derived from the Latin dismissal of the faithful, "*Ite, missa est.*"

VOCABULARY Continued

PENTECOST

A Jewish festival, fifty days after Passover, celebrating the giving of the Law to Moses at Sinai. On the fiftieth day after the Resurrection, the Holy Spirit was manifested, given, and communicated to the Apostles, fulfilling the mission of Christ. This is the "birthday" of the Church.

PEOPLE OF GOD

All the faithful from among humanity who seek and desire to know and love God.

PRIMACY OF PETER

The position of being first in rank or authority. The Gospels and the Acts of the Apostles bear witness to St. Peter's primacy among the Apostles.

ROCK

The literal meaning of the name Peter, taken from its Greek form *Petros*. Jesus gave St. Peter his name to indicate that he would be the "rock" upon which Jesus would build his Church.

SACRED SCRIPTURE

The Bible; the canonical writings validated by the Church as inerrant and inspired by the Holy Spirit. Together with Sacred Tradition, it makes up a single deposit of the Word of God—the *Deposit of Faith*—a single gift of God to the Church.

SACRED TRADITION

From the Latin *traditio* ("to hand down"); the Church's teachings that have been passed down through the ages through the successors of the Apostles. Together with Sacred Scripture, it makes up a single deposit of the Word of God—the *Deposit of Faith*—a single gift of God to the Church.

SAINT

In its more specific sense, any individual who has died and been canonized by the Catholic Church, meaning that the person is known to be in Heaven. The members of the Church on earth, the People of God, are also called saints (cf. CCC 823).

VICAR OF CHRIST

Term used for the Pope that emphasizes his role as a representative of Christ himself; from the Latin *vicarius*, meaning "in the person of."

The Martyrdom of St. Stephen by Daddi. "Then they cast him out of the city and stoned him; and the witnesses laid down their garments at the feet of a young man named Saul. And as they were stoning Stephen, he prayed, 'Lord Jesus, receive my spirit.' And he knelt down and cried with a loud voice, 'Lord, do not hold this sin against them.' And when he had said this, he fell asleep." (Acts 7: 58-60)

STUDY QUESTIONS

1. What did Jesus do during the forty days following his Resurrection?

2. What command did Jesus give the Apostles immediately before his Ascension into Heaven?

3. How has the Church fulfilled this command throughout the centuries? What implication does Christ's command have for the Christian today?

4. Which book of the Bible traces the development of the early Church?

5. Whom did the Apostles select as a replacement for Judas?

6. What did St. Peter tell his listeners at Pentecost that they must do in order to be saved?

7. How does the Holy Spirit continue working in the Church today?

8. What authority does Christ give St. Peter in Matthew 16:18-19?

9. Comparing Matthew 16:18-19 with Isaiah 22:21-22, what is the sign of authority that St. Peter is given as leader of the Christian Church?

10. Who was the first Christian martyr? How do martyrs participate in the life of Christ in a special way?

11. What was Saul's primary motive in persecuting Christians?

12. What is the name of the Gentile man St. Peter goes to meet after his vision in Acts 10:10-16?

13. To what question did the Council of Jerusalem provide a definitive answer?

14. Who was St. Polycarp, and how did he give Christian witness to his flock?

15. What was St. Peter's profession? What did Christ say that he would become?

16. St. Andrew is reported to have evangelized what country?

17. To whom did St. Philip first bring the Good News?

18. Why was St. Nathanael prejudiced against Jesus in the beginning?

19. What is unique about St. Matthew's Gospel?

20. Why is St. Judas' name often changed to Thaddeus or St. Jude?

21. What does the true restoration of the kingdom consist of?

22. What is the final goal of the Church?

23. What dangers do the faithful face during their pilgrimage on earth?

The Calling of St. Matthew by Terbrugghen "…and he said to him, 'Follow me.' And he rose and followed him." (Mt 9:9)

PRACTICAL EXERCISES

1. From the day of Pentecost, St. Peter was recognized as the Head of the Church, and he served as the final judge in deliberations among the Apostles. Why did Christ establish a single figure as the Head of the Church? Describe how this helped preserve the unity of the Church at the Council of Jerusalem (Acts 15).

2. Choose an episode from the Gospels in which the Risen Christ appears to his disciples. In what way is the Christ of this story different than before

his Crucifixion? In what way is he the same? What does the story indicate about the nature of the resurrection of the body?

3. In the Lord's Prayer, which is recited at every Mass, we pray, "Thy kingdom come." Why does the Church pray for the final coming of Christ in glory? In what ways do we already participate in heavenly glory as members of the Church on earth?

FROM THE CATECHISM

671 Though already present in his Church, Christ's reign is nevertheless yet to be fulfilled "with power and great glory" by the King's return to earth.[79] This reign is still under attack by the evil powers, even though they have been defeated definitively by Christ's Passover.[80] Until everything is subject to him, "until there be realized new heavens and a new earth in which justice dwells, the pilgrim Church, in her sacraments and institutions, which belong to this present age, carries the mark of this world which will pass, and she herself takes her place among the creatures which groan and travail yet and await the revelation of the sons of God."[81] That is why Christians pray, above all in the Eucharist, to hasten Christ's return by saying to him:[82] *Marana tha!* "Our Lord, come!"[83]

769 "The Church...will receive its perfection only in the glory of heaven,"[84] at the time of Christ's glorious return. Until that day, "the Church progresses on her pilgrimage amidst this world's persecutions and God's consolations."[85] Here below she knows that she is in exile far from the Lord, and longs for the full coming of the Kingdom, when she will "be united in glory with her king."[86] The Church, and through her the world, will not be perfected in glory without great trials. Only then will "all the just from the time of Adam, 'from Abel, the just one, to the last of the elect,'...be gathered together in the universal Church in the Father's presence."[87]

798 The Holy Spirit is "the principle of every vital and truly saving action in each part of the Body."[88] He works in many ways to build up the whole Body in charity:[89] by God's Word "which is able to build you up";[90] by Baptism, through which he forms Christ's Body;[91] by the sacraments, which give growth and healing to Christ's members; by "the grace of the apostles, which holds first place among his gifts";[92] by the virtues, which make us act according to what is good; finally, by the many special graces (called "charisms"), by which he makes the faithful "fit and ready to undertake various tasks and offices for the renewal and building up of the Church."[93]

1060 At the end of time, the Kingdom of God will come in its fullness. Then the just will reign with Christ for ever, glorified in body and soul, and the material universe itself will be transformed. God will then be "all in all" (1 Cor 15:28), in eternal life.

2818 In the Lord's Prayer, "thy kingdom come" refers primarily to the final coming of the reign of God through Christ's return.[94] But, far from distracting the Church from her mission in this present world, this desire commits her to it all the more strongly. Since Pentecost, the coming of that Reign is the work of the Spirit of the Lord who "complete[s] his work on earth and brings us the fullness of grace."[95]

Christ at the Sea of Galilee by Tintoretto. "But when the disciples saw him walking on the sea, they were terrified, saying, 'It is a ghost!' And they cried out for fear. But immediately he spoke to them, saying, 'Take heart, it is I; have no fear.'" (Mt 14: 26-27)

ENDNOTES - CHAPTER THREE

1. Jn 12: 13.
2. *LG* 4; cf. Jn 17: 4.
3. *AG* 4.
4. Cf. Mt 28: 19-20; *AG* 2; 5-6.
5. Acts 1: 3.
6. Lk 22: 30.
7. Mt 27: 3-5.
8. *LG* 4.
9. *LG* 5.
10. Acts 2: 38.
11. Cf. Jn 14: 18; 20: 22; Mt 28: 20; Acts 2: 33.
12. *LG* 7.
13. *LG* 4; cf. Jn 17: 4.
14. *AG* 4.
15. Cf. Mt 28: 19-20; *AG* 2; 5-6.
16. Acts 3: 2-10.
17. Acts 4: 1-12.
18. Mt 16: 18.
19. Mt 16: 19.
20. Jn 21: 15-17; cf. 10: 11.
21. Cf. Mt 18: 18.
22. CCC 882
23. Jn 15: 13.
24. CCC 852.
25. Acts 8: 3.
26. Cf. Acts 22: 25-29.
27. Acts 13: 47.
28. Jn 4: 22.
29. Dt 23: 1.
30. Mt 28: 19; Lk 24: 47.
31. Cf. Mk 1: 17; Mt 4: 19.
32. Mk 3: 13-14.
33. Jn 20: 21; cf. 13: 20; 17: 18.

34. Mt 10: 40; cf. Lk 10: 16.
35. Mt 28: 19.
36. Mt 28: 20.
37. Mt 16: 13.
38. Mt 16: 15.
39. Mt 16: 16.
40. Mk 3: 17-18.
41. Mk 10: 37.
42. Jn 19: 26.
43. Mk 10: 35-40.
44. Acts 12: 1-2.
45. Cf. Mt 4: 21; Mk 1: 19.
46. St. Irenæus of Lyons, *Adv. Hær.*, III, I, n. 1.
47. Jn 19: 25.
48. Jn 19: 26-27.
49. Gal 2: 8-9.
50. Cf. Acts 3: 1-4, 11; 4: 13, 19-20; 8: 14-15.
51. Jn 1: 40.
52. Jn 12: 20-22.
53. Jn 1: 44.
54. Jn 1: 45-46.
55. Jn 6: 8-14.
56. Jn 12: 20-22.
57. Jn 14: 8.
58. Jn 21: 2.
59. Jn 21: 5-6.
60. Jn 1: 46.
61. Mt 9: 10-11; 11: 19; Mk 2: 15-16; Lk 5: 30; 7: 34; 15: 1; 19: 2,7.
62. Mt 21: 31.
63. Jn 20: 25.
64. Jn 20: 27.

65. Jn 20: 28.
66. St. Eusebius of Cæsarea, H.E., 13. 12.
67. Jn 19: 25.
68. Mt 13: 55.
69. Ibid.
70. Mk 14: 3-10.
71. Mt 26: 24.
72. Acts 22: 3.
73. Acts 18: 3.
74. Cf. Acts 20: 34; 1 Cor 4: 12; 2 Cor 12: 13.
75. Rom 15: 24, 28.
76. *AA* 2.
77. Mk 1: 15.
78. *Roman Catechism* I, 10, 20.
79. Lk 21: 27; Mt 25: 31.
80. Cf. 2 Thes 2: 7.
81. *LG* 48 § 3; cf. 2 Pt 3: 13; Rom 8: 19-22; 1 Cor 15: 28.
82. Cf. 1 Cor 11: 26; 2 Pt 3: 11-12.
83. 1 Cor 16: 22; Rev 22: 17, 20.
84. *LG* 48.
85. St. Augustine, *De civ. Dei*, 18, 51: PL 41, 614; cf. *LG* 8.
86. *LG* 5; cf. 6; 2 Cor 5: 6.
87. *LG* 2.
88. Pius XII, encyclical, *Mystici Corporis*: DS 3808.
89. Cf. Eph 4: 16.
90. Acts 20: 32.
91. Cf. 1 Cor 12: 13.
92. *LG* 7 § 2.
93. *LG* 12 § 2; cf. *AA* 3.
94. Cf. Ti 2: 13.
95. *Roman Missal*, Eucharistic Prayer IV, 118.

The Church as Sacrament of Salvation

Each time that the Church gathers to celebrate the liturgy, especially the Eucharist liturgy, it becomes formed as the Body of Christ.

The Church

CHAPTER 4

The Church as Sacrament of Salvation

"The Church is in Christ like a sacrament or as a sign and instrument both of a very closely knit union with God and of the unity of the whole human race." (Lumen Gentium, n. 1)

sacrament "is a sign of a sacred reality and the visible expression of invisible grace" (cf. DS 1639)....[The Church] is a sign, but not only a sign; in herself she is also the fruit of redemption. The sacraments are means of sanctification; the Church, instead, is the assembly of the persons sanctified; thus, she constitutes the purpose of the saving action (cf. Eph 5: 25-27).

With these clarifications, the term *sacrament* can be applied to the Church. The Church is indeed the sign of the salvation accomplished by Christ and meant for all human beings through the work of the Holy Spirit. The sign is visible: the Church, as the community of God's People, has a visible character. The sign is also *efficacious*, inasmuch as belonging to the Church obtains for men union with Christ and all the graces necessary for salvation.

— Pope Bl. John Paul II, *L'Osservatore Romano*, n. 48, December 2, 1991.

IN THIS CHAPTER, WE WILL ADDRESS SEVERAL QUESTIONS:

✣ What does it mean to say that the Church is the Sacrament of Salvation?

✣ What is the meaning of the word *church*?

✣ How is the Church both visible and invisible?

✣ What is the role of the papacy in the Church?

✣ What are the three levels of the Church's hierarchy, and what is the function of each?

✣ What does it mean when we say, "Outside the Church there is no salvation"?

God gathers us together in a visible way each time we assemble as a local church community.

THE CHURCH IS THE SACRAMENT OF SALVATION

God's intent in creation was to share his divine life with all mankind through the Church that he would create through his Son, Jesus Christ:

> At the end of time... all the just, from Adam and "from Abel, the just one, to the last of the elect,"
> will be gathered together with the Father in the universal Church. (*Lumen Gentium*, 2)

But what exactly is the Church? A good starting point in answering this question is to look at the word that Christ and the New Testament writers used when speaking of the Church.

The Latin word used for *church* is *ecclesia*, which comes from Greek *ekklesia* and means an "assembly" or "to call out of." More significantly, as you recall, this was the word used throughout the Old Testament (*qahal* in Hebrew) to refer to Israel, the People of God. The Israelites were God's Chosen People, the assembly called by God to bear witness to his truth and his moral law.

The early Christians understood themselves to be the new People of God. They did not see a discontinuity between the Israel of the Old Covenant and Christ in the New Covenant; rather, they saw the new community of Christian believers as a fulfillment or completion of God's promises through Christ. God was not abolishing his Chosen People but rather perfecting them with his New and Everlasting Covenant. For this reason, they continued using the Old Testament terminology to describe their new assembly.

Later tradition also uses the Greek word *Kyriake* to describe the building wherein the community met and then the community itself, meaning "what belongs to the Lord."[1] This is the word from which the word "church" is derived. By choosing this word to describe the followers of Christ, the early Christians

A First Communion.
Christ, our salvation, acts through the Sacraments of his Church.

were emphasizing that Christians are a people gathered together and belonging to the Lord and that they are called to live in communion with Christ.

This "divine calling together" is the work of Jesus Christ, the incarnate Son of God; he establishes and builds "his" Church as a "calling together of all people in the new covenant." He chooses a visible foundation for this Church and entrusts to him the mandate of governing her. This Church, therefore, belongs to Christ and will always remain his. This is the conviction of the first Christian communities; this is their faith in the Church of Christ.

This calling together entails for each and everyone a call, which requires a response of faith and cooperation in the purpose of the new community, determined by him who gives the call: "It was not you who chose me, but I who chose you and appointed you to go and bear fruit." (Jn 15: 16).[2]

Although this gathering together of God's Church will not be complete until the end of time, it has already begun for us here on earth. God gathers us together in a visible way each time we assemble as a local church community. The *Catechism of the Catholic Church* describes this dual aspect of the Church. While she exists as a universal Church throughout the entire world, she also exists as a local community. Each time the Church gathers to celebrate a liturgy, especially the Eucharist liturgy, she becomes formed as the Body of Christ. This visible gathering of the Church on earth is both a foreshadowing of the future glory in Heaven as well as a participation of the heavenly Church's present glory.

> In Christian usage, the word "church" designates the liturgical assembly,[3] but also the local community[4] or the whole universal community of believers.[5] These three meanings are insep-arable. "The Church" is the People that God gathers in the whole world. She exists in local communities and is made real as a liturgical, above all a Eucharistic, assembly. She draws her life from the word and the Body of Christ and so herself becomes Christ's Body. (CCC 752)

THE MYSTERY OF THE CHURCH

When we think of the Church, often the first thoughts that come to mind are of the visible Church: the parish, the Mass, priests and nuns, catechism classes, or service projects. If we are really trying to think of the Church as "universal," perhaps we think of the Pope, or recall images of St. Peter's Square filled with pilgrims, or people in faraway countries attending Mass. However, the Church is what God wanted her to be: the People of God the Father, the Mystical Body of God the Son, and the Temple of God the Holy Spirit.

The Greek word *mysterion* is translated into Latin by two terms: *mysterium* and *sacramentum*. The term *sacramentum* describes the Church as a visible sign, while the term *mysterium* outlines the hidden reality of salvation.

St. Paul calls the union of Christ with his Bride, the Church, "a profound mystery."[6] Christ, our salvation, acts through the Sacraments of his Church, which are the signs and instruments of the Holy Spirit through which the grace of Christ is conveyed to the Church, his Mystical Body. Thus, the Church contains and distributes the grace that she signifies. Christ instituted his Church as the universal *Sacrament of Salvation*, and, through her, he joins all men more closely to himself. Nourishing them with his own Body and Blood, he makes them partakers of his glorious life.

A Visible and Invisible Society

The Church is both a visible and an invisible society. As a visible society, she is composed of members who are involved in the mission of the Church. She has a hierarchical structure of bishops, priests, and deacons, with the Pope, the Bishop of Rome, as her head. The Church establishes different institutions, such as Catholic schools and hospitals, which assist in her mission of ministering to the needs of both her own members and the world. Catholic churches and cathedrals are built to provide places of worship, and a variety of Catholic groups and organizations serve the spiritual, material, cultural, and social needs of the members.

As an invisible society, the Church includes all of her members, who are united in Jesus Christ, whether on earth, in Purgatory, or in Heaven. She is a spiritual community on which God has bestowed his grace.

The visible Church: St. Peter's Square filled with pilgrims. We can use our senses to perceive the visible realities of the Church, and we can use our reason to come to a deeper understanding of its invisible realities.

> **The Church is essentially both human and divine, visible but endowed with invisible realities, zealous in action and dedicated to contemplation, present in the world, but as a pilgrim, so constituted that in her the human is directed toward and subordinated to the divine, the visible to the invisible, action to contemplation, and this present world to that city yet to come, the object of our quest.**[7] **(CCC 771)**

Just as Christ is one divine Person with two natures, the Church is also a single reality with a dual composition. She is both human and divine; visible but endowed with invisible realities. These dimensions of the Church are a continuation of the Incarnation of the Word, Jesus Christ, who fulfilled the covenant between God and man. They are also in line with man's nature and deepest needs—as a social being desiring communion with God and neighbor.

Christ alluded to this "mixed composition" of the Church, comparing her to a field in which there were both wheat and weeds[8] and to a net that catches both good and bad fish.[9] The visible Church on earth is composed of human members who are sinners and subject to the weaknesses of the flesh. We are "already caught up in Christ's salvation but still on the way to holiness."[10]

Although the Church on earth is made up of sinful members, the Church herself is not sinful. The Church, united to Christ in Heaven, is truly holy and without sin, and she carries on Christ's work on earth, inviting all of those in need of the Divine Physician to be healed.

This brings us to another key point—namely, that the union between Christ and his Church is, as St. Paul called it, "a profound mystery." We can use our senses to perceive the visible realities of the Church, and we can use our reason to come to a deeper understanding of her invisible realities. However, neither our senses nor our reason can fully unveil the reality of the Church. In order to do that, we need the light of faith.

> **"The Church, in Christ, is like a sacrament—a sign and instrument, that is, of communion with God and of unity among all men."**[11] **The Church's first purpose is to be the sacrament of the *inner union of men with God*. Because men's communion with one another is rooted in that union with**

The Last Supper (detail) by Vouet.
By giving us his Body, the Lord transforms us into one body: the Church.

God, the Church is also the sacrament of the *unity of the human race*. In her, this unity is already begun, since she gathers men "from every nation, from all tribes and peoples and tongues";[12] at the same time, the Church is the "sign and instrument" of the full realization of the unity yet to come. (CCC 775)

Through Christ's Incarnation, God gave man the means to be reconciled with him. This reunification with God is achieved in the Church, especially through the Eucharist, when we are made one in Christ. Through Christ and his Mystical Body, the Church, the communion between God and man is restored. This is the sense in which we speak of the Church as *sacrament*, as a *Sacrament of Salvation*, for it is through the Church that the graces necessary for salvation are made available in Christ.

THE CHURCH AS THE SACRAMENT OF COMMUNION

The Church is fundamentally a community of men and women united in the fullness of the grace of Christ, who is the Head of his Mystical Body.

The New Testament word *koinonia* (in Latin, *communio*) meaning *communion* is adequate for expressing the essential core of the Church's mystery.[13] The notion entails both the *vertical dimension* (communion with God) and the *horizontal dimension* (communion among men).[14] This communion is above all a gift from God, a new relationship between humanity and God that has been established in Christ and is communicated through the Sacraments; it also extends a new relationship among human beings.

The Church's communion includes at the same time both the *invisible dimension* (intimate communion with the Holy Trinity and other human beings) and the *visible dimension* (communion in the teaching of the Apostles, the Sacraments, and in the hierarchical order). This communion, then, implies a spiritual solidarity among the members of the Church inasmuch as they are members of one Body, united in Christ.

Each individual enters into the Church's communion by faith and Baptism.[15] Through Baptism, the faithful are incorporated into a Body—the Church—which the risen Lord builds up and sustains through the Eucharist. The Eucharist, the root and center of the community, is the source of communion among the

POPE BENEDICT XVI
ON THE MEANING OF COMMUNION

"To be in communion with Christ is by its very nature to be in communion with one another as well."

The word *koinonia*—in Latin, *communio*—occurred to me as the fundamental concept that expresses the very essence of the Church.

Paul tells us: "The cup of blessing which we bless, is it not a *participation* [in Greek, *koinonia*; in Latin, *communio*] in the blood of Christ? The bread which we break, is it not a *participation* in the body of Christ? Because there is one bread, we who are many are one body, for we all *partake* of the one bread" (emphasis added). The concept of communion is anchored first and foremost in the most Blessed Sacrament of the Eucharist, which is why, in the language of the Church, we still describe the reception of this Sacrament today, and rightly so, simply as "going to communion."

Here we are told that through this Sacrament we enter, as it were, into a blood relationship with Jesus Christ, whereby blood, according to the Hebrew way of thinking, stands for "life." Thus the passage declares an interpenetration of Christ's life with ours.

We all "eat" the same man, not only the same thing; in this way we are wrested from our self-enclosed individuality and drawn into a greater one. We all are assimilated into Christ, and so through communion with Christ we are also identified with one another. To be in communion with Christ is by its very nature to be in communion with one another as well.[16]

members of the Church; it unites each one of them with Christ himself: "Because there is one bread, we who are many are one body, for we all partake of the one bread."[17] "When we share in the body and blood of Christ we become what we receive."[18]

By giving us his Body, the Lord transforms us into one Body: the Church. Hence St Paul's expression *the Church is the Body of Christ* means that the Church expresses herself principally in the Eucharist. While present everywhere, the Church is yet one, just as Christ is one.

THE HIERARCHICAL STRUCTURE OF THE CHURCH

A kingdom needs a certain organization, or it will fall apart. The Kingdom of God on earth was established by Christ to endure until the end of time, so Jesus Christ promised to guide and protect her. He also endowed her with an organization that would carry her through even the most difficult periods.

The New Testament writings speak of *bishops*, *priests*, and *deacons*. This hierarchy of the Church was developed while the Twelve were still alive. They used it to hand on their authority and their traditions so that the Church would continue on the course Jesus Christ had set for her. The bishops of the Church, as successors of the Apostles with the *Pope* as their head, form a single "college."[19] They continue to lead the church in an unbroken chain that leads back to the Twelve, a reality we call *Apostolic Succession*.

There are three distinct ministerial offices within the Church: bishops, priests, and deacons. Each of these offices corresponds to one of the three degrees of Holy Orders by which Christ bestows his authority on those men who are to serve his flock, giving them his own power to "do and give by God's grace what they cannot do and give by their own powers."[20]

> In order to shepherd the People of God and to increase its numbers without cease, Christ the Lord set up in his Church a variety of offices which aim at the good of the whole body. The holders of office, who are invested with a sacred power, are, in fact, dedicated to promoting the interests of their brethren, so that all who belong to the People of God...may attain to salvation."[21] (CCC 874)

Although there is a true equality of dignity among the faithful and their contributions to the Church's mission, the Church is organized in a governing structure of hierarchical authority, that is to say, certain members of the Church, because of the graces available through their ordained roles, possess greater authority in the Church than others.

THE HIERARCHY OF THE CHURCH IS ESTABLISHED BY CHRIST

In order to establish this His holy Church everywhere in the world till the end of time, Christ entrusted to the College of the Twelve the task of teaching, ruling and sanctifying. Among their number He selected Peter, and after his confession of faith determined that on him He would build His Church. Also to Peter He promised the keys of the Kingdom of Heaven, and after His profession of love, entrusted all His sheep to him to be confirmed in faith and shepherded in perfect unity. Christ Jesus Himself was forever to remain the chief cornerstone and shepherd of our souls.

Jesus Christ, then, willed that the Apostles and their successors—the bishops with Peter's successor at their head—should preach the Gospel faithfully, administer the sacraments, and rule the Church in love. It is thus, under the action of the Holy Spirit, that Christ wills His people to increase, and He perfects His people's fellowship in unity: in their confessing the one faith, celebrating divine worship in common, and keeping the fraternal harmony of the family of God.

— Second Vatican Council, *Unitatis Redintegratio*, 2

Twenty-nine Deacons are ordained to the priesthood by Pope Benedict XVI in St. Peter's Basilica. The Holy Father said to them, "Bring the Gospel to everyone so that they may experience the joy of Christ."

We must be careful not to think of the visible society of the Church on earth in terms of a democracy. The Church is instituted by Christ, and, unlike a democracy, the power of the Church comes from Christ, not from the people. The baptized share in Christ's priestly, prophetic, and kingly mission, but it is Christ himself who is the source of the Church's life and ministry.

It is through the Sacrament of Holy Orders that the ministerial authority of Christ, which he imparted to the Apostles, is passed down to the bishops, priests, and deacons of the Church. The clergy make up the Church's *hierarchy* (from the Greek word *hierarchia*, meaning "sacred order"), which derives its authority from Christ himself. It is Christ who established the Church's hierarchical structure, and he commanded the Apostles and their successors to exercise this authority in imitation of his own spirit of service. This is reflected in one of the Pope's titles, "Servant of the Servants of God."

> [Jesus] said to [the apostles], "The kings of the Gentiles exercise lordship over [their people]; and those in authority over them are called benefactors. But not so with you; rather let the greatest among you become as the youngest, and the leader as one who serves....I am among you as one who serves." (Lk 22:25-27)

The hierarchy of the Church is therefore different from any other hierarchical structure—such as a government or a corporation—for it is defined not by authoritarianism but rather by service performed out of love. The task of those who are "higher" is to serve those who are "lower," and not the other way around. We can see in this a reflection of God's own love, for, although God is infinitely greater than any of his creatures, he demonstrates his greatness by lifting us up and offering us his own divine life of grace.

> Sacramental ministry in the Church, then, is a service exercised in the name of Christ. It has a personal character and a collegial form. This is evidenced by the bonds between the episcopal college and its head, the successor of St. Peter, and in the relationship between the bishop's pastoral responsibility for his particular church and the common solicitude of the episcopal college for the universal Church. (CCC 879)

St. Peter Enthroned with Saints by Cima. St. Paul the Apostle (standing on the right) accepted wholeheartedly the position of St. Peter as first of the Apostles without any hesitation.

ST. PETER AND THE PAPACY

Christ instituted the Church as a collegial body with the Pope at her head.

> **When Christ instituted the Twelve, "he constituted [them] in the form of a college or permanent assembly, at the head of which he placed Peter, chosen from among them."[22] Just as "by the Lord's institution, St. Peter and the rest of the apostles constitute a single apostolic college, so in like fashion the Roman Pontiff, Peter's successor, and the bishops, the successors of the apostles, are related with and united to one another."[23] (CCC 880)**

> **The Lord made Simon alone, whom he named Peter, the "rock" of his Church. He gave him the keys of his Church and instituted him shepherd of the whole flock.[24] "The office of binding and loosing which was given to Peter was also assigned to the college of apostles united to its head."[25] This pastoral office of Peter and the other apostles belongs to the Church's very foundation and is continued by the bishops under the primacy of the Pope. (CCC 881)**

After the Ascension of Christ into Heaven, St. Peter began to fulfill his role as leader of the Church. The rest of the Apostles accepted his authority, even though before Christ's Death and Resurrection they had all been vying for the position of "greatest in the Kingdom of Heaven."

HOW A POPE IS ELECTED

Following the death of a Pope, the *cardinals* of the Church meet in Rome to decide on who will be the next Pope. These cardinals are generally archbishops who have been consecrated by a Pope to serve as a special adviser to the papacy; some remain at the helm of their archdiocese, while others are appointed to important administrative positions at the Vatican. One important duty of a cardinal, however, is to function as a papal elector.

A papal election, called a *conclave*, occurs between fifteen and twenty days after the death of a Pope. The cardinal electors first assemble in St. Peter's Basilica to celebrate the Mass. Afterwards, they proceed to the Sistine Chapel where the election will take place.

Upon entering the Sistine Chapel, each cardinal takes an oath to observe the correct procedures, to defend the liberty of the Holy See, to maintain secrecy, and to disregard all outside influences in the election process. The doors to the Sistine Chapel are then closed, and from this moment on absolute secrecy is maintained throughout the conclave. The electors may not speak with anyone outside the conclave until a new Pope is elected.

At some point during the election process, a call for voting will be made. Each cardinal elector writes down the name of the person he believes should be elected Pope and places it in a container. The ballots are then carefully counted. If the number does not correspond to the number of electors, the ballots are burnt unread, and the process is repeated. If the number is correct, the ballots are opened, and the numbers of votes received for each candidate are announced.

For a Pope to be elected, he must win a two-thirds majority of electors. If no candidate receives the necessary votes, the ballots are burnt. This is one of the ceremonious aspects of a papal election. Traditionally, large crowds gather in St. Peter's Square, waiting to learn the results of the papal election. Their first signal comes from the chimney atop the Sistine Chapel. If the smoke is white, a new Pope has been elected; if the smoke is black, it means a vote was taken but there was no clear winner. In the past, damp straw was added to the fire to produce dark smoke; today, certain chemicals are used to produce the effect.

If the vote has not resulted in the required majority, discussions among the cardinal electors will continue and another vote will be taken at a later time. This process is repeated until one candidate has received the two-thirds majority vote needed to elect a Pope. Once a Pope is elected, the cardinal dean asks the Pope-elect if he will accept the office of Pope. Upon indicating his acceptance, the new Pope immediately takes office. The ballots are burnt without additives, which produces the desired white smoke; this is followed by the ringing of the bells to announce the election to the world.

The first duty of the new Pope is to decide on the name by which he will be called. He then dresses himself in papal vestments and prepares to address the crowd gathered in St. Peter's Square. A cardinal will first appear on the main balcony of St. Peter's Basilica and proclaim to all gathered that a new Pope has been elected: *"Annuntio vobis gaudium magnum: Habemus papam!"* ("I announce to you a great joy: We have a Pope!")

The new Pope then steps out onto the balcony and speaks to the crowd, giving them his first papal blessing, known as *Urbi et Orbi* ("To the City [Rome] and the world").

Illustration: The Papal Coat of Arms is comprised of the Papal Tiara and the crossed keys of St. Peter.

✤ St. Peter was the one who decided that the Apostles must replace Judas with Matthias.

✤ St. Peter was the one who spoke for the Apostles at Pentecost.

✤ St. Peter was the one who defended the Christians before the Sanhedrin.

✤ St. Peter was the one who made the decision against circumcision at the Council of Jerusalem.

✤ St. Peter was the one who founded the church community in Rome, the capital of the civilized world.

✤ St. Paul the Apostle accepted wholeheartedly the position of St. Peter as first of the Apostles without any hesitation.

To ensure that the faithful would be truthfully taught, Christ guaranteed that St. Peter and his successors, the Popes, would be free from error—infallible—in their public teachings on matters of faith and morals. Papal *infallibility* is made possible by the work of the Holy Spirit in the Church. Hence, the *papacy* preserves the truth of God that liberates Church members from error.

ROMAN CURIA

The Roman Curia is the administrative or governing body of the Catholic Church, which assists the Pope in his role as pastor of the universal Church. While the Pope has primary authority over the Church, it is not possible for him to administer this authority in every detail. For this reason, the Popes have traditionally created various offices or ministries to assist them in this responsibility.

At present, the Roman Curia consists of:

✤ A Secretariat of State;

✤ Nine Congregations;

✤ Three Tribunals; and

✤ Eleven Pontifical Councils.

Secretariat of State

The Secretariat of State oversees the political and diplomatic functions of the Catholic Church. It is divided into two sections: the section for General Affairs and the section for Relations with States.

The *section for General Affairs* handles the everyday administrative functions of the Pope. This includes preparing papal documents and assisting with appointments within the Roman Curia. They publish official papal announcements through the Vatican Press Office and are responsible for keeping records. This section of the Secretariat also keeps the Papal Seal and the Fisherman's Ring.

The *section for Relations with States* attends to the Pope's diplomatic relations with civil governments. This includes establishing agreements with states and making the necessary arrangements for the Holy See's participation in international organizations.

Congregations

The *Congregation for the Doctrine of the Faith* assists the Pope in promoting and safeguarding the teachings of the Catholic Church in matters of Faith and morals.[26]

The *Congregation for the Oriental Churches* helps in the administration of matters concerning the Eastern Catholic Churches, sometimes referred to as the Oriental Catholic Churches.[27]

The *Congregation for Divine Worship and the Discipline of the Sacraments* oversees the "regulation and promotion of the sacred liturgy, primarily of the sacraments."[28]

The *Congregation for the Causes of Saints* handles matters regarding the canonization of servants of God to the sainthood. After conducting a thorough investigation and ensuring that the proper procedures have been followed, the congregation will make a recommendation to the Holy Father. This congregation also supervises the authentication of holy relics.[29]

The *Congregation for Bishops* helps in the establishment and provision of particular churches (dioceses) as well as the appointment of bishops.[30]

The *Congregation for the Evangelization of Peoples* coordinates the missionary work of the Catholic Church throughout the world. This congregation helps foster vocations to the missionary life and strives to help the faithful in fulfilling the missionary role of the Church.[31]

The *Sacred Congregation for the Clergy* deals with matters concerning the "life, conduct, rights, and obligations of clergy" as well as the religious education of the faithful.[32]

The *Congregation for Institutes of Consecrated Life and for Societies of Apostolic Life* promotes and supervises "the practice of the evangelical counsels" of poverty, chastity, and obedience. They are responsible for matters concerning the consecrated life (i.e., religious orders, congregations, and secular institutes) and societies of apostolic life.[33]

The *Congregation for Catholic Education* assists in the education of those preparing for the priesthood, including the establishment and administration of seminaries. It also assists other Catholic educational institutions, such as Catholic schools and universities.[34]

The Pontifical Swiss Guard is a department of the Roman Curia. The Guard serves not only as a Vatican Guard of Honor, but also keeps order whenever the Pope is in public, for liturgical celebrations in St. Peter's Basilica, at the General Audiences, during visits to the Pope by Heads of State, Foreign Ministers and Ambassadors.

Tribunals

The *Apostolic Penitentiary* is the tribunal of the Roman Curia that grants absolutions and dispensations in matters reserved to the Holy See. It also has authority over the granting and proper use of indulgences.[35]

The *Supreme Tribunal of the Apostolic Signatura* is the supreme tribunal of the Catholic Church, which "ensures that justice in the Church is correctly administered."[36]

The *Tribunal of the Roman Rota* is an appellate court charged with "safeguarding rights within the Church," and providing "assistance to lower tribunals."[37]

Pontifical Councils

The *Pontifical Council for the Laity* promotes and coordinates the apostolate of the laity.[38]

The *Pontifical Council for Promoting Christian Unity* assists the Church in its ecumenical activities.[39]

The *Pontifical Council for the Family* "promotes the pastoral care of families" and "protects their rights and dignity in the Church and in civil society."[40]

The *Pontifical Council for Justice and Peace* seeks to promote "justice and peace in the world in accordance with the Gospel and the social teaching of the Church."[41]

The *Pontifical Council "Cor Unum"* was established to help those in need, thus making manifest the love of Jesus Christ in the world.[42]

The *Pontifical Council for the Pastoral Care of Migrants and Itinerant People* is concerned with the pastoral care of those who have left their home countries or who do not have one.[43]

The *Pontifical Council for Pastoral Assistance to Health Care Workers* assists in the Church's apostolate to those who are suffering.[44]

The *Pontifical Council for Legislative Texts* is in charge of publishing the authentic interpretations of the Church's laws as directed by the Pope.[45]

The *Pontifical Council for Inter-Religious Dialogue* fosters dialogue with members of other religions.[46]

The *Pontifical Council for Dialogue with Non-Believers* looks into the causes for atheism and lack of faith and manifests the care of the Church for those who do not believe in God.[47]

The *Pontifical Council for Culture* helps to bring the message of the Gospel into human culture, especially in the areas of the sciences, literature, and the arts.[48]

The *Pontifical Council for Social Communications* seeks to advance the message by means of social communication.[49]

THE OFFICE OF BISHOP

When Christ began his ministry, he chose the Twelve Apostles to help him spread the Good News. He entrusted his Church to them and made St. Peter their leader. In turn, the Twelve chose others among their followers to help them and to continue their mission.

First among these is the office of bishop, also called the *episcopacy* (from the Greek *episkopos*, meaning "overseer," and the origin of the word "bishop"). As the direct successors of the Apostles, the bishops of the Church each possess the fullness of the Sacrament of Holy Orders, for they have received the full authority that Christ gave to the Twelve. Therefore, only those who have been validly ordained as bishops are able to confer the Sacrament of Holy Orders, whether to the episcopacy, the priesthood, or the diaconate.

The Martyrdom of St. Ignatius. St. Ignatius was the third Bishop of Antioch after St. Peter and St. Evodius. Because of his direct contact with the Apostles, St. Ignatius is an Apostolic Father. His letters are considered the most important documents linking the Twelve Apostles with the early Church.

"The individual *bishops* are the visible source and foundation of unity in their own particular Churches."[50] As such, they "exercise their pastoral office over the portion of the People of God assigned to them,"[51] assisted by priests and deacons. But, as a member of the episcopal college, each bishop shares in the concern for all the Churches.[52] The bishops exercise this care first "by ruling well their own Churches as portions of the universal Church," and so contributing "to the welfare of the whole Mystical Body, which, from another point of view, is a corporate body of Churches."[53] They extend it especially to the poor,[54] to those persecuted for the faith, as well as to missionaries who are working throughout the world. (CCC 886)

Generally, each bishop is entrusted with a "particular church," that is, a specific *diocese* (or *archdiocese*), in which he acts as Christ's chosen representative and the legitimate pastor of all the faithful within that diocese. He is the visible source of unity within the diocese and is responsible for the celebration of the Sacraments—most especially the Eucharist—as well as the teaching and governing of the flock entrusted to his care.

Individual bishops who have been entrusted with the care of a particular church—under the authority of the supreme pontiff—feed their sheep in the name of the Lord as their own, ordinary, and immediate pastors, performing for them the office of teaching, sanctifying, and governing. Nevertheless, they should recognize the rights which legitimately belong to patriarchs or other hierarchical authorities. (*Christus Dominus*, 11)

The bishops are often organized into a *bishops' conference*, which schedule regular meetings at which they discuss and adopt pastoral policies, issue statements on moral and social issues of concern, and both implement and make recommendations on practices and policies for the Church in their particular country.

WHAT IS A CATHEDRAL?

St. Louis Cathedral, first established in 1718, is the oldest continuously operating cathedral in the United States and the seat of the Archdiocese of New Orleans, Louisiana.

A *cathedral* is the official church of the local bishop. It is the seat of his authority, and it is usually in the city from which the diocese takes its name.

The word has a rich scriptural heritage. It comes from a Greek word meaning "seat of honor." Jesus used the word in this sense only once in the New Testament, but his choice is significant. "The scribes and the Pharisees sit on Moses' seat (*kathedra Mouseos*); so practice and observe whatever they tell you."[55] *Kathedra* here is a seat of religious and moral authority, from which wise men teach and guide. It refers today both to the cathedral church itself and to the literal and usually ornate chair that is reserved for the bishop.

In establishing the New Covenant, Jesus did not abolish the Old Covenant or the covenant structures. He fulfilled the Old Testament role of priest, prophet, and king, and delegated this ministry to his Apostles. Though the *kathedra* was superior to other seats of honor, he assigned to the Twelve something greater still. "Jesus said to them, 'Truly, I say to you, in the new world, when the Son of man shall sit on His glorious throne, you who have followed me will also sit on twelve thrones, judging the twelve tribes of Israel.'"[56] He promised them thrones (*thronoi*) that is, judgment seats suitable for kings.

The Apostles would occupy these exalted thrones, but called their position by a rather ordinary name: *episkope*, which is rendered as "bishopric" or "office" in English. The office-holder was an "overseer"—in Greek, *episkopos*, from which we get the word "bishop." These men—like St. Timothy, for example[57]—received their office from the hands of the Apostles themselves. They, in turn, each in his own city, would occupy the *kathedra* that was greater than the seat of Moses. They would, as St. Ignatius of Antioch said AD 107, "preside in the place of God."

Throughout the centuries, Christians have kept the *kathedra* as a furnishing in their places of worship. This seat was occupied by the bishop, whose throne represented his authority to teach, rule, and sanctify.

The Pope's *kathedra* in the Basilica of St. John Lateran, the cathedral of Rome.

ECUMENICAL COUNCILS

In order to address important doctrinal questions facing the early Church, the Church began calling *Ecumenical Councils*. As we saw in previous chapters, the archetype for an Ecumenical Council was the Council of Jerusalem AD 49 or 50, which discussed the requirements of Gentile converts. There was "much debate," St. Luke tells us,[58] and the opinions of all the leaders of the Church were heard. In the end, St. Peter pronounced the verdict of the whole Church. The decision of the council was written down and sent to the Christians in Antioch, where the question had arisen.

The first six Ecumenical Councils, beginning with the First Council of Nicæa AD 325, addressed various Christological heresies in an effort to preserve and clarify the true theological answer to the question, "Who is Jesus Christ?"

The word *ecumenical* comes from the Greek word *oikoumene*, meaning "the whole inhabited world." Ecumenical councils bring bishops under the leadership of the Pope together from all over the world to discuss central issues of the Church.

> When Christ instituted the Twelve, "he constituted [them] in the form of a college or permanent assembly, at the head of which he placed Peter, chosen from among them."[59] Just as "by the Lord's institution, St. Peter and the rest of the apostles constitute a single apostolic college, so in like fashion the Roman Pontiff, Peter's successor, and the bishops, the successors of the apostles, are related with and united to one another."[60] (CCC 880)

Opening of the Second Vatican Council, 1962-1965. 2,450 Counciliar Fathers from all over the world were present for what many consider to be the most important Council in the history of the Church. Opened under Pope Bl. John XXIII, four future pontiffs took part in the Council's opening session: Pope Paul VI, Pope John Paul I, Pope Bl. John Paul II, and Pope Benedict XVI.

The first seven councils are recognized by the Catholic and Orthodox Churches. However, Orthodox Christians do not recognize the ecumenical nature of any of the councils held in the West after 787 because they did not participate. At the time of the Reformation, most Protestant bodies recognized at least the special status of those first seven councils, though later Protestant churches chose largely to dismiss them.

> "The *college or body of bishops* has no authority unless united with the Roman Pontiff, Peter's successor, as its head." As such, this college has "supreme and full authority over the universal Church; but this power cannot be exercised without the agreement of the Roman Pontiff."[61] (CCC 883)

> "The college of bishops exercises power over the universal Church in a solemn manner in an ecumenical council."[62] But "there never is an ecumenical council which is not confirmed or at least recognized as such by Peter's successor."[63] (CCC 884)

The Church still refers important questions to an *Ecumenical Council* of the whole Church. The bishops meet and debate the questions before them, and ultimately the decision of the whole Church is expressed through the successor of St. Peter, the Pope. The most recent Ecumenical Council was the Second Vatican Council (1962-1965).

Current *canon law*, the law of the Church, grants the power to convene an Ecumenical Council only to the Pope. The Pope governs the council, and he alone has the power to accept or reject the decrees passed by it. If the Pope should die during a council, as happened during the Second Vatican Council, the council is halted until the election of a new Pope, who then decides whether to continue the council and selects the topics it will consider.

What distinguishes an Ecumenical Council from the other types of councils is that it convenes all of the bishops in the Catholic Church, and its teachings are regarded as having the highest authority, although its resolutions and conclusions must always be approved by the Supreme Pontiff.

THE OFFICE OF PRIEST

Closely joined to the episcopacy is the office of priest, sometimes referred to as the *presbyterate*. Through the Sacrament of Holy Orders, both bishops and priests are given a "ministerial participation in the priesthood of Christ,"[64] which empowers them to act *in persona Christi*—"in the Person of Christ."

Because the bishops alone have received the fullness of the Sacrament of Holy Orders, each priest depends upon his bishop for the proper exercise of this priestly power. The priests of the Church are co-workers of the bishops, assigned to carry out certain tasks of the apostolic ministry, often within an individual parish community. Principal among these tasks is the celebration of the Mass, which the priest offers in the Person of Christ and as the bishop's representative.

> From the beginning of his ministry, the Lord Jesus instituted the Twelve as "the seeds of the new Israel and the beginning of the sacred hierarchy."[65] Chosen together, they were also sent out together, and their fraternal unity would be at the service of the fraternal communion of all the faithful: they would reflect and witness to the communion of the divine persons.[66] For this reason every bishop exercises his ministry from within the episcopal college, in communion with the bishop of Rome, the successor of St. Peter and head of the college. So also priests exercise their ministry from within the *presbyterium* of the diocese, under the direction of their bishop. (CCC 877)

On Good Shepherd Sunday, April 2007, Pope Benedict XVI ordained twenty-two priests for the Diocese of Rome. A priest is empowered to act *in persona Christi*—"in the Person of Christ."

WHAT IS A PARISH?

"It [a parish] is the place where all the faithful can be gathered together for the Sunday celebration of the Eucharist." (CCC 2179)

A *parish* is a defined territorial district within a diocese, with its own church and congregation, which is placed in the sacramental care of a priest.

The *Catechism* teaches: "It is the place where all the faithful can be gathered together for the Sunday celebration of the Eucharist. The parish initiates the Christian people into the ordinary expression of the liturgical life: it gathers them together in this celebration; it teaches Christ's saving doctrine; it practices the charity of the Lord in good works and brotherly love."[67]

In the fourth century, St. John Chrysostom wrote: "You cannot pray at home as at church, where there is a great multitude, where exclamations are cried out to God as from one great heart, and where there is something more: the union of minds, the accord of souls, the bond of charity, the prayers of the priests."

THE OFFICE OF DEACON

Finally, there is the office of deacons, which, like the office of bishops and the office of priests, is bestowed through the Sacrament of Holy Orders. Unlike bishops and priests, however, deacons are not ordained for priestly ministry; rather, they are ordained for the ministry of service (in Greek, *diakonia*).

> It is the task of deacons to assist the bishop and priests in the celebration of the divine mysteries, above all the Eucharist, in the distribution of Holy Communion, in assisting at and blessing marriages, in the proclamation of the Gospel and preaching, in presiding over funerals, and in dedicating themselves to the various ministries of charity.[68] (CCC 1570)

There are two types of deacons. Men who are preparing for ordination to the priesthood are ordained as *transitional deacons* before receiving their ordination as priests. Other men, including married men, may be called to serve as *permanent deacons*.

THE TEACHING AUTHORITY OF THE CHURCH

The Church has been entrusted by Christ with the preaching of the word of God. As Christ was sent by the Father to be a witness to the truth, so also has the Church been sent by Christ to preach the Gospel to the whole human race, enabling all men to believe and be saved. To guide the faithful in this appreciation and to teach the truth, Christ endowed his Church with the teaching authority of the Pope and bishops called the *Magisterium*, Latin for "teaching office."[69]

> In order to preserve the Church in the purity of the faith handed on by the apostles, Christ who is the Truth willed to confer on her a share in his own infallibility. By a "supernatural sense of faith" the People of God, under the guidance of the Church's living Magisterium, "unfailingly adheres to this faith."[70] (CCC 889)

With the Incarnation of the Word, the world has been given the fullness of Divine Revelation in the Person of Jesus Christ. By his words, actions, and life, Christ instructed his Apostles and entrusted them

Christ Handing the Keys to St. Peter (detail) by Perugino. This fresco is located in the Sistine Chapel, the location since 1492 of the papal conclave, a meeting of the College of Cardinals convened to elect the Pope who is also the Bishop of Rome.

with the task of handing on all that he had taught them. And in order that they might fulfill this mission, the Father sent them the Holy Spirit, who empowered the Apostles to understand Christ's teaching and proclaim it. The definitive Revelation of Christ—given to the Apostles and through them to the entire Church—is found in Sacred Scripture and Sacred Tradition, and this is known as the *Deposit of Faith*.

The mandate for *evangelization* given by Christ to the Apostles and their successors is first accomplished through their task of teaching. During his time on earth, Christ revealed to his Apostles the truth of the Faith and instructed them on how they were to live as members of the Family of God. The Apostles, in turn, were given the responsibility of handing on the teaching of Christ, both through their oral preaching (preserved in the Church's Sacred Tradition) and through their written testimony (preserved in Sacred Scripture).

Christ entrusted his Church to the apostolic community of the Twelve, with St. Peter as its head, and this community continues in the assembly of the bishops, referred to as the *episcopal college*, which has as its head the successor of St. Peter, the Pope, the Bishop of Rome. United to the Pope, the bishops of the Church are each called to teach, sanctify, and govern the faithful of their own dioceses and also to work together in caring for the worldwide Church.

As the successors of the Apostles, the Pope and the bishops in union with him are the authentic custodians and interpreters of both Scripture and Tradition. They exercise the teaching office of the Church and maintain the Church's fidelity to the unchanging teaching of Christ passed down from the Apostles. In this way, the Church remains the "pillar and bulwark of the truth."[71]

The mission of the Magisterium is not to reveal new truths—Revelation ended with the death of the last Apostle—but rather to defend, guard, and interpret the received Deposit of Faith. The Church's Magisterium, even though carried out through human instruments, is not a human Magisterium: "The Counselor, the Holy Spirit, whom the Father will send in my name, he will teach you all things, and bring to your remembrance all that I have said to you."[72]

THE DEPOSIT OF FAITH

There is only one source of Revelation: God—Father, Son, and Holy Spirit.

The content of Divine Revelation is found in Sacred Scripture and Tradition as a single deposit, the Deposit of Faith: "So then, brethren, stand firm and hold to the traditions which you were taught by us, either by word of mouth or by letter."[73]

Sacred Scripture is the Word of God, written under the inspiration of the Holy Spirit and contained in the collection of sacred books that have God as their author, and it was entrusted to the Church as such.[74]

Tradition is the word of God, received from Christ himself through the Apostles. It is transmitted to us without alteration—as it were, from hand to hand—by the Church with the assistance of the Holy Spirit.[75] Thus, Revelation is kept alive in the midst of the Christian community and is handed down from generation to generation. This is the origin of the word *Tradition* (from *traditio*, "handing down").

The beliefs of the Church, unchanged for centuries, are either included in Scripture or belong to Tradition. It is often possible to find testimonies of Tradition dating back to the first centuries. Testimonies that are not explicitly contained in Sacred Scripture have been preserved in either ancient liturgical or disciplinary texts and practices or the writings of early Christian authors.

Through Tradition, we know which books are inspired by the Holy Spirit, that is, the list or canon of the books that make up Holy Scripture.

WHAT IS APOSTOLIC TRADITION?

Sacred Tradition or *Apostolic Tradition* (from the Latin *traditio*, meaning "to hand down") refers to the Church's teachings that have been passed down through the ages by the successors of the Apostles. Together with Sacred Scripture, Sacred Tradition makes up a single deposit of the Word of God—a single gift of God to the Church.

The Apostles were eyewitnesses to the teachings and events of Christ's public ministry and had been given the mission of faithfully preserving and handing on what they had received. This Tradition was at first transmitted by word of mouth, but, in time, much of the Deposit of Faith was put into written form. However, as St. Paul made clear, the written text was just one way that the Word of God lived in the Church. He told the Thessalonians: "Hold to the traditions which you were taught by us, either by word of mouth or by letter."[76]

For St. Paul, the Tradition that had been passed on by "word of mouth" was as authoritative as the Gospels and letters that had already been put in written form. The faith of the Church was much more than a book, it was a living faith that Christ had given to the Apostles.

The New Testament itself shows that the Apostles gave the faithful more than texts. They passed on rituals, like the Mass;[77] they pronounced blessings;[78] they conveyed authority to others;[79] and they healed the sick.[80]

The Second Vatican Council spoke of the fullness of Christian Tradition: "What was handed on by the Apostles includes everything which contributes toward the holiness of life and increase in faith of the people of God; and so the Church, in her teaching, life and worship, perpetuates and hands on to all generations all that she herself is, all that she believes."[81]

St. John on Patmos by Giovanni. Having escaped death in Rome and living in exile on the island of Patmos, the Apostle John wrote the Book of Revelation. Because of its association with St. John, Patmos is a destination for Christian pilgrims, and is often referred to as "the Jerusalem of the Aegean."

For instance, we can distinguish three stages in the formation of the Gospels:

✤ **The life and teaching of Jesus.** The Church holds firmly that the four Gospels, "whose historicity she unhesitatingly affirms, faithfully hand on what Jesus, the Son of God, while he lived among men, really did and taught for their eternal salvation, until the day when he was taken up."[82]

✤ **The oral tradition.** "For, after the ascension of the Lord, the apostles handed on to their hearers what he had said and done, but with that fuller understanding which they, instructed by the glorious events of Christ and enlightened by the Spirit of truth, now enjoyed."[83]

✤ **The written Gospels.** "The sacred authors, in writing the four Gospels, selected certain of the many elements which had been handed on, either orally or already in written form; others they synthesized or explained with an eye to the situation of the churches, the while sustaining the form of preaching, but always in such a fashion that they have told us the honest truth about Jesus."[84]

Tradition is of great importance. In fact, Tradition precedes Scripture, since the truths revealed by Christ were not immediately written down, but were first handed on orally. Thus, the word *Tradition* is also used to encompass the entire Deposit of Faith. The Second Vatican Council uses it in this sense:

> The apostolic preaching, which is expressed in a special way in the inspired books, was to be preserved by an unending succession of preachers until the end of time. Therefore the apostles, handing on what they themselves had received, warn the faithful to hold fast to the traditions which they had learned either by word of mouth or by letter (cf. 2 Thes 2:15); and to fight in defense of the faith handed on once and for all (cf. Jude 1:3).[85]

THE MAGISTERIUM

The Magisterium of the Church performs a very special function in the conservation and transmission of the Deposit of Faith. The Magisterium gives us the content of the official teaching of the Church. This teaching office is entrusted exclusively to the hierarchy of the Church, which was established by Christ and received his pledge of the special assistance of the Holy Spirit in order to prevent any error in its teachings.

Assisted by the Holy Spirit, the Church has continued to deepen her understanding of the Deposit of Faith. In every age, she scrutinizes the "signs of the times" and interprets them in light of the Gospel, thus developing her teaching in a gradual, organic way. Far from discarding earlier teachings, this development presupposes and builds upon them, using those earlier teachings as a sure path along which the Church can proceed in her growing understanding of the depth and inherent unity of the Faith.

> "No new public revelation is to be expected before the glorious manifestation of our Lord Jesus Christ."[86] Yet even if Revelation is already complete, it has not been made completely explicit; it remains for Christian faith gradually to grasp its full significance over the course of the centuries. (CCC 66)

INFALLIBILITY OF THE MAGISTERIUM

Through his gift of the Holy Spirit, the "Spirit of Truth," Christ bestowed authority upon the Apostles and their successors to teach in his name and to lead his Church in living in the truth. Further, "to fulfill this service, Christ endowed the Church's shepherds with the charism of infallibility in matters of faith and morals."[87]

Immaculate Conception by Rubens.
Pope Bl. Pius IX's definition of the Immaculate Conception in 1854 is an instance of the invocation of papal infallibility to define a matter of faith.

> "The Roman Pontiff, head of the college of bishops, enjoys this infallibility in virtue of his office, when, as supreme pastor and teacher of all the faithful—who confirms his brethren in the faith he proclaims by a definitive act a doctrine pertaining to faith or morals....The infallibility promised to the Church is also present in the body of bishops when, together with Peter's successor, they exercise the supreme Magisterium," above all in an Ecumenical Council.[88] When the Church through its supreme Magisterium proposes a doctrine "for belief as being divinely revealed,"[89] and as the teaching of Christ, the definitions "must be adhered to with the obedience of faith."[90] This infallibility extends as far as the deposit of divine Revelation itself.[91] (CCC 891)

> Divine assistance is also given to the successors of the apostles, teaching in communion with the successor of Peter, and, in a particular way, to the bishop of Rome, pastor of the whole Church, when, without arriving at an infallible definition and without pronouncing in a "definitive manner," they propose in the exercise of the ordinary Magisterium a teaching that leads to better understanding of Revelation in matters of faith and morals. To this ordinary teaching the faithful "are to adhere to it with religious assent"[92] which, though distinct from the assent of faith, is nonetheless an extension of it. (CCC 892)

Because the infallibility of the Magisterium's teachings comes from Christ himself, the faithful are to hold fast to these teachings with the *obedience of faith*.[93]

Two instances of the invocation of papal infallibility to define a matter of faith and morals would be Pope Bl. Pius IX's defining the dogma of the *Immaculate Conception* in 1854 and Pope Pius XII's defining the dogma of the *Assumption* in 1950. In both cases, the Popes were defining beliefs that had been held by the Catholics since the first centuries of Christianity.

Even when the Magisterium does not exercise the charism of infallibility, the faithful are obliged to accept their teaching with *religious assent*.[94]

By looking at Church history, we recognize the validity of Christ's guarantee of infallibility in matters of faith and morals. Since Christ founded his Church, she has taught the same truths without change. No other institution can demonstrate this claim.

SANCTIFYING AND GOVERNING ROLE OF THE CHURCH

When Christ commissioned the Apostles, he commanded them not only to teach, but also to sanctify, extending the life of grace to all mankind:

St. Augustine (354-430) was Bishop of Hippo (North Africa) He is a Doctor of the Church and one of the most prolific Latin authors. The list of surviving works consists of more than one hundred separate titles.

Go therefore and make disciples of all nations, baptizing them in the name of the Father and of the Son and of the Holy Spirit, teaching them to observe all that I have commanded you; and lo, I am with you always, to the close of the age. (Mt 28: 19-20)

The mission of the Church, like that of Christ, is the sanctification of mankind for the glory of God the Father. Although the entire life of Christ had a redemptive value, the redemption "was achieved principally by the paschal mystery of His blessed passion, resurrection from the dead, and glorious ascension, whereby 'dying he destroyed our death, and rising, restored our life.'"[95] To perpetuate that saving Death and Resurrection throughout history, and make the effects of his sacrifice reach all men our Lord entrusted precise means of sanctification to his Church—namely, the *Sacraments*. The Sacraments make present the redeeming sacrifice of Christ, unite us to his sacrifice, and apply the graces flowing from that sacrifice to our lives.

The bishops of the Church continue to carry out this mission through their faithful administration of the Sacraments and through their prayer, example, and preaching. Together with the priests, who are their co-workers, the bishops exercise the sanctifying office of the Church and work to lead all those entrusted to their care into the glory of Heaven.

The bishop and priests sanctify the Church by their prayer and work, by their ministry of the word and of the sacraments. They sanctify her by their example, "not as domineering over those in your charge but being examples to the flock."[96] Thus, "together with the flock entrusted to them, they may attain to eternal life."[97] (CCC 893)

Within a particular diocese, the bishop serves as the successor to the apostolic mission both in his administration of the Sacraments and in his governing of the local Church. Through ordination, he has received the authority to govern his flock in the name of Christ. This authority, however, "must be exercised in communion with the whole Church under the guidance of the pope."[98]

"The bishops, as vicars and legates of Christ, govern the particular Churches assigned to them by their counsels, exhortations, and example, but over and above that also by the authority and sacred power" which indeed they ought to exercise so as to edify, in the spirit of service which is that of their Master.[99] (CCC 894)

The bishops are representatives of Christ, and are therefore to model their governance after that of the Good Shepherd himself, who exercises his authority and sacred power not for his own benefit, but to give life to the Church. By establishing laws for the faithful—such as the precepts of the Church—the Church gives us basic moral norms for remaining in the grace of Christ.

In addition to the laws of the Church, there are specific disciplines prescribed by the Church that are intended to help us draw closer to Christ—for example, abstaining from meat during the Fridays of Lent. These disciplines, though binding for all the faithful, are left to the pastoral discretion of the Pope and the bishops, and can be adjusted by them according to the needs of the faithful.

Ultimately, the authority that the bishops have received from Christ is for the purpose of guiding Christ's Faithful on the road to Heaven. Assisted by the priests and the deacons, the bishops of the Church are sent by the Father to teach, sanctify, and govern his beloved children, and so lead us to eternal life.

PRECEPTS OF THE CHURCH[100]

1. You shall attend Mass on Sundays and holy days of obligation and rest from servile labor.

2. You shall confess your sins at least once a year.

3. You shall receive the Sacrament of the Eucharist at least during the Easter season.

4. You shall observe the days of fasting and abstinence established by the Church.

5. You shall help to provide for the needs of the Church.

SALVATION AND THE CHURCH

In the third century, St. Cyprian of Carthage wrote: "Outside the Church there is no salvation." In subsequent centuries, this doctrine was echoed by great saints, including St. Augustine and St. Thomas Aquinas.

What does it mean? The *Catechism of the Catholic Church* puts the answer in a positive form: "all salvation comes from Christ the Head through the Church which is his Body."[101]

The Catholic Church is indeed the universal Family of God, outside of which there is no salvation. This teaching simply clarifies the essential meaning of salvation and the Church—the Body of Christ, the community of God's children. Salvation means precisely to be counted as a son or daughter of God; therefore, those who are saved are necessarily members of the Church.

Basing itself upon Sacred Scripture and Tradition, it teaches that the Church, now sojourning on earth as an exile, is necessary for salvation. Christ, present to us in His Body, which is the Church, is the one Mediator and the unique way of salvation. In explicit terms He Himself affirmed the necessity of faith and baptism and thereby affirmed also the necessity of the Church, for through baptism as through a door men enter the Church. Whosoever, therefore, knowing that the Catholic Church was made necessary by Christ, would refuse to enter or to remain in it, could not be saved.[102]

Non-Catholic Christians, however, are considered *separated brethren*, united in an imperfect manner to the Church by the Sacrament of Baptism. The Catechism states this truth in moving terms: "All who have been justified by faith in Baptism...are accepted as brothers in the Lord by the children of the Catholic Church."[103]

> "The Church knows that she is joined in many ways to the baptized who are honored by the name of Christian, but do not profess the Catholic faith in its entirety or have not preserved unity or communion under the successor of Peter."[104] Those "who believe in Christ and have been properly baptized are put in a certain, although imperfect, communion with the Catholic Church."[105] *With the Orthodox Churches*, this communion is so profound "that it lacks little to attain the fullness that would permit a common celebration of the Lord's Eucharist."[106] (CCC 838)

In 1979, Pope Bl. John Paul II was welcomed by 2.5 million Catholics during a weekend trip to Ireland. He spoke directly to the young, "I say to you, with all the love I have for you, with all the trust I have in young people: Do not listen to voices which speak the language of hatred, revenge, retaliation. Do not follow any leaders who train you in the ways of inflicting death.... The true courage lies in working for peace."

Pope Bl. John Paul II wrote that salvation is "granted not only to those who explicitly believe in Christ and have entered the Church," but also "people of good will in whose hearts grace is secretly at work," people who "do not have an opportunity to come to know or accept the gospel revelation or to enter the Church."[107] To them, "salvation in Christ is accessible by virtue of a grace which, while having a mysterious relationship to the Church, does not make them formally part of the Church, but enlightens them in a way which is accommodated to their spiritual and material situation."

> Those also can attain to salvation who through no fault of their own do not know the Gospel of Christ or His Church, yet sincerely seek God and moved by grace strive by their deeds to do His will as it is known to them through the dictates of conscience.[108]

Nevertheless, said Pope Bl. John Paul, "It is still an urgent matter for the Church to evangelize all peoples, because salvation apart from the Church is arduous, uncertain, and accompanied by many dangers."[109]

The *Catechism*, quoting the Second Vatican Council, emphasizes "the necessity of faith and Baptism, and...the necessity of the Church which men enter through Baptism as through a door. Hence they could not be saved who, knowing that the Catholic Church was founded as necessary by God through Christ, would refuse either to enter it or to remain in it."[110]

Knowing that salvation comes only through union with Christ in his Mystical Body, the Church does not cease to proclaim the Gospel, repeating the affirmation of the early Christians, "Outside the Church there is no salvation."[111] She understands, though, that there are many people who, through no fault of their own, will never know Christ and his Church. The Church entrusts these men and women to the mercy of God, "who desires all men to be saved."[112]

> Every man who is ignorant of the Gospel of Christ and of his Church, but seeks the truth and does the will of God in accordance with his understanding of it, can be saved....Such persons would have *desired Baptism explicitly* if they had known its necessity. (CCC 1260)

In ways known only to God, it is possible that those who have not been baptized can still be given the grace to seek God and to receive the light of Christian Faith. However, this possibility in no way releases the Church from her obligation to evangelize all people, baptizing them in the name of the Father and of the Son and of the Holy Spirit. Commissioned by Christ to preach in his name, the Catholic Church has both the responsibility and the sacred right to make disciples of all nations, bringing them into the fullness of the Savior's Mystical Body.

ECUMENICAL AND INTERFAITH RELATIONS

Members of the various Protestant communities have not preserved all of the necessary elements of membership within the Church, and they cannot be considered as fully incorporated into Christ's Mystical Body. "Those 'who believe in Christ and have been properly baptized are put in a certain, although imperfect, communion with the Catholic Church.'"[113] Indeed, the Church professes "one Baptism"; she holds the rites of Baptism performed by any Christian community to be valid as long as flowing water and the Trinitarian formula were used.

The Church's imperfect communion with the Orthodox Churches is much closer than with Protestant communities. Although these Churches have not maintained unity with the successor of St. Peter, their hierarchies still maintains apostolic succession and therefore validly celebrate the Sacrament of the Eucharist.

In addition to her ecumenical efforts to unite all those who have been baptized, the Church constantly works to evangelize non-Christians, longing for them to know the Fatherhood of God as revealed by his Only-Begotten Son, Jesus Christ.

The people of Israel were the first to whom God revealed his plan for salvation. The Church therefore has a unique bond with the Jewish religion, and she rejoices over their Faithful response to God in the Old Covenant and invites them to share in the fullness of the New and Everlasting Covenant of Jesus Christ.

During Pope Benedict's Apostolic visit to the Holy Land in 2009, he met with Muslims and Christians living in the Aida Refugee Camp, Bethlehem. Muslims have been recognized in a special way by Pope Benedict because of their acknowledgment of a single God.

The Last Sermon of Our Lord by Tissot.
"Let not your hearts be troubled; believe in God, believe also in me. In my Father's house are many rooms; if it were not so, would I have told you that I go to prepare a place for you? And when I go and prepare a place for you, I will come again and will take you to myself, that where I am you may be also. And you know the way where I am going." (Jn 14: 1-4)

Among the other non-Christian religions, Muslim have also been recognized in a special way by recent Popes because of their acknowledgment of a single God. Muslims recognize Jesus as a holy man and a prophet, and the Church continuously prays that, through the gift of the Holy Spirit, they will come to know him as the Son of God, their Savior.

> The Catholic Church recognizes in other religions that search, among shadows and images, for the God who is unknown yet near since he gives life and breath and all things and wants all men to be saved. Thus, the Church considers all goodness and truth found in these religions as "a preparation for the Gospel."[114] (CCC 843)

CONCLUSION

The Church is both a sign and instrument of the communion between God and men, the link between the invisible and visible elements of ecclesial communion. The Church is a font of grace through which we receive the Sacraments and, thus, herself a Sacrament of Salvation. The Church is also our "mother and teacher"—*Mater et Magistra*. She is indeed our mother, for through the Sacrament of Baptism we are given a new birth in Christ. The Church is our teacher, for she teaches us as Christ taught, lovingly and authoritatively, pointing the way to truth and salvation. Through her teachings and wise counsel we grow in maturity in the Faith.

In keeping with the intention of Christ, the bishops, as successors of the Apostles, continue the teaching and salvific ministry of Christ in an unbroken line emanating from Christ himself. The Pope, as the successor of St. Peter, stands at the Head of the Church, its chief shepherd on earth. It is through the bishops' ministry of teaching, sanctifying, and governing that we can be assured of the continued and steady hand of the Holy Spirit in guiding the Church through the centuries and preserving it in truth and fidelity. Salvation is granted by virtue of Christ working through his Church and the sanctifying grace that flows through it. It is in this sense that the Church is necessary for salvation.

SUPPLEMENTARY READING

1. The Bishops Were Appointed by the Apostles

The apostles appointed the first fruits [of their labours], having first proved them by the Spirit, to be bishops and deacons of those who should afterwards believe. Nor was this any new thing, since indeed many ages before it was written concerning bishops and deacons. For thus says the Scripture in a certain place, "I will appoint their bishops in righteousness, and their deacons in faith."

Our apostles also knew, through our Lord Jesus Christ, that there would be strife on account of the office of the episcopate. For this reason, therefore, inasmuch as they had obtained a perfect foreknowledge of this, they appointed those [ministers] already mentioned, and afterwards gave instructions, that when these should fall asleep, other approved men should succeed them in their ministry.

— St. Clement of Rome, *To the Corinthians* 42, 44

Pope St. Clement Adoring the Trinity (detail) by Tiepolo. According to Tertullian, Pope St. Clement I was ordained by St. Peter. He became Bishop of Rome in 92 and was the first Apostolic Father of the Early Church. He was martyred ca. 99.

2. The Teaching Authority of the Magisterium

Bishops, teaching in communion with the Roman Pontiff, are to be respected by all as witnesses to divine and Catholic truth. In matters of faith and morals, the bishops speak in the name of Christ and the faithful are to accept their teaching and adhere to it with a religious assent. This religious submission of mind and will must be shown in a special way to the authentic Magisterium of the Roman Pontiff, even when he is not speaking *ex cathedra*; that is, it must be shown in such a way that his supreme Magisterium is acknowledged with reverence, the judgments made by him are sincerely adhered to, according to his manifest mind and will.

Although the individual bishops do not enjoy the prerogative of infallibility, they nevertheless proclaim Christ's doctrine infallibly whenever, even though dispersed through the world, but still maintaining the bond of communion among themselves and with the successor of Peter, and authentically teaching matters of faith and morals, they are in agreement on one position as definitively to be held. This is even more clearly verified when, gathered together in an Ecumenical Council, they are teachers and judges of faith and morals for the universal Church, whose definitions must be adhered to with the submission of faith.

And this infallibility with which the Divine Redeemer willed His Church to be endowed in defining doctrine of faith and morals, extends as far as the deposit of Revelation extends, which must be religiously guarded and faithfully expounded. And this is the infallibility which the Roman Pontiff, the head of the college of bishops, enjoys in virtue of his office, when, as the supreme shepherd and teacher of all the faithful, who confirms his brethren in their faith, by a definitive act he proclaims a doctrine of faith or morals.

— *Lumen Gentium*, 25

SUPPLEMENTARY READING Continued

3. Papal Infallibility

"The Roman Pontiff, head of the College of Bishops, enjoys this infallibility in virtue of his office, when, as supreme pastor and teacher of all the faithful—who confirms his brethren in the faith (cf. Lk 22:32)—he proclaims in an absolute decision a doctrine pertaining to faith or morals. For that reason his definitions are rightly said to be irreformable by their very nature and not by reason of the assent of the Church, inasmuch as they were made with the assistance of the Holy Spirit...and as a consequence they are in no way in need of the approval of others, and do not admit of appeal to any other tribunal. For in such a case the Roman Pontiff does not utter a pronouncement as a private person, but rather does he expound and defend the teaching of the Catholic faith as the supreme teacher of the universal church, in whom the Church's charism of infallibility is present in a singular way" (*Lumen Gentium*, n. 25).

It should be noted that the Second Vatican Council also calls attention to the Magisterium of the Bishops in union with the Roman Pontiff, stressing that they too enjoy the Holy Spirit's assistance when they define a point of faith in conjunction with the Successor of Peter: "The infallibility promised to the Church is also present in the body of Bishops when, together with Peter's Successor, they exercise the supreme Magisterium....When the Roman Pontiff, or the body of Bishops together with him, define a doctrine, they make the definition in conformity with Revelation itself...and this revelation is transmitted integrally either in written form or in oral tradition through the legitimate succession of Bishops...and through the light of the Spirit of truth it is scrupulously preserved in the Church and unerringly explained" (*Lumen Gentium*, n. 25).

— Pope Bl. John Paul II, *L'Osservatore Romano*, n. 12, March 24, 1993.

4. The Message of Pope Benedict XVI to Representatives of Other Religions

Through the ministry of the Successors of Peter, including the work of the Pontifical Council for Interreligious Dialogue, and the efforts of local Ordinaries and the People of God throughout the world, the Church continues to reach out to followers of different religions. In this way she gives expression to that desire for encounter and collaboration in truth and freedom. In the words of my venerable Predecessor, Pope Paul VI, the Church's principal responsibility is service to the Truth—"truth about God, truth about man and his hidden destiny, truth about the world, truth which we discover in the Word of God" (*Evangelii Nuntiandi*, 78).[115]

The broader purpose of dialogue is to discover the truth. What is the origin and destiny of mankind? What are good and evil? What awaits us at the end of our earthly existence? Only by addressing these deeper questions can we build a solid basis for the peace and security of the human family, for "wherever and whenever men and women are enlightened by the splendor of truth, they naturally set out on the path of peace" (*Message for the 2006 World Day of Peace*, 3).[116]

We are living in an age when these questions are too often marginalized. Yet they can never be erased from the human heart. Throughout history, men and women have striven to articulate their restlessness with this passing world. In the Judeo-Christian tradition, the Psalms are full of such expressions: "My spirit is overwhelmed within me" (Ps 143:4; cf. Ps 6:6; 31:10; 32:3; 38:8; 77:3); "why are you cast down, my soul, why groan within me?" (Ps 42:5). The response is always one of faith: "Hope in God, I will praise him still; my Savior and my God" (Ps 42:5, 11; cf. Ps 43:5; 62:5). Spiritual leaders have a special duty, and we might say competence, to place the deeper questions at the forefront of human consciousness, to reawaken mankind to the mystery of human existence, and to make space in a frenetic world for reflection and prayer.[117]

Confronted with these deeper questions concerning the origin and destiny of mankind, Christianity proposes Jesus of Nazareth. He, we

SUPPLEMENTARY READING Continued

believe, is the eternal *Logos* who became flesh in order to reconcile man to God and reveal the underlying reason of all things. It is he whom we bring to the forum of interreligious dialogue. The ardent desire to follow in his footsteps spurs Christians to open their minds and hearts in dialogue (cf. Lk 10: 25-37; Jn 4: 7-26).[118]

Message to the Jewish Community

By her very nature the Catholic Church feels obliged to respect the Covenant made by the God of Abraham, Isaac, and Jacob. Indeed, the Church herself is situated within the eternal Covenant of the Almighty, whose plans are immutable, and she respects the children of the Promise, the children of the Covenant, as her beloved brothers and sisters in the faith. She compellingly repeats, through my voice, the words of the great Pope Pius XI, my beloved predecessor: Spiritually, we are Semites (*Allocution to the Belgian Pilgrims*, 16 September 1938). The Church therefore is opposed to every form of anti-Semitism, which can never be theologically justified. The theo-logian Henri de Lubac, in a time of darkness, as Pius XII (*Summi Pontificatus*, 10 October 1939) described it, added that to be anti-Semitic also signifies being anti-Christian (cf. *Un nuovo fronte religioso* in: *Israele e la Fede Cristiana* [1942]).[119]

Message to the Muslim Community

"The Church looks upon Muslims with respect. They worship the one God living and subsistent, merciful and almighty, creator of heaven and earth, who has spoken to humanity and to whose decrees, even the hidden ones, they seek to submit themselves whole-heartedly, just as Abraham, to whom the Islamic faith readily relates itself, submitted to God.... Although considerable dissensions and enmities between Christians and Muslims may have arisen in the course of the centuries, the Council urges all parties that, forgetting past things, they train themselves towards sincere mutual understanding and together maintain and promote social justice and moral values as well as peace and freedom for all people" (Declaration *Nostra Ætate*, n. 3).[120]

Pope Benedict XVI praying at the Western Wall in Jerusalem, May 2009.

The Holy Father read a Psalm in Latin, then prayed in silence and placed a prayer in the Wall.

This site is also known as the "Wailing Wall" because of the Jewish practice of coming to the Wall to mourn the destruction of the Temple by the Roman Empire in AD 70.

Just over half the wall, including seventeen courses located below street level, dates from the end of the Second Temple period, around 19 BC, built by Herod the Great.

VOCABULARY

APOSTOLIC SUCCESSION
The truth that the Catholic bishops today can trace their authority in a direct line back to the Apostles and ultimately from Christ himself, each consecrated a bishop by another bishop.

ARCHBISHOP
A bishop of the highest rank, generally the bishop of an archdiocese.

ARCHDIOCESE
A larger diocese, under the care of an archbishop, which has an elevated status over the dioceses in its region.

BISHOP
A consecrated successor to the Apostles, usually given charge of the pastoral and catechetical care of a particular jurisdiction, or diocese; he is called to teach, sanctify, and govern the faithful of his own diocese, and also to work together in caring for the worldwide Church.

CANON
The definitive list of the books of the Bible, by virtue of having been declared by the Church as inspired by the Holy Spirit; the term also refers to an official law of the Church (canon law).

CARDINAL
A bishop or archbishop who has been selected by a Pope to become part of the College of Cardinals and thus an adviser. The main purpose of a cardinal is to serve as a papal elector. Some cardinals lead archdioceses; others serve in the administration at the Vatican.

CATHEDRAL
The official church of the local bishop, his seat of authority, usually located in the city from which the diocese takes its name.

CHURCH
A name given the assembly of the People of God called together from the ends of the earth. This word has three meanings: the people that God gathers together, the local church (diocese), and the liturgical assembly. When we speak of "the Church," it normally refers to the Catholic Church. The word is a translation of the Latin *ecclesia*, the Greek *ekklesia*, and the Hebrew *qahal* ("assembly" or "convocation"); it is derived from the Greek *Kyriake* ("what belongs to the Lord").

CLERGY
The faithful of the Church who have received the Sacrament of Holy Orders; that is, bishops, priests, and deacons.

COLLEGIALITY
The principle that all the bishops of the Church with the Pope at their head form a single "college," which succeeds in every generation the "college" of the Twelve Apostles, with Peter at their head, which Christ instituted as the administrative foundation of the Church.

COMMUNION
A new relationship between man and God that has been established in Christ, is communicated through the Sacraments, and also extends a new relationship of men among themselves; it implies a spiritual solidarity among the members of the Church inasmuch as they are members of one Body, united in Christ. It is a translation of the Greek *koinonia*.

COMMUNION OF SAINTS
The unity in Christ of all the redeemed, those on earth and those who have died, especially the unity of faith and charity through the Eucharist.

CONCLAVE
A gathering of the world's cardinals in St. Peter's Basilica in Rome for the purpose of electing a new Pope.

CONSECRATED LIFE
A permanent state of life recognized by the Church, characterized by the profession of the evangelical counsels.

COUNCIL OF JERUSALEM
A council of the Church held AD 49 or 50 to decide whether Gentile converts to the Church would have to abide by the Jewish requirement of circumcision. It is the archetype for the later Ecumenical Councils.

DEACON
A man who is ordained to assist the mission of the Church; transitional deacons are men who are preparing for ordination to the priesthood; permanent deacons are mature men, married or unmarried, who are ordained deacons in a permanent capacity; from the Greek for "helper."

VOCABULARY Continued

DEPOSIT OF FAITH
The definitive Revelation of Christ given to the Apostles and, through them, to the entire Church as Sacred Scripture and Sacred Tradition; the heritage of faith handed on in the Church from the time of the Apostles, from which the Magisterium draws all that it proposes for belief as being divinely revealed.

DIACONATE
The office of deacon in the Catholic Church.

DIOCESAN COUNCIL
Often called a *synod*; a meeting of the bishop and representatives of the clergy, religious, and laity in which matters of diocesan Church discipline and procedure are discussed.

DIOCESE
The territory and the churches under a bishop's authority; a community of the Christian faithful in communion of faith and Sacraments with their bishop ordained in apostolic succession; also called a "particular church." In the East, it is often called an *eparchy*.

EASTERN CATHOLIC CHURCHES
Often called the Eastern Rites of the Catholic Church, any of the various Churches in union with the Pope whose rites, devotions, customs, and culture developed in connection to the lands associated with the eastern half of the Roman Empire (especially centered in Antioch, Alexandria, and Constantinople).

ECUMENICAL COUNCIL
A meeting of Church leaders. The Council of Jerusalem described in Acts is the scriptural archetype of a council of the whole Church. The most recent Ecumenical Council was the Second Vatican Council.

EFFICACIOUS
When speaking of the Sacraments, the term indicates an action or sign that confers the grace it signifies; for example, the pouring of the water and reciting with proper intent the words of Baptism confer the sanctifying grace of the Sacrament.

EPISCOPACY
The office of bishop in the Catholic Church; from the Greek *episkopos* ("overseer"), from which also is derived the word "bishop."

EPISCOPAL COLLEGE
The assembly of the world's bishops.

EVANGELIZATION
The mission given to the Apostles by Christ to preach the Gospel to the whole world and make converts of every nation; also, witnessing to our faith in the Gospel in our daily lives.

EX CATHEDRA
A definitive teaching by the Pope when he speaks as pastor of the Universal Church on matters of faith and morals, with the intention of officially teaching a certain truth for all Catholics to believe, which is therefore an infallible teaching; Latin for "from the chair."

EXTRAORDINARY MAGISTERIUM
The teaching office of all the bishops gathered with the Pope, as happens in an Ecumenical Council, or the Pope alone speaking *ex cathedra* in an exercise of infallibility.

HIERARCHY
The order of teaching authority in the Church, given such authority by Christ himself, with the Pope as its head, followed by bishops, priests, and deacons; from the Greek *hierarchia* ("sacred order").

HOLY ORDERS
The Sacrament by which men are ordained to the episcopacy, priesthood, or diaconate.

INFALLIBILITY
Immunity from error and any possibility of error. The gift of the Holy Spirit to the Church whereby the Magisterium can definitively proclaim a doctrine in faith or morals without error. The Church possesses this character as promised by Christ, as does the Pope as defined by the Twentieth Ecumenical Council (Vatican I, 1870).

VOCABULARY Continued

IN PERSONA CHRISTI
Literally, "in the Person of Christ"; refers to the fact that by virtue of the Sacrament of Holy Orders, the ordained priest participates in the priesthood of Christ and acts in the place of Christ, particularly in the Mass and in conferring the Sacraments.

MAGISTERIUM
The name given to the ordinary and universal teaching authority of the Pope and the bishops in communion with him, who guide the members of the Church without error in matters of faith and morals through the interpretation of Sacred Scripture and Tradition.

NICENE CREED
The symbol or formula of the Catholic Faith that was developed at the Ecumenical Councils of Nicæa I (325) and Constantinople I (381). It is sung or said by the congregation during the Mass/Divine Liturgy.

OBEDIENCE OF FAITH
The obligation of the faithful to accept and believe in the authoritative and infallible teachings of the Magisterium.

ORDINARY MAGISTERIUM
The teaching office of the bishops in their own dioceses, teaching the same doctrine with moral unanimity, or that of the Pope for the whole Church.

PAPACY
The office of Pope in the Catholic Church.

PARISH
A defined territorial district within a diocese, with its own church and congregation, which is placed in the care of a priest.

PLENARY COUNCIL
A council involving all the bishops of a particular nation.

POPE
Successor of St. Peter; Bishop of Rome; supreme pontiff of the Catholic Church. The Pope exercises a primacy of authority as Vicar of Christ and shepherd of the whole Church; he receives the divine assistance promised by Christ.

PRESBYTERATE
The office of priest in the Catholic Church; the priesthood.

PRIEST
One of the tribe of Levi. In the New Testament, an abbreviation of the Greek *presbyteros* ("elder"). A member of the order of presbyters; this baptized and confirmed male is ordained to be a co-worker with his bishop, to preside at public liturgies in his stead, and otherwise to assist the bishop in priestly service to the People of God.

PRIMACY
The highest rank. The Acts of the Apostles shows the "primacy" of St. Peter, that is, it shows he had the highest rank among the Apostles.

PURGATORY
A state of final purification after death and before entrance into Heaven for those who died in God's friendship but owe raparation for confessed sins; a final cleansing of human imperfection before one is able to enter the joy of Heaven.

RELIGIOUS ASSENT
The obligation of the faithful to accept teachings of the Magisterium even when the teaching is not solemnly and infallibly defined.

SACRAMENT OF SALVATION
Refers to the Catholic Church because she is the sign and the instrument of the communion of God and men, established by Christ as a means to achieve the salvation of souls.

VOCABULARY Continued

SACRED SCRIPTURE

The Bible; the canonical writings validated by the Church as inerrant and inspired by the Holy Spirit; together with Sacred Tradition, it makes up a single deposit of the Word of God—the *Deposit of Faith*—a single gift of God to the Church.

SACRED TRADITION

The Church's teachings that have been passed down through the ages through the successors of the Apostles; together with Sacred Scripture, it makes up a single deposit of the Word of God—the *Deposit of Faith*—a single gift of God to the Church; from the Latin *traditio* ("to hand down").

SECOND VATICAN COUNCIL

The most recent of the Ecumenical Councils of the Catholic Church, held in Rome in 1962-65. It produced documents and teachings on a wide range of concerns, including the nature of the Church, the role of the laity, the liturgy, and the Church's relationship with other faith traditions.

SEPARATED BRETHREN

Those who are properly baptized and known by the name Christian, but who do not profess the entirety of the Catholic Faith or have not preserved unity with the Pope. Separated Brethern possess a certain, albeit imperfect, communion with the Catholic Church.

St. Jerome as a Scholar by El Greco. St. Jerome, ca. 345-420, was ordained a priest in Antioch. He is best known for his translation of the Bible from its original languages into Latin, known as the *Vulgate*. He translated the Old Testament from Hebrew, the Psalms and New Testament from Greek. He was a prolific writer and is second only to St. Augustine in the quantity of Latin Christian works.

STUDY QUESTIONS

1. Who established the Church's organization?

2. Why can the Church be called the *Sacrament of Salvation*?

3. In what way is the Church simultaneously a visible society and an invisible society?

4. Summarize the teaching of Pope Benedict XVI on the meaning of *communion*.

5. When was the hierarchy of the Church developed?

6. Whom do the Twelve Apostles represent?

7. When did Christ make St. Peter the head of the Apostles?

8. When did St. Peter begin to act as leader of the Church?

9. Who is the successor to St. Peter, and what is his role in the Church?

10. List several instances from Scripture when St. Peter exercised his authority in the early Church.

11. Describe the process involved in electing a new Pope.

12. What is a diocese? Who leads a diocese?

13. What is the relationship between the Pope and the bishops?

14. Why would the Church call an *Ecumenical Council*? Who is authorized to convene it?

15. What happens when a Pope dies in the middle of an Ecumenical Council?

16. What does the word *apostle* mean?

17. What was the first council of the whole Church?

18. Name the three levels of ordained ministry in the Church.

19. Name the two kinds of deacons in the Church, and how they are distinguished.

20. What is the *Deposit of Faith*?

21. Identify the three stages by which the Gospels were formed.

22. When can the Church expect there to be new public Revelation?

23. Define *Magisterium*. Why is the Magisterium logically necessary to the Church?

24. Distinguish between the ordinary Magisterium and extraordinary Magisterium.

25. Under what conditions does the Pope and/or the bishops teach infallibly?

26. Name the two Marian doctrines that have been defined by a Pope invoking the charism of infallibility.

27. List the precepts of the Church.

28. What is a *cathedral*? What does *ex cathedra* mean?

29. Comment on this statement: "A bishop is simply the Pope's representative to the local diocese."

30. Are Catholics the only ones who will be saved?

31. What does the Church mean when it teaches, "Outside the Church there is no salvation"?

32. With what Churches does the Catholic Church feel an "especially profound" bond? Why?

33. What is the general position of the Catholic Church toward the Protestant churches?

34. How does the Church regard other faith traditions, such as Islam, Judaism, and the various Eastern traditions?

PRACTICAL EXERCISES

1. Learn the name of your bishop and say a prayer that he will be a faithful leader of the People of God in your diocese. Research your bishop to review his apostolic succession: which bishop consecrated him, which bishop consecrated that bishop, etc., all the way back to the sixteenth century. What stands out in this apostolic succession? Were there any Popes in that line? Reference a list of all the Popes from St. Peter to the present. Select two Popes you have never heard of before from different centuries in Church history, research them and write a one-paragraph summary of each one's life.

2. Visit the cathedral of your diocese or archdiocese. Call ahead to request a tour; many cathedrals have someone on staff who can give a guided tour of the cathedral. Identify the *cathedra* and study the architecture. Review some of the literature available either in person or online about the architectural, artistic, and historic features of the cathedral. Write a brief report on your impressions of the cathedral.

3. Read the sidebar in this chapter listing the precepts of the Church. Based on what you have learned in this course, explain why each of these precepts is an important requirement for members of the faithful.

4. Do some research on the more recent Ecumenical Councils of the Church and answer the following questions:

a. What were the major documents of the Second Vatican Council?

b. When was the First Vatican Council held, and what two topics were discussed?

c. What is the name of the Ecumenical Council previous to Vatican I? What was its purpose?

5. Do some research on the two Marian dogmas that the Popes have defined infallibly. What process did they go through before they made these infallible statements? How is this process an exercise in collegiality?

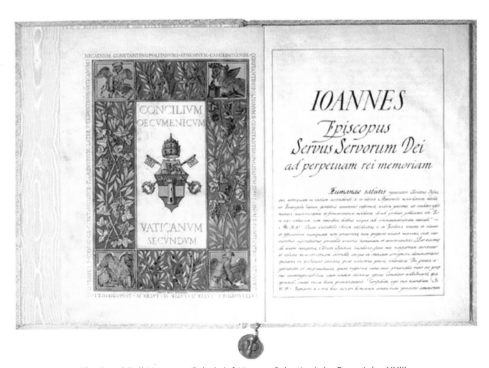

The Papal Bull *Humanæ Salutis* (of Human Salvation), by Pope John XXIII to summon the Second Vatican Council, December 25, 1961.

FROM THE CATECHISM

552 Simon Peter holds the first place in the college of the Twelve;[121] Jesus entrusted a unique mission to him. Through a revelation from the Father, Peter had confessed: "You are the Christ, the Son of the living God." Our Lord then declared to him: "You are Peter, and on this rock I will build my Church, and the gates of Hades will not prevail against it."[122] Christ, the "living Stone,"[123] thus assures his Church, built on Peter, of victory over the powers of death. Because of the faith he confessed Peter will remain the unshakable rock of the Church. His mission will be to keep this faith from every lapse and to strengthen his brothers in it.[124]

731 On the day of Pentecost when the seven weeks of Easter had come to an end, Christ's Passover is fulfilled in the outpouring of the Holy Spirit, manifested, given, and communicated as a divine person: of his fullness, Christ, the Lord, pours out the Spirit in abundance.[125]

732 On that day, the Holy Trinity is fully revealed. Since that day, the Kingdom announced by Christ has been open to those who believe in him: in the humility of the flesh and in faith, they already share in the communion of the Holy Trinity. By his coming, which never ceases, the Holy Spirit causes the world to enter into the "last days," the time of the Church, the Kingdom already inherited though not yet consummated.

> We have seen the true Light, we have received the heavenly Spirit, we have found the true faith: we adore the indivisible Trinity, who has saved us.[126]

739 Because the Holy Spirit is the anointing of Christ, it is Christ who, as the head of the Body, pours out the Spirit among his members to nourish, heal, and organize them in their mutual functions, to give them life, send them to bear witness, and associate them to his self-offering to the Father and to his intercession for the whole world. Through the Church's sacraments, Christ communicates his Holy and sanctifying Spirit to the members of his Body. (This will be the topic of Part Two of the Catechism.)

816 "The sole Church of Christ [is that] which our Savior, after his Resurrection, entrusted to Peter's pastoral care, commissioning him and the other apostles to extend and rule it.... This Church, constituted and organized as a society in the present world, subsists in (*subsistit in*) the Catholic Church, which is governed by the successor of Peter and by the bishops in communion with him."[127]

The Second Vatican Council's *Decree on Ecumenism* explains: "For it is through Christ's Catholic Church alone, which is the universal help toward salvation, that the fullness of the means of salvation can be obtained. It was to the apostolic college alone, of which Peter is the head, that we believe that our Lord entrusted all the blessings of the New Covenant, in order to establish on earth the one Body of Christ into which all those should be fully incorporated who belong in any way to the People of God."[128]

Statue of St. Peter by Arnolfo di Cambio.
St. Peter is the "the unshakable rock of the Church."

ENDNOTES - CHAPTER FOUR

1. Cf. CCC 751.
2. Pope Bl. John Paul II, *L'Osservatore Romano*, n. 29, July 22, 1991.
3. Cf. 1 Cor 11: 18; 14: 19, 28, 34, 35.
4. Cf. 1 Cor 1: 2; 16: 1.
5. Cf. 1 Cor 15: 9; Gal 1: 13; Phil 3: 6.
6. Eph 5: 32.
7. *SC* 2; cf. Heb 13: 14.
8. Mt 13: 24-30, 36-43.
9. Mt 13: 47-48.
10. CCC 827.
11. *LG* 1.
12. Rev 7: 9.
13. Bl. John Paul II, *Address to the Bishops of the United States of America*, n. 1, September 16, 1987: *Insegnamenti di Giovanni Paolo II*, X, 3 (1987), p. 553.
14. Ratzinger, Joseph, *Letter to the Bishops of the Catholic Church on some Aspects of the Church Understood as Communion*, 3.
15. Cf. Eph 4: 4-5; Mk 16: 16.
16. Pope Benedict XVI, *On the Way to Jesus Christ* (Ignatius Press: San Francisco, 2005) p. 113-117.
17. 1 Cor 10: 17; *LG* 7.
18. St. Leo the Great, *Sermo* 63,7.
19. Cf. CCC 880.
20. CCC 875.
21. *LG* 18.
22. *LG* 19; cf. Lk 6: 13; Jn 21: 15-17.
23. *LG* 22; cf. CIC, 330.
24. Cf. Mt 16: 18-19; Jn 21: 15-17.
25. *LG* 22 § 2.
26. Cf. *Pastor Bonus*, Art. 48.
27. Cf. *Pastor Bonus*, Art. 56.
28. *Pastor Bonus*, Art. 62.
29. Cf. *Pastor Bonus*, Art. 71-74.
30. Cf. *Pastor Bonus*, Art. 71.
31. Cf. *Pastor Bonus*, Art. 85, 87-88.
32. Cf. *Pastor Bonus*, Art. 94, 95.
33. Cf. *Pastor Bonus*, Art. 105.
34. Cf. *Pastor Bonus*, Art. 112, 113, 115, 116.
35. Cf. *Pastor Bonus*, Art. 117, 118.
36. Cf. *Pastor Bonus*, Art. 121.
37. Cf. *Pastor Bonus*, Art. 126.
38. Cf. *Pastor Bonus*, Art. 131.
39. Cf. *Pastor Bonus*, Art. 135.
40. Cf. *Pastor Bonus*, Art. 139.
41. *Pastor Bonus*, Art. 142.
42. *Pastor Bonus*, Art. 145.
43. *Pastor Bonus*, Art. 149.
44. *Pastor Bonus*, Art. 152.
45. Cf. *Pastor Bonus*, Art. 154, 155.
46. Cf. *Pastor Bonus*, Art. 159.
47. Cf. *Pastor Bonus*, Art. 163.
48. Cf. *Pastor Bonus*, Art. 166.
49. Cf. *Pastor Bonus*, Art. 169.
50. *LG* 23.
51. Ibid.
52. Cf. *CD* 3.
53. *LG* 23.
54. Cf. Gal 2: 10.
55. Mt 23: 2-3.
56. Mt 19: 28.
57. Cf. 1 Tm 3: 1.
58. Acts 15: 7.
59. *LG* 19; cf. Lk 6: 13; Jn 21: 15-17.
60. *LG* 22; cf. CIC, can. 330.
61. *LG* 22; cf. CIC, can. 336.
62. CIC, can. 337 § 1.
63. *LG* 22.
64. CCC 1554.
65. *AG* 5.
66. Cf. Jn 17: 21-23.
67. CCC 2179.
68. Cf. *LG* 29; *SC* 35 § 4; *AG* 16.
69. Cf. *LG* 12; CCC 785, 888-892.
70. *LG* 12; cf. *DV* 10.
71. 1 Tm 3: 15.
72. Jn 14: 26.
73. 2 Thes 2: 15.
74. Cf. DS 3006.
75. Cf. DS 1501; *DV* 9.
76. 2 Thes 2: 15.
77. Cf. 1 Cor 11: 23-26.
78. Acts 6: 6.
79. Acts 13: 3.
80. Acts 28: 8.
81. *DV* 8.
82. *DV* 19; cf. Acts 1: 1-2.
83. *DV* 19.
84. CCC 126.
85. *DV* 8.
86. *DV* 4; cf. 1 Tm 6: 14; Ti 2: 13.
87. CCC 890.
88. *LG* 25; cf. Vatican Council I: DS 3074.
89. *DV* 10 § 2.
90. *LG* 25 § 2.
91. Cf. *LG* 25.
92. *LG* 25.
93. CCC 891.
94. CCC 892.
95. *SC* 5.
96. 1 Pt 5: 3.
97. *LG* 26 § 3.
98. CCC 895.
99. *LG* 27; cf. Lk 22: 26-27.
100. Cf. CCC 2041; CCC 2042-2043.
101. CCC 846.
102. *LG* 14
103. CCC 818.
104. *LG* 15.
105. *UR* 3.
106. Paul VI, Discourse, December 14, 1975; cf. *UR* 13-18.
107. *Redemptoris Missio*, 10.
108. *LG* 16.
109. Ibid.
110. CCC 846.
111. Ibid.
112. 1 Tm 2: 4.
113. CCC 838.
114. *LG* 16; cf. *NA* 2; *EN* 53.
115. Pope Benedict XVI, *Address of His Holiness Benedict XVI to Participants in the Tenth Plenary Assembly of the Pontifical Council for Interreligious Dialogue*, Consistory Hall, June 7, 2008.
116. Pope Benedict XVI, *Meeting with Representatives of Other Religions*, Bl. John Paul II Cultural Center of Washington, DC, Apr. 17, 2008.
117. Ibid.
118. Ibid.
119. Pope Benedict XVI, *Meeting With Representatives of the Jewish Community*, Sept. 12, 2008.
120. Pope Benedict XVI, *Meeting with Representatives of Some Muslim Communities*, Cologne, Aug. 20, 2005.
121. Cf. Mk 3: 16; 9: 2; Lk 24: 34; 1 Cor 15: 5.
122. Mt 16: 18.
123. 1 Pt 2: 4.
124. Cf. Lk 22: 32.
125. Cf. Acts 2: 33-36.
126. Byzantine liturgy, Pentecost, Vespers, *Troparion*, repeated after communion.
127. *LG* 8 § 2.
128. *Unitatis redintegratio* 3 § 55.

The Four Marks of the Church:
One, Holy, Catholic, and Apostolic

The Catholic Church is the one and only true Church.
The fullness of the means of salvation are to be found only within her.

The Church

CHAPTER 5

The Four Marks of the Church: One, Holy, Catholic, and Apostolic

The sole Church of Christ which in the Creed is professed as one, holy, catholic, and apostolic... subsists in the Catholic Church. (*Lumen Gentium*, 8)

 he one Church established by Christ is present both on earth and in Heaven. She is at the same time a visible community and an invisible spiritual communion, made up of both "the earthly Church and the Church endowed with heavenly riches."[1]

From the Church's earliest centuries, Christians have identified four characteristics, called *marks*, that are essential to the whole Church, both in Heaven and on earth. These four marks are that the Church is *One*, *Holy*, *Catholic*, and *Apostolic*, and they help distinguish the true pilgrim Church on earth from any others that claim to be Christ's Church.

The marks are essential and visible signs that allow the true Church founded by Christ to be distinguished from other churches. Only faith can recognize that the Church possesses these marks because of her divine origin, but the historical manifestations of these marks are signs that speak clearly to human reason.

Although these characteristics are of the Church's very essence, she does not possess them on her own. All that the Church has, she receives from God. Through the gift of the Holy Spirit, Christ sustains the Church and continues to make her One, Holy, Catholic, and Apostolic. As we will see, it is to the Catholic Church alone that Christ gives these characteristics in their fullness.

"This is the sole Church of Christ, which in the Creed we profess to be one, holy, catholic and apostolic."[2] These four characteristics, inseparably linked with each other,[3] indicate essential features of the Church and her mission. The Church does not possess them of herself; it is Christ who, through the Holy Spirit, makes his Church one, holy, catholic, and apostolic, and it is he who calls her to realize each of these qualities. (CCC 811)

The one Church established by Christ is present both on earth and in Heaven.

The Voice from on High by Tissot.
"This voice has come for your sake, not for mine. Now is the judgment of this world, now shall the ruler of this world be cast out;
and I, when I am lifted up from the earth, will draw all men to myself." (Jn 12: 30-32)

IN THIS CHAPTER, WE WILL ADDRESS SEVERAL QUESTIONS:

✠ What are the four marks of the Catholic Church?

✠ What does it mean that the Church is *One*?

✠ How has the unity of the Church been wounded?

✠ What ecumenical efforts are being made at present?

✠ What does it mean that the Church is *Holy*?

✠ What does it mean that the Church is *Catholic*?

✠ What does it mean that the Church is *Apostolic*?

✠ What is apostolic succession, and why is it important?

✠ What is apostolic Tradition?

Christ Handing the Keys to St. Peter (detail) by Master of the Legend of the Holy Prior.
It is evident from the Gospel that Christ desired "one flock, one shepherd."

THE FIRST MARK: THE CHURCH IS ONE

When we recite the *Nicene Creed* at Sunday Mass, we profess our belief in the four marks of the Church: "We believe in One, Holy, Catholic, and Apostolic Church." Of these four characteristics, the first—that the Church is One—is of foundational importance for understanding the other three.

What do we mean when we say, "The Church is One"? First, we are acknowledging the uniqueness and singularity of the Church. Just as we profess faith in one God and not in multiple gods, so too we believe that Jesus has instituted One Church and not multiple churches. The Church's unity has its source in the *one* God in three Persons.

The Church founded by Christ is One and unique because of her origin. The *unicity* or uniqueness of the Church means that there is only one true Church of Christ that is constituted exactly in agreement with her divine Founder's will. It is evident from the Gospel that Christ desired "one flock, one shepherd."[4]

Christ himself said that he is the only way to salvation:

> **I am the way, and the truth, and the life; no one comes to the Father, but by me. (Jn 14: 6)**

In establishing the Church on earth, Jesus gives all mankind the opportunity to be united to him, the one Savior of the world, by becoming part of his one Mystical Body.

Second, by saying that the Church is One, we are affirming the unity and solidarity of the Church. In any social group or organization, a certain degree of unity must exist among its members. Whether we are talking about a political party, a school club, a bowling league, or a neighborhood association, every group exists by being united around common goals, interests, or opinions.

The Church, however, is different. Although her members might indeed be united around common goals, interests, or opinions, the Church's unity does not originate in these things. Rather, the Church's unity comes from her divine source, God, who in his Trinity is perfect unity, one God in three Persons.

UNITY IN THE MYSTICAL BODY

Of all the names and images of the Church that we have encountered so far, the image of the Church as the Mystical Body of Christ, a reality we have explored in previous chapters, is perhaps best for expressing this unity that the Church receives from God. We can see both how closely united the Church is to her founder and how closely united each of her members is to one another. In the Mystical Body of Christ, the many diverse members of the Church are united to Jesus, our head, to form the whole Christ, united and animated by the Holy Spirit, the "soul" of the Mystical Body.

We can see the unity of the Mystical Body of Christ visibly expressed in a number of different ways or attributes:

✤ **Unity of faith.** In the Creed, the Church professes the one faith that has been passed down from the Apostles. The Catholic Church is the only Church with unity of doctrine, of Sacraments, and of government under a single head.

✤ **Unity of worship.** The pilgrim Church celebrates in common the same Seven Sacraments that were instituted by Christ during his time on earth. The eucharistic sacrifice, while always offered in a particular community, is never a celebration of that community alone. The community is the image and true presence of the One, Holy, Catholic, and Apostolic Church. Wherever the Eucharist is celebrated, the totality of the mystery of the Church becomes present.

✤ **Unity of leadership.** Through the Sacrament of Holy Orders, the Church's apostolic succession ensures uninterrupted continuity with the teaching and leadership of St. Peter and the Apostles.[5]

The Savior by Juanes.
Wherever the Eucharist is celebrated, the totality of the mystery of the Church becomes present.

The Church has always held, in faithfulness to Christ's teachings, that the Church is One and unique. "The sacred Council begins by professing that God himself has made known to the human race how men serving him can be saved and reach happiness in Christ. We believe that this one true religion continues to exist in the Catholic and Apostolic Church, to which the Lord Jesus entrusted the task of spreading it among all men."[6]

The essential value of this unity achieved at the beginning of the Church's life, will never disappear. The Second Vatican Council repeated that: "Christ the Lord founded one Church and one Church only" (*Unitatis Redintegratio*, n. 1). It must, however, be observed that this original unity has suffered deep lacerations in the course of history. Love of Christ must spur his followers today to reconsider together their past, to return to the way of unity with renewed vigour.[7]

The Saints
PILLARS OF THE CHURCH

Pope St. Leo the Great
"PETER HAS SPOKEN"

Pope St. Leo the Great lived in the fifth century and was Pope AD 440-461. The capital of the Roman Empire had moved to Constantinople more than one century earlier, and the Western half of the empire was rapidly approaching collapse. In addition to the heresies he had to combat as Pope, one of Leo's biggest challenges was to ensure the continued survival and growth of the Church amidst the chaos resulting from the empire's disintegration.

As Pope, Leo's primary goal was to preserve the Church's unity and adherence to the teaching of Christ. The heresies of Pelagianism, Nestorianism, Monophysitism, and Manichæism were raging throughout the Church, and Leo understood that it was his pastoral responsibility to defend the faithful from these dangerous errors. He convoked the Council of Chalcedon in 451 and issued a lengthy explanation— often referred to as the "Tome of Leo"—that clarified the Church's teaching on the disputed issues. When

those present heard Pope Leo's letter, they readily assented to his teaching and exclaimed, "Peter has spoken through Leo."

Pope Leo's accomplishments were not limited to Church doctrine. In perhaps the most memorable event of his papacy, Leo was called upon to intercede with Attila the Hun, who had rampaged through northern and central Italy and was now threatening the Eternal City. Leo went to meet the notorious barbarian outside the walls of the city, and although we do not know what was said during their encounter, his words prevented the Huns' invasion; Attila and his men left Rome without a fight.

Because of his pastoral and political achievements, after his death Pope Leo was hailed as "the Great," the first of only three Popes to have received such acclamation. He was declared a saint, and in 1754 Pope Benedict XIV conferred upon him the further honor of being named a Doctor of the Church.

Pope St. Leo the Great, pray for us.

WOUNDS TO UNITY

Since the beginning of the Church's ministry, divisions and disagreements have arisen among Christians that threaten and, in some cases, seriously wound the visible unity of the pilgrim Church. As we saw earlier, some of the members of the early Church in Jerusalem disagreed as to whether or not Gentiles should undergo circumcision in order to become Christians. The resolution of this dispute at the Council of Jerusalem is a good example of how the authority given by Christ to St. Peter and his successors is intended to maintain and strengthen the pilgrim Church's visible unity.

The Council of Nicæa (325) was called by Emperor Constantine to unite the Christian empire which was divided over Arianism. The council concluded with the Nicene Creed proposed by St. Athanasius.

In fact, "in this one and only Church of God from its very beginnings there arose certain rifts, which the Apostle strongly censures as damnable. But in subsequent centuries much more serious dissensions appeared and large communities became separated from full communion with the Catholic Church—for which, often enough, men of both sides were to blame."[8] The ruptures that wound the unity of Christ's Body—here we must distinguish *heresy*, *apostasy*, and *schism*[9]—do not occur without human sin:

> Where there are sins, there are also divisions, schisms, heresies, and disputes. Where there is virtue, however, there also are harmony and unity, from which arise the one heart and one soul of all believers.[10] (CCC 817)

There have been times, however, when some Christians rejected the teaching and leadership of the Church's shepherds—the Pope and the bishops in union with him. In doing so, they rejected Christ himself[11] and wounded the unity of the whole Mystical Body. These wounds to the Church's unity usually take the form of the following:

✤ **Apostasy,** the total rejection of the Christian Faith by someone already baptized.

✤ **Heresy,** the deliberate and persistent postbaptismal denial of a truth of the Faith taught by the Church.

✤ **Schism,** the postbaptismal refusal of unity with the Pope or the refusal of communion with the members of the Church.

All of these are very grave sins that result from the choices and actions of individuals, but schism is especially tragic, for it often involves entire communities of people who choose to separate themselves from Christ and his Church. Nevertheless, one cannot charge with the sin of separation those who are born into these communities and in them are instructed in the Faith of Christ.

In the history of the Church, there have been two main periods of schism. The first, with the Orthodox Churches, took place in the eleventh century. The second was with the various denominations that were founded during the Protestant Reformation in the sixteenth century.

Catholics today must be careful to distinguish between those who initially separated themselves from the Church (called *schismatics*) and those members of later generations who were born into these schismatic communities (called *separated brethren*). These separated brethren cannot be considered *prima facie* guilty of the sin of separation; it is often through no fault of their own that they remain unaware of the truth of the Catholic Faith. Rather, provided they are baptized, they are to be recognized as fellow Christians and brothers and sisters in Christ.

It is with great joy that the Catholic Church acknowledges elements of sanctification and truth within these separated churches and communities of *Protestantism* and *Orthodoxy*. Included among these elements are the Sacred Scriptures, some or all of the Seven Sacraments, the *theological virtues* of faith, hope, and charity, and the gifts of the Holy Spirit. However, all these elements, which come from Christ and lead back to him, belong by right to the Catholic Church, the one Church founded by Christ, which possesses them in their fullness. The fact that some of these elements are present to some degree within other communities is evidence of those communities' origins (i.e., they separated from the Catholic Church) and may provide an avenue for their eventual return to Catholic unity.

THE FOUR MARKS OF THE CHURCH

"Let us pray so that the primacy of Peter, entrusted to poor human beings, may always be exercised in this original sense desired by the Lord, so that it will be increasingly recognised in its true meaning by brothers who are still not in communion with us."
(Pope Benedict XVI, General Audience, June 7, 2006)

This is the one Church of Christ which in the Creed is professed as one, holy, catholic and apostolic, which our Saviour, after His Resurrection, commissioned Peter to shepherd, and him and the other Apostles to extend and direct with authority, which He erected for all ages as "the pillar and mainstay of the truth." This Church constituted and organized in the world as a society, subsists in the Catholic Church, which is governed by the successor of Peter and by the Bishops in communion with him, although many elements of sanctification and of truth are found outside of its visible structure. These elements, as gifts belonging to the Church of Christ, are forces impelling toward catholic unity.

— *Lumen Gentium*, 8

HERESIES IN THE EARLY CHURCH

Catholic doctrine derives from the revealed truths contained in the Deposit of Faith that Christ entrusted to his Church and which is found in Sacred Scripture and Sacred Tradition. However, from the earliest days of Christianity, there are some who corrupt these teachings.

Heresy is the denial or alteration of some part or parts of the Deposit of Faith. The first heresies that afflicted the early Church were especially dangerous because they struck at the heart of Christianity—the Person of Jesus Christ.

The early Christians frequently utilized the Greek linguistic and philosophical traditions in explaining the doctrines of Christianity. St. Paul's Epistles and St. John's Gospel show how the richness of the Greek language allowed for the articulation of the Christian message. Later, the philosophies of Plato and Aristotle would prove valuable for the development of Christian theology.

However, beginning in the second century, proponents of neo-Platonic religious thought sought to incorporate certain elements of Christian teaching into their own beliefs. They held that there was a Supreme Being who created through lesser beings, one of which was the *logos*.

St. John had used the word *Logos* (in Greek, "Word") to refer to God the Son. Jesus Christ is God the Son, the Second Person of the Blessed Trinity, equal to and consubstantial with God the Father. However, the neo-Platonists conflated the *Logos* from the Gospel of St. John with the philosophical *logos* of the Greeks, thereby denying the true divinity of Christ.

Neo-Platonists also viewed the created world as an obstacle to contemplation and personal perfection. Thus, besides denying Christ's true divinity, they also de-emphasized—if not completely denied—Christ's humanity.

Gnosticism

The word *Gnosticism* is derived from the Greek word *gnosis* ("knowledge") and refers to a set of beliefs that salvation may be achieved through secret knowledge and only by some people. By the second century, Gnostics had incorporated elements of the Old and New Testaments into their religious teachings. Gnosticism taught that there were two gods: the creator god who propagated evil (the god of the Old Testament) and the unknowable divine being (the god of the New Testament).

According to Gnostics, the *Logos* (Christ) had been sent to give secret knowledge to a select few so that they could return to the unknowable divine being. This was only possible if the individuals understood the secret knowledge of the Redeemer's teaching and performed the appropriate Gnostic rituals.

Gnosticism rejected the Church's teaching regarding Christ's two natures: human and divine. According to Gnostic thought, Jesus did not have a human nature because it would be material and therefore evil. Additionally, he could not have inhabited a human body nor die on the Cross; instead, his body was an apparition.

The early Church vigorously opposed these Gnostic teachings, emphasizing the goodness of the created world, the existence and supremacy of the one true God, the clear meaning of the Old and New Testament Scriptures, and the reality of Christ's human and divine natures, along with his redemptive Passion, Death, and Resurrection.

This principle of secret knowledge gained through pagan or ritual ceremony is the essence of the contemporary New Age movement. These practices teach that hidden powers are released through amulets, crystals, and secret incantations; that knowledge

Baptism of Christ by Piero. The first heresies that afflicted the early Church were especially dangerous because they struck at the heart of Christianity—the Person of Jesus Christ.

can be gained through fortunetelling, horoscopes, zodiac signs, and tarot cards; and that salvation ultimately comes from within oneself, thus eliminating the need for a Redeemer.

Gnostic thought has also resurfaced in the form of quasi-historical novels, movies, and other media. Some make use of various interpretations of the Gnostic gospels to propound erroneous views about the life, nature, and teachings of Jesus Christ.

The Church today, just as in the first centuries, proclaims the perennial truth that salvation comes from Jesus Christ, the only Son of God, who shared fully in our humanity and died on the Cross for our Redemption.

St. Basil the Great and St. Athanasius by Coello.
St. Basil (ca. 330-379) was Bishop of Caesarea and St. Athanasius (ca. 296-373) was Bishop of Alexandria. Both saints are Doctors of the Church and staunchly defended the Church against Arianism in the fourth century. St. Basil authored the Divine Liturgy of St. Basil the Great, which greatly influenced the Eucharistic Prayer IV used in the Roman Missal.
The Nicene Creed, the decisive document of the First Ecumenical Council of Nicæa, was the lifelong work of St. Athanasius.

Arianism (fourth century)

Arius (ca. 250-336) was a priest from Alexandria in Egypt whose study of neo-Platonism and familiarity with Gnosticism prepared the way for his erroneous interpretation of the son's relation to the Father. Selecting certain passages from the New Testament, Arius claimed that Jesus Christ was not eternally God and thus not equal to the Father.

Arius' belief in a transcendent, supreme God could not conceive that anything coming from God could be equal to God. He taught that Jesus was a supreme creation of God, but not his eternally begotten Son, Second Person of the Blessed Trinity. This denial of Christ's divinity was at the root of the Arian heresy, which invariably led to a rejection of almost all of the Church's central tenets, especially her doctrines on the Blessed Trinity and the Redemption.

Arianism quickly became the greatest doctrinal crisis the Church would experience until the sixteenth-century Reformation. Arianism first ravaged the Church in the East and was later adopted by many of the Visogothic tribes in the West that dominated central and northern Europe, thereby becoming a serious threat to the existence of orthodox Christianity. So pervasive was this heresy, St. Athanasius once remarked, "The whole world has gone Arian; then it is Athanasius against the world."

The Church responded to this threat by reaffirming the traditional belief in the divinity of Jesus Christ in the Nicene and Athanasian Creeds, which proclaim that Christ is consubstantial with the Father. Through clear and consistent teaching, along with the catechetical and missionary work and sacrifices of many saintly men and women, this heresy was ultimately eliminated in the sixth and seventh centuries.

Periodically, however, there has resurged a certain tendency among some to stress Christ's humanity at the expense of his divinity. These tendencies are often manifested today in the mistaken search for the *historical Jesus*, which views Christ as a wise teacher but denies his divinity, his redemptive Death on the Cross, and his Resurrection.

Certain modern Christian sects, such as the Jehovah's Witnesses or the Church of Jesus Christ of Latter Day Saints (Mormons), view Christ as "the son of God," but not equal to or consubstantial with the Father, making them incompatible with the teachings of the Catholic Church in regard to the divinity of Jesus Christ.

Apollinarianism (ca. 360-381)

Apollinaris (ca. 310-390), bishop of Laodicea in Syria, ardently supported the orthodox position regarding the divinity of Christ against the Arians, but his unguided fervor led him into heresy. Though he affirmed that Christ had a human body, Apollinaris denied the existence of a human mind and will in Christ. Therefore, it would follow that Christ did not live a complete human life as a man.

This teaching is incompatible with the Church's teaching that Christ is true God and true man, sharing completely our human experience. Apollinarianism was declared erroneous and was officially condemned at the First Ecumenical Council of Constantinople (381).

Nestorianism (ca. 351–ca. 451)

As Bishop Apollinaris had done, Patriarch Nestorius of Constantinople strove to emphasize the full divinity and full humanity of Christ. He maintained Christ was the unity of two persons: one divine and one human. Because of this, he attempted to eliminate the Marian title *Theotokos* ("Bearer of God"), which had always been used in orthodox circles in the East. Although he allowed Mary to be called the Mother of Christ ("*Christotokos*"), he would not allow her to be called the Mother of God.

Summoned by Emperor Theodosius II, the Third Ecumenical Council at Ephesus (431) condemned Nestorius' teachings and declared Mary as the true Mother of God (*Theotokos*). In 436, Nestorius was exiled to Egypt.

The Church responded by reemphasizing that Jesus Christ is one divine Person with two natures, human and divine. This relationship of the two natures is called the *hypostatic union*, a doctrine formally accepted by the Church at the Ecumenical Council of Chalcedon (451).

The Church has always proclaimed that Jesus Christ is true man and true God—God the Son—and, therefore, Mary is the Mother of God. The East celebrates the Feast of the *Theotokos* on December 26, the day after the Nativity of Christ; the West celebrates the Solemnity of Mary, Mother of God, on January 1, the octave of the Nativity of Christ.

The errors of Nestorius are propagated by some Christians today who, while accepting that Mary is the Mother of Jesus ("*Christotokos*," Bearer of Christ), will deny that she is the Mother of God ("*Theotokos*"). As seen in the heresy of Nestorianism, such a denial is actually a rejection of the belief that Jesus Christ is one divine Person with two natures, human and divine.

Monophysitism (400s-600s)

Monophysites claimed that there is only one nature in Christ, not two. The name means "only one nature" (*monos*, "alone" or "single"; *physis*, "nature"). This heresy taught the human nature of Christ was "incorporated" into the divine nature, in the same way a drop of water is absorbed into an ocean.

The heresy of monophysitism was the primary issue at the Council of Chalcedon (451). Pope St. Leo's legates spoke first, and his *Tome* (written in 449) was recognized as teaching the orthodox Faith by the Council Fathers. It declared that Jesus Christ was the God-man, one Person with two natures. Thereafter it was said, "Peter has spoken through Leo."

THE PROTESTANT REFORMATION

Martin Luther Nailing His Ninety-Five Theses to the Wittenburg Church Door by Hugo Vogel.

The Protestant Reformation was an interrelated series of schisms that took place from 1517 to 1648. At the time, Catholic practice was in need of reform. Indeed, several Popes and saints of the time had attempted to curb abuses that were occurring within the Church.

At the same time, a new social class was emerging in Europe. Princes found themselves reaping the benefits of the prosperity of the Renaissance, and wealth was now available in greater quantities to far more people. These princes and other emerging rulers were dissatisfied with the old social order in which the Church played a major role as a land-owner and moral judge.

In 1517, Martin Luther began publishing criticisms against the sale of *indulgences*, which are a means for the faithful to obtain remission from the temporal punishment due to sins whose guilt has already been forgiven. Luther was right to criticize the sale of indulgences, but he erred when he began arguing against the validity of indulgences themselves. About the same time, a Swiss priest by the name of Huldrych Zwingli started a similar campaign in Switzerland. Both Luther and Zwingli began their criticisms hoping to correct abuses within the Church. However, their theological reasoning led them to dismiss the very authority of the Church, and they soon began to attack the teaching, worship, and structure of the Church herself.

Within the next several decades, many other "reformers" arose throughout Europe. Two of the most famous were John Calvin and King Henry VIII. Soon, full-blown schisms broke out in Germany, Switzerland, England, Denmark, Sweden, and Scotland.

It is important to remember that even before the time of the Reformation, there was a growing tension between these rising nation-states and the Church as rulers wished to consolidate control of the local churches under their own power. Protestantism offered an opportunity for these leaders to seize control of the lands and power formally held by local churches and religious orders and to extend temporal control over matters of justice and moral legislation.

Once independent of the central authority of the Catholic Church, these new Christian communities found that they disagreed with one another as well. The movements they started remained separated from one another, and often these communities are still limited to their country of origin. In many ways, the Christian communities that emerged from this period have continued the pattern of splintering that they inherited from their founders, for today there are more than thirty thousand different Protestant denominations throughout the world.

The visible unity of the Church on earth was deeply wounded by these schismatic movements, but this period also saw the beginnings of the true reform that the Church had needed. God gave the world saints like Ignatius of Loyola, Francis Xavier, John of the Cross, Teresa of Avila, and Francis de Sales to assist the pilgrim Church. The emergence of the Catholic Reformation (also called the Counter-Reformation) brought with it new religious fervor on the part of Catholics throughout Europe, new clarification of Church doctrine at the Council of Trent, and new religious orders of men and women—such as the Jesuits and the Discalced Carmelites—dedicated to living in imitation of Christ.

TOWARD GREATER CHRISTIAN UNITY

The task of working toward Christian unity is called ecumenism. As members of the Church, we are called to engage in *ecumenism*.

> "The sole Church of Christ [is that] which our Savior, after his Resurrection, entrusted to Peter's pastoral care, commissioning him and the other apostles to extend and rule it....This Church, constituted and organized as a society in the present world, subsists in (*subsistit in*) the Catholic Church, which is governed by the successor of Peter and by the bishops in communion with him." [12]

> The Second Vatican Council's *Decree on Ecumenism* explains: "For it is through Christ's Catholic Church alone, which is the universal help toward salvation, that the fullness of the means of salvation can be obtained. It was to the apostolic college alone, of which Peter is the head, that we believe that our Lord entrusted all the blessings of the New Covenant, in order to establish on earth the one Body of Christ into which all those should be fully incorporated who belong in any way to the People of God." [13] (CCC 816)

In Jerusalem, January 1964, Pope Paul VI met with Patriarch of Constantinople Athenagoras I. They issued a joint statement withdrawing mutual excommunications that had formalized the Catholic-Orthodox split in 1054.

In the writings of the Second Vatican Council—and particularly in the Decree on Ecumenism—we are able to identify some principles for engaging in ecumenical work. First, each of us is called to greater conversion of heart. Divisions are brought about because of sin, but the cultivation of virtue and holiness gives us unity of life and moves each of us toward greater Christian unity with others.

A deeper understanding between Catholics and our separated brethren is also encouraged, both in terms of theological dialogue and personal knowledge of one another. As has been the case in the past, simple misunderstandings between Catholics and non-Catholics have given rise to suspicion and greater division. Therefore, efforts should be made to understand the positions of our separated brethren and to look for areas of agreement. Reflection on St. Paul's advice to the Philippians can be helpful in these instances of ecumenical dialogue:

> Finally, brethren, whatever is true, whatever is honorable, whatever is just, whatever is pure, whatever is lovely, whatever is gracious, if there is any excellence, if there is anything worthy of praise, think about these things. (Phil 4: 8)

Although we are to seek common ground with our separated brethren, it is essential that the truth of the Catholic Faith always be represented accurately and in its entirety. The Catholic Church is the pillar and foundation of truth, and the infallible teaching authority given to her by Christ is essential for preserving the

CONTEMPORARY EFFORTS IN ECUMENISM AND INTERFAITH DIALOGUE

Schisms are easily made but very difficult to heal. The Second Vatican Council acknowledged the need for an increased effort on the part of the Catholic Church to seek reconciliation between the various groups of Christians in schism with the Catholic Church.

Pope Bl. John Paul II took up this call during his papacy and made great efforts to reach out to the Eastern Orthodox Churches by opening dialogues that someday may lead to healing this ancient schism. In a historic visit to Greece in May 2001, the Pope met with the Orthodox Patriarch of Constantinople and Holy Synod in Athens. The Church has had cordial and friendly dialogue with several leaders of the Orthodox Churches and continues to seek inroads to foster unity.

Ecumenical dialogue has taken place at the international, national, and local levels in various parts of the world. The Catholic Church has issued joint statements with several Protestant bodies on matters of agreement, including the question of justification by faith.

A certain difficulty in ecumenism is the nature of Orthodoxy and Protestantism. Orthodoxy comprises not one church but more than a dozen national Churches

In May 2001, following in the footsteps of St. Paul, Pope Bl. John Paul II made a pilgrimage to Greece, Syria and Malta. He was the first Pope to visit Greece since the Great Schism of 1054.

that are not all united among themselves; various Orthodox Churches do not recognize the legitimacy of each other.

Likewise, the Protestant communities are numerous, having undergone continuous ruptures among themselves ever since the Reformation began. Even dialogue with mainstream Protestants—Episcopalian, Presbyterian, Lutheran, Baptist, Methodist, etc.—must generally be done with each individual body. Complicating matters further is that the Protestant communities generally lack the kind of hierarchy or teaching authority that can speak in the name of an entire denomination. Some degree of official dialogue can be had with their governing bodies, but the fruits of such dialogue would not be binding on their own followers.

Such difficulties, however, do not excuse us from seeking unity as Christ willed for all Christians. However slow the progress or unlikely the success, ecumenical dialogue is a duty of all the faithful.

The Church even carries out interfaith dialogue with Jewish and Muslim leaders and representatives of the Oriental religions. Although unity is even less likely, the search for common ground and mutual respect is also a moral imperative.

In May 2006, Pope Benedict XVI visited the Auschwitz-Birkenau death camp memorial in Poland. He met with Jewish Holocaust survivors and called for the world to unite against anti-Semitism. Poland's chief rabbi called the Pope's speech "a great moment in the process of reconciling" Jews and Christians.

visible unity of the pilgrim Church. "Nothing is so foreign to the spirit of ecumenism as a false conciliatory approach which harms the purity of Catholic doctrine and obscures its assured genuine meaning."[14]

Finally, the Church affirms the responsibility of all Christians to pray for a greater manifestation of the unity that Christ wills for the Church on earth. At times, praying in common with our separated brethren can be an appropriate means of fostering communion, because the "spiritual ecumenism" of prayer helps to remind us that true Christian unity comes from God alone. The pilgrim Church therefore places all her hope in the Son's prayer for unity, the Father's love for his children, and the Holy Spirit's power of uniting all men in charity.

> Christ always gives his Church the gift of unity, but the Church must always pray and work to maintain, reinforce, and perfect the unity that Christ wills for her. This is why Jesus himself prayed at the hour of his Passion, and does not cease praying to his Father, for the unity of his disciples: "That they may all be one. As you, Father, are in me and I am in you, may they also be one in us...so that the world may know that you have sent me."[15] (CCC 820)

THE SECOND MARK: THE CHURCH IS HOLY

St. Augustine and St. Monica by Scheffer. St. Augustine detailed his spiritual journey from a life of sin to Catholicism in his famous *Confessions,* a classic of both Christian theology and world literature.

The second mark of the Church is her holiness, which she receives from Christ her founder through the indwelling of the Holy Spirit. As with her unity, the Church's holiness comes solely from God.

Christ sanctifies the Church and fills her with his grace so completely that she becomes sanctifying herself. The Church is Holy in that her origin is Christ. The Church is Holy because her goal is the glory of God. The Church is also Holy in the means she has been given to bring all men into communion with God. These means include the teachings of Christ, passed on by the Apostles and preserved by the Church's Magisterium; the Sacraments, instituted by Christ to impart grace to all who receive them; and the life of prayer that is cultivated by the Holy Spirit.

> "The Church...is held, as a matter of faith, to be unfailingly holy. This is because Christ, the Son of God, who with the Father and the Spirit is hailed as 'alone holy,' loved the Church as his Bride, giving himself up for her so as to sanctify her; he joined her to himself as his body and endowed her with the gift of the Holy Spirit for the glory of God."[16] The Church, then, is "the holy People of God,"[17] and her members are called "saints."[18] (CCC 823)

The Church is made up of the members of the faithful. But we know these members, like ourselves, are sinful. So how can we say that the Church is Holy? We must remember that the Church, in her very essence, is the Mystical Body of Christ, and like Christ himself is Holy and without sin. The Church's holiness is not defiled by the presence of sinners; rather, her holiness is so complete that it transforms them. The Catholic Church is where sinners are enabled to become saints, a process that continues for those being purified in Purgatory.

> The Church is holy, even though she embraces sinners in her bosom, for she enjoys no other life but the life of grace. If, then, they live her life her members are sanctified.[19]

It is also important to remember that the Church consists of more than just the members of the pilgrim Church on earth and in Purgatory. All of the Church's members who are in Heaven—the saints, or "holy ones"—have already reached the perfection of holiness; they are no longer sinners. They have reached their state of perfection precisely because of the life of grace offered to them by Christ through the ministry of the pilgrim Church.

> The Church is...holy, though having sinners in her midst, because she herself has no other life but the life of grace. If they live her life, her members are sanctified; if they move away from her

life, they fall into sins and disorders that prevent the radiation of her sanctity. This is why she suffers and does penance for those offenses, of which she has the power to free her children through the blood of Christ and the gift of the Holy Spirit.[20] (CCC 827)

Far too often, the sins of individual members of the Church obscure her holiness in the eyes of the world. The Church therefore calls her members to purification, penance, and renewal, so that the perfect holiness she has received from Christ might be made manifest among all the faithful. It is only when we cooperate with God's grace that the light of Christ will shine out in the members of his Mystical Body, drawing all people into the unity of the Church.

In 2000, Pope Bl. John Paul II publicly asked forgiveness for the sins committed by members of the Church throughout history.

> As the Successor of Peter, I asked that "in this year of mercy the Church, strong in the holiness which she receives from her Lord, should kneel before God and implore forgiveness for the past and present sins of her sons and daughters."[21] Today, the First Sunday of Lent, seemed to me the right occasion for the Church, gathered spiritually round the Successor of Peter, to implore divine forgiveness for the sins of all believers. *Let us forgive and ask forgiveness!* [22]

> At the same time, as we confess our sins, *let us forgive the sins committed by others against us.* Countless times in the course of history Christians have suffered hardship, oppression and persecution because of their faith. Just as the victims of such abuses forgave them, so let us forgive as well. The Church today feels and has always felt obliged to *purify her memory* of those sad events from every feeling of rancour or revenge.[23]

PARTICIPATION IN THE HOLINESS OF CHRIST

From the time of St. Peter's first sermon on the day of Pentecost, the Resurrection of Christ has occupied a central place within the Church's teaching. As St. Paul explained to the Corinthians, Christ's Resurrection is "of first importance," because "if Christ has not been raised, your faith is futile and you are still in your sins."[24]

The Resurrection of Jesus is not the only one contained in the Scriptures. Jesus himself raised other people from the dead—for example, Lazarus[25] and the daughter of Jairus.[26] However, the nature of Christ's own Resurrection was completely different from these.

> Christ's Resurrection was not a return to earthly life, as was the case with the raisings from the dead that he had performed before Easter....These actions were miraculous events, but the persons miraculously raised returned...to ordinary earthly life. At some particular moment they would die again. Christ's Resurrection is essentially different. In his risen body he passes from the state of death to another life beyond time and space. (CCC 646)

Apostles on the Day of Pentecost. From the day of Pentecost, Christ's Holy Spirit has empowered the Apostles and their successors to proclaim the saving truth of the Gospel to the entire human race.

After his Resurrection, Jesus was still fully human and fully divine, but his humanity more completely reflected the glory of his divinity. His body bore the scars of the Crucifixion, but it also possessed new properties. No longer limited by time and space, Jesus had not merely come back from the dead, but had entered into his resurrected body—the perfected form of his being meant for dwelling in the eternity of Heaven.

Jesus' Resurrection is the foundation of our belief that Christ will raise us up "at the last day."[27] The "resurrection of the dead," which we profess every Sunday in the Nicene Creed, refers to the bodily resurrection of all the faithful, when our bodies will become like Christ's, sharing in the glory of Heaven. We will not just live again after death, we will be given our own resurrected bodies so that we may dwell with Christ eternally.

We know that this resurrection will ultimately take place only at the end of history, but in a certain way, the Church already shares in Christ's Resurrection. This is because the same Holy Spirit that fills Christ's resurrected body also fills his Mystical Body and each of her members.

> United with Christ by Baptism, believers already truly participate in the heavenly life of the risen Christ, but this life remains "hidden with Christ in God."[28] The Father has already "raised us up with him, and made us sit with him in the heavenly places in Christ Jesus."[29] Nourished with his body in the Eucharist, we already belong to the Body of Christ. When we rise on the last day we "also will appear with him in glory."[30] (CCC 1003)

The Resurrected Christ by Rosa.
The same Holy Spirit that fills Christ's resurrected body also fills his Mystical Body and each of her members.

It is through the Sacraments, particularly the Eucharist, that the pilgrim Church on earth participates in the glory of Heaven. Together with the faithful who have died, we patiently but eagerly await the final unveiling of Christ's glorious kingdom.

THE CHURCH WILL RECEIVE HER PERFECTION IN THE GLORY OF HEAVEN

It was at the very dawn of the creation of man that God saw the future of the Church, the definitive gathering together of God's family, the fulfillment of the plan to bring mankind back in communion with him after the Fall. When viewed in the context of salvation history, we can see the Church as the ultimate expression of God's continuous call to bring man back into communion with him. God had gradually prepared the world for the coming of Christ and the unveiling of the Church.

But the establishment of the Church on earth is still not the end of God's vision for mankind's future. The Church is an echo of things to come, a gathering together of God's people in a way that participates in what is the final goal of our human existence: eternal communion with God in Heaven.

> "The Church...will receive its perfection only in the glory of heaven,"[31] at the time of Christ's glorious return. Until that day, "the Church progresses on her pilgrimage amidst this world's persecutions and God's consolations."[32] Here below she knows that she is in exile far from the Lord, and longs for the full coming of the Kingdom, when she will "be united in glory with her king."[33] The Church, and through her the world, will not be perfected in glory without great trials. Only then will "all the just from the time of Adam, 'from Abel, the just one, to the last of the elect,'...be gathered together in the universal Church in the Father's presence."[34] (CCC 769)

As a result of her divine origin, the Church is *immutable*, meaning she will never change in her essential aspects; *indefectible*, meaning she has no flaw or defect; and *perennial*, meaning she will exist until the end of time.

THE THIRD MARK: THE CHURCH IS CATHOLIC

"All men are called to this catholic unity of the People of God.... And to it, in different ways, belong or are ordered: the Catholic faithful, others who believe in Christ, and finally all mankind, called by God's grace to salvation."[35] (CCC 836)

Today, the word "Catholic" is typically used as a denominational term, much like "Baptist" or "Lutheran," referring to a specific, limited group of Christians. But this common usage communicates exactly the opposite of what the word really means. The term *catholic* comes from the Greek word *katholikos*, meaning "universal" or "pertaining to the whole."

The Church is said to be *Catholic* in two ways. First, the Church is Catholic because she is whole and complete. Christ has united himself to her entirely and has given her the fullness of his holiness. Second, the Church is Catholic because she has received universal authority from Christ to fulfill her universal mission. "All authority in heaven and on earth has been given to me. Go therefore and make disciples of all nations."[36]

From the day of Pentecost, Christ's Holy Spirit has empowered the Apostles and their successors to proclaim the saving truth of the Gospel to the entire human race. All men in every age are invited to become a part of Christ's Mystical Body, which is the universal or "Catholic" Church. No one nation, ethnicity, or language can claim the Church as its alone because, like Christ, the universal Church transcends these human boundaries. "There is no distinction between Jew and Greek; the same Lord is Lord of all and bestows his riches upon all who call upon him."[37]

We encounter evidence of the Church's universality in numerous places in the New Testament, particularly in its references to the many local communities of Christians (in Rome, Corinth, Galatia, etc.). Insofar as these communities preserved Christian unity in their teaching, worship, and leadership, each was appropriately identified as the Church of Christ by the New Testament authors. Today the local Churches throughout the world are called "dioceses."

THE CATHOLICITY OF THE CHURCH

[The Church] is called catholic because it extends over all the world, from one end of the earth to the other; and because it teaches universally and completely one and all the doctrines which ought to come to men's knowledge, concerning things both visible and invisible, heavenly and earthly; and because it brings into subjection to godliness the whole race of mankind, governors and governed, learned and unlearned; and because it universally treats and heals the whole class of sins, which are committed by soul or body, and possesses in itself every form of virtue which is named, both in deeds and words, and in every kind of spiritual gifts.

— St. Cyril of Jerusalem, *Catechetical Lectures*, 18.23

St. Cyril of Jerusalem (ca. 313-386).
St. Cyril was declared a Doctor of the Church by Pope Leo XIII in 1883.

Early Church Fathers Icon. The Church Fathers share these characteristics: orthodoxy in doctrine, holiness, notoriety, and antiquity. The Golden Age of the Church Fathers was 320 to 461. Because of their proximity in time to the teachings of the Apostles, the Fathers' clarification and interpretation of Scripture will always serve as a standard reference point for Church teaching.

"The Church of Christ is really present in all legitimately organized local groups of the faithful, which, in so far as they are united to their pastors, are also quite appropriately called Churches in the New Testament." [38] (CCC 832)

The universal Church is not simply the total of these local churches; each local Church possesses the presence of Christ in his fullness. This means, too, that the Church's universality goes beyond merely "being international." Through her unity with Christ, the Church fills both time and space. Included among her members are all the faithful on earth as well as the faithful departed, who are now being purified in Purgatory or sharing in the glory of Heaven.

Finally, because the universal Church exists locally in a multitude of different nations and cultures, her external expressions of faith and worship often take on a diversity of appearance, according to the culture in which the Church has taken root. This diversity reflects both the Church's universality and her unity of mission.

The rich variety of ecclesiastical disciplines, liturgical rites, and theological and spiritual heritages proper to the local churches "unified in a common effort, shows all the more resplendently the catholicity of the undivided Church." [39] (CCC 835)

WHY DOES THE CHURCH HAVE DIFFERENT RITES?

From the earliest days of the Church, when the followers of Christ spread throughout and beyond the Roman Empire, the Catholic Faith has found expressions and modes of worship that are distinctive to individual cultures. This has resulted in the development of many different forms of worship, which together make up the Church's rich liturgical tradition. Though each rite shares the same apostolic origin and Sacraments, they differ in external form, each preserving its own linguistic, artistic, architectural, spiritual, and cultural heritage.

Included among the many liturgical rites in the Catholic Church are these:

THE ALEXANDRIAN RITE: This rite, sometimes called the Coptic Rite, originated in Egypt and includes the Ethiopian Rite. Its liturgical languages are Coptic, Arabic, and Ge'ez.

THE ANTIOCHENE RITE: Named for Antioch in ancient Syria, it developed under the influence of the Church of Jerusalem. Originating from the Antiochene Rite are Syro-Malankara, Maronite, and Syrian Catholics. Its liturgical languages are Syriac (a dialect of Aramaic) and Arabic.

THE ARMENIAN RITE: This rite traces its origins back to the early Fathers of the Church and uses classical Armenian as its liturgical language.

THE BYZANTINE RITE: Originating in the ancient imperial see of Constantinople (Byzantium), it is the most widely used Eastern liturgical form. Catholic Churches using liturgies originating from the Byzantine Rite include the Albanian, Belarussian, Bulgarian, Greek, Hungarian, Italo-Albanian, Melkite, Romanian, Russian, Ruthenian, Slovak, and Ukrainian Catholic Churches.

THE CHALDEAN (OR EAST SYRIAN) RITE: The Chaldean Rite is concentrated in the Middle East and India. It includes the Chaldean Catholic and Syro-Malabar Catholic Churches, and its liturgical languages are classical Syriac, Arabic, and Malayalam.[40]

THE TWENTY-ONE RITES OF THE CATHOLIC CHURCH

ROMAN	ALEXANDRIAN	ANTIOCHENE	ARMENIAN	BYZANTINE	CHALDEAN
Latin	Coptic Ethiopian	Malankar Maronite Syrian	Armenian	Albanian Belarusian Bulgarian Greek Greek-Melkite Hungarian Italo-Albanian Romanian Russian Ruthenian Slovak Ukrainian	Chaldean Malabar

Appearance While the Apostles Are at Table by Duccio.
"Then he said to them, 'These are my words which I spoke to you, while I was still with you, that everything written about me in the law of Moses and the prophets and the psalms must be fulfilled.' Then he opened their minds to understand the scriptures, and said to them, 'Thus it is written, that the Christ should suffer and on the third day rise from the dead, and that repentance and forgiveness of sins should be preached in his name to all nations, beginning from Jerusalem.'" (Lk 24:44-47)

THE FOURTH MARK: THE CHURCH IS APOSTOLIC

The fourth mark of the Church is that she is *Apostolic*. This mark relates primarily to Christ's selection of the Twelve Apostles as the foundation of his Church. He chose these twelve men to be witnesses to his Resurrection, sent out as his ambassadors to the entire world. Like the twelve ministers who assisted Solomon, the son of David, in ruling the Kingdom of Israel, the Twelve Apostles were given the task of assisting Christ, the new son of David, in ruling his kingdom. They were appointed as symbolic rulers of the Twelve Tribes of Israel, and were entrusted with Christ's own authority to teach, sanctify, and govern his Church.

> "In order that the mission entrusted to them might be continued after their death, [the apostles] consigned, by will and testament, as it were, to their immediate collaborators the duty of completing and consolidating the work they had begun, urging them to tend to the whole flock, in which the Holy Spirit had appointed them to shepherd the Church of God. They accordingly designated such men and then made the ruling that likewise on their death other proven men should take over their ministry."[41] (CCC 861)

The Church is called Apostolic because she is founded on the Apostles in a threefold sense:[42]

✤ **Apostolic Foundation.** She was built and remains on the foundation of the Apostles.

✤ **Apostolic Faith.** She guards and transmits, with the help of the Holy Spirit who dwells in her, the teachings of the Apostles.

✤ **Apostolic Succession.** She continues being taught, sanctified, and directed by the Apostles in the persons of their successors in the pastoral ministry: the college of bishops, presided over by St. Peter's successor, the Pope.

Pope Benedict XVI Ordains a New Bishop.
During the installation of a bishop, the ritual of laying on of hands reflects the direct linkage with the Apostles.

The Church goes back in a living continuity to the Twelve whom Christ established as shepherds of his flock. Thus, it is only in the body of shepherds, who received their mission and powers from the Apostles through an uninterrupted chain of lawful succession, that the true Church of Jesus Christ can be found.

In this manner, the Church's Apostolic nature is manifested through the Apostles' successors, the bishops of the Church, whose office can be traced back to the Twelve. During the installation of a bishop, the ritual of laying on of hands reflects this direct linkage with the Apostles. Each bishop has been touched by his predecessor in an unbroken line all the way back to the Apostles. Although they are not "eyewitnesses" in the same sense as the Apostles, the bishops, united with the successor of St. Peter, the Pope, are called to carry on the Apostles' mission of proclaiming the Gospel and shepherding Christ's flock on earth.

The Church teaches that "the bishops have by divine institution taken the place of the apostles as pastors of the Church, in such wise that whoever listens to them is listening to Christ and whoever despises them despises Christ and him who sent Christ."[43] (CCC 862)

Aided by the Holy Spirit, the Pope and the bishops are responsible for preserving and proclaiming the teaching of Christ that has been passed down from the Apostles in Scripture and in the Church's Sacred Tradition.

CONCLUSION

These four marks of the Church—One, Holy, Catholic, and Apostolic—belong to the Catholic Church alone. No other church can validly make this claim. The divisions within Christianity are wounds to unity of the Church founded by Christ. All Christians of good will must pray and work to heal the unity of the Church in keeping with Christ's own prayer "that they may all be one; even as thou, Father, art in me, and I in thee, that they also may be in us, so that the world may believe that thou hast sent me."[44]

> This Church constituted and organized as a society in the present world, subsists in the Catholic Church, which is governed by the successor of Peter and by the bishops in communion with him. Nevertheless, many elements of sanctification and of truth are found outside her visible confines. Since these are gifts belonging to the Church of Christ, they are forces impelling towards Catholic unity.[45]

The Catholic Church is the one and only true Church. The fullness of the means of salvation are to be found only within her, and in her every single distinctive mark of the true Church is found in their fullest degree. This Catholic Church is united to the Pope. As St. Ambrose wrote, "Where Peter is, there is the Church; and where the Church is, not death but eternal life reigns." Where Peter and the Church are, there Christ is; and he is salvation, the only way.[46]

Crucifixion by Titian.
The Church is an echo of things to come, a gathering together of God's people in a way that
participates in what is the final goal of our human existence: eternal communion
with God in Heaven.

SUPPLEMENTARY READING

1. The Apostolicity of the Church

The *Catechism of the Catholic Church*, in explaining how the Church is apostolic—founded on the Apostles—sees three meanings in this expression. First, "she was and remains built on 'the foundation of the Apostles' (Eph 2:20), the witnesses chosen and sent on mission by Christ himself."

The second sense in which the Church is apostolic, as the Catechism points out, is that "with the help of the Spirit dwelling in her, the Church keeps and hands on the teaching, the 'good deposit,' the salutary words she has heard from the Apostles."…This faith remains unchanged and it is essential for the Church that it remain unchanged.

Lastly, the Church is apostolic in the sense that she "continues to be taught, sanctified and guided by the Apostles until Christ's return, through their successors in pastoral office: the college of Bishops assisted by priests, in union with the Successor of Peter, the Church's supreme pastor." Succession to the Apostles in the pastoral mission necessarily entails the sacrament of Holy Orders, that is, the uninterrupted sequence, from the very beginning, of valid episcopal ordinations. This succession is essential for the Church to exist in a proper and full sense.

— Pope Bl. John Paul II, *Ecclesia de Eucharistia*, 27-28

2. The Church Brings the Light of Christ to All Men

Christ is the Light of nations. Because this is so, this Sacred Synod gathered together in the Holy Spirit eagerly desires, by proclaiming the Gospel to every creature, to bring the light of Christ to all men, a light brightly visible on the countenance of the Church. Since the Church is in Christ like a sacrament or as a sign and instrument both of a very closely knit union with God and of the unity of the whole human race, it desires now to unfold more fully to the faithful of the Church and to the whole world its own inner nature and universal mission. This it intends to do following faithfully the teaching of previous councils. The present-day conditions of the world add greater urgency to this work of the Church so that all men, joined more closely today by various social, technical and cultural ties, might also attain fuller unity in Christ.

— *Lumen Gentium*, 1

3. The Church as Communion

The Church of Christ, which we profess in the Creed to be one, holy, catholic and apostolic, is the universal Church, that is, the worldwide community of the disciples of the Lord, which is present and active amid the particular characteristics and the diversity of persons, groups, times and places. Among these manifold particular expressions of the saving presence of the one Church of Christ, there are to be found, from the times of the Apostles on, those entities which are in themselves Churches, because, although they are particular, the universal Church becomes present in them with all its essential elements. They are therefore constituted "after the model of the universal Church," and each of them is "a portion of the People of God entrusted to a bishop to be guided by him with the assistance of his clergy."

The universal Church is therefore the Body of the Churches. Hence it is possible to apply the concept of communion in analogous fashion to the union existing among particular Churches, and to see the universal Church as a Communion of Churches. Sometimes, however, the idea of a "communion of particular Churches" is presented in such a way as to weaken the concept of the unity of the Church at the visible and institutional level. Thus it is asserted that every particular Church is a subject complete in itself, and that the universal Church is the result of a reciprocal recognition on the part of the particular Churches. This ecclesiological unilateralism, which impoverishes not only the concept of the universal Church but also that of the particular Church, betrays an insufficient understanding of the concept of communion. As history shows, when a particular Church has sought to become self-sufficient,

SUPPLEMENTARY READING Continued

and has weakened its real communion with the universal Church and with its living and visible centre, its internal unity suffers too, and it finds itself in danger of losing its own freedom in the face of the various forces of slavery and exploitation.

— Congregation for the Doctrine of the Faith, *On Some Aspects of the Church Understood as Communion*, 7-8

4. Worthy Reception of the Eucharist

The celebration of the Eucharist, however, cannot be the starting-point for communion; it presupposes that communion already exists, a communion which it seeks to consolidate and bring to perfection. The sacrament is an expression of this bond of communion both in its *invisible* dimension, which, in Christ and through the working of the Holy Spirit, unites us to the Father and among ourselves, and in its *visible* dimension, which entails communion in the teaching of the Apostles, in the sacraments and in the Church's hierarchical order. The profound relationship between the invisible and the visible elements of ecclesial communion is constitutive of the Church as the sacrament of salvation.[47] Only in this context can there be a legitimate celebration of the Eucharist and true participation in it. Consequently it is an intrinsic requirement of the Eucharist that it should be celebrated in communion, and specifically maintaining the various bonds of that communion intact.

Invisible communion, though by its nature always growing, presupposes the life of grace, by which we become "partakers of the divine nature" (2 Pt 1: 4), and the practice of the virtues of faith, hope and love. Only in this way do we have true communion with the Father, the Son and the Holy Spirit. Nor is faith sufficient; we must persevere in sanctifying grace and love, remaining within the Church "bodily" as well as "in our heart";[48] what is required, in the words of Saint Paul, is "faith working through love" (Gal 5: 6).

Keeping these invisible bonds intact is a specific moral duty incumbent upon Christians who wish to participate fully in the Eucharist by receiving the body and blood of Christ. The Apostle Paul appeals to this duty when he warns: "Let a man examine himself, and so eat of the bread and drink of the cup"(1 Cor 11: 28). Saint John Chrysostom, with his stirring eloquence, exhorted the faithful: "I too raise my voice, I beseech, beg and implore that no one draw near to this sacred table with a sullied and corrupt conscience. Such an act, in fact, can never be called 'communion,' not even were we to touch the Lord's body a thousand times over, but 'condemnation,' 'torment' and 'increase of punishment.'"[49]

Along these same lines, the *Catechism of the Catholic Church* rightly stipulates that "anyone conscious of a grave sin must receive the sacrament of Reconciliation before coming to communion."[50] I therefore desire to reaffirm that in the Church there remains in force, now and in the future, the rule by which the Council of Trent gave concrete expression to the Apostle Paul's stern warning when it affirmed that, in order to receive the Eucharist in a worthy manner, "one must first confess one's sins, when one is aware of mortal sin."[51]

— Pope Bl. John Paul II, *Ecclesia de Eucharistia*, 35-36

5. The Catholic Church and Other Christian Churches

The Catholic faithful *are required to profess* that there is an historical continuity—rooted in the apostolic succession[52]—between the Church founded by Christ and the Catholic Church: "This is the single Church of Christ...which our Saviour, after his resurrection, entrusted to Peter's pastoral care (cf. Jn 21: 17), commissioning him and the other Apostles to extend and rule her (cf. Mt 28: 18ff.), erected for all ages as 'the pillar and mainstay of the truth' (1 Tm 3: 15). This Church, constituted and organized as a society in the present world, subsists in [*subsistit in*] the Catholic Church, governed by the Successor of Peter and by the Bishops in communion with him."[53] With the expression *subsistit in*, the Second Vatican Council sought to harmonize two doctrinal statements: on the one hand, that the Church of Christ, despite the divisions which exist

SUPPLEMENTARY READING Continued

among Christians, continues to exist fully only in the Catholic Church, and on the other hand, that "outside of her structure, many elements can be found of sanctification and truth,"[54] that is, in those Churches and ecclesial communities which are not yet in full communion with the Catholic Church.[55] But with respect to these, it needs to be stated that "they derive their efficacy from the very fullness of grace and truth entrusted to the Catholic Church."[56]

Therefore, there exists a single Church of Christ, which subsists in the Catholic Church, governed by the Successor of Peter and by the Bishops in communion with him.[57] The Churches which, while not existing in perfect communion with the Catholic Church, remain united to her by means of the closest bonds, that is, by apostolic succession and a valid Eucharist, are true particular Churches.[58] Therefore, the Church of Christ is present and operative also in these Churches, even though they lack full communion with the Catholic Church, since they do not accept the Catholic doctrine of the Primacy, which, according to the will of God, the Bishop of Rome objectively has and exercises over the entire Church.[59]

On the other hand, the ecclesial communities which have not preserved the valid Episcopate and the genuine and integral substance of the Eucharistic mystery,[60] are not Churches in the proper sense; however, those who are baptized in these communities are, by Baptism, incorporated in Christ and thus are in a certain communion, albeit imperfect, with the Church.[61] Baptism in fact tends per se toward the full development of life in Christ, through the integral profession of faith, the Eucharist, and full communion in the Church.[62]

— Congregation for the Doctrine of the Faith, *Dominus Iesus*, 16-17

6. Papal Succession

It is within the power of all, therefore, in every Church, who may wish to see the truth, to contemplate clearly the tradition of the apostles manifested throughout the whole world; and we are in a position to reckon up those who were by the apostles instituted bishops in the Churches, and [to demonstrate] the succession of these men to our own times.

The blessed apostles [**Peter and Paul**], then, having founded and built up the Church, committed into the hands of **Linus** the office of the episcopate. Of this Linus, Paul makes mention in the Epistles to Timothy. To him succeeded **Anacletus**; and after him, in the third place from the apostles, **Clement** was allotted the bishopric. This man, as he had seen the blessed apostles, and had been conversant with them, might be said to have the preaching of the apostles still echoing [in his ears], and their traditions before his eyes. Nor was he alone [in this], for there were many still remaining who had received instructions from the apostles....To this Clement there succeeded **Evaristus**. **Alexander** followed Evaristus; then, sixth from the apostles, **Sixtus** was appointed; after him, **Telephorus**, who was gloriously martyred; then **Hyginus**; after him, **Pius**; then after him, **Anicetus**. **Soter** having succeeded Anicetus, **Eleutherius** does now, in the twelfth place from the apostles, hold the inheritance of the episcopate. In this order, and by this succession, the ecclesiastical tradition from the apostles, and the preaching of the truth, have come down to us. And this is most abundant proof that there is one and the same vivifying faith, which has been preserved in the Church from the apostles until now, and handed down in truth.

— St. Irenæus of Lyons, *Against the Heresies*, 3.3.1, 3

VOCABULARY

APOSTASY
The total repudiation of the Christian Faith. This is forbidden by the First Commandment and is against the theological virtue of faith.

APOSTLE
From the Greek for "one sent forth." Refers to the Twelve chosen by Jesus during the course of his public ministry to be his closest followers, as well as Sts. Matthias, Paul of Tarsus, Barnabas, and the enlighteners of whole nations.

APOSTOLIC
The fourth mark of the Church, indicating that the Church was founded by Christ and given to the Apostles. The Church is Apostolic in three ways. It has an *Apostolic foundation*, having been built and remaining on the foundation of the Apostles; it has *Apostolic faith*, because she guards and transmits the teachings of the Apostles with the help of the Holy Spirit who dwells in her; and it has an *Apostolic succession*, because she continues to be taught, sanctified, and directed by the Apostles in the persons of their successors in the pastoral ministry: the College of Bishops, presided over by St. Peter's successor, the Pope.

APOLLINARIANISM
A fourth-century heresy advanced by Apollinaris, himself a fourth-century opponent of Arianism, which held that Christ had only a divine mind and will, not a human mind and will, and thus was not truly man.

ARIANISM
A fourth-century heresy claiming that Jesus Christ was neither God nor equal to the Father, only that he was sent by the Father and only did the will of the Father; it also taught that Christ was an exceptional creature and was raised to the level of "Son of God" because of his heroic fidelity to the Father's will and his sublime holiness.

ATHANASIAN CREED
An enumeration of Christian beliefs authored by St. Athanasius, a key fourth-century opponent of the Arian heresy.

CANON LAW
The official internal law of the Catholic Church; the Code of Canon Law. Currently, there are two bodies of canon law: one for the Latin Rite of the Church and one for the Eastern Catholic Churches.

CATHOLIC CHURCH
The Church established by Christ on the foundation of the Apostles, possessing the fullness of the means of salvation which he has willed; the pilgrim Church on earth, in which the One, Holy, Catholic, and Apostolic Church subsists. Literally, "universal," in the sense of "according to the whole." The Church is Catholic in the dual sense that it (a) possesses the fullness of the means of salvation and (b) has been sent by Christ to the whole human race.

DEPOSIT OF FAITH
The revealed truths contained in Sacred Scripture and Sacred Tradition that are entrusted to the care of the Church.

DIOCESE
A portion of the People of God that is entrusted to a bishop to be nurtured by him, with the cooperation of his priests, in such a way that, remaining close to its pastor the bishop and gathered by him through the Gospel and the Eucharist in the Holy Spirit, it constitutes a particular Church. In this Church, the One, Holy, Catholic, and Apostolic Church of Christ truly exists and functions (cf. CIC, 369).

ECUMENICAL
From the Greek word *oikoumene*, meaning "the whole inhabited world." In one sense, the term refers to the twenty-one councils of the world's bishops that have been held since the fourth century to discuss important issues affecting the whole Church. In another sense, it refers to Ecumenism.

ECUMENISM
The efforts to reunite all Christians on earth and to cooperate among Christian faith traditions in achieving common goals.

VOCABULARY Continued

GNOSTICISM

An ancient heresy that taught, among other things, that salvation came from obtaining secret experiential knowledge and that the material world was evil, a corruption of spirit. Jesus was the Redeemer, but he was neither true God nor true man; he was an apparition, a lesser divine being who inhabited a human body; he neither had a body nor died on the Cross.

HERESY

The obstinate denial by a baptized person of some truth that must be believed with divine faith.

HOLY SEE

The diocese of the Pope, Bishop of Rome; also, a term used to refer to the central administration of the worldwide Catholic Church.

IMMUTABLE

Will never change in its essential aspects; an attribute of the Catholic Church as a result of its divine origin.

INDEFECTIBLE

Having no flaw or defect; an attribute of the Catholic Church as a result of its divine origin.

INDULGENCE

The remission before God of the temporal punishment due to sin whose guilt has already been forgiven, available to the faithful under certain conditions prescribed by the Church. The prescribed conditions usually involve particular prayers, devotions, pilgrimages, timely reception of the Sacraments, acts of charity, or some combination thereof, all done with the proper disposition. "Temporal punishment due to sin" refers to time spent after death in Purgatory, a place of purification for those who are saved before entering Heaven; in life, when sins are sacramentally forgiven, the temporal punishment remains. A partial indulgence removes part of this punishment, while a plenary indulgence removes all the punishment.

LOGOS

In the New Testament, a reference to Jesus Christ, the Son of God, the Word made flesh; it is a Greek term meaning *word*. In pagan neo-Platonic thought, the *logos* was an elevated being, created by but inferior to the Supreme Being; this etymology led some early Christians to doubt the true divinity of Christ and fall into heresy.

MARKS OF THE CHURCH

The four attributes of the Church mentioned in the Nicene Creed ("I believe in *One*, *Holy*, *Catholic*, and *Apostolic* Church").

MONOPHYSITISM

A heresy arising in the fifth century that claimed there is only one nature in the Person of Christ, his human nature having been incorporated into his divine nature.

NEO-PLATONISM

A pagan school of thought based upon the ideas of the Greek philosopher Plato that held the existence of a Supreme Being, "the One," who creates through an emanation of lesser beings, one of which is the *logos*.

NESTORIANISM

A heresy arising in the fourth century advanced by Nestorius, who taught Christ was the unity of a divine Person and a human person—in other words, Jesus was two persons united in one nature rather than one Person with both a divine nature and a human nature. He opposed the title *Theotokos* (Bearer of God) for Mary, teaching that Mary was the Mother of Christ, but not of God.

ORTHODOXY, EASTERN

The various Churches of the Eastern Roman (Byzantine) Empire and other associated lands that broke from communion with the Catholic Church in the eleventh century; they retain many elements of the Catholic Church, including apostolic succession and the Seven Sacraments.

VOCABULARY Continued

PERENNIAL
Will exist until the end of time; an attribute of the Catholic Church as a result of its divine origin.

PROTESTANTISM
The general name given to any of the Christian denominations that broke from the Catholic Church during the sixteenth-century Reformation and to the splinter churches from these communities; today these include the Lutherans, Anglicans (Episcopalians), Methodists, Presbyterians, Baptists, and many others. More generally, the term refers to any Western Christian community not in union with the Catholic Church.

REFORMATION
An interrelated series of schisms from the Catholic Church that took place from 1517 to 1648. These include the breaking away of Martin Luther and other reformers in the sixteenth century as well as the schism of King Henry VIII.

SCHISM
A breach of the unity of the visible Church; the refusal to submit to the Pope or be united with the Church.

SCHISMATIC
An individual who is part of an organized group that breaks away from the unity of the Catholic Church and thus creates a schism.

SEPARATED BRETHREN
Persons who were born into schismatic communities, including Protestant communities and Orthodox Churches, and thus cannot be considered guilty *prima facie* of the sin of separation because it is often through no fault of their own that they remain unaware of the truth of the Catholic Faith.

THEOLOGICAL VIRTUES
The virtues of faith, hope, and love (charity).

THEOTOKOS
Greek for "Bearer of God." This title of the Blessed Virgin Mary was confirmed at the Council of Ephesus AD 431; it acknowledges Jesus Christ is true God and true man.

UNICITY
Uniqueness; the term is sometimes used to describe the Church because it is the only Church founded by Christ.

The Black Madonna of Czestochowa, Poland.

The Black Madonna icon is Poland's holiest relic and one of the country's national symbols. Several legends surround the origins of the icon and the cause of the facial scars. One legend is that the icon was painted by St. Luke.

The Virgin Mary is shown as the *Hodegetria* (*She Who Shows the Way*). *Hodegetria* is an iconographic depiction of the *Theotokos* holding the Child Jesus at her side while pointing to Him as the source of salvation for mankind.

STUDY QUESTIONS

1. Name the four marks of the Church. In what important statement of belief, which is prayed during Sunday Mass, are these marks mentioned?

2. Explain: What does it mean to say the Church is *One*?

3. Cite the three ways in which the Mystical Body of Christ bears witness to the unity of the Church.

4. Re-read the sidebar on Pope St. Leo the Great. What aspects of his story show how the Church of his day recognized the papacy and its teaching authority?

5. Name the three primary types of "wounds" to unity. Which, according to the text, is the most tragic of the three?

6. Give the two major examples of schism in the Church and the approximate period in which they occurred.

7. What are some of the "elements of sanctification and truth" that the Church recognizes within the Protestant and Orthodox Churches?

8. Describe the basic beliefs of Gnosticism. What belief system today bears resemblance to Gnosticism?

9. Explain why the followers of Arianism did not believe in the full divinity of Jesus Christ.

10. Why was the Arian heresy a particularly grave threat to the unity of the Church?

11. Apollinaris was an ardent opponent of the Arian heresy. How did he manage to slip into heresy himself?

12. What is the meaning of *Theotokos*, and to whom does it apply?

13. Why did Nestorius disagree with the title *Theotokos*? Explain.

14. List four of the major Protestant "reformers" and the roles they each played in the schisms from the Catholic Church.

15. What sociopolitical issues helped spur the Reformation?

16. Name five saints who led reforms within the Catholic Church in the years after the Reformation.

17. What is *ecumenism*?

18. What is the cause of divisions within Christianity? What can we do to build "unity of life" and move toward greater Christian unity?

19. What must all Christians do for the sake of unity?

20. How can we say that the Church is Holy even though it is made up of sinful members?

21. What great public act of humility did Pope Bl. John Paul II make in the year 2000?

22. Explain: Christians participate in the holiness of Christ.

23. When will the Church be perfected?

24. What four attributes or marks does the Church have because of her divine origin?

25. Define *Catholic* in the general sense. Why does this word apply to the Church?

26. Describe the threefold sense in which the Church is founded on the Apostles.

PRACTICAL EXERCISE

Perform an Internet search using topics such as "Catholic-Anglican Dialogue," "Catholic-Orthodox Dialogue," "Catholic-Lutheran Dialogue," "Catholic-Jewish Dialogue," and "Catholic-Muslim Dialogue." Choose two of these topics and write a brief summary of what you have learned from your sources: What kind of dialogue has taken place, and at what level? What are the topics they have discussed or will discuss? What progress do those involved feel has been made up to this time?

FROM THE CATECHISM

812   Only faith can recognize that the Church possesses these properties from her divine source. But their historical manifestations are signs that also speak clearly to human reason. As the First Vatican Council noted, the "Church herself, with her marvelous propagation, eminent holiness, and inexhaustible fruitfulness in everything good, her catholic unity and invincible stability, is a great and perpetual motive of credibility and an irrefutable witness of her divine mission."[63]

818   "However, one cannot charge with the sin of the separation those who at present are born into these communities [that resulted from such separation] and in them are brought up in the faith of Christ, and the Catholic Church accepts them with respect and affection as brothers.... All who have been justified by faith in Baptism are incorporated into Christ; they therefore have a right to be called Christians, and with good reason are accepted as brothers in the Lord by the children of the Catholic Church."[64]

819   "Furthermore, many elements of sanctification and of truth"[65] are found outside the visible confines of the Catholic Church: "the written Word of God; the life of grace; faith, hope, and charity, with the other interior gifts of the Holy Spirit, as well as visible elements."[66] Christ's Spirit uses these Churches and ecclesial communities as means of salvation, whose power derives from the fullness of grace and truth that Christ has entrusted to the Catholic Church. All these blessings come from Christ and lead to him,[67] and are in themselves calls to "Catholic unity."[68]

822   Concern for achieving unity "involves the whole Church, faithful and clergy alike."[69] But we must realize "that this holy objective—the reconciliation of all Christians in the unity of the one and only Church of Christ—transcends human powers and gifts." That is why we place all our hope "in the prayer of Christ for the Church, in the love of the Father for us, and in the power of the Holy Spirit."[70]

825   "The Church on earth is endowed already with a sanctity that is real though imperfect."[71] In her members perfect holiness is something yet to be acquired: "Strengthened by so many and such great means of salvation, all the faithful, whatever their condition or state—though each in his own way—are called by the Lord to that perfection of sanctity by which the Father himself is perfect."[72]

830   The word "catholic" means "universal," in the sense of "according to the totality" or "in keeping with the whole." The Church is catholic in a double sense:

First, the Church is catholic because Christ is present in her. "Where there is Christ Jesus, there is the Catholic Church."[73] In her subsists the fullness of Christ's body united with its head; this implies that she receives from him "the fullness of the means of salvation"[74] which he has willed: correct and complete confession of faith, full sacramental life, and ordained ministry in apostolic succession. The Church was, in this fundamental sense, catholic on the day of Pentecost[75] and will always be so until the day of the Parousia.

831   Secondly, the Church is catholic because she has been sent out by Christ on a mission to the whole of the human race:[76]

All men are called to belong to the new People of God. This People, therefore, while remaining one and only one, is to be spread throughout the whole world and to all ages in order that the design of God's will may be fulfilled: he made human nature one in the beginning and has decreed that all his children who were scattered should be finally gathered together as one....The character of universality which adorns the People of God is a gift from the Lord himself whereby the Catholic Church ceaselessly and efficaciously seeks for the return of all humanity and all its goods, under Christ the Head in the unity of his Spirit.[77]

834   Particular Churches are fully catholic through their communion with one of them, the Church of Rome "which presides in charity."[78] "For with this church, by reason of its pre-eminence, the whole Church, that is the faithful everywhere, must necessarily be in accord."[79] Indeed, "from the incarnate Word's descent to us, all Christian churches everywhere have held and hold the great Church that is here [at Rome] to be their only basis and foundation since, according to the Savior's promise, the gates of hell have never prevailed against her."[80]

ENDNOTES - CHAPTER FIVE

1. CCC 771.
2. *LG* 8.
3. Cf. DS 2888.
4. Jn 10:16.
5. Cf. CCC 815
6. *DH* 1.
7. Pope Bl. John Paul II, *L'Osservatore Romano*, n. 29, July 19, 1995.
8. *UR* 3 § 1.
9. Cf. CIC, can. 751.
10. Origen, *Hom. in Ezech.* 9, 1: PG 13, 732.
11. Cf. Lk 10:16.
12. *LG* 8 § 2.
13. *UR* 3 § 5.
14. *UR* 11.
15. Jn 17:21; cf. Heb 7:25.
16. *LG* 39; cf. Eph 5:25-26.
17. *LG* 12.
18. Acts 9:13; 1 Cor 6:1; 16:1.
19. Paul VI, *The Creed of the People of God*, no. 19; cf. CCC 823-829.
20. Paul VI, *CPG* § 19.
21. *Incarnationis Mysterium*, 11.
22. Homily of the Holy Father, March 12, 2000, n. 3.
23. Ibid., n. 4.
24. 1 Cor 15:17.
25. Jn 11:1-44.
26. Lk 8:40-59.
27. Jn 6:54.
28. Col 3:3; cf. Phil 3:20.
29. Eph 2:6.
30. Col 3:4.
31. *LG* 48.
32. St. Augustine, *De civ. Dei*, 18, 51: PL 41, 614; cf. *LG* 8.
33. *LG* 5; cf. 6; 2 Cor 5:6.
34. *LG* 2.
35. *LG* 13.
36. Mt 28:18-19.
37. Rom 10:12.
38. *LG* 26.
39. *LG* 23.
40. *The Catholic Almanac*.
41. *LG* 20; cf. Acts 20:28; St. Clement of Rome, *Ad Cor.* 42, 44: PG 1, 291-300.
42. Cf. CCC 857.

43. *LG* 20 § 2.
44. Jn 17:21.
45. *LG* 8.
46. Cf. St Ambrose, *In Ps. 12 Enarratio*, 40. 30.
47. Cf. Congregation for the Doctrine of the Faith, Letter to the Bishops of the Catholic Church on Some Aspects of the Church Understood as Communion *Communionis Notio* (28 May 1992), 4: AAS 85 (1993), 839-840.
48. *LG* 14.
49. *Homiliæ in Isaiam*, 6, 3: PG 56, 139.
50. No. 1385; cf. CIC, can. 916; *Code of Canons of the Eastern Churches*, can. 711.
51. Address to the Members of the Sacred Apostolic Penitentiary and the Penitentiaries of the Patriarchal Basilicas of Rome (30 January 1981): AAS 73 (1981), 203; cf. Ecumenical Council of Trent, Sess. XIII, *Decretum de ss. Eucharistia*, Chapter 7 and Canon 11: DS 1647, 1661.
52. LG 20; cf. also St. Irenaeus, *Adversus hæreses*, III, 3, 1-3: SC 211, 20-44; St. Cyprian, *Epist.* 33, 1: CCSL 3B, 164-165; St. Augustine, *Contra adver. legis et prophet.*, 1, 20, 39: CCSL 49, 70.
53. *LG* 8.
54. Ibid.; cf. Bl. John Paul II, Encyclical Letter *Ut Unum Sint*, 13; cf. also *LG* 15, *UR* 3.
55. The interpretation of those who would derive from the formula *subsistit in* the thesis that the one Church of Christ could subsist also in non-Catholic Churches and ecclesial communities is therefore contrary to the authentic meaning of *Lumen Gentium*. "The Council instead chose the word *subsistit* precisely to clarify that there exists only one 'subsistence' of the true Church, while outside her visible structure there only exist *elementa Ecclesiae*, which—being elements of that same Church—tend and lead toward the Catholic Church" (Congregation for the Doctrine of the Faith, Notification on the Book "Church: Charism and Power" by Father Leonardo Boff: AAS 77 [1985], 756-762).

56. *UR* 3.
57. Cf. Congregation for the Doctrine of the Faith, Declaration *Mysterium Ecclesiæ*, 1: AAS 65 (1973), 396-398.
58. *UR* 14, 15; Congregation for the Doctrine of the Faith, Letter *Communionis notio*, 17: AAS 85 (1993), 848.
59. Cf. First Vatican Council, Constitution Pastor *Æternus*: DS 3053-3064; *LG* 22.
60. Cf. *UR* 22.
61. Cf. ibid., 3.
62. Cf. ibid., 22.
63. Vatican Council I, *Dei Filius* 3: DS 3013.
64. *UR* 3 § 1.
65. *LG* 8 § 2.
66. *UR* 3 § 2; cf. *LG* 15.
67. Cf. *UR* 3.
68. Cf. *LG* 8.
69. *UR* 5.
70. *UR* 22 § 2.
71. *LG* 48 § 3.
72. *LG* 11 § 3.
73. St. Ignatius of Antioch, *Ad Smyrn.* 8, 2: Apostolic Fathers, II/2, 311.
74. *UR* 3; *AG* 6; Eph 1:22-23.
75. Cf. *AG* 4.
76. Cf. Mt 28:19.
77. *LG* 13 §§ 1-2; cf. Jn 11:52.
78. St. Ignatius of Antioch, *Ad Rom.* 1, 1: Apostolic Fathers, II/2, 192; cf. *LG* 13.
79. St. Irenæus, *Adv. hæres.* 3, 3, 2: PG 7/1, 849; cf. Vatican Council I: DS 3057.
80. St. Maximus the Confessor, *Opuscula Theo.*: PG 91: 137-140.

The Church

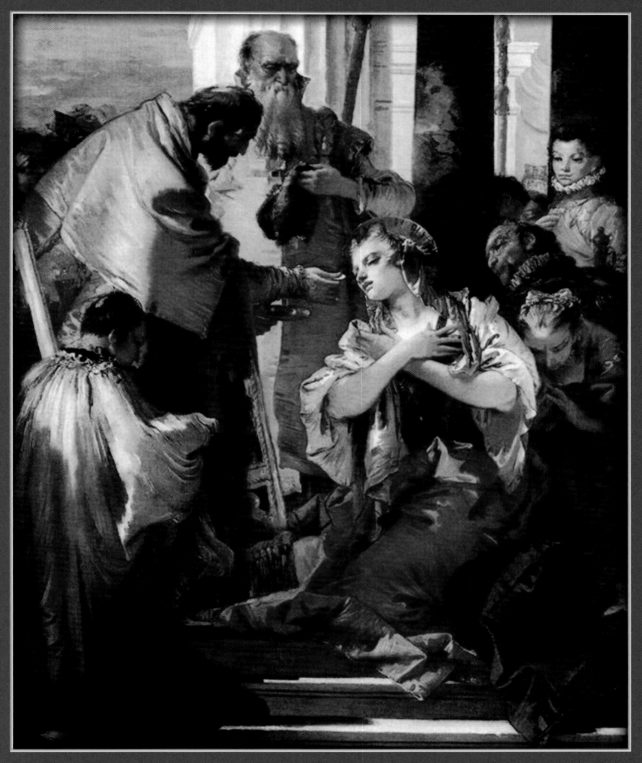

The Church in the Life of the Faithful

The pilgrim Church on earth is a visible society, structured and given order by Christ for the purpose of extending the Kingdom of God over the entire world.

The Church

CHAPTER 6

The Church in the Life of the Faithful

The faith of the faithful is the faith of the Church, received from the apostles. Faith is a treasure of life which is enriched by being shared. (CCC 949)

e have already learned about the history and the foundation of the Church as well as those first Apostles who helped establish the Church in her infancy and began the spread of the Word of God. We have also learned that the Church is Christ's Mystical Body. Through the Sacrament of Baptism, all of the faithful become a part of the Church—true members of God's family and adopted sons and daughters of the Father.

"See what love the Father has given us," St. John writes in his Gospel, "that we should be called children of God; and so we are."[1]

"In virtue of their rebirth in Christ there exists among all the Christian faithful a true equality with regard to dignity and the activity whereby all cooperate in the building up of the Body of Christ in accord with each one's own condition and function."[2] (CCC 872)

God loves each of us so much that he sent his Son, Jesus Christ, to redeem us. Because each person is uniquely created in the image and likeness of God, every member of the Church is given *charisms*, special

graces and gifts from the Holy Spirit that enable the People of God to build up the Body of Christ. These different charisms are given to each individual in keeping with the circumstances of his or her particular state of life. In this chapter, we will take a look at some of the different vocations and states of life within the Church and examine the many and various ways in which God calls each person to live in communion with him.

To live as a Christian in the world has never been easy. Concupiscence, our human inclination to sin that is a result of Original Sin, often clouds our discernment, distorts our intellect, and weakens our will. If we are inattentive or lukewarm about the Faith, we inevitably will find ourselves led astray by our tendency to sin. However, if we embrace the Faith and conscientiously devote ourselves to seeking personal holiness and be of service to God and neighbor, we will find ourselves strengthened against temptation and drawing ever closer in our relationship to Christ, our communion with God.

That is the lifelong challenge and goal that faces every Christian in living as a member of the Church: to know, love, and serve God in this life so that we may live happily forever with him in the next life.

Christ Carrying the Cross by Morales. To live as a Christian in the world has never been easy.

The Baptism of Christ (detail) by Corot.
Along with the Eucharist and Confirmation, Baptism is one of the three Sacraments of Initiation, and a person is not fully initiated as a member of the Church until all three Sacraments have been received.

IN THIS CHAPTER, WE WILL ADDRESS SEVERAL QUESTIONS:

✤ What is the *common priesthood of the faithful*?

✤ What is the role of the laity in the Church?

✤ How do we respond to the call of Christ?

✤ What is the *universal call to holiness*?

✤ What is our basis for stating that Christ instituted the Seven Sacraments?

✤ What is the meaning of the Latin term *ex opere operato*?

✤ What is the role of prayer in the Christian life?

✤ What is the *liturgical year*?

✤ What does it mean to be an apostle?

✤ How can we participate in the missionary activity of the Church?

✤ What is the consecrated life?

St. Peter Enthroned by Guido of Siena.
Faith is first and foremost, Jesus says, a gift from God.

PART I: THE UNIVERSAL CALL TO HOLINESS

FAITH REQUIRES A RESPONSE

Throughout his public ministry, Christ repeatedly emphasized the importance of faith. He grieved over the lack of faith that he found in many of his hearers[3] but was always moved when he encountered those who did believe. He marveled at the faith of the Roman centurion and immediately granted the centurion's request that his servant be healed.[4] When Jesus saw the faith of the men who lowered their paralytic friend through the roof, not only did he heal the paralytic, but he also forgave his sins.[5] And when a woman touched the hem of his garment in order to be made well, Jesus said that it was her faith that had healed her.[6] Because of the dignity of the human person, which is unique among visible creation, people are able to believe. To believe is a conscious and free human act.

The Gospel of St. Matthew tells us another story about faith.

> **When Jesus came in to the district of Caesarea Philippi, he asked his disciples...“Who do you say that I am?” Simon Peter replied, “You are the Christ, the Son of the living God.” And Jesus answered him, “Blessed are you, Simon Bar-Jona! For flesh and blood has not revealed this to you, but my Father who is in heaven. And I tell you, you are Peter, and on this rock I will build my church.” (Mt 16: 13, 15-18)**

Christ's response to St. Peter's profession of faith is different from other similar episodes in the Gospel. Not only does Jesus' response give us an insight into the nature of faith, it marks the first time that Jesus spoke of the Church that he was going to establish.

It is important to note that Jesus did not praise St. Peter's intelligence or ingenuity in coming to the realization that he [Christ] is the Son of God. Rather, Jesus told him that it was not "flesh and blood" that had revealed this to him, but rather it was from his "Father who is in heaven." Faith is first and foremost, Jesus says, a gift from God. This supernatural gift is freely given, and the interior helps of the Holy Spirit are necessary for people to believe.

But faith is a gift that must be accepted; in other words, it requires a response, the adherence of the whole person to God. God has revealed himself in deeds and words, and each person must turn his intellect and will toward God.

> Believing is possible only by grace and the interior helps of the Holy Spirit. But it is no less true that believing is an authentically human act. Trusting in God and cleaving to the truths he has revealed are contrary neither to human freedom nor to human reason. (CCC 154)

> What moves us to believe is not the fact that revealed truths appear as true and intelligible in the light of our natural reason: we believe "because of the authority of God himself who reveals them, who can neither deceive nor be deceived."[7] (CCC 156)

The above passage from St. Matthew marks the first time that Jesus made explicit reference to the Church, and he did so by proclaiming that St. Peter was to be the rock on which it is built. As we have seen, this is the basis for the Catholic understanding that the Church on earth was to be led by St. Peter, the first Pope, and his successors, who are a visible sign of the Church's unity. But note especially *how* Jesus said that the Church was to be built. It is Christ himself who is building the Church.

The Church is Jesus' greatest work. Not only is it the gathering place for all those who believe in him, it is also the instrument he has chosen to continue his work on earth and to reveal himself to the world. In the Church, each member of the faithful is supported and nourished by the whole Church's faith, which precedes and engenders her members' faith; the Church is a loving Mother to her children. Thus, Christ instituted the Church as a means of salvation for all people.

THE CHURCH IS THE PEOPLE OF GOD

Christ Handing the Keys to St. Peter by Rubens. The Church on earth was to be led by St. Peter, the first Pope, and his successors, who are a visible sign of the Church's unity. The Church is Jesus' greatest work.

Who is *the Church*? We often use these words, *the Church*, in a variety of ways depending upon the context. When we speak of what *the Church* teaches, we are referring to the Magisterium, the teaching authority given by Christ to his Apostles and now vested in their successors, the Pope and the bishops of the Catholic Church in union with him, who teach the truths of the Faith on the basis of Sacred Scripture and Sacred Tradition.

However, *the Church* also means the communion of all the faithful in Christ; the Church is the *People of God*. This concept, which we introduced in earlier chapters, refers to the Old Testament reckoning of the Israelites as the *People of God* (or "God's Chosen People"). This understanding of the Church as the *People of God* can be found in the First Letter of St. Peter:

Christ instituted this new covenant, the new testament, that is to say, in His Blood (cf. 1 Cor 11:25), calling together a people made up of Jew and gentile, making them one, not according to the flesh but in the Spirit. This was to be the new People of God. For those who believe in Christ, who are reborn not from a perishable but from an imperishable seed through the word of the living God (cf. 1 Pt 1:23), not from the flesh but from water and the Holy Spirit (cf. Jn 3:5-6), are finally established as "a chosen race, a royal priesthood, a holy nation, a purchased people...who in times past were not a people, but are now the people of God" (1 Pt 2:9-10).[8]

To speak of the Church as the People of God is in many ways a logical extension of the idea of members of the Church as the Mystical Body of Christ. Both concepts convey that all the Christian faithful are bound together in a mystical way, sharing a common purpose and goal in the salvific mission of Jesus Christ.

What *People of God* expresses clearly is that it indicates a pilgrim Church (another term introduced previously in this text), a Church of believers seeking holiness and redemption, a Church of the faithful on a journey toward God, as Joseph Cardinal Ratzinger—who was later to become Pope Benedict XVI—once said:

> The Church is not identical with Christ, but she stands before Him. She is a Church of sinners, ever in need of purification and renewal, ever needing to become Church....The phrase conveys the unity of salvation history which comprises both Israel and the Church in her pilgrim journey. The phrase expresses the historical nature of the pilgrim Church that will not be wholly herself until the paths of time have been traversed and have blossomed in the hands of God. It describes the unity of the People of God amid the variety, as in all peoples, of different ministries and services; yet above and beyond all distinctions, all are pilgrims in the one community of the pilgrim People of God.[9]

The Second Vatican Council, after describing the Church as the Mystical Body of Christ and the People of God, explains that the Church is also hierarchical.

> In order to shepherd the People of God and to increase its numbers without cease, Christ the Lord set up in his Church a variety of offices which aim at the good of the whole body. The holders of office, who are invested with a sacred power, are, in fact, dedicated to promoting the interests of their brethren, so that all who belong to the People of God, and are consequently endowed with true Christian dignity, may, through their free and well ordered efforts towards a common goal, attain to salvation.[10]

The document goes on to situate the various roles that the bishops and priests fulfill in service to the People of God and in the governance of the Church. As we have seen, these roles developed from the teachings of Christ and have been in practice since the apostolic age. But there is another phrase in the First Letter of St. Peter that is applied to the whole Church and requires a deeper look. From what we have read already, we can understand the Church as the "People of God," the "chosen race," and a "holy nation." But what does it mean when we call the members of the Church "a royal priesthood"?

St. Peter's Square overflowing with the *People of God*—a Church of the faithful on a journey toward God.

COMMON PRIESTHOOD OF THE FAITHFUL

When God established the covenant with Moses on Mount Sinai after the Israelites were liberated from Egypt, he said the Israelites would be to him "a kingdom of priests, a holy nation."[11] Yet God also established seventy elders[12] and an order of priests led by Aaron and his sons,[13] assisted by the Levites, to serve this "kingdom of priests." Aaron and the Levites were consecrated to the responsibility of offering the sacrifices before God, leading the people in worship, and taking care of the Ark of the Covenant and other sacred objects. In other words, these priests were "appointed to act on behalf of men in relation to God, to offer gifts and sacrifices for sins.... And one does not take the honor upon himself, but he is called by God, just as Aaron was."[14]

So it is with the Church that Jesus established. There is a common priesthood shared by all the faithful, and there is a ministerial priesthood of ordained leaders at the service of the faithful. Together they participate in the one priesthood of Christ.

All of the faithful share in the common priesthood by virtue of their Baptism. In the Rite of Baptism, the celebrant prays: "As Christ was

The Fall of Jericho (detail) by Fouquet.
An order of priests established by God took care of the Ark of the Covenant and other sacred objects even in battle.

anointed priest, prophet and king, so may you live always as a member of his holy people, sharing everlasting life." The newly baptized Christian thus receives a real participation in the priesthood of Christ. He or she is truly a priest, and that embrace of the common priesthood, if lived faithfully, will shape his or her other occupations and relationships in this world.

How does one live out this participation in the priesthood of Christ? The same way Christ himself lived out his priesthood. Every priest offers sacrifices for himself and for others in order to lead all to salvation. Christ sacrificed himself for the life of the world. We who are baptized, as members of the common priesthood, are called to do likewise, offering ourselves—our possessions, our work, our prayer, our suffering, our relationships with others, our very selves, our very lives, our every thought, word, and deed—to God. By our sacrifices, prayers, apostolic work, and loving example, we thus are commissioned to lead our families, our friends, our co-workers, our neighbors, our classmates, and all whom we encounter to salvation.

Pope Bl. John Paul II described this baptismal commitment quite beautifully:

> With this spiritual "unction" [anointing], Christians can repeat in an individual way the words of Jesus: "The Spirit of the Lord is upon me, because he has anointed me to preach the good news to the poor. He has sent me to proclaim release to captives and recovering of sight to the blind, to set at liberty those who are oppressed to proclaim the acceptable year of the Lord" (Lk 4:18-19; cf. Is 61:1-2). Thus with the outpouring of the Holy Spirit in Baptism and Confirmation, the baptized share in the same mission of Jesus as the Christ, the Savior-Messiah.[15]

The *Catechism of the Catholic Church* summarizes well the relationship between the common priesthood and the ministerial priesthood:

> The ministerial or hierarchical priesthood of bishops and priests, and the common priesthood of all the faithful participate, "each in its own proper way, in the one priesthood of Christ." While being "ordered one to another," they differ essentially.[16] In what sense? While the common priesthood of the faithful is exercised by the unfolding of baptismal grace—a life of faith, hope,

and charity, a life according to the Spirit—the ministerial priesthood is at the service of the common priesthood. It is directed at the unfolding of the baptismal grace of all Christians. The ministerial priesthood is a *means* by which Christ unceasingly builds up and leads his Church. For this reason it is transmitted by its own sacrament, the sacrament of Holy Orders. (CCC 1547)

The Laity

The *laity*—meaning all the faithful except for those in Holy Orders or consecrated religious life—are characterized by their completely *secular* nature, a different vocation or calling from God. Priests are ordained for sacred ministry; the vocation of men and women in religious life is in living the evangelical counsels of poverty, chastity, and obedience in the spirit of the Beatitudes. The vocation of the laity, however, is to "seek the Kingdom of God by engaging in temporal affairs and by ordering them according to the plan of God."[17]

> They live in the world, that is, in each and in all of the secular professions and occupations. They live in the ordinary circumstances of family and social life, from which the very web of their existence is woven. They are called there by God that by exercising their proper function and led by the spirit of the Gospel they may work for the sanctification of the world from within as a leaven. In this way they may make Christ known to others, especially by the testimony of a life resplendent in faith, hope and charity. Therefore, since they are tightly bound up in all types of temporal affairs it is their special task to order and to throw light upon these affairs in such a way that they may come into being and then continually increase according to Christ to the praise of the Creator and the Redeemer.[18]

The laity (we may also speak of people in the *lay state*, *lay persons*, or of *lay men* and *lay women*) are those members of the Church who are called to engage in everyday family and professional activities, evangelizing and sanctifying the world "from within." The laity includes the old and the young, the married and the single. All who live and work in the midst of the world are in the "front lines" of the Church's evangelical

Christ commands the entire Church, but especially the laity, to be salt and light to the world.

mission.[19] Christ commands the entire Church, but especially the laity, to be salt and light to the world. "Let your light so shine before men, that they may see your good works and give glory to your Father who is in heaven."[20] We can see, then, that an essential way in which lay people are to evangelize is through the witness of their lives.

UNIVERSAL CALL TO HOLINESS

The Council Fathers went on to state explicitly the implications of the common priesthood. "In the Church everyone does not proceed by the same path, nevertheless all are called to sanctity and have received an equal privilege of faith through the justice of God."[21] The term often used to express this call of all the faithful to sanctity is the *universal call to holiness*. The council sought to invite the laity into a greater sense of their own vocation and their own role in continuing the mission of Christ.

The universal call to holiness is firmly rooted in Sacred Scripture and Sacred Tradition. During his earthly ministry, Christ constantly called the people to greater holiness through prayer, repentance, self-denial, charitable works, the Beatitudes, detachment from the things of this world, and the keeping of the Commandments, particularly the great New Commandment of Love, even so far as loving their enemies. As he told the crowds in his Sermon on the Mount, "Be perfect, as your heavenly Father is perfect."[22] As perfection is something we as humans can aspire to but will never achieve in this life, our call to perfection is a call to greater and greater holiness. "All Christians in any state or walk of life are called to the fullness of Christian life and to the perfection of charity."[23]

Jesus Preaching on the Mount (detail) by Doré. Jesus told the crowds in his Sermon on the Mount, "Be perfect, as your heavenly Father is perfect." Our call to perfection is a call to greater and greater holiness.

To seek holiness as a member of the laity, then, requires more than simply attending Mass, reciting an occasional prayer, and volunteering every once in a while at the parish fundraiser or the downtown soup kitchen, as if the "holy" part of our lives were somehow separate from the secular aspects of study, work, recreation, and family obligations. Instead, God calls us to sanctify ourselves in every part of our lives:

> "The laity, dedicated as they are to Christ and anointed by the Holy Spirit, are marvelously called and prepared, so that even richer fruits of the Spirit may be produced in them. For all their works, prayers, and apostolic undertakings, family and married life, daily work, relaxation of mind and body, if they are accomplished in the Spirit—indeed even the hardships of life, if patiently borne—all these become spiritual sacrifices acceptable to God through Jesus Christ. In the celebration of the Eucharist these may most fittingly be offered to the Father along with the body of the Lord. And so, worshiping everywhere by their holy actions, the laity consecrate the world itself to God, everywhere offering worship by the holiness of their lives."[24] (CCC 901)

The proper response to the universal call to holiness calls for:

✤ Active and regular participation in the liturgy of the Church, especially the Holy Mass;

✤ Frequent reception of the Sacraments, particularly the Sacraments of the Eucharist and Reconciliation;

The Saints
PILLARS OF THE CHURCH

St. Gianna Beretta Molla

"Greater love has no man than this, that a man lay down his life for his friends." (Jn 15:13)

St. Gianna Beretta Molla was a wife, mother, and medical doctor who lived in the mid-twentieth century. She was born in Italy in 1922 to a large, devout Catholic family—the tenth of thirteen children— that would also produce two priests and one nun. (Gianna herself considered entering the religious life but ultimately decided to pursue medicine instead.)

Although she remained focused on her medical studies, Gianna also volunteered much of her free time to charity work. She graduated from medical school in 1949 and immediately went to work among the poor and the elderly, opening a clinic near her hometown in 1950. She received an additional degree in children's medicine in 1952 in order to give special attention to the mothers with young children who came to her for help.

It was around this time that Gianna met her future husband, Pietro Molla, an engineer who lived across the street from her clinic. They were married at their local parish in late 1955 in a ceremony presided over by her older brother Guiseppe. Little more than a year later, Gianna gave birth to her first child, Pierluigi. Gianna and Pietro welcomed this new addition to their family with great joy, and over the next three years, they would celebrate the births of two more children, Mariolina and Laura.

In the fall of 1961, after two miscarriages, Gianna again became pregnant. During the course of this pregnancy, however, Gianna's doctors discovered that she had developed a tumor that was threatening both her life and the life of her unborn child. The doctors recommended that she abort her child and undergo surgery to remove the tumor. But for Gianna, this was unacceptable: "If you must decide between me and the child, do not hesitate. Choose the child—I insist on it. Save the baby."

On Good Friday in 1962, after nine months of pregnancy, Gianna checked into the hospital, giving birth the following day to a baby girl, Gianna Emanuela. And although the doctors struggled to save the lives of both mother and child, in the end, the complications of the delivery proved too much for the elder Gianna. She died exactly one week after the birth of her infant daughter, having indeed been called by Christ to lay down her life for the life of another.

At her canonization in 2004—at which Gianna's husband and children were present—Gianna Molla was praised by Pope Bl. John Paul II for this heroic act of self-giving, "following the example of Christ, who 'having loved his own... loved them to the end.'" [25]

St. Gianna Beretta Molla, pray for us.

✤ A well-formed life of prayer as a focal point of each day;

✤ The practice of sacrifice and self-denial;

✤ The sanctification of ordinary life—family life, professional work, and all human relationships; and

✤ Our witness and apostolate in the church community and in society.

THE LITURGY OF THE CATHOLIC CHURCH

As in all states of Christian life, the lay faithful can neither respond to the universal call to holiness nor contribute to the mission of the Church without a life of constant prayer, both individually and as a community. Our worship of God has both a personal dimension and a communal dimension. Private prayers and devotions complement, but do not replace, our need for communal worship—and vice versa.

The term *liturgy* comes from the Greek *ergos* ("work"), and *leiton* ("of the people"), meaning essentially "public work," or any work performed for the common good. In the third-century BC Greek translation of the Old Testament, *leitourgia* designated the worship led by the Levite priests of the Temple on behalf of the people. Since the days of the early Church, liturgy has come to mean the Church's public and official worship of God, including the Mass and all her official rites and ceremonies—the worship of God by the People of God.

The *Ecce Agnus Dei* during the Mass. "Behold, the Lamb of God, who takes away the sin of the world!" (Jn 1: 29)

In the liturgy, as the public action (*leitourgia*) of the Church as such, Christ exercises his threefold office as prophet, priest, and king. In celebrating the liturgy the Church participates in the worship offered by Jesus and at the same time proclaims God's wonderful works and furthers the establishment of the Kingdom. Insofar as it is worship, liturgy has a priestly aspect, but it is not reducible to worship alone. Under a second aspect it is a participation in the prophetic office of Christ, who addresses his people by word and gesture. Under still a third aspect, thanks to the active presence of the risen Christ and the Holy Spirit, liturgy serves to transform the old world into the new creation. It gives fresh actuality to the fruits of Christ's Paschal mystery.[26]

The purpose of the liturgy is diverse. It gives glory and honor to God, builds up the faith of the people, and instructs the faithful in the Faith. The Christian liturgy is the response of faith and love to the "spiritual blessings" with which the Father constantly enriches us. At the same time, the Church unceasingly offers to the Father her own gifts "to the praise of the glory of his grace."

The liturgy is an exercise of the priestly office of Jesus Christ, continued in and by the Church under the impulse of the Holy Spirit. In the liturgy of the Mass, led by ordained ministers and involving the prayer and participation of the entire assembly of the People of God, the Holy Spirit prepares the assembly to encounter Christ, recalls and manifests Christ to the faith of the assembly, makes the saving work of Christ present and active by his transforming power, and makes the gift of communion bear fruit in the Church.[27]

In the *liturgy of the New Covenant* every liturgical action, especially the celebration of the Eucharist and the sacraments, is an encounter between Christ and the Church. The liturgical assembly derives its unity from the "communion of the Holy Spirit" who gathers the children of God into the one Body of Christ. (CCC 1097)

JESUS CHRIST, THE ONE MEDIATOR BETWEEN GOD AND MAN

Before the Fall, Adam and Eve performed all their acts according to the will of God and were in communion with God. After they sinned, their relationship with God was severed, and they were no longer in this communion. They would need a Redeemer, a mediator, to restore that relationship with God. As we have seen in earlier chapters, the Incarnation of Jesus as true God and true man, having both a divine nature and a human nature in the unity of the divine Person, is the one and only mediator between God and man and is God's means of restoring that relationship with humanity. Jesus, as our Redeemer, became our sole Mediator and Priest to heal the wounds of sin.

Jesus' entire life—in particular, his Passion, Death, and Resurrection—reflected one uninterrupted priestly action. His priestly work is not merely something that happened in the past that has no bearing upon our present life; rather, it continues in the liturgy of the Church, particularly in the Holy Sacrifice of the Mass, where Christ brings about the effects of salvation and accomplishes the perfect worship of God.[28]

THE LITURGICAL YEAR

In the course of each year, the Church celebrates the whole mystery of Christ, from his Incarnation until the day of Pentecost and the expectation of his coming again. In the ordinary form of the Latin Rite, this cycle begins each year on the first Sunday of Advent and continues through the Feast of Christ the King, the last Sunday before Advent begins again. We call this cycle of observances the *liturgical year*.

The liturgical year comprises the following seasons in the ordinary form of the Latin Rite:

✤ **Advent** begins on the fourth Sunday before Christmas and continues until Christmas Eve. Advent has a twofold character: It is a season to prepare for Christmas, the commemoration of Christ's "first coming"; it also directs the mind and heart to await his second coming at the end of time. Advent is thus a period of devout and joyful expectation that calls the faithful to prepare themselves spiritually for the coming of the Lord through prayer and repentance.

✤ **The Christmas Season** begins with the vigil Mass of Christmas. On the Sunday after Christmas, the Feast of the Holy Family of Jesus, Mary, and Joseph honors and presents the virtues of the family of Nazareth as a model for every Christian family; the Solemnity of Mary, Mother of God, is on the octave of Christmas; and the Epiphany recalls the Magi's visit to the Christ child and focuses on the universal nature of the salvation accomplished by Christ. The Christmas Season ends with the Feast of the Baptism of the Lord.

✤ **Lent** begins with Ash Wednesday, a day on which the faithful receive ashes on their foreheads, calling them to a conversion of heart, inviting them to pray, and announcing that Christ's Resurrection will follow the mystery of the Cross. Lent is a penitential season, recalling the forty days Christ spent in the desert in prayer and fasting to prepare for his public ministry. The faithful use this time to prepare for the Resurrection of Christ by interior conversion and participation especially in the Sacrament of Penance. Many spiritual practices are common

Good Friday Liturgy—Prayers of Intercession by Cistercian monks at Abbey Heiligenkreuz, Austria.

during this season: listening to and meditating on the word of God, prayer, abstinence, fasting, almsgiving, and devotions such as the Way of the Cross. The last Sunday of Lent is Palm Sunday, which inaugurates Holy Week and the commemoration of Christ's Passion.

✣ **The Easter Triduum** is celebrated on the three days leading to Easter Sunday, the "Feast of feasts." It begins with the Evening Mass of the Lord's Supper, at which Christ instituted the Holy Eucharist. The liturgy of Good Friday, the only day of the year on which the Mass is not celebrated, comprises three parts: (a) the readings, psalms, and prayers of intercession; (b) the adoration of the Cross; and (c) Holy Communion, the Hosts having been reserved from Holy Thursday. The Easter Triduum reaches its pinnacle in the Easter Vigil, which commemorates the holy night when Christ rose from the dead. Those who desire to be in full communion with the Church receive the Sacraments of Initiation during the vigil. The liturgy of this solemn vigil comprises four parts: (a) the service of light, with the blessing of the fire and procession with the Paschal candle and Easter proclamation; (b) the Liturgy of the Word; (c) the Rite of Baptism, with the blessing of the water and renewal of the baptismal promises; and (d) the Liturgy of the Eucharist. The Easter Triduum concludes with evening prayer of Easter Sunday.

✣ **The Easter Season** is a continuation of the Easter joy. The Ascension of Christ into Heaven is celebrated, and preparation is made for the Feast of Pentecost, on which the faithful celebrate the descent of the Holy Spirit on the Apostles and the Blessed Virgin Mary.

✣ **Ordinary Time** refers to the weeks outside the seasons already described that do not celebrate a specific aspect of the mystery of Christ; rather, especially on Sunday as the day of the Resurrection, they are devoted to the mystery of Christ in all its aspects. Ordinary Time begins after the Baptism of the Lord and continues until Ash Wednesday; it resumes on the Monday after Pentecost and lasts until Advent.

In the course of each year, the Church celebrates the whole mystery of Christ, from his Incarnation until the day of Pentecost and the expectation of his coming again. The Easter Season follows the Easter Triduum. The Ascension of Christ into Heaven is celebrated, and preparation is made for the Feast of Pentecost.

✤ **The Proper of Saints** is observed throughout the year. The Proper of Saints is a yearly cycle of days dedicated to the Blessed Virgin Mary, the martyrs, and other saints. When the Church, in the annual cycle, brings to memory the martyrs and all the saints, "she proclaims the Paschal Mystery completed in them; they suffered and have been glorified with Christ. She proposes them to the faithful as examples, who draw all men to the Father through Christ, and through their merits she begs for God's favors."[29] This shows the Church's liturgy on earth is united to the liturgy of Heaven.

In the Eastern Catholic Churches, the liturgical year begins on September 1 and follows the life of the Mother of God, beginning with her Nativity on September 8 through her Dormition on August 15. There are four seasons of fasting; two correspond to Advent and Lent (above) as preparations for Christmas and Easter, and two shorter fasts precede the Feast of Sts. Peter and Paul on June 29 and the Dormition of the Blessed Virgin Mary. As in the West, Easter Sunday (often called *Pascha*, Greek for "Passover") is the pinnacle of the Church year.

THE SEVEN SACRAMENTS

The purpose of the sacraments is to sanctify men, to build up the body of Christ, and, finally, to give worship to God; because they are signs they also instruct. They not only presuppose faith, but by words and objects they also nourish, strengthen, and express it; that is why they are called "sacraments of faith." They do indeed impart grace, but, in addition, the very act of celebrating them most effectively disposes the faithful to receive this grace in a fruitful manner, to worship God duly, and to practice charity.[30]

What Is a Sacrament?

The definition for *Sacrament* used in this text begins with the definition given by the *Catechism of the Catholic Church*: "The sacraments are efficacious signs of grace, instituted by Christ and entrusted to the Church, by which divine life is dispensed to us" (CCC 1131). Among Christians of the early Church, the word *mysterion* ("mystery") was used, which is Greek for "a sign of something sacred or hidden"; to this day, Eastern Catholics and the Orthodox often call the Sacraments *"the holy mysteries."*

As Latin increasingly became the language of the Western Church in the fourth and fifth centuries, Christians found there was no equivalent word for *mysterion*, so they used the term *sacramentum*, meaning "oath." It was the word used to describe the ceremony in which a recruit was accepted into the Roman army. The soldier would take an oath and be branded behind the ear with the number of his legion. Thus initiated into the army, the soldier would immediately acquire particular responsibilities and benefits—the responsibility to follow the commands of the military, and certain social and legal privileges including veterans' benefits. The Roman army ritual, which included certain signs (oath, branding), had an automatic effect upon the soldier (responsibilities, benefits)—a causal relationship that loosely correlated with the *mysterion* of the Church.

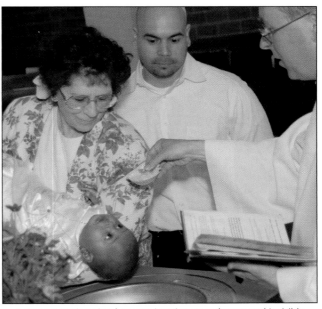

A Sacrament is a sign because it points to a deeper and invisible reality. In Baptism, the primary sign is the water being poured on the one being baptized.

Ex Opere Operato

A closer look at the *Catechism*'s definition of Sacrament can deepen our understanding.

✤ A Sacrament is a *sign* because it points to a deeper and invisible reality. In Baptism, for example, the primary sign is the water being poured on the one being baptized. We associate water with washing and cleansing, among other things. The sign of cleansing by water points to the deeper invisible reality that the person's sins, including Original Sin, are being washed away by the waters of Baptism.

✤ A Sacrament is a *sign of grace* because through it *divine life is dispensed to us*. By participating in the sign of the Sacrament, the participant receives grace, a share in the life of God. To the extent that we are properly disposed to receive the Sacrament, this grace draws us closer to Christ, strengthens us to seek God's will in our lives, and helps us to live according to the example of Christ.

✤ A Sacrament is an *efficacious sign of grace* because it dispenses the grace it signifies. The validity of the Sacrament does not depend upon the holiness of the minister nor on the holiness of the

The Miracle of the Loaves and Fishes by Tissot.
This feeding of the five thousand (Jn 6:1-14) was an early foreshadowing of the institution of the Eucharist.
"I am the living bread which came down from heaven; if any one eats of this bread, he will live for ever; and the bread which I shall give for the life of the world is my flesh." (Jn 6: 51)

person receiving the Sacrament. It is Christ himself who acts in the Sacraments. The grace given is efficacious as long as the minister(s) of the Sacrament intend(s) to convey the Sacrament and the participant is properly disposed to receive it.

> Celebrated worthily in faith, the sacraments confer the grace that they signify.[31] They are *efficacious* because in them Christ himself is at work; it is he who baptizes, he who acts in his sacraments in order to communicate the grace that each sacrament signifies. (CCC 1127)

The Latin term that has been used since the thirteenth century to describe this truth is *ex opere operato*, meaning "from the work performed." As the Council of Trent stated so simply in the sixteenth century, the Sacraments "confer Grace on those who do not place an obstacle thereunto."

✚ A Sacrament is *instituted by Christ and entrusted to the Church*; Sacred Scripture and Sacred Tradition attest to this. As we have seen, the word Sacrament did not originate in the New Testament. However, it is clear that Christ, in establishing his New Covenant, left us these seven signs as particular fonts of grace and expected the Church he founded to continue to exercise them as the primary means of building communion between God and man.

> The mysteries of Christ's life are the foundations of what he would henceforth dispense in the sacraments, through the ministers of his Church, for "what was visible in our Savior has passed over into his mysteries."[32] (CCC 1115)

> Sacraments are "powers that come forth" from the Body of Christ,[33] which is ever-living and life-giving. They are actions of the Holy Spirit at work in his Body, the Church. They are "the masterworks of God" in the new and everlasting covenant. (CCC 1116)

The Seven Sacraments were part of the practice of the Church from the very beginning and were understood as originating with Christ, even if the fuller understanding of the Sacraments—like the fuller understanding of Christ as true God and true man—took time to develop.

> As she has done for the canon of Sacred Scripture and for the doctrine of the faith, the Church, by the power of the Spirit who guides her "into all truth," has gradually recognized this treasure received from Christ and, as the faithful steward of God's mysteries, has determined its "dispensation."[34] Thus the Church has discerned over the centuries that among liturgical celebrations there are seven that are, in the strict sense of the term, sacraments instituted by the Lord. (CCC 1117)

Why the Sacraments?

But why Sacraments? Why did God institute these particular signs as ways of dispensing his grace? Can he not give us grace in any way that he pleases?

God surely can—and does—dispense his grace as he sees fit in countless ways, and he is by no means restricted to the Sacraments he instituted. Yet, God directed his Church to use these signs as special avenues of grace. The reason has to do with the nature of humanity.

By nature, every person is composed of two elements, body and soul—a physical, visible body and a nonphysical, invisible soul. As St. Thomas Aquinas explained, humanity is led by things that are physical, that can be seen and experienced by the senses. Furthermore, God provides for everything in accordance with its nature. He could have redeemed the world in other ways, for example, but he sent his Son to be born of a woman and become part of humanity, to suffer and experience physical Death on the Cross, and to rise bodily from the dead.

Sacred oil used in the Sacraments is consecrated by the bishop of the diocese during the Chrism Mass on Holy Thursday. Sacred Chrism is used for Confirmation, Baptism, Holy Orders, and Anointing the Sick.

Man has an elementary need to understand that which is invisible by experiencing that which is visible. Consider the experience of love. One person can tell another "I love you" with great frequency, but it becomes difficult to believe that love is genuine if it is not expressed in tangible ways: through acts of kindness, self-sacrifice, and affection. We have a natural need to "ritualize" the significant events and realities in our lives. That is why we have graduation ceremonies, awards banquets, Thanksgiving dinners, and pledges of allegiance. These rituals signify something deeper in our lives: academic or athletic achievement, the joy of having family together for the holidays, or loyalty to our country. So it is with the Sacraments. They give form to spiritual "events" and serve as signs of deeper realities, with the added supernatural dimension of conveying the very grace they signify.

There are Seven Sacraments: Baptism, Confirmation, Eucharist, Penance (Reconciliation), Anointing of the Sick, Holy Orders, and Matrimony (marriage). We will briefly examine each in turn.

BAPTISM

Jesus began his public ministry by seeking baptism from St. John the Baptist, his cousin, an ascetic preacher who recognized him as the Messiah. Although St. John protested, Jesus insisted on receiving baptism, at which time there occurred a *theophany*—a divine manifestation or appearance of all three Persons of the Blessed Trinity.

The Disciples of Jesus Baptize by Tissot.
"After this Jesus and his disciples went into the land of Judea; there he remained with them and baptized. John [the Baptist] also was baptizing at Aenon near Salim, because there was much water there; and people came and were baptized." (Jn 3: 22-23)

Jesus came from Galilee to the Jordan to John, to be baptized by him. John would have prevented him, saying, "I need to be baptized by you, and do you come to me?" But Jesus answered him, "Let it be so now; for thus it is fitting for us to fulfill all righteousness." Then he consented. And when Jesus was baptized, he went up immediately from the water, and behold, the heavens were opened and he saw the Spirit of God descending like a dove, and alighting on him; and lo, a voice from heaven, saying, "This is my beloved Son, with whom I am well pleased." (Mt 3: 13-17)

St. John's Baptism, however, was not the sacramental Baptism instituted by Jesus; rather, it is a voluntary act of a person indicating his or her repentance from sin. It was not efficacious. Instead, it merely symbolized the recipient's desire to live more virtuously. St. John admitted as much when he told the crowds, "I baptize you with water for repentance, but he who is coming after me is mightier than I, whose sandals I am not worthy to carry; he will baptize you with the Holy Spirit and with fire."[35]

Jesus himself spoke of the Baptism that he would institute when he told the Pharisee Nicodemus, "Truly, truly, I say to you, unless one is born of water and the Spirit, he cannot enter the kingdom of God."[36] As he was about to ascend into Heaven, Christ clearly instituted the Sacrament of Baptism when he gave his Apostles his command to preach the Gospel to the whole world.

Jesus approached and said to [the Eleven], "All authority in heaven and on earth has been given to me. Go therefore and make disciples of all nations, baptizing them in the name of the Father

and of the Son and of the Holy Spirit, teaching them to observe all that I have commanded you; and lo, I am with you always, to the close of the age." (Mt 28: 18-20)

Scripture reveals how the Apostles baptized new Christian believers at the very beginning of their ministry. On the day of Pentecost, after St. Peter preached that Jesus was the Messiah, three thousand converts were baptized.[37] We later find even the Gentiles, including the Ethiopian eunuch and Cornelius, requesting Baptism from the Apostles.[38]

The Sacrament of Baptism instituted by Christ is a new birth in water and the Spirit. It removes all sin, Original and actual; unites one to the Death, Burial, and Resurrection of Christ, giving birth to new life in Christ; and incorporates a person into the Mystical Body of Christ, the Church, by which one becomes an adoptive son or daughter of God, a temple of the Holy Spirit, and a sharer in the priesthood of Christ. Along with the Eucharist and Confirmation, it is one of the three *Sacraments of Initiation*, and a person is not fully initiated as a member of the Church until all three Sacraments have been received. Along with Confirmation and Holy Orders, Baptism leaves an indelible *sacramental character* or *seal* that configures the recipient to Christ and his Church, remains in the Christian as a positive disposition for grace, and grants him or her a vocation to the worship of God and the service of the Church.[39] Because of this indelible seal, Baptism can only be received once.

Baptism of Christ (detail) by Perugino. A *theophany* occurred when St. John baptized Jesus—the appearance of all three Persons of the Blessed Trinity.

The Catechumenate

The Baptism of the Neophytes (detail) by Masaccio. On the day of Pentecost, after St. Peter preached that Jesus was the Messiah, three thousand converts were baptized.

In the early Church, persons who wished to become members of the Church went through a process called the *catechumenate* in which they were instructed in the teachings of the Faith and prepared for the Sacraments of Initiation. It became customary for the Church to initiate these new members at the Easter Vigil, the night before the commemoration of Christ's Resurrection. More recently, in the wake of the Second Vatican Council, the form of the catechumenate has been restored in the Rite of Christian Initiation for Adults (RCIA).

The Rite of Baptism centrally involves the pouring of water on the head of the recipient and the pronouncement of the words of Baptism by the minister: "I baptize you in the name of the Father, and of the Son, and of the Holy Spirit." Today, as in the early Church, Baptism can also be accomplished by immersion, and this practice has become common in many churches. The full rite also includes a recommitment of all present to their baptismal promises, the lighting of a candle symbol-izing the light of Christ, the wearing of a white garment symbolizing new life in Christ, and the anointing with Sacred Chrism.

The water of Baptism symbolizes not only cleansing from sin but also a sharing in the Passion, Death, and Resurrection of Christ. This is a symbol more explicit in Baptism by immersion, in which the individual is immersed in the water and then "rises again" out of the water to new life.

In the Eastern Rites, the three Sacraments of Initiation are given consecutively, even to infants. In the Latin Rite, they often are conferred simultaneously on adults or older minors who are baptized at the Easter Vigil; in the case of infants, Confirmation and Eucharist are usually deferred until after they have reached the age of reason (about seven years old). In the Latin Rite, Confirmation is sometimes administered in Catholic schools and parish religious education programs during the junior high or high school years.

The Church also teaches that the Sacrament of Baptism is necessary for salvation. Sacramental grace makes the faithful "partakers in the divine nature by uniting them in a living union with the only Son, the Savior."[40] The *Catechism* explains this necessity:

> Baptism is necessary for salvation for those to whom the Gospel has been proclaimed and who have had the possibility of asking for this sacrament.[41] The Church does not know of any means other than Baptism that assures entry into eternal beatitude; this is why she takes care not to neglect the mission she has received from the Lord to see that all who can be baptized are "reborn of water and the Spirit." God *has bound salvation to the sacrament of Baptism, but he himself is not bound by his sacraments.* (CCC 1257)

Baptism of Blood, Baptism of Desire, and Unbaptized Infants

The Church recognizes that those who die for the sake of the Faith but have not yet received sacramental Baptism "are baptized by their death for and with Christ" in a *Baptism of blood*.[42] The Church also teaches that an uncatechized person of good will, under certain conditions, can receive what is called a *Baptism of desire*:

> Every man who is ignorant of the Gospel of Christ and his Church, but seeks the truth and does the will of God in accordance with his understanding of it, can be saved. It may be supposed that such persons would have *desired Baptism explicitly* if they had known its necessity. (CCC 1260)

Theologians have long pondered the question of salvation for unbaptized infants, who can neither willfully die for the Faith nor implicitly desire Baptism. The *Catechism of the Catholic Church* states simply that the "great mercy of God and Jesus' tenderness toward children ... allow us to hope that there is a way of salvation for children who have died without Baptism."[43]

BAPTISM: THE DOORWAY OF THE CHURCH

Baptism as a Sacrament, as a visible sign of invisible grace, is the door through which God acts in the human soul—even in the soul of a newborn—to unite it to himself in Christ and the Church. In Baptism, we share in redemption, and "new life" is infused into the soul.

With Christ's life, Baptism fills the new soul with his holiness, as the new condition of belonging to God through liberation and purification, as St. Paul reminds the Corinthians: "You were washed, you were sanctified, you were justified in the name of the Lord Jesus Christ and in the Spirit of our God."[44]

According to the Apostle's teaching, Christ purifies the entire church "by the bath of water with the word": she becomes "holy and without blemish" in her members since they receive Baptism (Eph 5: 27), which is deliverance from sin and also benefits the entire community, for which it is the basis of a continual process of spiritual growth (cf. Eph 2: 21). It is clear that, from baptismal sanctification, Christians—individuals and the community—obtain the ability and the obligation of leading a holy life.[45]

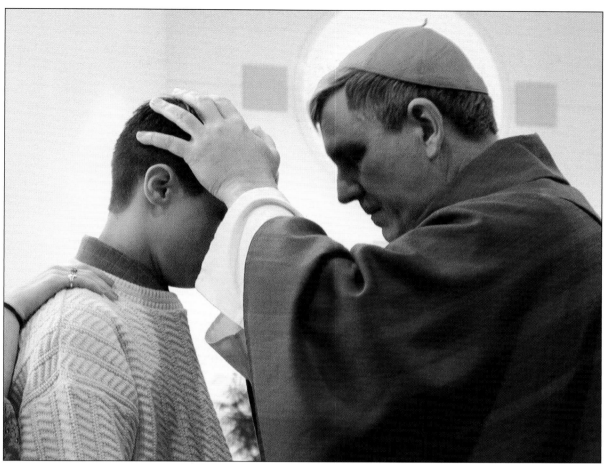

The signs of the Sacrament of Confirmation, which "confirms" one's Baptism with an indelible character, are the laying on of hands and the anointing with Sacred Chrism.

CONFIRMATION

The institution by Christ of the Sacrament of Confirmation can be seen in Jesus' promise to the Apostles that he would send the Holy Spirit after he returned to the Father. He told them just before his Ascension. "You shall receive power when the Holy Spirit has come upon you; and you shall be my witnesses in Jerusalem and in all Judea and Samaria and to the end of the earth."[46]

The dramatic fulfillment of this promise came at Pentecost, when the Spirit descended in a mighty wind upon the Apostles in the Upper Room and was imparted to each in the form of "tongues as of fire, distributed and resting on each one of them." Thus filled with the Holy Spirit, the Apostles went outside and began to preach the Gospel. To the amazement of everyone, persons of every tongue and culture were able to understand them in their own languages.[47]

Pope Paul VI affirmed the apostolic roots of Confirmation:

> The apostles, in fulfillment of Christ's wish, imparted to the newly baptized by the laying on of hands the gift of the Spirit that completes the grace of baptism. This is why the Letter to the Hebrews listed among the first elements of Christian instruction the teaching about baptisms and the laying on of hands (Heb 6: 2). This laying on of hands is rightly recognized by reason of Catholic tradition as the beginning of the sacrament of confirmation, which in a certain way perpetuates the grace of Pentecost in the Church.[48]

In addition to Baptism, Scripture shows the Apostles administered this Sacrament. The Acts of the Apostles recounts, after an Apostle had baptized a convert, he laid his hands on his new brother or sister:

> They were baptized in the name of the Lord Jesus. And when Paul had laid his hands upon them, the Holy Spirit came on them; and they spoke with tongues and prophesied. (Acts 19:5-6)

But when the Apostles were not present, and other believers had baptized the new followers of Christ, then the Apostles would "lay hands on," or confirm, the newly baptized when they were in the area.

> When the apostles at Jerusalem heard that Samaria had received the word of God, they sent to them Peter and John, who came down and prayed for them that they might receive the Holy Spirit; for it had not yet fallen on any of them, but they had only been baptized in the name of the Lord Jesus. Then they laid their hands on them and they received the Holy Spirit. (Acts 8:14-17)

From these two accounts, we can see that Confirmation (sometimes called *Chrismation* after the Sacred Chrism used) completes Baptism. The *confirmand*—the person receiving this Sacrament—receives the same outpouring of the Holy Spirit experienced by the Apostles at Pentecost. The Sacrament of Confirmation, through the action of the Holy Spirit, perfects the graces received at Baptism, incorporates one more fully into the Mystical Body of Christ, the Church, associates one more closely to the Church's mission, reaffirms one's identity as a child of God, and strengthens the person to bear faithful witness to Christ in word and deed. The bishops, the successors of the Apostles, are responsible for the administration of this Sacrament.

> In the first centuries Confirmation generally comprised one single celebration with Baptism, forming with it a "double sacrament," according to the expression of St. Cyprian. Among other reasons, the multiplication of infant baptisms all through the year, the increase of rural parishes, and the growth of dioceses often prevented the bishop from being present at all baptismal celebrations. In the West the desire to reserve the completion of Baptism to the bishop caused the temporal separation of the two sacraments. The East has kept them united, so that Confirmation is conferred by the priest who baptizes. But he can do so only with the "myron" consecrated by a bishop.[49] (CCC 1290)

The signs of the Sacrament of Confirmation, which "confirms" one's Baptism with an indelible character, are the laying on of hands and the anointing with Sacred Chrism (sometimes called by its Greek equivalent *myron*); the sweet-smelling Sacred Chrism signifies the gift of the Holy Spirit.[50] In the Latin Rite, the ordinary minister of Confirmation is a bishop, although a priest may be delegated by his bishop to confer this Sacrament.

Pentecost by Duccio.
The *confirmand*—the person receiving the Sacrament of Confirmation—receives the same outpouring of the Holy Spirit experienced by the Apostles at Pentecost.

The Last Supper (detail) by Tiepolo. The word *eucharist* means "thanksgiving." In a mysterious but real way, the bread and wine become Jesus' Body and Blood, which the faithful receive as a sharing and participation in Christ's Death and Resurrection.

EUCHARIST

Early in his public ministry, Jesus performed the miracle of the multiplication of the loaves and fishes. Having drawn a crowd of five thousand who came to hear him teach, he asked St. Philip where they could find enough food to feed the crowds. St. Andrew found a boy who had five barley loaves and two fishes, hardly enough even for a small family. But Jesus "took the loaves, and when he had given thanks, he distributed them to those who were seated; so also the fish, as much as they wanted."[51] When the disciples collected the leftovers, they filled twelve baskets of food.

This feeding of the five thousand was an early foreshadowing of the institution of the Eucharist—particularly in light of the passages that follow. The next day, when the crowds returned to hear him again, Jesus spoke of himself as the Bread of Life. Comparing himself to the manna given to the Israelites in the desert, he told the people:

> **Your fathers ate the manna in the wilderness, and they died. This is the bread which comes down from heaven, that a man may eat of it and not die. I am the living bread which came down from heaven; if any one eats of this bread, he will live for ever; and the bread which I shall give for the life of the world is my flesh. (Jn 6: 49-51)**

When some in the crowd objected to this teaching—"How can this man give us his flesh to eat?"—Jesus became even more unequivocal.

> **Jesus said to them, "Truly, truly, I say to you, unless you eat the flesh of the Son of man and drink his blood, you have no life in you; he who eats my flesh and drinks my blood has eternal life, and I will raise him up at the last day. For my flesh is food indeed, and my blood is drink indeed. He who eats my flesh and drinks my blood abides in me, and I in him. As the living Father sent me, and I live because of the Father, so he who eats me will live because of me. This is the bread which came down from heaven, not such as the fathers ate and died; he who eats this bread will live for ever." (Jn 6: 53-58)**

Many of his disciples who had followed him up to this point left him after hearing this teaching. It is interesting to note that Christ did nothing to dissuade them of their understanding that he was speaking literally of eating his flesh and drinking his blood. The Apostles stayed with Christ, perhaps not fully understanding his words, but placing their full trust in him as their Messiah.

Adoration of the Lamb (detail) by Van Eyck.
In a mysterious but real way, the bread and wine become Jesus' Body and Blood, which the faithful receive
as a sharing and participation in Christ's Death and Resurrection.

The New Passover

Christ instituted the Sacrament of the Eucharist at the Last Supper, a Passover meal. Using the unleavened bread and wine from the Passover celebration, a thanksgiving to God for having spared and delivered his faithful people, Christ gave the meal of the Old Covenant an entirely new meaning under his New Covenant.

> As they were eating, Jesus took bread, and blessed, and broke it, and gave it to the disciples and said, "Take, eat; this is my body." And he took a cup, and when he had given thanks he gave it to them, saying, "Drink of it, all of you; for this is my blood of the covenant, which is poured out for many for the forgiveness of sins. I tell you I shall not drink again of the fruit of the vine until that day when I drink it new with you in my Father's kingdom." (Mt 26:26-29)

In the Mass, the unique sacrifice of Christ on the Cross is perpetually re-presented (made present) on the altar.

> The sacrifice of Christ and the sacrifice of the Eucharist are *one single sacrifice*: "The victim is one and the same: the same now offers through the ministry of priests, who then offered himself on

THE MASS IN THE EARLY CHURCH

As we read in previous chapters, the "breaking of the bread"—the Mass, the Eucharistic Liturgy—was the central activity of the early Christian community and was celebrated every Sunday, the first day of the week.[52] St. Justin Martyr, a Christian convert living in the second century whose writings open a marvelous window to the practices of the early Church, described what this celebration entailed:

✤ **Gathering on Sunday.** "On the day we call the day of the sun, all who dwell in the city or country gather in the same place."

✤ **Readings from Scripture.** "Memoirs of the Apostles and the writings of the prophets are read."

✤ **A Homily.** "When the reader has finished, he who presides over those gathered admonishes and challenges them to imitate these beautiful things."

✤ **Prayers of the Faithful.** "Then we all rise together and offer prayers for ourselves...and for others, wherever they may be."

✤ **An Offertory.** "Then someone brings bread and a cup of water and wine mixed together to him who presides over the brethren."

✤ **Eucharistic Prayer.** "He takes them and offers praise and glory to the Father of the universe, through the name of the Son and of the Holy Spirit and for a considerable time he gives thanks (in Greek, *eucharistian*) that we have been judged worthy of these gifts."

✤ **Reception of the Eucharist.** "When he who presides has given thanks and the people have responded, those whom we call deacons give to those present the 'eucharisted' bread and wine and water."

This liturgy of the early Christians exhibits the very same structure as the Mass today. In obedience to Christ, who at the Last Supper told the Apostles, "Do this in memory of me," the Church has celebrated the Eucharist from the very beginning of her existence.

The Last Supper by Juan de Juanes.
In obedience to Christ, who at the Last Supper told the Apostles, "Do this in memory of me," the Church has celebrated the Eucharist from the very beginning of her existence.

the cross; only the manner of offering is different." "And since in this divine sacrifice which is celebrated in the Mass, the same Christ who offered himself once in a bloody manner on the altar of the cross is contained and is offered in an unbloody manner...this sacrifice is truly propitiatory."[53] (CCC 1367)

The Mass is also a sacrifice of praise and thanksgiving. The word *eucharist*, in fact, means "thanksgiving." Jesus' own words at the Last Supper, repeated by the priest in the words of Consecration, clearly indicate that the bread is his "body" and the wine is his "blood of the covenant," thus giving a supernatural meaning to his earlier self-identification as the Bread of Life.

In a mysterious but real way, the bread and wine become Jesus' Body and Blood, which the faithful receive as a sharing and participation in Christ's Death and Resurrection. Although the bread and wine do not change in appearance or any other observable property, they become the Body and Blood of Christ. The Church calls this change *transubstantiation* to indicate a change in substance but not in appearance. *Real Presence* is the term used to describe Christ's true and substantial presence under the appearance of bread and wine.

> By celebrating the Last Supper with his apostles in the course of the Passover meal, Jesus gave the Jewish Passover its definitive meaning. Jesus' passing over to his Father by his death and Resurrection, the new Passover, is anticipated in the Supper and celebrated in the Eucharist, which fulfills the Jewish Passover and anticipates the final Passover of the Church in the glory of the kingdom. (CCC 1340)

"Do This in Memory of Me"

At the Last Supper, Christ commissioned his Apostles, whom we acknowledge as the first priests and bishops of the Church, to "do this in memory of me"—a command bishops and priests today fulfill whenever they celebrate Holy Mass.

> The command of Jesus to repeat his actions and words "until he comes" does not only ask us to remember Jesus and what he did. It is directed at the liturgical celebration, by the apostles and their successors, of the memorial of Christ, of his life, of his death, of his Resurrection, and of his intercession in the presence of the Father.[54] (CCC 1341)

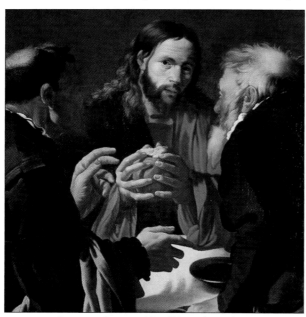

Supper at Emmaus (detail) by Terbrugghen.
Because the Eucharist unites us more closely to Christ, it also unites us to the entire Mystical Body of Christ, the People of God, our fellow members of the Church.

Scripture indicates that the Apostles understood this command from the very beginning, as the faithful "devoted themselves to the apostles' teaching and fellowship, to the breaking of bread and the prayers."[55] They soon established Sunday, the day of Christ's Resurrection, as the appropriate day each week to celebrate the Eucharist, which today and throughout time "remains the center of the Church's life."[56] The Mass is a single act of worship, which includes the proclamation of the Word of God in the Liturgy of the Word, thanksgiving for the great gifts God has bestowed upon his people, especially for the gift of his Son, whom he sent for our redemption, the consecration of bread and wine, which will become the Body and Blood of Christ, and the reception of the Eucharist in Holy Communion.

The faithful benefit profoundly from participating in the Mass and receiving the Eucharist worthily. To receive the Eucharist worthily, one must be in full communion with the Church and free from mortal sin. Holy Communion increases our union with Christ; it forgives our venial sins and strengthens us against future temptations to commit mortal sins. Because the Eucharist unites us more closely to Christ, it also unites us to the entire Mystical Body of Christ, the People of God, our fellow members of the Church. It "identifies us with [Christ's] Heart, sustains our strength along the pilgrimage of this life, makes us long for eternal life, and unites us even now to the Church in heaven, the Blessed Virgin Mary, and all the saints."[57]

Communal prayer, hearing the Word of God proclaimed, and receiving the Eucharist are so vital to the spiritual life that the Church obliges the Catholic faithful to attend Holy Mass every Sunday and on Holy Days of Obligation and to receive the Eucharist at least once a year, although, if properly disposed, weekly or even daily reception is greatly encouraged.

THE EUCHARIST: THE SOURCE AND SUMMIT OF THE CHURCH'S LIFE

The Liturgy of the Eucharist—Institution Narrative and Consecration
This prayer recalls the Last Supper of the Lord in which the celebration of the Eucharist was instituted.

The Eucharist is the *summit* of the whole Christian life because the faithful bring to it all their prayers and good works, their joys and sufferings. These modest offerings are united to the perfect sacrifice of Christ and are thus completely sanctified and lifted up to God in an act of perfect worship which brings the faithful into the divine intimacy (cf. Jn 6:56-57). Therefore, as St. Thomas Aquinas writes, the Eucharist is "the culmination of the spiritual life and the goal of all the sacraments" (*Summa Theol.*, III. Q. 66, a. 6).

The Eucharist requires the participation of the Church's members. According to the Council, "both in the offering and in Holy Communion, each in his own way, though not of course indiscriminately, has his own part to play in the liturgical [Eucharistic] action" (*LG* 11).

Participation is common to the entire "priestly people," who have been allowed to unite themselves to the offering and the communion. But this participation differs according to the condition of the Church's members, in accord with the sacramental institution. There is a specific role for the priestly ministry; however, it does not eliminate, but rather promotes the role of the common priesthood.

In virtue of Baptism and Confirmation... the Christian is qualified to participate...in divine worship, which has its centre and culmination in the sacrifice of Christ made present in the Eucharist.

— Pope Bl. John Paul II, *L'Osservatore Romano*, n. 15, April 15, 1992.

PENANCE

As Christians, we know that we are sinners. Although Baptism washes away our sins, it does not make us perfect. We still commit actual sins, even after Baptism, because the Sacrament does not change our human nature, which, due to the effects of Original Sin, still suffers from an inclination to sin, called *concupiscence*. Therefore, we still need to be sorry for, confess, and seek forgiveness for those sins on a regular basis.

The principal purpose of Christ's mission of redemption was to release humanity from its bondage to sin and to bestow the possibility of entering eternal life with God in Heaven. As an integral part of this ministry, Jesus often forgave the sins of the men and women whom he encountered.

After he rose from the dead, Jesus spent his remaining time on earth preparing his Apostles to lead his Church. As a part of that preparation, Christ granted the Apostles, his first priests and bishops, his power and authority—including the authority to forgive sins.

He breathed on them, and said to them, "Receive the Holy Spirit. If you forgive the sins of any, they are forgiven; if you retain the sins of any, they are retained." (Jn 20: 22-23)

A confessor may not reveal what has been told to him in Confession, even upon the threat of death to himself or others as in the story of St. John Nepomucene.

Through the very explicit commissioning of this authority to forgive sins, Christ instituted the Sacrament of Penance and Reconciliation. "Penance" and "reconciliation" emphasize different elements in the Sacrament itself. The penitent, who is aware of his or her sins and has true sorrow for having committed them, confesses his or her sins to a priest; the priest pronounces the forgiveness of Christ, the words of *absolution*, and assigns the penitent a penance—usually particular prayers, Scripture reading, or virtues to practice; and the absolution and the completion of the penance, through the power of the Holy Spirit, complete the reconciliation between the penitent and God.

The Apostles exercised this authority and preached confession to the first Christians. "If we confess our sins, [God] is faithful and just," taught St. John, "and will forgive our sins and cleanse us from all unrighteousness."[58] St. Paul made the further clarification that "confession" is something you do "with your lips," not just with your heart and mind.[59]

Confession of sins is also taught in the *Didache*—an ancient Christian document that dates back to the first century. It states, "Thou shalt confess thy transgressions in the Church and shalt not come unto prayer with an evil conscience." A later chapter speaks of the importance of confession before receiving Communion: "On the Lord's Day gather together, break bread and give thanks, first confessing your sins so that your sacrifice may be pure."

The Sacrament of Penance is also tied to Jesus' solemn words to St. Peter, the Head of the Apostles and the first Pope, when he said, "I will give you the keys of the kingdom of heaven, and whatever you bind on earth shall be bound in heaven, and whatever you loose on earth shall be loosed in heaven."[60]

The words *bind* and *loose* mean: whomever you exclude from your communion, will be excluded from communion with God; whomever you receive anew into your communion, God will welcome back into his. *Reconciliation with the Church is inseparable from reconciliation with God.* (CCC 1445)

Cain and Abel by Titian.
A mortal sin such as murder is a sin that breaks our communion with God and his Church, rendering us unable to receive the Eucharist in Holy Communion until the mortal sin is forgiven and our communion restored.

Venial and Mortal Sins

The Church recognizes two types of sin: *venial sin* and *mortal sin*. Venial sins are lesser offenses that harm our relationship with God, while mortal sins—sins of a grave matter that we commit with forethought and full consent of the will—break our communion with God and his Church, rendering us unable to receive the Eucharist in Holy Communion until those mortal sins are forgiven and our communion restored. The only way to restore that communion is through God's forgiveness in the Sacrament of Penance.

The concrete form of the Sacrament of Penance has changed over the centuries, but its fundamental structure has remained the same:

✤ The one who has sinned undergoes an interior conversion, which leads him or her to *contrition* (true sorrow), confession, and *satisfaction* (penance and/or *restitution*);

✤ God acts through the ministry of the Church as the priest forgives the penitent in the name of Jesus Christ, assigns the manner of satisfaction, and prays for and with the sinner, thus healing the penitent and bringing him or her back into communion with God and his Church.

✤ The Sacrament of Penance effects, through the grace of the Holy Spirit, the forgiveness of sin, the reconciliation of the sinner with God and the Church, the remission of the eternal punishment due to mortal sin as well as the restoration of sanctifying grace, the remission of the temporal punishment, at least in part, due to all sin, venial and mortal, peace, serenity of conscience, spiritual consolation, strength to resist temptation, and an increase in actual grace.

In the early Church, penance for particularly grave sins such as murder or adultery was extremely rigorous and public, sometimes lasting for years. Centuries later, Irish missionaries introduced the practice of private and frequent confession. This practice made the Sacrament of Penance a regular part of the devotional lives of the faithful.

Because Jesus gave his Apostles the authority to forgive and retain sins, the Church uses that power to bring Christians back into a right relationship with God. Only a priest who has received the authority from the Church can pronounce the forgiveness of sins in Christ's name.

ANOINTING OF THE SICK

Just as the Gospels report that Christ often forgave the sins of the people he met, they also attest to the many times he cured people of their diseases and disabilities. Healing was an integral part of Christ's public ministry and a foreshadowing of the coming Kingdom of God, a proof, as it were, that Jesus was the promised Messiah. In the Gospel of St. Luke, the works of healing are mentioned right alongside Christ's ministry of preaching.

> When the men had come to [Jesus], they said, "John the Baptist has sent us to you, saying, 'Are you he who is to come, or shall we look for another?'" In that hour he cured many of diseases and plagues and evil spirits, and on many that were blind he bestowed sight. And he answered them, "Go and tell John what you have seen and heard: the blind receive their sight, the lame walk, lepers are cleansed, and the deaf hear, the dead are raised up, the poor have good news preached to them. And blessed is he who takes no offense at me." (Lk 7: 20-23)

Jesus often used physical signs to heal, such as the laying on of hands, mud, washing, even his own spittle. Often, he asked the person seeking healing to believe in him. On one occasion, a woman of great faith was cured merely by touching his garment.

Christ Healing the Sick by West.
Healing was an integral part of Christ's public ministry and a foreshadowing of the coming Kingdom of God.

Jesus also empowered the Apostles to heal the sick and cast out demons. As in Jesus' own example, preaching and healing went hand in hand.

> They went out and preached that men should repent. And they cast out many demons, and anointed with oil many that were sick and healed them. (Mk 6: 12-13)

The Acts of the Apostles relate how the Apostles were able to do great "works" of healing in much the same way that Christ did, including the remarkable story of how St. Peter first cured a man who had been paralyzed for eight years and then raised a woman from the dead.[61]

The Sacrament of the Anointing of the Sick has its institution in Christ, who gave the power to heal to his Apostles. The Letter of St. James also bears witness to the use of this Sacrament in the early Church and how the elders (in Greek, *presbyteros*, from which the word "priest" originates) used oil in the healing ritual.

> **Is any among you sick? Let him call for the elders of the church, and let them pray over him, anointing him with oil in the name of the Lord; and the prayer of faith will save the sick man, and the Lord will raise him up; and if he has committed sins, he will be forgiven.** (Jas 5: 14-15)

Not Just "Extreme Unction"

The Church continues to exercise Christ's healing power today by anointing the sick through the ministry of a priest, who confers the Sacrament by the laying on of hands and the anointing with the Oil of the Sick. As is the case with the Sacrament of Penance, the Sacrament of the Anointing of the Sick has gone through some development over the centuries. Following the apostolic era, the anointing became more and more associated with imminent death; for that reason, it acquired the name *Extreme Unction*, sometimes called *Last Anointing* or *Last Rites*. Today the Church emphasizes that the Sacrament can be celebrated with any illness or condition, even prior to surgery, where there is any danger of death.

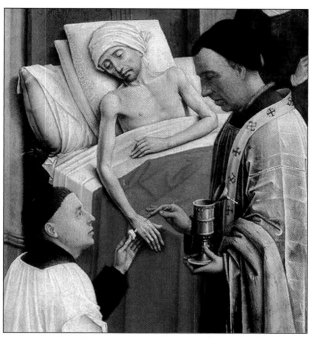

Anointing of the Sick, Seven Sacraments Triptych (detail) by Weyden. The Sacrament of the Anointing of the Sick has its institution in Christ, who gave the power to heal to his Apostles.

> *Extreme unction*, which may also and more fittingly be called *anointing of the sick*, is not a sacrament for those only who are at the point of death. Hence, as soon as any one of the faithful begins to be in danger of death from sickness or old age, the fitting time for him to receive this sacrament has certainly already arrived. (*Sacrosanctum Concilium*, 73)

There are several spiritual benefits of the Sacrament of the Anointing of the Sick. It gives grace to strengthen the individual, granting peace and courage to overcome the trials and difficulties of illness or infirmity. It unites the patient's suffering with the Passion of Christ, allowing him or her to participate in the saving work of Christ; it helps make the entire Church holy, as the Church prays for healing and as the patient offers his or her suffering for others; and it prepares the patient for the final journey, forgiving his or her sins if he or she was not able to obtain it through the Sacrament of Penance (as would be the case with an unconscious patient, for example). In some instances, the Sacrament may even help restore the patient to health, if it is God's will.

It is important to remember that physical healing is not always part of God's plan. Even St. Paul, who was famous for healings and, like St. Peter, even raised a man from the dead, was not healed when he prayed to be rid of the "thorn" that tormented him. Instead, Christ gave him this answer to his prayers: "My grace is sufficient for you, for my power is made perfect in weakness."[62]

In the Sacrament of Holy Orders, a man is ordained to the ministry of the Church. The rite is called *ordination* after the ancient Roman term *ordo*, which referred to an established civil body, particularly a governing body.

HOLY ORDERS

By the very act of calling together the Twelve Apostles and making St. Peter the head of the Apostles, Jesus constituted the pastoral office of the Church—the apostolic college, the successors of whom are the bishops in union with the Pope. This was the beginning of the Church hierarchy, which in the New Testament era developed into the three degrees of *episcopate*, *presbyterate*, and *diaconate*—stated simply, the orders of bishop, priest, and deacon. These ministries conferred in the Sacrament of Holy Orders are essential for the life of the Church, and, in fact, without bishops, priests, and deacons, the Church cannot exist. It can readily be seen as a fulfillment of the priesthood of Aaron and the Levites under the Old Covenant.

The Sacrament is called "Holy Orders" and the rite is called *ordination* after the ancient Roman term *ordo*, which referred to an established civil body, particularly a governing body.

Throughout the course of his public ministry, Jesus conferred upon the Apostles the power and obligation to baptize, to forgive sins, to anoint with oil, and to celebrate the Eucharist. The conferral of the Sacraments is central to the ministry of Holy Orders. To help them in their pastoral ministry, the Apostles chose men to be bishops, priests, and deacons.

St. Stephen, who was the first Christian martyr, was chosen to become one of the first deacons of the Church, and St. Paul, in his First Letter to St. Timothy and his Letter to Titus, sets forth the personal qualities to be sought in men who would serve as bishops, presbyters (priests), and deacons.[63]

The Sacrament of Holy Orders consecrates a man for service in the sacramental ministry of the Church. Through this Sacrament, bishops and priests are given the mission and faculty to act *in persona Christi* ("in the Person of Christ"), and deacons are given strength to serve the People of God through liturgy, the Word, and charity in communion with the bishops and priests. Because Christ chose only men to be his Apostles, the Church is bound to continue this example by ordaining only men in the Sacrament of Holy Orders.

Characters of Ecclesial Ministry

The sacramental nature of ecclesial ministry is marked by three characters:[64]

✣ **A character of service,** since the ordained are servants of the faithful who, in the course of being "slaves for Christ" and acting as ministers of the word and grace that are not their own, freely become the slaves of all;

✤ **A collegial character,** bonded in a fraternal unity at the service of the faithful—priests serving collegially among the presbyterate, deacons serving collegially among the diaconate, each under the direction of their bishops, and bishops serving collegially with one another and with the successor to St. Peter—that reflects and witnesses the communion of the Trinity;

✤ **A personal character,** in that they were personally called by Christ to this life of service and must bear personal witness to fulfill the mission they have been given by Christ.

Men who believe they may be called to the ordained ministry ordinarily go through a discernment process with their local diocese or a religious community. If accepted as a seminarian, they would embark on a course of study and formation that normally includes some pastoral experience. When a seminarian has finished his studies, and when those responsible for his formation believe that the candidate is ready for ordination, they present the candidate to the bishop, who makes the final decision and celebrates the rite of ordination.

In the Sacrament of Holy Orders, the bishop lays his hands on the *ordinand* (the person receiving the Sacrament) and prays that God will pour out his Holy Spirit and the gifts of the Spirit that will be needed for the ordinand's ministry. The ordained deacon, priest, or bishop is enabled to act in the Person of Christ, shepherd and bridegroom of his Church.

> The sacrament of Holy Orders is conferred by the laying on of hands followed by a solemn prayer of consecration asking God to grant the ordinand the graces of the Holy Spirit required for his ministry. Ordination imprints an indelible sacramental character. (CCC 1597)

MATRIMONY

Like Holy Orders, the Sacrament of Matrimony is a vocation of service. Husbands and wives are to assist each other in living the Faith.

From the beginning of creation, human beings were created male and female with a mission to "be fruitful and multiply, and fill the earth." In the story of Adam and Eve, God brought the animals to Adam, but none of them was a suitable companion. Finally, God created woman from Adam's side, and he immediately recognized that she was a part of him: "This at last is bone of my bones and flesh of my flesh."[65]

Then the Sacred Author explains in straightforward manner that marriage—the union of one man and one woman—is part of God's original plan for creation:

A man leaves his father and his mother and cleaves to his wife, and they become one flesh (Gn 2: 24).

Sin, however, took its toll on this original unity of man and woman. Original Sin broke the communion not only between humanity and God but between man and woman. Instead of the equality and complementarity that man and woman were meant to enjoy, sins of lust, domination, disrespect, and discord entered male-female relationships. God's plan for the marriage of man and woman continues, but sin also continues to disrupt his plan and causes a great distortion of what marriage is meant to be. Only by the grace of God through the power of the Holy Spirit can we overcome these disturbances and rediscover that original unity that God intended for men and women in marriage.

In the Old Testament, we can see that the restoration of marriage to its original dignity was a work in progress. *Polygamy* among some of Israel's kings and patriarchs was tolerated, and divorce was allowed in

The Marriage of the Virgin (detail) by Raphael.
St. Paul writes of married love extensively in his Letter to the Ephesians, comparing the love between husbands and wives to the relationship between Christ and his Church.

some conditions under the Law of Moses. The idea of marriage as a lifelong and exclusive relationship between man and woman had not yet been incorporated into the lives of God's people. All the while, sexual sins including adultery, fornication, prostitution, homosexual behavior, and acts of bestiality—all grave sins against marriage that arise from a disordered conscience and a lack of God's grace—seemed to flourish.

At the same time, however, some of the Old Testament prophets began to prepare the Israelites for the restoration of God's original vision for marriage.

> Seeing God's covenant with Israel in the image of exclusive and faithful married love, the prophets prepared the Chosen People's conscience for a deepened understanding of the unity and indissolubility of marriage.[66] The books of Ruth and Tobit bear moving witness to an elevated sense of marriage and to the fidelity and tenderness of spouses. Tradition has always seen in the Song of Solomon a unique expression of human love, insofar as it is a reflection of God's love—a love "strong as death" that "many waters cannot quench."[67] (CCC 1611)

We have no clear indication in Scripture that Christ ever performed a marriage or commanded the Apostles to preside at Christian weddings. What is clear, however, is that Christ, in announcing his New Covenant, reestablished matrimony as it was originally intended by God.

"One Flesh"

Christ taught that, in marriage, a man and a woman "become one flesh" and that this union is meant to be permanent. Although the Law of Moses made provision for divorce, Christ reminded us, "From the beginning it was not so":

> Pharisees came up to [Jesus] and tested him by asking, "Is it lawful to divorce one's wife for any cause?" He answered, "Have you not read that he who made them from the beginning made them male and female, and said, 'For this reason a man shall leave his father and mother and be joined to his wife, and the two shall become one flesh'? So they are no longer two but one flesh. What therefore God has joined together, let not man put asunder." They said to him, "Why then did Moses command one to give a certificate of divorce, and to put her away?" He said to them, "For your hardness of heart Moses allowed you to divorce your wives, but from the beginning it was not so. And I say to you: whoever divorces his wife, except for unchastity, and marries another, commits adultery." (Mt 19:3-9)

St. Paul writes of married love extensively in his Letter to the Ephesians, comparing the love between husbands and wives to the relationship between Christ and his Church. In marriage, as in the Mystical Body of Christ, the "two become one," a reality that St. Paul calls "a great mystery, and I mean in reference to Christ and the church."[68]

The Church, from her apostolic beginnings, considered Christian marriage to be elevated by Christ to its former sacred dignity in a manner that was quite different from the marriage that existed between non-Christians. The Sacrament of Matrimony signifies the union that exists between Christ and his Church, which St. Paul refers to as the bride of Christ. The Sacrament, entered into between a baptized man and a baptized woman, gives them the grace through the Holy Spirit to love each other as Christ loves his Church, thus perfecting the human love of the spouses. It strenghtens their indissouble union, sanctifies them, and gives them the graces needed to help each other on their way to Heaven and to raise a Christian family.

A Vocation of Service

Like Holy Orders, the Sacrament of Matrimony is a vocation of service. Husbands and wives are to assist each other in living the Faith, helping each other to grow in sanctity so as to someday enter eternal life. If blessed with children, they are also called to raise them lovingly in the Catholic Faith.

> **"By reason of their state in life and of their order, [Christian spouses] have their own special gifts in the People of God."[69] This grace proper to the sacrament of Matrimony is intended to perfect the couple's love and to strengthen their indissoluble unity. By this grace they "help one another to attain holiness in their married life and in welcoming and educating their children."[70] (CCC 1641)**

The Sacrament of Matrimony is unique in the Western Church in that it is the man and woman themselves who are the ministers of the Sacrament. Through marriage preparation programs, the Church helps the couple discern their call to marriage and prepares them for the Sacrament. In the wedding itself, the Church, through a bishop, priest, or deacon, blesses the marriage covenant that the couple willfully enters before the community of the faithful.

A LIFE OF PRAYER

Prayer is the raising of one's mind and heart to God or the requesting of good things from God.[71] Prayer and Christian life are inseparable, for they concern the same love and the same renunciation, proceeding from love.[72]

Pope Bl. John Paul II described the nature of prayer in this way:

> [Prayer] is commonly held to be a conversation. In a conversation there are always an "I" or a "We" and a "thou" or "you." In this case the "Thou" is with a capital "T." If at first the "I" seems to be the most important element in prayer, prayer teaches that the situation is actually different. The "Thou" is more important, because our prayer begins with God.
>
> In prayer, then, the true protagonist is God. The protagonist is Christ, who constantly frees creation from slavery to corruption and leads it toward liberty, for the glory of the children of God. The protagonist is the Holy Spirit, who "comes to the aid of our weakness."
>
> We begin to pray, believing that it is our own initiative that compels us to do so. Instead, we learn that it is always God's initiative within us, just as St. Paul has written. This initiative restores in us our true humanity; it restores in us our unique dignity.[73]

Pope Bl. John Paul II in Prayer at the Vatican.
Prayer is the raising of one's mind and heart to God or the requesting of good things from God.

Christian prayer tries above all to meditate on the mysteries of Christ: to get to know him, to love him, and to be united to him. We learn what prayer is by reviewing the life of Christ. He taught us how to pray. When Jesus prayed to his Father, he was already teaching us how to pray.[74]

The Lord's Prayer by Tissot.
"Pray then like this: Our Father who art in heaven," (Mt 6: 9)

A recurring theme throughout Christ's life was his devotion to prayer, especially before the great events in his life. When one of his disciples asked, "Lord, teach us to pray," Jesus responded by teaching his followers the words of the Lord's Prayer, or the Our Father:

> **Our Father who art in heaven,**
> **Hallowed be thy name.**
> **Thy kingdom come,**
> **Thy will be done,**
> **On earth as it is in heaven.**
> **Give us this day our daily bread;**
> **And forgive us our debts,**
> **As we also have forgiven our debtors;**
> **And lead us not into temptation,**
> **But deliver us from evil. (Mt 6: 9-13)**

The Our Father is a gift from Christ and the Holy Spirit to the Church and, thus, the quintessential prayer of Christians. It is a model for all Christian prayer and, therefore, sometimes called the perfect prayer as it sums up the entire Gospel of Jesus Christ. It teaches prayer is a communication with the Father and people should rely upon him for everything, both material and spiritual. The Lord's Prayer helps resist temptation and is an effective petition for personal forgiveness that rests on one's willingness to forgive others. It contains the most essential petitions for holiness, which pertain to everyone.

> The Lord's Prayer "is truly the summary of the whole gospel"[75] "Since the Lord...after handing over the practice of prayer, said elsewhere, 'Ask and you will receive,' and since everyone has petitions which are peculiar to his circumstances, the regular and appropriate prayer [the Lord's Prayer] is said first, as the foundation of further desires"[76] (CCC 2761)

From that moment on, the Lord's Prayer has been the most important prayer in the life of the Church. St. Thomas Aquinas called it the most perfect prayer, and one of the early Christian writers, Tertullian of North Africa, called it "truly the summary of the whole gospel."[77]

Although the Lord's Prayer is the perfect prayer, it is not the only type of prayer that Jesus gave his disciples. Jesus taught his followers by his example, and he practiced many forms of prayer.

In the Gospels, we see Jesus using the formal or traditional prayers of Judaism.[78] Scripture also records that he prayed spontaneously, raising heartfelt prayers of thanks to his Father in Heaven.[79] He sometimes prayed alone in silence,[80] but he also prayed with groups of friends.[81] Jesus prayerfully read the Scriptures,[82] and he prayed the Psalms.[83] He celebrated holy days, made pilgrimages, and attended the Jewish liturgy.[84] Jesus also practiced fasting,[85] as did his Apostles,[86] which Christianity has traditionally called the "prayer of the senses."

TYPES OF PRAYER

Just as Jesus' prayer life was rich and varied, the Church too presents us with many different ways to pray. In fact, it is the Holy Spirit, acting through the living transmission of the faith, that is, the Church's Tradition, that we learn to pray.

We generally can speak of prayer taking one or a combination of four main types—*petition, adoration, contrition,* and *thanksgiving*. In petition, we humbly ask for God to heal us, to take away our doubts and fears, to help us become more virtuous, and to fill our own needs or those of others; in adoration, we praise God for his infinite goodness and his perfect attributes; in contrition, we sincerely ask forgiveness for our sins; in thanksgiving, we express our gratitude to God for having created us, for blessing us, for sustaining us, for forgiving us, and for redeeming us.

We can categorize prayer in several ways. In form, prayer may be formal, using memorized prayers like the *Our Father* or the *Hail Mary*; spontaneous, speaking to God straight from the heart; or a combination of both. It may be mental, spoken, or sung; it may be done alone or with others, in a church or in the privacy of one's home; one may pray sitting or kneeling with eyes closed or while carrying on ordinary tasks, such as working, driving, or performing household chores. Other times, we may simply listen for God to speak to us, usually following a period of prayer or meditation.

> The Christian tradition comprises three major expressions of the life of prayer:…
>
> VOCAL PRAYER, founded on the union of body and soul in human nature, associates the body with the interior prayer of the heart, following Christ's example of praying to his Father and teaching the Our Father to his disciples.
>
> MEDITATION is a prayerful quest engaging thought, imagination, emotion, and desire. Its goal is to make our own, in faith, the subject considered, by confronting it with the reality of our own life.
>
> CONTEMPLATIVE PRAYER is the simple expression of the mystery of prayer. It is a gaze of faith fixed on Jesus, an attentiveness to the Word of God, a silent love. It achieves real union with the prayer of Christ to the extent that it makes us share in his mystery. (CCC 2721-2724)

We can read from Scripture or from the writings of the saints and pray afterward about what we have read, asking the Holy Spirit to enlighten our minds and hearts; we can use a method such as the *lectio divina*, a technique whereby one meditates on individual words and phrases of a scriptural reading and then imagines oneself at the very scene of the scriptural event described.

Prayer may take the form of popular devotions, such as the *Rosary*, the *Chaplet of Divine Mercy*, or any of a number of *novenas*, nine-day devotions asking the intercession of God or particular saints for particular needs. With the consent of a spiritual director, Christians may also undertake some other form of pious activity in conjunction with prayer, such as fasting. There are prayers for certain times of day, such as morning or night prayers, grace before meals, or the *Angelus*. Special journeys may serve as extended periods of prayer, such as retreats or pilgrimages to religious sites or shrines.

The Mass, of course, is the ultimate prayer of the Church, and all liturgies of the Church invite us into communal prayer. We are recommended to spend time before the Blessed Sacrament, reserved in the tabernacle, praying in the presence of Christ; we can pray our devotions using sacramentals (sacred signs instituted by the Church), such as statuary or the *Stations of the Cross*, to help focus our prayer.

We can pray our devotions using sacramentals to help focus our prayer.

> Prayer in the events of each day and each moment is one of the secrets of the kingdom revealed to "little children," to the servants of Christ, to the poor of the Beatitudes. It is right and good to pray so that the coming of the kingdom of justice and peace may influence the march of history, but it is just as important to bring the help of prayer into humble, everyday situations; all forms of prayer can be the leaven to which the Lord compares the kingdom.[87] (CCC 2660)

Prayer is an indispensable component of the Christian life. Jesus' example of daily prayer is a model that will help us understand and live the teachings of Christ and his Church more fully. The Church, through her liturgical year, Sacraments, and pious practices, provides many opportunities for both private and communal prayer and emphasizes the importance of scheduling and integrating prayer into our daily lives.

> The Tradition of the Church proposes to the faithful certain rhythms of praying intended to nourish continual prayer. Some are daily, such as morning and evening prayer, grace before and after meals, the Liturgy of the Hours. Sundays, centered on the Eucharist, are kept holy primarily by prayer. The cycle of the liturgical year and its great feasts are also basic rhythms of the Christian's life of prayer. (CCC 2698)

SACRIFICE AND SELF-DENIAL

The way of perfection passes by way of the cross. There is no holiness without renunciation and spiritual battle.[88] **Spiritual progress entails the ascesis and mortification that gradually lead to living in the peace and joy of the Beatitudes. (CCC 2015)**

Mortification, which in its Latin roots literally means "to make [the flesh] dead," is a means of seeking holiness through self-discipline and self-denial. Its purpose is not only to avoid sin but also to subdue the body so as to strengthen the soul. Just as a dieter builds self-control by turning down a delicious dessert, we can build spiritual self-control by controlling our own appetites. St. Paul compared growth in the spiritual life to the training of an athlete:

Do you not know that in a race all the runners compete, but only one receives the prize? So run that you may obtain it. Every athlete exercises self-control in all things. They do it to receive a perishable wreath, but we an imperishable. Well, I do not run aimlessly, I do not box as one beating the air; but I pommel my body and subdue it, lest after preaching to others I myself should be disqualified. (1 Cor 9: 24-27)

St. Jerome by Perugino.
St. Jerome became a hermit in the desert of Palestine dedicating his attention to learning Hebrew and studying Scripture. As penance, he practiced self-denial and mortification.

Mortification can be practiced frequently, even continually. When it is directed at training ourselves to avoid temptation, it usually involves an additional measure of prudence in avoiding the "near occasions" of sin—for example, averting our eyes from an immodestly dressed person or image in order to negate any opportunity for temptation to sexual sin, or biting our tongue when tempted to join in gossip or to voice an uncharitable criticism. It can also be simply an intentional self-denial of a perfectly innocent pleasure, such as drinking our morning coffee black instead of adding cream and sweetener or arising in the morning at the first sound of the alarm instead of hitting the snooze button and sleeping a few more minutes.

Self-denial can also involve accepting opportunities to practice virtue, such as bearing a headache or a small inconvenience without complaining, or keeping patient while waiting in line at the supermarket. The prescribed fasting and abstinence associated with Lent, as well as the required one-hour fast prior to receiving Holy Communion, are also examples of mortification. Even making the effort to attend daily Mass or to pray every day when we otherwise feel tired or overwhelmed requires self-discipline.

As St. Paul advised Timothy, "Train yourself in godliness; for while bodily training is of some value, godliness is of value in every way, as it holds promise for the present life and also for the life to come."[89]

Self-denial will be more precious if it is united to charity according to the teaching of St. Leo the Great: "Let us give to virtue what we refuse to self-indulgence. Let what we deny ourselves by fast be the refreshment of the poor." When we fast from a meal or choose to live in a simpler fashion than we can otherwise afford, we can do so in solidarity with the poor of the world and thus offer these mortifications for their intention.

Let us listen to our Lord: "He who is faithful in a very little thing is faithful also in much; and he who is dishonest in a very little thing is dishonest also in much." It is as if he were saying to us: "Fight continuously in the apparently unimportant things which are to my mind important; fulfill your duty, punctually; smile at whoever needs cheering up, even though there is sorrow in your soul; devote the necessary time to prayer, without haggling; go to the help of anyone who looks for you; practice justice, and go beyond it with the grace of charity." (St. Josemaria Escriva, *Christ Is Passing By*, 77)

THE ROLE OF YOUTH IN THE CHURCH

On Palm Sunday, April 5, 2009, Pope Benedict XVI presided at Holy Mass in St. Peter's Square on the occasion of the XXIV World Youth Day. At the end of the Eucharistic Concelebration, the World Youth Day Cross and the Icon of Our Lady were passed on from the youth of Sydney to the youth of Madrid for World Youth Day 2011.

The young "are the hope of the Church" (Decree *Gravissimum Educationis*, n. 2). What are the reasons for this hope? One could say the first is of a demographic order. Young people, "in a great many countries of the world...represent half the entire population, and often constitute in number half of the People of God living in those countries" (*CL* 46).

But there is another even stronger reason of a psychological, spiritual and ecclesiological kind. The Church today observes the generosity of many young people, their desire to make the world a better place and to make the Christian community advance (cf. ibid.). Thus she focuses her attention on them, seeing in them a privileged participation in the hope which comes to her from the Holy Spirit. The grace operating in young people paves the way for the Church's progress as regards both her expansion and her quality.

Very rightly we can speak of the Church of the young, remembering that the Holy Spirit renews in everyone—even in the elderly, provided they remain open and receptive—the vibrance of grace.

I hope that young people will find ever wider openings in the apostolate. The Church must introduce them to the message of the Gospel with its promises and demands. In turn, young people must express their aspirations and their plans to the Church. "This mutual dialogue, by taking place with great cordiality, clarity and courage, will provide a favourable setting for the meeting and exchange between generations, and will be a source of richness and youthfulness for the Church and for civil society" (*CL* 46).

— Pope Bl. John Paul II, *L'Osservatore Romano*, n. 36, September 7, 1994.

PART II: SEEKING HOLINESS IN DAILY LIFE

LIVING WITNESSES OF JESUS CHRIST

Scenes from the Life of St. Francis (detail) by Gozzoli.
"Preach the Gospel always; and if necessary, use words."

The missionary or evangelizing role of the Church is founded on the command that Christ gave to his Apostles before his Ascension into Heaven:

Go therefore and make disciples of all nations, baptizing them in the name of the Father and of the Son and of the Holy Spirit, teaching them to observe all that I have commanded you; and lo, I am with you always, to the close of the age. (Mt 28: 19-20)

While this teaching of Christ was issued to the Apostles nearly two thousand years ago, it is just as relevant to the Church today. As the Second Vatican Council stated, "In the present state of affairs, out of which there is arising a new situation for mankind, the Church, being the salt of the earth and the light of the world,[90] is more urgently called upon to save and renew every creature, that all things may be restored in Christ and all men may constitute one family in him and one People of God."[91]

Missionary work has been at the forefront of the Church's activity in the world throughout her history. This work of evangelization, however, is not solely the responsibility of the institutional Church, rather, it is part of the baptismal vocation shared by all Christians. "Side by side with the collective proclamation of the Gospel, the other form of transmission, the person-to-person one, remains valid and important."[92]

A Christian participates in the missionary activity of the Church, first and foremost, by his or her witness. Through their Christian witness in the midst of society, the followers of Christ show understanding and acceptance of others and a willingness to share in their lives in solidarity with all that is good and noble. Through their example, Christians exhibit God's values that surpass the values of the world. Such Christian witness is a paradox that inevitably touches other people and causes irresistible questions to rise in their hearts.[93] This approach of silent witness to Christ coincides with St. Francis of Assisi's famous dictum, "Preach the Gospel always; and if necessary, use words."

> Let everyone know that their first and most important obligation for the spread of the Faith is this: to lead a profoundly Christian life. For their fervor in the service of God and their charity toward others will cause a new spiritual wind to blow for the whole Church, which will then appear as a sign lifted up among the nations (cf. Is 11: 12), "the light of the world" (Mt 5: 14) and "the salt of the earth" (Mt 5: 13). This testimony of a good life will more easily have its effect if it is given in unison with other Christian communities.[94]

In addition to being a living witness to Christ, a person must also know the Faith and be prepared to defend it if he or she is to effectively transmit the message of Christ. As St. Peter said, "Always be prepared to make a defense to any one who calls you to account for the hope that is in you."[95] For the missionary work of the Church to be effective, it must remain centered on Jesus Christ, and the truth of his teachings, as transmitted by the Catholic Church, must be proclaimed in the fullness of their understanding.

EVANGELIZING TRUTHS

In speaking about the work of evangelization in the Church, Pope Bl. John Paul II detailed several basic truths that are derived from the command to teach and baptize all nations that Christ gave to his disciples:[96]

✤ God desires the salvation of all.

✤ Jesus Christ is the "only Mediator," the one who "gave himself as a ransom for all" (1 Tm 2:5-6), since "there is salvation in no one else" (Acts 4:12).

✤ Everyone, therefore, ought to be converted to Christ, who is known through the preaching of the Church, and they ought, by Baptism, to become incorporated into him and into the Church which is his Body.

✤ He confirmed the role of the Church into which one ought to enter and persevere if one desires salvation (cf. *AG* 7).

Pope Bl. John Paul II greets the People of God in Assisi, Italy.
The pilgrim Church on earth is a visible society.

HOLINESS WITHIN ONE'S STATE OF LIFE

The pilgrim Church on earth is a visible society, structured and given order by Christ for the purpose of extending the Kingdom of God over the entire world. As we have seen, within this visible society there exists a great diversity of functions, each of which serves to sustain and strengthen the Church. Some are called to be pastors and shepherds of Christ's flock as bishops, priests, and deacons; others are called to witness to the Gospel by permanently embracing poverty, chastity, and obedience in the consecrated life, sometimes in conjunction with Holy Orders; still others are called to engage in everyday family and professional activities, bringing the light of Christ to all they encounter. These general categories of Christian living are referred to as *states of life*, and the calling we receive to a specific state of life is referred to as our *vocation* (from the Latin *vocatio*, meaning "call").

The specific tasks that each of us are given correspond to our state of life. "Having gifts that differ according to the grace given to us, let us use them."[97]

For Christians, the exercise of the common priesthood means offering all the circumstances of their lives to God. In the words of Christ, "If any man would come after me, let him deny himself and take up his cross daily and follow me."[98]

There are two necessary components to this lived witness: First, each of us must live according to the teachings of Christ as handed down and proclaimed by the Church; second, we must work to fulfill each of our duties to the best of our abilities. But it is not only by our example that we as Christians are called to evangelize those around us; we must also be prepared to witness to Christ when the opportunity presents itself.

> This witness of life, however, is not the sole element in the apostolate; the true apostle is on the lookout for occasions of announcing Christ by word, either to unbelievers...or to the faithful.[99] (CCC 905)

The vast majority of the members of the Church are the laity, both married and unmarried, who are called to live as Christ's witnesses in every activity according to their state of life—in family life, in ordinary daily work, in the lay apostolate, and in the public square.

HOLINESS IN FAMILY LIFE

The combination of evangelization by word and example finds a special expression within the state of married and family life. Sanctified by the Sacrament of Matrimony, husbands and wives "find their proper vocation in being witnesses of the faith and love of Christ to one another and to their children."[100] As the primary teachers of their children, parents have the unique role of educating them in the Faith, both through their example and through their verbal instruction, and encouraging them to fulfill their own common priesthood and call to holiness:

> It is here that the father of the family, the mother, children, and all members of the family exercise the *priesthood of the baptized* in a privileged way "by the reception of the sacraments, prayer and thanksgiving, the witness of a holy life, and self-denial and active charity."[101] Thus the home is the first school of Christian life and "a school for human enrichment."[102] Here one learns endurance and the joy of work, fraternal love, generous—even repeated—forgiveness, and above all divine worship in prayer and the offering of one's life. (CCC 1657)

Parents are to provide for the physical and spiritual needs of their children and, as they grow, to educate them in the proper use of their free will and their power of reason. Calling upon the grace of the Sacrament of Matrimony, they have the responsibility of "creating a home where tenderness, forgiveness, respect, fidelity, and disinterested service are the rule. The home is well suited for education in the virtues. This requires an apprenticeship in self-denial, sound judgment, and self-mastery—the preconditions of true freedom."[103]

Children living at home are to regard their parents with love and gratitude, showing their respect by docility and obedience. Grown children must look after their sick or aging parents and provide both material and moral support to them. As adults, children have the right and duty to select for themselves their profession and their state of life, although in doing so they should seek the advice of their parents. For their part, parents must not pressure their children to pursue any particular path but should encourage them to prayerfully discern their options.

ST. PAUL'S TEACHINGS CONCERNING THE UNMARRIED

"Concerning the unmarried, I have no command of the Lord, but I give my opinion as one who by the Lord's mercy is trustworthy.... Are you bound to a wife? Do not seek to be free. Are you free from a wife? Do not seek marriage. But if you marry, you do not sin, and if a girl marries she does not sin. Yet those who marry will have worldly troubles, and I would spare you that....

"I want you to be free from anxieties. The unmarried man is anxious about the affairs of the Lord, how to please the Lord; but the married man is anxious about worldly affairs, how to please his wife, and his interests are divided. And the unmarried woman or girl is anxious about the affairs of the Lord, how to be holy in body and spirit; but the married woman is anxious about worldly affairs, how to please her husband. I say this for your own benefit, not to lay any restraint upon you, but to promote good order and to secure your undivided devotion to the Lord."[104]

Opportunities for sanctity in family life are available also to the childless. "Spouses to whom God has not granted children can nevertheless have a conjugal life full of meaning, in both human and Christian terms. Their marriage can radiate a fruitfulness of charity, of hospitality, and of sacrifice." [105]

FINDING HOLINESS IN OUR WORK

Work can be sanctified because it is part of God's will for humanity. After God created Adam, "the LORD God took the man and put him in the garden of Eden to till it and keep it," Genesis tells us. [106]

St. Josemaria Escriva.
"Your human vocation is a part—and an important part—of your divine vocation."

Human work proceeds directly from persons created in the image of God and called to prolong the work of creation by subduing the earth, both with and for one another. [107] Hence work is a duty: "If any one will not work, let him not eat." [108] Work honors the Creator's gifts and the talents received from him. It can also be redemptive. By enduring the hardship of work [109] in union with Jesus, the carpenter of Nazareth and the one crucified on Calvary, man collaborates in a certain fashion with the Son of God in his redemptive work. He shows himself to be a disciple of Christ by carrying the cross, daily, in the work he is called to accomplish. [110] Work can be a means of sanctification and a way of animating earthly realities with the Spirit of Christ. (CCC 2427)

Because we are called to be witnesses to the Faith wherever we happen to be, the workplace is a particular opportunity to reflect the virtues of Christ. By performing our duties well and maintaining a cheerful and positive attitude, we can sanctify our work, ourselves, and those who may find in us inspiration and exemplary behavior.

When we deal with others fairly and ethically, showing great courtesy and kindness, we model proper Christian virtue that may lead to friendships and acquaintances in the workplace that provide opportunities to witness to our Faith more directly. Attracted to our example and good spirit, classmates and friends may want to learn more about us and the source of our virtue and happiness. Such moments can be entry points to mentioning our Faith, our Church, and our commitment to Christ, and continued interest may invite a deeper discussion on the issues of faith, whether it be with other Catholics, our separated brethren, or persons of non-Christian faith traditions.

Our witness to Christ extends to all our outside relationships—whether it be with neighbors, members of clubs or other organizations, or anyone else with whom we come in contact, keeping aware of the presence of Christ and our mission to witness the love of Christ at all times.

Christian faith and calling affect our whole existence, not just a part of it. Our relations with God necessarily demand giving ourselves, giving ourselves completely. The man of faith sees life, in all its dimensions, from a new perspective: that which is given us by God....Your human vocation is a part—and an important part—of your divine vocation. That is the reason why you must strive for holiness, giving a particular character to your human personality, a style to your life; contributing at the same time to the sanctification of others, your fellow men; sanctifying your work and your environment: the profession or job that fills your day, your home and family and the country where you were born and which you love. (St. Josemaria Escriva, *Christ Is Passing By*, 46)

The Saints

PILLARS OF THE CHURCH

St. Thomas More

"PATRON OF LAWYERS AND POLITICIANS"

One statesman who lived just after the Middle Ages, a layman, stands out as a giant of the Faith—St. Thomas More (1478-1535). He was Lord Chancellor of England, lawyer, theologian, philosopher, author, diplomat, counselor, teacher, sheriff of London, Member of Parliament, and a friend of the great men of his time. His public speaking abilities were unmatched. He was married with one daughter and three sons, though he had once considered the priesthood; he even lived in a monastery for four years. He was an ordinary Christian trying to balance daily Mass and prayer, family life, his work as a lawyer, and his literary and historical studies. While known for his integrity, his splendid court garments often hid a hair shirt and his smile sometimes hid his hunger from regular fasting.

Though he was old friends with King Henry VIII, he decided to resign his post as Chancellor because he opposed the king's divorce. Later, when he refused to sign the Act of Succession because the act asserted Parliament's authority to legislate in matters of religion, challenging the authority of the Pope. He was imprisoned in the Tower of London. He also refused to acknowledge Henry VIII as the supreme head of the Church in England. St. Thomas More was thoroughly convinced that no worldly ruler had jurisdiction over the Church of Jesus Christ—so convinced that he was willing to give up his life.

While he was imprisoned awaiting his trial, he continued to keep his good humor. He would dress up on feast days and continued to wear his hair shirt. It was during this time that he composed a beautiful prayer in which he exclaimed: "Grant me, my Lord, a desire to be with you, not so as to avoid the calamities of this world, nor even to avoid the pains of purgatory nor those of hell, not to gain the joys of heaven, not out of consideration for my own profit, but simply through true love for Thee."

After a hasty trial, he was sentenced to death by beheading. In a letter to his daughter Margaret (Meg) about his unworthiness to be a martyr, he wrote: "Although I know well, Margaret, that because of my past wickedness I deserve to be abandoned by God, I cannot but trust in his merciful goodness....I will not mistrust him, Meg, though I shall feel myself weakening and on the verge of being overcome with fear....I trust he shall place his holy hand on me and in the stormy seas hold me up from drowning....Nothing can come but what God wills. And I am very sure that whatever that be, however bad it may seem, it shall indeed be the best."

On the scaffold before the executioner's blade fell, Thomas More said to the crowd: "I die the king's good servant, but God's first."

St. Thomas More, pray for us.

THE LAY APOSTOLATE

The task of building up the Church is called *apostolate*. There are as many different ways of doing apostolate as there are members of the Church. The Holy Spirit offers many gifts to the faithful, each suited to the talents with which God has created us.

> "Christ, sent by the Father, is the source of the Church's whole apostolate"; thus the fruitfulness of apostolate for ordained ministers as well as for lay people clearly depends on their vital union with Christ.[111] In keeping with their vocations, the demands of the times and the various gifts of the Holy Spirit, the apostolate assumes the most varied forms. But charity, drawn from the Eucharist above all, is always "as it were, the soul of the whole apostolate."[112] (CCC 864)

Catholic high school students help prepare meals at a nutrition center. Any work of service or charity, either within the parish or the local community, can be an apostolic work.

The Church unifies these diverse talents and gifts by directing them toward the single purpose of serving God and accomplishing his will on earth. We recall from earlier chapters how St. Paul, in explaining the Mystical Body of Christ, said that all the faithful are unified in these different forms of apostolate because the diversity of their charisms comes from the unity of the one Holy Spirit.[113]

All are "sent out" and commissioned by Christ to continue his work on earth, but it is only in the fulfillment of those duties proper to our own God-given vocation that we are truly able to build up the Body of Christ. For lay men and women, the call to apostolate is not only a right but a duty of their sacramental commitment.

> Since, like all the faithful, lay Christians are entrusted by God with the apostolate by virtue of their Baptism and Confirmation, they have the right and duty, individually or grouped in associations, to work so that the divine message of salvation may be known and accepted by all men throughout the earth. This duty is the more pressing when it is only through them that men can hear the Gospel and know Christ. Their activity in ecclesial communities is so necessary that, for the most part, the apostolate of the pastors cannot be fully effective without it.[114] (CCC 900)

Any work of service or charity, either within the parish or the local community, can be an apostolic work. However, those apostolates with a specifically Catholic character are particularly appropriate in that they allow the believer to "make of their apostolate, through the vigor of their Christian spirit, a leaven in the world."[115]

Some of the apostolates in which the laity may engage include catechist; direct service to the homeless, the poor, the sick, the disabled, the elderly; spiritual reading libraries, pro-life initiatives, care for the bereaved, and emergency assistance programs. Some of these are sponsored by Catholic organizations such as the Knights of Columbus, the St. Vincent de Paul Society, the Catholic Worker Movement, and the Council for Catholic Women.

> Wherever there are people in need of food and drink, clothing, housing, medicine, employment, education; wherever men lack the facilities necessary for living a truly human life or are afflicted with serious distress or illness or suffer exile or imprisonment, there Christian charity should seek them out and find them, console them with great solicitude and help them with appropriate relief....In order that the exercise of charity on this scale may be unexceptionable in appearance as well as in fact, it is altogether necessary to consider in one's neighbor the image of God in which he has been created, and also Christ the Lord to whom is really offered whatever is given to a needy person.[116]

THEY WILL KNOW YOU ARE MY DISCIPLES

**All men will know that you are my disciples,
if you have love for one another. (Jn 13:35)**

All genuine witness to Christ entails charity; it requires the will to avoid inflicting any harm on love. And so the whole Church must be distinguished by charity.

Charity also requires a willingness to serve one's neighbour. In the Church throughout history there have always been numerous people who have dedicated themselves to this service. We can say that no religious society has ever inspired as many works of charity as the Church has: service to the sick, the disabled, service to young people in schools, to people struck by natural disasters and other misfortunes, support for all kinds of poor and needy. Today we see a repetition of this phenomenon, which seems prodigious at times: every new need which appears in the world is met with new endeavours of relief and assistance by Christians who live according to the spirit of the Gospel. It is a charity which is often witnessed to with heroism in the Church. She has many martyrs of charity.

— Pope Bl. John Paul II, *L'Osservatore Romano*, n. 23, June 10, 1992.

LIVING OUR FAITH IN THE MIDST OF THE WORLD

In addition to their responsibilities in the family, the workplace, and in apostolate, an important aspect of the laity's vocation is found in their involvement in the *public square*—that is, in the areas of culture and politics. As Christians living and working in the midst of the world, the lay faithful are called to shape these areas according to the will of God, for "there is no human activity which can be withdrawn from God's dominion."[117]

Although the bishops and clergy can and must address issues of public policy insofar as they involve questions of morality and the common good, it is up to the laity to advance this discussion more fully in society, getting involved in the political and policy-making process at every level of government and society. "It is the duty of citizens to work with civil authority for building up society in a spirit of truth, justice, solidarity, and freedom."[118]

In her social teaching, the Church supports legitimate political authority, which she defines as authority that "is committed to the common good of society" and seeks to attain this common good by "morally acceptable means."[119] She also defines *common good* as "the sum of those conditions of social life which allow social groups and their individual members relatively thorough and ready access to their own fulfillment."[120] "The common good consists of three essential elements: respect for and promotion of the fundamental rights of the person; prosperity, or the development of the spiritual and temporal goods of society; the peace and security of the group and of its members."[121]

The common good, however, is not the sole responsibility of the government; rather, it is an obligation of every individual to participate in achieving the common good, an ethical obligation "inherent in the dignity of the human person."[122] The faithful must begin by being conscientious in their personal responsibilities, including the education of their families and their daily work, for these duties also support the common good of society.

To the extent possible, the faithful should participate in the public life of society. Such participation can include informed voting, campaigning for just causes and worthy candidates, or even running for public office. In whatever capacity, the faithful must call for a continued conversion of the members of society, condemning injustice where it is found and always promoting a defense of human dignity and improvements to the conditions of human life.[123]

VOCATION TO THE CONSECRATED LIFE

As we have seen, the universal call of all the Christian faithful is to live in imitation of Christ, pursuing holiness of life and the perfection of charity. For certain men and women within the Church, this calling comes in the form of a vocation to the *consecrated life*, a permanent state of life characterized by the profession of *poverty*, *chastity*, and *obedience*. These three practices are known as the *evangelical counsels*, and they have been given to the Church by Christ as a means of assisting our growth in charity.

> "The state of life which is constituted by the profession of the evangelical counsels, while not entering into the hierarchical structure of the Church, belongs undeniably to her life and holiness."[124] (CCC 914)

Some examples of those in consecrated life include *women religious* (often referred to as *sisters* or *nuns*), religious brothers, clergy who are members of a religious order or institute, and *consecrated virgins*. Certainly, there are many different forms of the consecrated state of life, but what they share in common is the commitment to a radical imitation of Christ that bears witness to the Gospel and enables them to better serve the Church's mission.

St. Rose of Lima by Dolci.
St. Rose (1586-1617) was the first Catholic saint of the Americas. Born in Lima, Peru, she was permitted to enter a Dominican convent in 1602. She was canonized by Pope Clement X in 1671. Many places are named Santa Rosa in the New World and pay homage to her.

We know from the Gospels that, during his time on earth, Christ embraced a life of material poverty, chastity, and obedience to the Father. Far from demeaning the value of wealth, marriage, or personal freedom, Christ's example reveals to us their true dignity. Our possessions, sexuality, and independence are among God's greatest natural gifts to us, and they are therefore especially worthy to be offered to God. Further, in a world that worships money, sex, and power in place of God, this offering gives testimony to the truth that communion with God is worth infinitely more than even the greatest of his gifts.

> Christ proposes the evangelical counsels, in their great variety, to every disciple. The perfection of charity, to which all the faithful are called, entails for those who freely follow the call to consecrated life the obligation of practicing chastity in celibacy for the sake of the Kingdom, poverty and obedience. (CCC 915)

For the faithful, the lived example of the person consecrated to God also serves as a reminder of the glorious life to come, a life in which we already participate through our sacramental life in Christ.

> [The consecrated state of life] reveals more clearly to all believers the heavenly goods which are already present in this age, witnessing to the new and eternal life which we have acquired through the redemptive work of Christ and preluding our future resurrection and the glory of the heavenly kingdom.[125] (CCC 933)

By their celibacy in particular, those called to the consecrated life give "prophetic witness" to how all of us will live in Heaven. "In the resurrection they neither marry nor are given in marriage, but are like angels in heaven."[126] As we will see in the next section, the married state of life plays an important part in fulfilling the mission of the Church on earth. But as St. Paul explains to the Corinthians, it also brings with it many additional obligations—such as providing for one's spouse and children. Those who are called to celibacy "for the sake of the Kingdom of Heaven" are less constrained by the concerns of this world, and they can therefore devote themselves more completely to prayer and to assisting the growth of the Church.

"From the God-given seed of the counsels a wonderful and wide-spreading tree has grown up in the field of the Lord, branching out into various forms of the religious life lived in solitude or in community. Different religious families have come into existence in which spiritual resources are multiplied for the progress in holiness of their members and for the good of the entire Body of Christ."[127] (CCC 917)

TYPES OF CONSECRATED LIFE

St. Benedict (detail) by Fra Angelico.
St. Benedict of Nursia (480-547). The Rule of St. Benedict became one of the most influential religious rules in Western Christendom. Benedict is often called the founder of Western Christian monasticism. In 1964, Pope Paul VI named St. Benedict patron saint of Europe.

A vocation to the consecrated life is one way of living out the baptismal commitment and involves following one or more of the evangelical counsels of poverty, chastity, and obedience. It can take various forms depending on the particular charism or spirit of each congregation, society, or institute. The consecrated life can also be lived individually or with others in a community. The main types of consecrated life are *religious orders and congregations*, *societies for apostolic life*, and *secular institutes*.

✛ **Religious orders (or congregations)** are communities whose members make vows of poverty, chastity, and obedience and live a life of prayer centered on the Eucharist. Although there are some differences between orders and congregations, the terms are often used interchangeably. These communities are specifically for men or for women. Members in men's communities are referred to as *brothers*, although some are usually chosen to receive Holy Orders in order to serve the sacramental needs of their community. Members of women's communities are called *sisters*, *nuns*, or *women religious*. Religious orders or congregations have their origin in the monasticism of the early Church, when certain individuals felt a call to leave society to live a life of solitude and prayer. Eventually organized according to a rule, they strove to live a life of holiness in community. Many of the first monastic orders in the West were organized according to the Rule of St. Benedict. In addition to a special focus on prayer and penance, some orders may be involved in particular works of mercy, such as service to the poor, education, and preaching. Some of these religious orders would include the Benedictines, the Franciscans, and the Dominicans.

✛ **Societies for Apostolic Life** were founded to serve society and the world outside of the traditional cloistered life (monastery). Like religious orders, societies for apostolic life are specifically for men or women, and as in the case of religious orders, some of the men are ordained to the priesthood. However, unlike those in religious orders or congregations, they do not take public vows of poverty, chastity, and obedience, although they may embrace these vows privately. The distinguishing characteristic of societies for apostolic life is their involvement in the world. Their members normally perform works of service, such as missionary activities, charity, social work, education, and health care. Examples of societies for apostolic life would include the Priestly Fraternity of St. Peter or the Missionaries of the Precious Blood.

✤ **Secular institutes** are institutes of consecrated life in which the Christian faithful living in the world strive for the perfection of charity and work for the sanctification of the world, especially from within.[128]

God also calls certain individuals to a specific missionary vocation. These missionaries are aided in their vocation by the Holy Spirit who distributes his gifts for the good of the Church.

> He inspires the missionary vocation in the hearts of individuals, and at the same time he raises up in the Church certain institutes which take as their own special task the duty of preaching the Gospel, a duty belonging to the whole Church. (*Ad Gentes*, 23)

CONCLUSION

The *Catechism of the Catholic Church* aptly summarizes a critical truth about the Church:

> It is in the Church, in communion with all the baptized, that the Christian fulfills his vocation. From the Church he receives the Word of God containing the teachings of "the law of Christ."[129] From the Church he receives the grace of the sacraments that sustains him on the "way." From the Church he learns the *example of holiness* and recognizes its model and source in the all-holy Virgin Mary; he discerns it in the authentic witness of those who live it; he discovers it in the spiritual tradition and long history of the saints who have gone before him and whom the liturgy celebrates in the rhythms of the sanctoral cycle. (CCC 2030)

To seek holiness is to seek after Christ, and to seek Christ is to follow him and model ourselves after his example. If we follow Christ closely, we inevitably keep company with his Apostles, who were his closest companions during his ministry on earth; and if we stay close to his Apostles, we inevitably remain close to the successors of the Apostles, the Pope and bishops of today, and therefore to the teachings and pastoral guidance of the Catholic Church herself.

"Stay close to the Sacraments!" is sound pastoral advice for every member of the faithful, for it is in the Sacraments that we find our greatest source of grace that draws us ever closer to the divine life of Christ. Many have the great privilege of attending Holy Mass and receiving the Body and Blood, Soul and Divinity of Jesus Christ *every day*.

We also have the great benefit of being able to confess our sins and receive Christ's forgiveness in the Sacrament of Penance. In addition to the priest's absolution, the spiritual direction that we may receive at confession can strengthen us to continue the battle against temptation and sin that plagues every one of us. We can continually call upon the gifts of the Holy Spirit received in Baptism and Confirmation to aid us in developing greater virtue.

"Stay close to the Sacraments!" is sound pastoral advice for every member of the faithful, for it is in the Sacraments that we find our greatest source of grace that draws us ever closer to the divine life of Christ.

The life of the laity lived in accord with Christ will be a life centered on the Mass, on prayer, the Sacraments, the sacramentals, of sanctifying ourselves and others through our ordinary daily work and family duties, through a sense of apostolic service to others in keeping with the evangelizing mission handed to us by Christ. Such a life would most assuredly be a truly happy life, for there is no true happiness apart from doing the will of God, and no true happiness on this earth unless we are preparing ourselves for eternal happiness in communion with God in the next life.

SUPPLEMENTARY READING

1. The Eucharist as the Center of the Christian Life

Every commitment to holiness, every activity aimed at carrying out the Church's mission, every work of pastoral planning, must draw the strength it needs from the Eucharistic mystery and in turn be directed to that mystery as its culmination. In the Eucharist we have Jesus, we have his redemptive sacrifice, we have his resurrection, we have the gift of the Holy Spirit, we have adoration, obedience and love of the Father. Were we to disregard the Eucharist, how could we overcome our own deficiency?

The mystery of the Eucharist—sacrifice, presence, banquet—does not allow for reduction or exploitation; it must be experienced and lived in its integrity, both in its celebration and in the intimate converse with Jesus which takes place after receiving communion or in a prayerful moment of Eucharistic adoration apart from Mass. These are times when the Church is firmly built up and it becomes clear what she truly is: one, holy, catholic and apostolic; the people, temple and family of God; the body and bride of Christ, enlivened by the Holy Spirit; the universal sacrament of salvation and a hierarchically structured communion....

By giving the Eucharist the prominence it deserves, and by being careful not to diminish any of its dimensions or demands, we show that we are truly conscious of the greatness of this gift. We are urged to do so by an uninterrupted tradition, which from the first centuries on has found the Christian community ever vigilant in guarding this "treasure." Inspired by love, the Church is anxious to hand on to future generations of Christians, without loss, her faith and teaching with regard to the mystery of the Eucharist. There can be no danger of excess in our care for this mystery, for "in this sacrament is recapitulated the whole mystery of our salvation."

— Pope Bl. John Paul II, *Ecclesia de Eucharistia*, 60-61

2. The Presence of Christ in the Eucharist

In the conversation that the Gospel just recounted, [Jesus] says: "He who eats my flesh and drinks my blood abides in me, and I in him" (Jn 6:56). How can we not rejoice over such a promise? However, we heard that, in the face of that first proclamation, instead of rejoicing, the people began to argue and protest: "How can this man give us his flesh to eat?" (Jn 6:52).

To tell the truth, that attitude has been repeated many times in the course of history. It would seem that, deep down, people do not want to have God so close, so available, so present in their affairs. People want him to be great and, in a word, rather distant. Then they ask themselves questions to demonstrate that in fact such closeness is impossible.

However, the words Christ pronounced specifically in that circumstance retain all their graphic clarity: "Truly, truly, I say to you, unless you eat the flesh of the Son of man and drink his blood, you have no life in you" (Jn 6:53). Facing the murmur of protest, Jesus could have backed down with tranquilizing words. "Friends, he could have said, don't worry! I spoke of flesh, but it is only a symbol. What I wish to say is only a profound communion of sentiments."

But Jesus did not take recourse to such sweeteners. He maintained his affirmation with firmness, even in face of the defection of his own Apostles, and did not change at all the concrete character of his discourse: "Will you also go away?" (Jn 6:67), he asked. Thank God, Peter gave an answer that we also assume today with full awareness: "Lord, to whom shall we go? You have the words of eternal life" (Jn 6:68).

In the Eucharist, Christ is really present among us. His presence is not static. It is a dynamic presence, which makes us his, he assimilates us to himself. Augustine understood this very well. Coming from a Platonic formation, it was difficult for him to accept the "incarnate" dimension of Christianity. In particular, he reacted before the

SUPPLEMENTARY READING Continued

prospect of the "Eucharistic meal," which seemed to him unworthy of God. In ordinary meals man becomes stronger, as it is he who assimilates the food, making it an element of his own corporal reality. Only later did Augustine understand that in the Eucharist the exact opposite occurs: the center is Christ who attracts us to himself; he makes us come out of ourselves to make us one with him (cf. *Confessions*, VII, 10, 16). In this way, he introduces us into the community of brothers.

— Pope Benedict XVI, Homily at the Closing Mass of the Italian National Eucharistic Congress, May 29, 2005

3. Ministerial Priesthood and the Common Priesthood

The baptized, by regeneration and the anointing of the Holy Spirit, are consecrated as a spiritual house and a holy priesthood, in order that through all those works which are those of the Christian man they may offer spiritual sacrifices and proclaim the power of Him who has called them out of darkness into His marvelous light. Therefore all the disciples of Christ, persevering in prayer and praising God, should present themselves as a living sacrifice, holy and pleasing to God. Everywhere on earth they must bear witness to Christ and give an answer to those who seek an account of that hope of eternal life which is in them.

Though they differ from one another in essence and not only in degree, the common priesthood of the faithful and the ministerial or hierarchical priesthood are nonetheless interrelated: each of them in its own special way is a participation in the one priesthood of Christ. The ministerial priest, by the sacred power he enjoys, teaches and rules the priestly people; acting in the person of Christ, he makes present the Eucharistic sacrifice, and offers it to God in the name of all the people. But the faithful, in virtue of their royal priesthood, join in the offering of the Eucharist. They likewise exercise that priesthood in receiving the sacraments, in prayer and thanksgiving, in the witness of a holy life, and by self-denial and active charity.

— *Lumen Gentium*, 10

4. The Lay Apostolate

The lay apostolate, however, is a participation in the salvific mission of the Church itself. Through their Baptism and Confirmation all are commissioned to that apostolate by the Lord Himself. Moreover, by the sacraments, especially holy Eucharist, that charity toward God and man which is the soul of the apostolate is communicated and nourished. Now the laity are called in a special way to make the Church present and operative in those places and circumstances where only through them can it become the salt of the earth. Thus every layman, in virtue of the very gifts bestowed upon him, is at the same time a witness and a living instrument of the mission of the Church itself "according to the measure of Christ's bestowal."

— *Lumen Gentium*, 33

5. The Universal Call to Holiness

Therefore, all the faithful of Christ are invited to strive for the holiness and perfection of their own proper state. Indeed they have an obligation to so strive. Let all then have care that they guide aright their own deepest sentiments of soul. Let neither the use of the things of this world nor attachment to riches, which is against the spirit of evangelical poverty, hinder them in their quest for perfect love. Let them heed the admonition of the Apostle to those who use this world; let them not come to terms with this world; for this world, as we see it, is passing away.

— *Lumen Gentium*, 42

SUPPLEMENTARY READING Continued

6. Christians in Society

For the Christians are distinguished from other men neither by country, nor language, nor the customs which they observe. For they neither inhabit cities of their own, nor employ a peculiar form of speech, nor lead a life which is marked out by any singularity. The course of conduct which they follow has not been devised by any speculation or deliberation of inquisitive men; nor do they, like some, proclaim themselves the advocates of any merely human doctrines. But, inhabiting Greek as well as barbarian cities, according as the lot of each of them has determined, and following the customs of the natives in respect to clothing, food, and the rest of their ordinary conduct, they display to us their wonderful and confessedly striking method of life. They dwell in their own countries, but simply as sojourners. As citizens, they share in all things with others, and yet endure all things as if foreigners. Every foreign land is to them as their native country, and every land of their birth as a land of strangers.

They marry, as do all [others]; they beget children; but they do not destroy their offspring. They have a common table, but not a common bed. They are in the flesh, but they do not live after the flesh. They pass their days on earth, but they are citizens of Heaven. They obey the prescribed laws, and at the same time surpass the laws by their lives. They love all men, and are persecuted by all.

They are unknown and condemned; they are put to death, and restored to life. They are poor, yet make many rich; they are in lack of all things, and yet abound in all; they are dishonoured, and yet in their very dishonour are glorified. They are evil spoken of, and yet are justified; they are reviled, and bless; they are insulted, and repay the insult with honour; they do good, yet are punished as evildoers. When punished, they rejoice as if quickened into life; they are assailed by the Jews as foreigners, and are persecuted by the Greeks; yet those who hate them are unable to assign any reason for their hatred.

To sum up all in one word—what the soul is in the body, that are Christians in the world. The soul is dispersed through all the members of the body, and Christians are scattered through all the cities of the world. The soul dwells in the body, yet is not of the body; and Christians dwell in the world, yet are not of the world. The invisible soul is guarded by the visible body, and Christians are known indeed to be in the world, but their godliness remains invisible. The flesh hates the soul, and wars against it, though itself suffering no injury, because it is prevented from enjoying pleasures; the world also hates the Christians, though in nowise injured, because they abjure pleasures. The soul loves the flesh that hates it, and [loves also] the members; Christians likewise love those that hate them.

—*Epistle to Diognetus*, chapters 5-6

St. Dominic and His Friars Fed by Angels (detail) by Sogliani.
St. Dominic (1170-1221) was the founder of the Friars Preachers, popularly called the Dominicans or Order of Preachers (OP). For centuries the Rosary has been at the heart of the Dominican Order. St. Dominic is the patron saint of astronomers.

SUPPLEMENTARY READING Continued

7. Catechetical Instruction

A means of evangelization that must not be neglected is that of catechetical instruction. The intelligence, especially that of children and young people, needs to learn through systematic religious instruction the fundamental teachings, the living content of the truth which God has wished to convey to us and which the Church has sought to express in an ever richer fashion during the course of her long history. No one will deny that this instruction must be given to form patterns of Christian living and not to remain only notional. Truly the effort for evangelization will profit greatly—at the level of catechetical instruction given at church, in the schools, where this is possible, and in every case in Christian homes—if those giving catechetical instruction have suitable texts, updated with wisdom and competence, under the authority of the bishops. The methods must be adapted to the age, culture and aptitude of the persons concerned, they must seek always to fix in the memory, intelligence and heart the essential truths that must impregnate all of life. It is necessary above all to prepare good instructors—parochial catechists, teachers, parents—who are desirous of perfecting themselves in this superior art, which is indispensable and requires religious instruction. Moreover, without neglecting in any way the training of children, one sees that present conditions render ever more urgent catechetical instruction, under the form of the catechumenate, for innumerable young people and adults who, touched by grace, discover little by little the face of Christ and feel the need of giving themselves to Him.

— Pope Paul VI, *Evangelii Nuntiandi*, 44.

8. The Family as the Domestic Church

The family has well deserved the beautiful name of "domestic Church." This means that there should be found in every Christian family the various aspects of the entire Church. Furthermore, the family, like the Church, ought to be a place where the Gospel is transmitted and from which the Gospel radiates.

In a family which is conscious of this mission, all the members evangelize and are evangelized. The parents not only communicate the Gospel to their children, but from their children they can themselves receive the same Gospel as deeply lived by them.

And such a family becomes the evangelizer of many other families, and of the neighborhood of which it forms part. Families resulting from a mixed marriage also have the duty of proclaiming Christ to the children in the fullness of the consequences of a common Baptism; they have moreover the difficult task of becoming builders of unity.

— Pope Paul VI, *Evangelii Nuntiandi*, 71

"The family has well deserved the beautiful name of 'domestic Church.' This means that there should be found in every Christian family the various aspects of the entire Church." —Pope Paul VI

VOCABULARY

ABSOLUTION
An essential element of the Sacrament of Penance in which the priest, by the power entrusted to the Church by Christ, pardons the sins of the penitent.

ADORATION
The loving acknowledgement of God as God, Creator and Savior, the Lord and Master of everything that exists. Through worship and prayer, the Church and individual persons give to God the adoration which is the first act of the virtue of religion. It is one of the four main types of prayer.

ANOINTING OF THE SICK
A Sacrament administered by a priest to a baptized person who begins to be in danger of death because of illness or old age, celebrated with prayer and anointing with oil in the name of Christ; it provides the recipient with grace for healing, strength, forgiveness of sins, and, if near death, preparation for death and the afterlife; one of the Seven Sacraments of the Church.

APOSTOLATE
The work of the laity toward building up the Church through initiatives and efforts that evangelize, educate, or serve the needs of others.

ASCESIS
The practice of penance, mortification, and self-denial to promote greater self-mastery and to foster the way of perfection by embracing the way of the cross.

BAPTISM
The first Sacrament received by a Christian, involving immersion or the pouring of water on the recipient's head while pronouncing the invocation of the Trinity; it forgives sins, including Original Sin, begins a new life in Christ, and incorporates the new Christian into the life of the Church, the Body of Christ; it is one of the Seven Sacraments of the Church and the first of the three Sacraments of Initiation.

BAPTISM BY BLOOD
The martyrdom of an unbaptized person who thereby receives the graces of Baptism for having died or been killed for the Faith.

BAPTISM OF DESIRE
The graces of Baptism received by an unbaptized person who would have sought Baptism explicitly had he or she been aware of the Gospel of Christ but has sought the truth and tried to follow God's will in keeping with his level of understanding it.

CATECHUMENATE
A process used in the early Church; persons who wished to join the Church were instructed in the teachings of the Faith and prepared for the Sacraments of Initiation. It became customary for the Church to initiate these new members at the Easter Vigil, the night before the commemoration of Christ's Resurrection. The process was restored in the late twentieth century as the Rite of Christian Initiation for Adults (RCIA).

CHAPLET OF DIVINE MERCY
A devotion that comes to us from St. Faustina Kowalska, the "Apostle of Divine Love," involving a set of beads, meditations on the Passion of Christ, and prayers for his mercy "on us and on the whole world."

CHARISMS
Special graces from the Holy Spirit that enable the People of God to build up the Body of Christ.

CHASTITY
The moral virtue that provides for the successful integration of sexuality within the person leading to the inner unity of the bodily and spiritual being; in other words, a commitment to the moral use of one's sexuality in keeping with one's state of life. For unmarried men and women, including those in Holy Orders and the consecrated life, this means complete abstinence from all sexual activity; for married Christians, it means complete fidelity to one's spouse and respect for both the unitive and procreative purposes of married love.

CHRISM
Perfumed oil used for Consecration in the Sacraments of Baptism, Confirmation, and Holy Orders; the oil is consecrated by the bishop and signifies the gift of the Holy Spirit.

CHRISMATION
This alternative name for the Sacrament of Confirmation, named for the Sacred Chrism used, is often used in the East.

VOCABULARY Continued

COMMON GOOD
The sum total of social conditions which allow people, either as groups or individuals, to reach their fulfillment more fully and more easily. It consists of three essential elements: respect for and promotion of the fundamental rights of the person; prosperity, or the development of the spiritual and temporal goods of society; the peace and security of the group and of its members.

COMMON PRIESTHOOD
The priesthood of all the faithful; by virtue of our Baptism and Confirmation, the laity and those in the ministerial priesthood (bishops, priests, deacons) share in the one priesthood of Christ and share in his mission of salvation.

CONCUPISCENCE
Human appetites or desires that remain disordered due to the temporal consequences of Original Sin that remain after Baptism and produce an inclination to sin.

CONFIRMATION
Sacrament that completes the grace of Baptism by a special outpouring of the Holy Spirit that "confirms" the baptized in union with Christ and equips them for active participation in the worship and apostolic life of the Church; it is one of the Seven Sacraments of the Church and one of the three Sacraments of Initiation.

CONSECRATED LIFE
A permanent state of life recognized by the Church, entered into freely in response to the call of Christ to perfection, and characterized by the profession of the evangelical counsels of poverty, chastity, and obedience.

CONSECRATION
The dedication of a person or thing to divine service by a prayer or blessing, as in the Consecration of priests and bishops or the Consecration of the bread and wine on the altar into the Body and Blood of Christ during the Mass.

CONSECRATED VIRGIN
A woman who, with the Church's approval, has decided to cling only to the Lord and to live in a state of virginity "for the sake of the Kingdom of Heaven" and is consecrated in that state by a solemn rite.

CONTRITION
Sorrow of the soul and hatred for the sin committed, together with a resolution not to sin again. It is the most important act of the penitent and is necessary for the reception of the Sacrament of Penance. It is one of the four main types of prayer.

DEACON
A degree of the Sacrament of Holy Orders after bishop and priest for men who are ordained to ministry and service, assisting bishops by preaching and doing charitable works. Transitional deacons are celibate men who will soon be ordained priests; permanent deacons are either married or unmarried men who serve in the diaconate for life.

DIACONATE
The order of deacon, one of the Holy Orders in the Catholic Church.

EFFICACIOUS
When speaking of the Sacraments, the term indicates an action or sign that confers the grace it signifies; for example, the pouring of the water and reciting with proper intent the words of Baptism confer the sanctifying grace of the Sacrament.

EPISCOPACY
The office of bishop in the Catholic Church; from the Greek *episkopos* ("overseer"), from which also is derived the word "bishop."

EUCHARIST
The Sacrament by which bread and wine are consecrated by a priest and become the true Body and Blood of Christ, which the faithful consume in Holy Communion; more broadly, Eucharist, which means "thanksgiving," refers to the Catholic Mass itself.

EVANGELIZATION
The proclamation of Christ and his Gospel by word and the testimony of one's life in fulfillment of Christ's command; from the Greek word *evangelion*.

EVANGELICAL COUNSELS
The practices of poverty, chastity, and obedience, proposed by Christ in his own life and given to the Church for assisting our growth in charity.

EXAMINATION OF CONSCIENCE
Prayerful self-reflection on our words and deeds in light of the Gospel and the Commandments to determine how we may have sinned against God. It is a recommended daily practice and should also be done in preparation for the Sacrament of Penance.

EX OPERE OPERATO
Latin term used to state that a Sacrament dispenses the grace it signifies and does not depend upon the holiness of the minister, nor on the holiness of the person receiving the Sacrament, as long as the minister(s) of the Sacrament intend to convey the Sacrament and the participant intends to receive it; literally, it means "from the work performed."

EXTREME UNCTION
A term formerly used for the Sacrament of the Anointing of the Sick; it is no longer used because it refers to the use of the Sacrament only in instances of imminent death, whereas the Church encourages the Sacrament for anyone in danger of death from disease, infirmity, or old age.

GRACE
The free and unmerited favor of God given, first of all, through the Sacraments. Grace is a share in the divine life infused into the soul by the Holy Spirit to heal from sin and sanctify.

HOLY ORDERS
The Sacrament by which the mission entrusted by Christ to his Apostles continues to be exercised in the Church through the laying on of hands in ordination; the Sacrament has three distinct orders—bishop (episcopate), priest (presbyterate), and deacon (diaconate)—and confers an indelible character on the soul.

LAITY
All the faithful, except those in Holy Orders and those in the state of religious life specially approved by the Church. These faithful are by Baptism made one body with Christ and are constituted among the People of God, and are in their own way made sharers in the priestly, prophetical, and kingly functions of Christ. They carry out for their own part the mission of the whole Christian people in the Church and in the world.

LAY MEN, LAY WOMEN
See Laity.

LECTIO DIVINA
A method of Scripture reading practiced by monastics since the beginning of the Church. It involves four stages: *lectio* (reading), *meditatio* (meditation), *oratio* (prayer), and *contemplatio* (contemplation).

LITURGY
The priestly action of Jesus Christ, continued in and by the Church under the impulse of the Holy Spirit. In the liturgy, the Holy Spirit himself brings about his work of salvation through effective signs, thus giving a most perfect cult to God and salvation to mankind; more generally, the word indicates the Mass, as in "eucharistic liturgy," which itself comprises the Liturgy of the Word and the Liturgy of the Eucharist; or an official prayer of the church outside of Mass, such as the Liturgy of the Hours. It comes from the Greek *ergos* ("work") and *leiton* ("of the people"). In the Greek Christian culture, it meant "public work," any work performed for the common good; in the Greek translation of the Old Testament it refers to the Levitical cult of the Jewish Temple on behalf of the people.

MATRIMONY
The Sacrament by which a man and a woman are joined in Christian marriage, a lifelong and exclusive bond recognized by the Church; one of the Seven Sacraments of the Catholic Church.

MINISTERIAL PRIESTHOOD
The priesthood of those who have received Holy Orders, which is at the service of all the faithful; along with the common priesthood of all the baptized, all share in the one priesthood of Christ and in his mission of salvation.

VOCABULARY Continued

MYRON
The Greek name for Sacred Chrism, which is used in the Sacraments of Baptism, Confirmation, and Holy Orders.

MORTIFICATION
The practice of self-denial as a way to discipline our bodies and appetites so as to strengthen the soul and focus more on interior life.

NOVENA
A devotional series of prayers, usually done over a period of nine days, to a particular saint, group of saints, or devotional seeking intercession for a particular request or need.

OBEDIENCE
As one of the evangelical counsels, it refers to a vow to obey and respect one's religious superiors, an element of consecrated life.

ORDERS
See Holy Orders.

ORDINAND
The man to be ordained in the Sacrament of Holy Orders.

ORDINATION
The rite by which the Sacrament of Holy Orders is conferred upon a man to a share in the high priesthood of Jesus Christ as a bishop, priest, or deacon.

PASCHAL MYSTERY
Christ's work of redemption accomplished principally by his Passion, Death, Resurrection, and Ascension, whereby, "dying he destroyed our death, rising he restored our life" (CCC 1067; cf. 654). The Paschal Mystery is celebrated and made present in the liturgy of the Church, and its saving effects are communicated through the Sacraments, especially the Eucharist, which renews the Paschal Sacrifice of Christ as the sacrifice offered by the Church (CCC 571, 1362-1372).

PENANCE
The Sacrament of God's forgiveness of sins that reconciles the penitent with God and with the Church; the acts of the penitent—contrition, confession of sins, and satisfaction or reparation—together with the prayer of absolution by the priest, constitute the essential elements of the Sacrament of Penance. The word penance also refers to the particular prayers or acts the penitent is assigned by the priest as satisfaction for the sins confessed.

PENITENT
A sinner who repents of his or her sin and seeks forgiveness.

PETITION
Prayer that asks a favor from God or the intercession of one or more of the saints; it can also make a request for the general needs of the community or the world. One of the four main types of prayer.

POLYGAMY
The practice of a man having more than one wife. (If a woman has more than one husband, it's called polyandry.)

POVERTY
As one of the evangelical counsels, a commitment to detachment from worldly goods and simplicity of life as a way of seeking justice and solidarity with the world's poor.

PRESBYTER
Word used in the New Testament for "priest" or "elder."

PRESBYTERATE
The order of the Catholic priesthood, one of the three Holy Orders.

PRIEST
A man who has been ordained to the presbyterate and assists his bishop in the service to the People of God, particularly through celebrating the Eucharist and conferring the Sacraments.

REAL PRESENCE
Name given to the truth that Christ is fully, truly, and substantially present in the Eucharist under the appearance of bread and wine.

VOCABULARY Continued

RELIGIOUS LIFE
See Consecrated Life.

RELIGIOUS INSTITUTE
A society whose members, in accord with Church law, live a life consecrated to Christ and shared with one another by the public profession of the evangelical counsels of poverty, chastity, and obedience.

RESTITUTION
The act of compensation by a penitent, whenever possible, for the damage done to another person, or to his or her possessions or reputation as a result of sin. *See* Satisfaction.

SACRAMENTAL
A sacred sign that bears a certain resemblance to the Sacraments and by means of which spiritual effects are signified and obtained not efficaciously but through the disposition of the recipient and the intercession of the Church.

SACRAMENTAL CHARACTER (or SEAL)
An indelible mark conferred by the Sacraments of Baptism, Confirmation, and Holy Orders that configures the Christian to Christ and his Church, remains within him or her as a positive disposition for grace, promises and guarantees divine protection, and grants him or her a vocation to divine worship and to the service of the Church; therefore, these Sacraments can be received validly only once in a lifetime.

SACRAMENTS OF INITIATION
The three Sacraments that fully incorporate a Christian into the Catholic community: Baptism, Eucharist, and Confirmation.

SATISFACTION
In the context of the Sacrament of Penance, an act whereby the sinner makes amends for sin, especially in reparation to God for offenses against him; the penance assigned by the priest during confession is the reparation for that sin.

SECULAR INSTITUTE
A form of consecrated life in which the Christian faithful living in the world strive for the perfection of charity and work for the sanctification of the world, especially from within.

STATE OF LIFE
A general category of structured Christian living, used primarily in reference to the clerical, consecrated, and married states.

STATIONS OF THE CROSS
A traditional devotion, popular during Lent, involving prayers and meditations at each of fourteen "stations" depicting Jesus' Passion and Death.

THANKSGIVING
Prayer that expresses gratitude to God for his blessings and care; one of the four main types of prayer.

THEOPHANY
A revelation or visible appearance of God, as in the case of Moses at Mount Sinai, at the Transfiguration, or at the Baptism of Jesus.

TRANSUBSTANTIATION
Scholastic term used by the Church to describe how the bread and wine are changed into the Eucharist; Consecration of the bread and wine by a priest at Mass changes the substance of the bread and wine into the Body and Blood of Christ while leaving the appearances as bread and wine.

VOCATION
The particular plan or calling that God has for each individual in this life and hereafter. All people have a vocation to love and serve God and are called to the perfection of holiness. The vocation of the laity consists in seeking the Kingdom of God by engaging in temporal affairs and by directing them according to God's will. Priestly and religious vocations are dedicated to the service of the Church.

WOMEN RELIGIOUS
Women who have entered religious life, often called *sisters* or *nuns*.

STUDY QUESTIONS

1. What are some of the meanings of the term "the Church"? What term(s) or model(s) of the Church were used extensively by the Second Vatican Council?

2. Describe the *ministerial priesthood* and the *common priesthood*. How are they different? How are they similar?

3. Who are the *laity*?

4. Summarize the meaning of the *universal call to holiness*.

5. Name several aspects of what we would consider a "proper response" to the universal call to holiness by a lay person.

6. Who is St. Gianna Molla, and what example of holiness did she leave for us?

7. What are the requirements for receiving the Eucharist?

8. Name the beginning, the end, and the major seasons of the liturgical year.

9. What is the "high point" of the Easter Triduum? Why?

10. What was the meaning of the word that the Greeks used for *Sacrament*? How does that meaning relate to our understanding of the Sacraments?

11. Explain the meaning of *ex opere operato*.

12. What does the word *efficacious* mean?

13. What are the Sacraments of Initiation? Explain how the administration of these Sacraments, in the case of infants, differs between the Latin and Eastern Rites of the Catholic Church.

14. How was the baptism practiced by St. John the Baptist different from the Baptism instituted by Christ?

15. What is *Baptism of blood*?

16. What is *Baptism of desire*?

17. Explain the teachings of the Church on the question of babies who die without Baptism.

18. Why is Baptism called the "doorway" to the Church?

19. What event in Scripture do we associate with the institution of the Sacrament of Confirmation?

20. What miracle in the New Testament foreshadowed the institution of the Eucharist?

21. Why does the Church require the faithful to attend Mass every Sunday?

22. Explain the scriptural basis for the Sacrament of Penance.

23. Who should receive the Sacrament of the Anointing of the Sick?

24. Name and explain the three levels of Holy Orders.

25. Describe the three characteristics of the nature of ecclesial ministry.

26. What image is said to be reflected in the sacramental union of a man and a woman in Matrimony?

27. Describe Jesus' example of prayer and mortification.

28. What are the four main types of prayer?

STUDY QUESTIONS Continued

29. How should we pray? What are different methods of prayer?

30. What role can reading Scripture or the writings of the saints have in our prayer life?

31. What does the Latin root for *mortification* mean? Why is that an appropriate means of explaining mortification?

32. Name some ways in which a person could practice self-denial.

33. What does Jesus' command to teach and baptize all nations have to do with us today?

34. What is the primary way in which a Christian can participate in the missionary activity of the Church?

35. Why do we need to "know our Faith" if we are to be part of this mission?

36. Name the two necessary components of being a living witness for Christ.

37. Describe the various *states of life*.

38. What is *apostolate* and who is supposed to practice it?

39. What is the role of the faithful in the *public square*?

40. What are the *evangelical counsels*?

41. Name and briefly describe the three major forms of *consecrated life*.

Station of the Cross, No. 7: Jesus Falls the Second Time.
Walking the Stations of the Cross is a popular meditation on the Passion, Death, and Burial of Our Lord throughout the year, especially during Lent. Many Popes—notably Clement XII, Pius XI, and Bl. John Paul II—have prescribed and lauded this devotion.

PRACTICAL EXERCISES

1. Ponder the universal call to holiness; consider especially what is at stake in pursuing this call—namely, our eternal destiny—and how well or poorly we have striven to be holy thus far in life. Consider also the state of humanity today, and how many people seem to reject or at least be lukewarm about their relationship with God and their attention to the Ten Commandments. In light of the evangelizing mission of the Church and our common priesthood, what obligations do we bear in the course of our ordinary daily life and our human relationships therein?

2. What does the Sacrament of the Eucharist imply about the Catholic understanding of the Church of Christ? Who is included in the Church? Where does the Church exist? How are we called to demonstrate our fidelity to the Church?

3. We know from Scripture, the *Catechism*, and our own experience that all members of the pilgrim Church are sinners. Is it possible for the sinfulness of the Church's members to invalidate the truth of Christ's teaching? How would you respond to someone who thinks that all Christians are hypocritical because they are sinners?

4. Christ told his disciples, "Where two or three are gathered in my name, there am I in the midst of them" (Mt 18: 20). Imagine a friend uses this quote from Scripture to challenge the hierarchical structure of the Church. If Christ is available to all of us simply by gathering in his name, why does the Church retain a hierarchical structure to administer the Sacraments?

5. "In this sacrament, the sinner, placing himself before the merciful judgment of God, anticipates in a certain way the judgment to which he will be subjected at the end of his earthly life. For it is now, in this life, that we are offered the choice between life and death, and it is only by the road of conversion that we can enter the Kingdom, from which one is excluded by grave sin"[130] (CCC 1470). This quote is referring to the Sacrament of Penance. What main point is the quote trying to get across? How are we to stay on the road of conversion?

6. Scripture teaches us that the Sacrament of Confirmation brings the gifts of the Holy Spirit, just as the Spirit came to the Apostles at Pentecost. If you have been confirmed, what have you done with those gifts since your Confirmation? If you have not been confirmed yet, how have you used the gifts God has given you in Baptism to prepare yourself for Confirmation and your life of service to him?

7. Review the meaning of the term *ex opere operato* with regard to the Sacraments. Then explain: What role does the disposition of the recipient play in the effects of the Sacraments?

8. Make a chart with four columns. In the first column, write the name of each of the Seven Sacraments. In the second column, write the major *signs* of each Sacrament. In the third column, list the *ordinary minister* of each Sacrament. In the fourth, write one or more of the *effects* of this Sacrament on the recipient. How many of these Sacraments have you received in your life? Take a moment to pray briefly that the Holy Spirit will grant you a more effective use of the graces of each Sacrament you have received.

FROM THE CATECHISM

850 *The origin and purpose of mission.* The Lord's missionary mandate is ultimately grounded in the eternal love of the Most Holy Trinity: "The Church on earth is by her nature missionary since, according to the plan of the Father, she has as her origin the mission of the Son and the Holy Spirit."[131] The ultimate purpose of mission is none other than to make men share in the communion between the Father and the Son in their Spirit of love.[132]

851 *Missionary motivation.* It is from God's love for all men that the Church in every age receives both the obligation and the vigor of her missionary dynamism, "for the love of Christ urges us on."[133] Indeed, God "desires all men to be saved and to come to the knowledge of the truth";[134] that is, God wills the salvation of everyone through the knowledge of the truth. Salvation is found in the truth. Those who obey the prompting of the Spirit of truth are already on the way of salvation. But the Church, to whom this truth has been entrusted, must go out to meet their desire, so as to bring them the truth. Because she believes in God's universal plan of salvation, the Church must be missionary.

895 "The power which they exercise personally in the name of Christ, is proper, ordinary, and immediate, although its exercise is ultimately controlled by the supreme authority of the Church."[135] But the bishops should not be thought of as vicars of the Pope. His ordinary and immediate authority over the whole Church does not annul, but on the contrary confirms and defends that of the bishops. Their authority must be exercised in communion with the whole Church under the guidance of the Pope.

898 "By reason of their special vocation it belongs to the laity to seek the Kingdom of God by engaging in temporal affairs and directing them according to God's will....It pertains to them in a special way so to illuminate and order all temporal things with which they are closely associated that these may always be effected and grow according to Christ and may be to the glory of the Creator and Redeemer."[136]

909 "Moreover, by uniting their forces let the laity so remedy the institutions and conditions of the world when the latter are an inducement to sin, that these may be conformed to the norms of justice, favoring rather than hindering the practice of virtue. By so doing they will impregnate culture and human works with a moral value."[137]

912 The faithful should "distinguish carefully between the rights and the duties which they have as belonging to the Church and those which fall to them as members of the human society. They will strive to unite the two harmoniously, remembering that in every temporal affair they are to be guided by a Christian conscience, since no human activity, even of the temporal order, can be withdrawn from God's dominion."[138]

1076 The Church was made manifest to the world on the day of Pentecost by the outpouring of the Holy Spirit.[139] The gift of the Spirit ushers in a new era in the "dispensation of the mystery": the age of the Church, during which Christ manifests, makes present, and communicates his work of salvation through the liturgy of his Church, "until he comes."[140] In this age of the Church Christ now lives and acts in and with his Church, in a new way appropriate to this new age. He acts through the sacraments in what the common Tradition of the East and the West calls "the sacramental economy"; this is the communication (or "dispensation") of the fruits of Christ's Paschal mystery in the celebration of the Church's "sacramental" liturgy.

FROM THE CATECHISM Continued

1084 "Seated at the right hand of the Father" and pouring out the Holy Spirit on his Body which is the Church, Christ now acts through the sacraments he instituted to communicate his grace. The sacraments are perceptible signs (words and actions) accessible to our human nature. By the action of Christ and the power of the Holy Spirit they make present efficaciously the grace that they signify.

1088 "To accomplish so great a work"—the dispensation or communication of his work of salvation—"Christ is always present in his Church, especially in her liturgical celebrations.

He is present in the Holy Sacrifice of the Mass not only in the person of his minister, 'the same now offering, through the ministry of priests, who formerly offered himself on the cross,' but especially in the Eucharistic species. By his power he is present in the sacraments so that when anybody baptizes, it is really Christ himself who baptizes. He is present in his word since it is he himself who speaks when the holy Scriptures are read in the Church. Lastly, he is present when the Church prays and sings, for he has promised 'where two or three are gathered together in my name there am I in the midst of them.'"[141]

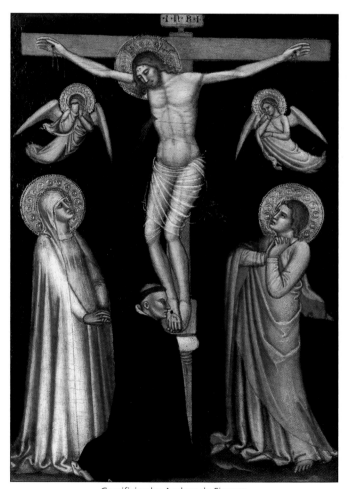

Crucifixion by Andrea da Firenze.
"...he [Christ] is present when the Church prays and sings, for he has promised 'where two or three are gathered together in my name there am I in the midst of them.'" (CCC 1088)

ENDNOTES - CHAPTER SIX

1. 1 Jn 3:1.
2. CIC, can. 208; cf. *LG* 32.
3. Cf. Mt 6:30; 13:58.
4. Cf. Mt 8:5-13.
5. Cf. Mt 9:2-6.
6. Cf. Mt 9:20.
7. *Dei Filius* 3: DS 3008.
8. *LG* 9.
9. Cardinal Joseph Ratzinger, "The Ecclesiology of Vatican II," address to the Pastoral Congress of the Diocese of Aversa, Italy, Sept. 15, 2001.
10. *LG* 18.
11. Dt 18:6.
12. Nm 11:24-25.
13. Ex 28:1.
14. Heb 5:1, 4.
15. Pope Bl. John Paul II, *Christifidelis Laici*, 13.
16. *LG* 10 § 2.
17. *LG* 3.
18. *LG* 31.
19. Cf. CCC 899.
20. Mt 5:16.
21. *LG* 32.
22. Mt 5:48.
23. *LG* 40 § 2.
24. Cf. *LG* 34, 10; 1 Pt 2:5.
25. Jn 13:1.
26. Avery Cardinal Dulles, "The Ways We Worship," *First Things* (March 1998).
27. CCC 1112.
28. Cf. *SC* 5-7.
29. *SC* 104; CCC 1173; cf. *SC* 108 and 111.
30. *SC* 59.
31. Cf. Council of Trent (1547) DS 1605; DS 1606.
32. St. Leo the Great, *Sermo.* 74, 2: PL 54, 398.
33. Cf. Lk 5:17; 6:19; 8:46.
34. Jn 16:13; cf. Mt 13:52; 1 Cor 4:1.
35. Mt 3:11.
36. Jn 3:5.
37. Acts 2:41.
38. Acts 8:26-40; 10:1-48.
39. CCC 1272.
40. CCC 1129.
41. Cf. Mk 16:16.
42. CCC 1258.
43. CCC 1261.
44. 1 Cor 6:11.

45. Pope Bl. John Paul II, *L'Osservatore Romano*, n. 13, April 1, 1992.
46. Acts 1:8.
47. Acts 2:1-41.
48. Pope Paul VI, Apostolic Constitution *Divinæ Consortium Naturæ*, 659.
49. Cf. CCEO, can. 695 § 1; 696 § 1.
50. CCC 1289.
51. Jn 6:11.
52. Acts 2:42, 46; 20:7, 11; 27:35.
53. Council of Trent (1562), *Doctrina de Ss. Missæ Sacrificio*, c. 2: DS 1743; cf. Heb 9:4, 27.
54. Cf. 1 Cor 11:26.
55. Acts 2:42.
56. CCC 1343
57. CCC 1419.
58. 1 Jn 1:9.
59. Rom 10:10.
60. Mt 16:19.
61. Acts 9:32-42.
62. 2 Cor 12:9.
63. 1 Tm 3:1-13; Ti 1:5-9.
64. Cf. CCC 876-878.
65. Gn 2:23.
66. Cf. Hos 1-3; Is 54; 62; Jer 2-3; 31; Ez 16; 23; Mal 2:13-17.
67. Sg 8:6-7.
68. Eph 5:25-26, 31-32.
69. *LG* 11 § 2.
70. *LG* 11 § 2; cf. *LG* 41.
71. St. John Damascene, *De Fide Orth.* 3, 24 (PG 94, 1089C).
72. Cf. CCC 2745.
73. CTH, 16-17.
74. Cf. CCC, 2607, 2708.
75. Tertullian, *De orat.* 1: PL 1, 1155.
76. Tertullian, *De orat.* 10: PL 1, 1165; cf. Lk 11:9.
77. *De orat.* 1: PL 1, 1155.
78. Cf. Mk 12:29.
79. Cf. Jn 11:41-42.
80. Cf. Lk 3:21-22; Lk 5:16; Lk 6:12; Lk 11:1.
81. Cf. Lk 9:18.
82. Lk 4:16-20.
83. Mk 15:34.
84. Cf. Jn 7:10-14.
85. Mt 4:2.
86. Cf. Acts 13:2, 14:23.
87. Cf. Lk 13:20-21.
88. Cf. 2 Tm 4.
89. 1 Tm 4:7-8.
90. Cf. Mt 5:13-14.

91. *AG* 1.
92. *Evangelii Nuntiandi*, 46.
93. Cf. *Evangelii Nuntiandi*, 21.
94. *AG* 36.
95. 1 Pt 3:15.
96. Bl. John Paul II, *Missionary Activity*, General Audience, May 10, 1995.
97. Rom 12:6.
98. Lk 9:23.
99. *AA* 6 § 3; cf. *AG* 15.
100. *LG* 35.
101. *LG* 10.
102. *GS* 52 § 1.
103. CCC 2223.
104. 1 Cor 7:25-28, 32-35.
105. CCC 1654.
106. Gn 2:15.
107. Cf. Gn 1:28; *GS* 34; *CA* 31.
108. 2 Thes 3:10; cf. 1 Thes 4:11.
109. Cf. Gn 3:14-19.
110. Cf. *LE* 27.
111. *AA* 4; cf. Jn 15:5.
112. *AA* 3.
113. 1 Cor 12:4-7, 12.
114. Cf. *LG* 33.
115. CCC 940.
116. *AA* 8.
117. *LG* 36.
118. CCC 2255.
119. CCC 1921.
120. *GS* 26.
121. CCC 1925.
122. CCC 1913.
123. CCC 1916.
124. *LG* 44 § 4.
125. *LG* 44 § 3.
126. Mt 22:30.
127. *LG* 43.
128. CCC 928.
129. Gal 6:2.
130. Cf. 1 Cor 5:11; Gal 5:19-21; Rev 22:15.
131. *AG* 2.
132. Cf. Bl. John Paul II, *RMiss* 23.
133. 2 Cor 5:14; cf. *AA* 6; *RMiss* 11.
134. 1 Tm 2:4.
135. *LG* 27.
136. *LG* 31 § 2.
137. *LG* 36 § 3.
138. *LG* 36 § 4.
139. Cf. *SC* 6; *LG* 2.
140. 1 Cor 11:26.
141. *SC* 7; Mt 18:20.

The Church as a Communion of Saints

The Church on earth is on the journey toward Heaven, and with the example of the saints, who have already completed this journey, she continuously points to our heavenly reward.

The Church

CHAPTER 7

The Church as a Communion of Saints

In all you do, remember the end of your life, and then you will never sin. (Sir 7:36)

cclesial communion, into which each individual is introduced by faith and by Baptism, has its root and centre in the Blessed Eucharist. Indeed, Baptism is an incorporation into a body that the risen Lord builds up and keeps alive through the Eucharist, so that this body can truly be called the Body of Christ. The Eucharist is the creative force and source of *communion* among the members of the Church, precisely because it unites each one of them with Christ himself: "Really sharing in the body of the Lord in the breaking of the eucharistic bread, we are taken up into communion with him and with one another. 'Because the bread is one, we, though many, are one body, all of us who partake of the one bread' (1 Cor 10:17)."

Hence, the Pauline expression *the Church is the Body of Christ* means that the Eucharist, in which the Lord gives us his Body and transforms us into one Body, is where the Church expresses herself permanently in most essential form. While present everywhere, she is yet only *one*, just as Christ is *one*.

The Church is a *Communion of the saints*, to use a traditional expression that is found in the Latin versions of the Apostles' Creed from the end of the fourth century. The common visible sharing in the goods of salvation (*the holy things*), and especially in the Eucharist, is the source of the invisible communion among the sharers (*the saints*). This communion brings with it a spiritual solidarity among the members of the Church, insofar as they are members of one same Body, and it fosters their effective union in charity by constituting "*one heart and soul.*" Communion tends also towards union in prayer, inspired in all by one and the same Spirit, the Holy Spirit "*who fills and unites the whole Church.*"

In its invisible elements, this communion exists not only among the members of the pilgrim Church on earth, but also between these and all who, having passed from this world in the grace of the Lord, belong to the heavenly Church or will be incorporated into it after having been fully purified. This means, among other things, that there is a *mutual relationship* between the pilgrim Church on earth and the heavenly Church in the historical-redemptive mission. Hence the ecclesiological importance not only of Christ's intercession on behalf of his members, but also of that of the saints and, in an eminent fashion, of the Blessed Virgin Mary's. *Devotion to the saints*, which is such a strong feature of the piety of the Christian people, can thus be seen to correspond in its very essence to the profound reality of the Church as a mystery of communion.

Our Lord Jesus Christ (detail) by Tissot. The entire Church—in Heaven, in Purgatory, and on earth—works to continue the saving work of Jesus Christ.

— Congregation for the Doctrine of the Faith, *On Some Aspects of the Church Understood as Communion*, 5-6.

Virgin and Child with Saints by Boccaccino.
Saints represented in this painting are St. Catherine of Alexandria, St. Christine of Tyre, St. Peter, and St. John the Baptist.
The word *saint* literally means "holy one," and this title refers primarily to those Christian men and women who remained faithful during their time on earth and have reached the glory of Heaven.

IN THIS CHAPTER, WE WILL ADDRESS SEVERAL QUESTIONS:

✤ What is the *Communion of Saints*?

✤ How do we participate in the heavenly liturgy?

✤ What does the "end of time" signify for Christians?

✤ What are the Particular Judgment, the second coming, and the Last Judgment?

✤ What are *Heaven*, *Hell*, and *Purgatory*?

✤ Why do we pray for the *Holy Souls* in Purgatory?

✤ How can a merciful God send anyone to an eternal Hell?

✤ What is the meaning of *koinonia* or *communio*, and how do these words describe the reality of the Church?

✤ How can the saints intercede for us?

Madonna with Angels and Saints, The Maesta (front central panel) by Duccio.
The *Church Triumphant* is the heavenly Church in glory.

THE CHURCH AS A COMMUNION OF SAINTS

After confessing "the holy catholic Church," the Apostles' Creed adds "the communion of saints." In a certain sense this article is a further explanation of the preceding: "What is the Church if not the assembly of all the saints?"[1] The communion of saints is the Church. (CCC 946)

When we think of our personal experiences of the Church, it is easy to limit our conception of the Church to the visible Church on earth. However, the Church does not exist only on earth, but rather it exists in three different states:

✤ The **Church Militant**, which is the pilgrim Church on earth, is composed of Christ's Faithful here on earth;

✤ The **Church Suffering** includes those in Purgatory who have died in communion with God but who have not yet been fully purified; and

✤ The **Church Triumphant**, which is the heavenly Church in glory.

This union within the Church—both between God and man, and among men—is called the Communion of Saints. The entire Church, that is, in Heaven, in Purgatory, and on earth, works to continue the saving work of Jesus Christ.

These different parts of the Church form one and the same Church and one single body, because they have the same head, Jesus Christ; the same spirit, which gives them life and unity; and the same aim—eternal happiness—which some already enjoy and others await.[2]

The Church Militant, Suffering, and Triumphant are not three churches but *only one Church*. For the members of the Church who are in Heaven, this work consists of intercession, which means praying for the Church on earth. For members of the Church on earth, our work is twofold: to remain united to Christ and to bring the entire world into union with him. Even in these different states, however, the Church is united as a single community in Christ. Just as the Body of Christ is one, the faithful on earth, in Purgatory, and in Heaven form one family and one People of God. For members of the Church in Purgatory, Masses and prayers offered and indulgences earned for them—by those on earth—can ease their suffering or even release their souls to Heaven.

United in grace with Christ and the Church in Heaven, the pilgrim Church on earth longs for the glory of Heaven, and at the same time she strives to continue Christ's work on earth, bringing grace and salvation to all mankind. Established and sustained by Christ himself, the Church "is the visible plan of God's love for humanity," a sign of the love that has existed from the very beginning.

WHAT IS AN INDULGENCE?

"An indulgence is a remission before God of the temporal punishment due to sins whose guilt has already been forgiven, which the faithful Christian who is duly disposed gains under certain prescribed conditions through the action of the Church which, as the minister of redemption, dispenses and applies with authority the treasury of the satisfactions of Christ and the saints."[3]

"An indulgence is partial or plenary according as it removes either part or all of the temporal punishment due to sin."[4] The faithful can gain indulgences for themselves or apply them to the dead.[5] (CCC 1471)

Within the one Church, we "bear one another's burdens."[6] The saints in Heaven intercede for us who are on earth. And we on earth pray for those who are undergoing purification in Purgatory, so that their burden may be lighter.

An indulgence is an act of faith that requires an offering of some prayer, sacrifice, or work of service, in imitation of Christ and the saints. By doing these things, we can develop virtues—good habits—and become more like Christ. An indulgence is an act by which we dispose ourselves to receive God's grace of conversion. On behalf of Christ, the Church rewards us from the "treasury of merits"—the abundance of grace won for us by Christ and by his faithful people down through the ages. Indulgences may also be applied to other people, whether on earth or in Purgatory.

When the Israelites sinned, Moses himself offered acts of atonement on behalf of the people, but the people still had to fulfill acts of penance.[7] A bishop of the early Church, St. John Chrysostom, eloquently preached about our solidarity across the generations: "If Job's sons were purified by their father's sacrifice,[8] why would we doubt

that our offerings for the dead bring them some consolation? Let us not hesitate to help those who have died and to offer our prayers for them."

An indulgence is *partial* or *plenary* depending on whether it removes part or all of the debt due to sin, and the Church requires that those seeking indulgences should also go to confession and receive Holy Communion near the time they complete the indulgenced act.[9]

The Church frequently makes indulgences available to mark certain feast days or special celebrations. The Church's official list of indulgenced actions is called the *Enchiridion (or Handbook) of Indulgences.* Among the "indulgenced acts" on the current list are praying the Stations of the Cross or visiting the Blessed Sacrament for half an hour.

St. John Chrysostom
Statue at St. Patrick's Cathedral, New York City. St. John Chrysostom (ca. 347-407), born in Antioch, was Archbishop of Constantinople and an important early Church Father and Doctor of the Church. He is known for his eloquence in preaching and public speaking. He emphasized charitable giving and was concerned with the spiritual and temporal needs of the poor. He also spoke out against abuse of wealth and personal property.

WHAT DOES IT MEAN TO BE A SAINT?

For members of the pilgrim Church on earth, our communion with the Church in Heaven is most fully realized in the Liturgy of the Mass and in our reception of the Eucharist. This is the first meaning of the Communion of Saints. We profess in the Creed an acknowledgement of our shared participation in the Holy Communion of the heavenly liturgy.

The second meaning of the phrase *Communion of Saints* is closely related to the first. Through our union with Christ, we are brought into communion with everyone else who is united to him, that is, the entire Church. This includes those members still on earth, those in Purgatory, and those in Heaven. We enter into this Communion of Saints by virtue of our Baptism, when through the power of the Holy Spirit we are adopted as sons and daughters of the Father, thus making us brothers and sisters in Christ.

The word *saint* literally means "holy one," and this title refers primarily to those Christian men and women who remained faithful during their time on earth and have reached the glory of Heaven. The Church's official process for declaring someone a saint is called "canonization."

> By *canonizing* some of the faithful, i.e., by solemnly proclaiming that they practiced heroic virtue and lived in fidelity to God's grace, the Church recognizes the power of the Spirit of holiness within her and sustains the hope of believers by proposing the saints to them as models and intercessors.[10] "The saints have always been the source and origin of renewal in the most difficult moments in the Church's history."[11] Indeed, "holiness is the hidden source and infallible measure of her apostolic activity and missionary zeal."[12] (CCC 828)

St. Vincent de Paul Helping the Plague-Ridden by Ansiaux. St. Vincent de Paul (1581-1660), a French priest, founded the Daughters of Charity in 1633 to care for the poor and provide hospital care for them. He was canonized in 1737. In 1885, Pope Leo XIII named St. Vincent de Paul patron of all charitable societies.

On the Solemnity of All Saints, celebrated each year on November 1 in the Latin Rite of the Church and the first Sunday after Pentecost in the Eastern Rites, the Church rejoices in all of the unknown saints who are now in Heaven. The Church reminds us that sanctity is within everyone's reach, and that through the communion of the saints, we help one another achieve sanctity.

Having already passed through their period of trial and pilgrimage, the saints in Heaven are our models for how we should lead Christian lives—they have reached the perfection in Heaven to which all of us are called. With the exception of the Blessed Virgin Mary, who was conceived without Original Sin, all the saints were sinners just like us. They had to work to overcome temptation with the help of God's grace, and when they sinned, they relied on God's mercy in the Sacrament of Penance. Through the presence of the Holy Spirit in our souls, we are saints-in-the-making. In examining the lives of the saints, we should be inspired by their victory in Christ to more closely follow him ourselves.

> Since we are surrounded by so great a cloud of witnesses, let us also lay aside every weight, and sin which clings so closely, and let us run with perseverance the race that is set before us, looking to Jesus the pioneer and perfecter of our faith, who for the joy that was set before him endured the cross, despising the shame, and is seated at the right hand of the throne of God. (Heb 12:1-2)

Nevertheless, it is not only for their example that we honor the saints. The work of the saints in Heaven is to constantly intercede for the Church on earth. We are encouraged, therefore, to ask for their intercession so that, with the grace of God, each of us—and the entire Church—might attain our perfection in the glory of Heaven. For this reason, everyone should pray to his or her patron saint and guardian angel regularly.

INTERCESSION OF THE SAINTS

Those in the Church Triumphant can intercede before God for the members of the Church Suffering, the Holy Souls in Purgatory; besides, they present to God the sufferings and prayers of the pilgrim members on earth so that he may have mercy on them—hence the importance not only of Christ's intercession on behalf of his members but also of that of the saints, especially the Blessed Virgin Mary. Devotion to the saints corresponds in its very essence to the profound reality of the Church as a mystery of communion.

> The Church has always believed that the apostles and Christ's martyrs, who gave the supreme witness of faith and charity by the shedding of their blood, are closely united with us in Christ; she has always venerated them, together with the Blessed Virgin Mary and the holy angels, with a special love, and has asked piously for the help of their intercession.[13]

In addition to the Apostles and martyrs, there are all those who have heroically practiced the Christian virtues and those whose divine charisma commend them to the devotion of Christians.

> It is most fitting, therefore, that we love those friends and co-heirs of Jesus Christ who are also our brothers and outstanding benefactors, and that we give due thanks to God for them, "humbly invoking them, and having recourse to their prayers, their aid and help in obtaining from God through his Son, Jesus Christ, our Lord, our only Redeemer and Savior, the benefits we need."[14]

Why should we seek the intercession of the saints? Because God wishes us to pray for one another. St. Paul instructed his disciple St. Timothy:

> First of all, then, I urge that supplications, prayers, intercessions, and thanksgivings be made for all men, for kings and all who are in high positions, that we may lead a quiet and peaceable life, godly and respectful in every way. This is good, and is acceptable in the sight of God our Savior. (1 Tm 2: 1-3)

Intercessory Prayer

The Bible is full of stories of people praying for others. One memorable moment of prayer occurred when the Roman centurion came to Jesus and asked for his servant to be healed. Because of the man's great faith revealed in his prayer, Christ answered his prayer and healed the servant.[15] This type of prayer is called *intercessory prayer*—praying to God on behalf of another.

God already knows our needs and the needs of our neighbor, but praying for our families, friends, and neighbors is one way that we express our love for them. Prayer reflects also our faith and hope in God's will in our lives. It

Virgin and Child in Glory with Saints by Carlone. The represented saints are St. George, St. John the Baptist, St. Bernard and St. Lawrence.

is one way that we live the way God made us to live. For God is love,[16] and he made us to share in his divine nature.[17] He also became man in order to show us how human beings can love as God loves. He prayed for his persecutors[18] and urged us to do the same.[19] Jesus asked his followers to "bear one another's burdens."[20] When we pray for the needs of others, we are following Christ's teachings and imitating him.[21]

Praying for others is one kind of intercessory prayer. Another kind is practiced when we ask others to pray for us. In addition to asking friends and family to remember us in their prayers, we may also ask the saints

The Saints
PILLARS OF THE CHURCH

St. Therese of Lisieux
"I WANT TO SPEND MY HEAVEN IN DOING GOOD ON EARTH"

St. Therese of Lisieux, commonly called the "Little Flower," was a Carmelite nun who lived in the late nineteenth century. She was born in France in 1873 into a devout Catholic family, and from an early age she demonstrated great virtue and holiness. Her mother died when Therese was only four years old, and afterward her older sister Pauline looked after her.

Therese thought of Pauline as "a second mother," and after Pauline left home to join the Carmelites when Therese was nine, she too wanted to become a nun. At the age of fifteen, after being told she was too young to enter the Carmelite convent, she went with her father to Rome and obtained approval from the Pope himself.

The account of her years as a religious sister is given in her autobiography, which her religious superiors had requested she write. In it, St. Therese details the many graces she had received as well as her great love for God. St. Therese was not to remain in the convent for long, however. She soon developed tuberculosis, and, in 1897, at the age of twenty-four, she died.

Her autobiography, *Story of a Soul*, was discovered and published shortly after her death, and it was soon translated into dozens of languages and made available all over the world. St. Therese was canonized by Pope Pius XI in 1925 and was declared a Doctor (or "Teacher") of the Church—only the third woman to be so named—by Pope Bl. John Paul II in 1997.

Before she died, Therese expressed her wish of interceding for the souls of those in the world, which is the work of the Church in Heaven. She said, "I want to spend my heaven in doing good on earth." During her time on earth, Therese led an exemplary life of holiness, always trying to draw closer to Christ. Perfectly united to him now in Heaven, she continues to assist all of us by her constant prayer and intercession.

St. Therese of Lisieux, pray for us.

to pray for us. In this context, the word *saint* refers to all people who are part of the Body of Christ—those who have been given a share in God's sanctity, his holiness. In the Letter to the Colossians, St. Paul uses the word *saint* four times—three times to refer to the living members of the Church, and once to refer to the saints "in light," those who are now in Heaven.

In the Book of Revelation, we learn that the saints in glory are already praying for us before the altar of God in Heaven. The angels bear the "golden bowls full of incense, which are the prayers of the saints."[22]

St. Paul Preaching in Athens (detail) by Raphael. Everywhere the Gospel reached, Christians raised their voices to the saints, saying, "Pray for us!"

The Book of Revelation shows us that the saints in Heaven continue to be aware of life on earth and intercede for God's blessings on their brothers and sisters in the Faith. Revelation relates how the saints in Heaven cry out to God to right the wrongs that have been committed on earth,[23] and the Letter to the Hebrews refers to the saints in glory as our "great cloud of witnesses,"[24] which watches over us and cheers us on to finish the good race. In Heaven, united to Christ, they pray for us, and their prayers are effective.

> "Being more closely united to Christ, those who dwell in heaven fix the whole Church more firmly in holiness....They do not cease to intercede with the Father for us, as they proffer the merits which they acquired on earth through the one mediator between God and men, Christ Jesus....So by their fraternal concern is our weakness greatly helped."[25] (CCC 956)

The *Catechism* goes on to quote St. Dominic and St. Therese of Lisieux:

> Do not weep, for I shall be more useful to you after my death and I shall help you then more effectively than during my life.[26]

> I want to spend my heaven in doing good on earth.[27]

Veneration of the Saints

The Church has always believed in the intercession of the saints. The early Christians reverently preserved the relics of the martyrs and every year celebrated their "birthdays" into Heaven. In the third century, Origen (an Egyptian) and St. Cyprian (an African) attested to the custom of seeking the intercession of the saints. The ancient liturgies invoked the witness and intercession of the saints of both the Old and New Testaments as well as that of the martyrs.

In the fourth century, St. Cyril of Jerusalem, St. Ambrose, St. Epiphanius, St. John Chrysostom, and St. Gregory Nazianzen exhorted their congregations to seek the help of the saints in glory. We can still look upon early images of those saints, painted on the walls of the catacombs, engraved on tombstones, and etched into the sides of pilgrim flasks and oil lamps. Everywhere the Gospel reached, Christians raised their voices to the saints, saying, "Pray for us!"

The saints, who have died in Christ, now live in light and are now more alive than we are. It is our privilege, as the saints on earth, to share in the one Church, the one Body of Christ, with the saints in Heaven.

In summary, our veneration of the saints is:

✤ an expression of the Communion of the Saints;

✤ a channel of petitions through which their intercession is entreated; and

✤ a means of providing the faithful with examples of virtue to emulate.

Last Judgment by Michelangelo.
For those who are united to Christ, the end of history is a promise, not a threat.

THE END OF HISTORY:
A New Heaven and a New Earth

> I saw a new heaven and a new earth; for the first heaven and the first earth had passed away, and the sea was no more. (Rev 21: 1)

The Church waits for the coming of Christ and the end of history, but what is the end of history? For what is the Church waiting?

From Sacred Scripture, we know a little about what the end of history will be like. First, Jesus himself has told us that it is impossible for us to know when the end of the world will take place:

> Of that day and hour no one knows, not even the angels of heaven, nor the Son, but the Father only. (Mt 24: 36)

The second thing we know about the end of the world is that on that Last Day the Final Judgment of the living and the dead will take place. At that time, all of our thoughts and actions—both good and evil—will be brought to light.

We should remember that Jesus did not come to condemn the world but to give us the grace to share in the divine life of the Blessed Trinity. Through the Sacraments, the Church continues Christ's work of offering this grace to mankind. It is according to our acceptance or refusal of this grace that we will be judged. Those who have rejected grace in this life will have condemned themselves to Hell, while those who have accepted and cultivated the gift of grace will be welcomed into Christ's heavenly kingdom.

Third, we know that after the Final Judgment, all things will be perfectly reestablished.

> He will wipe away every tear from their eyes, and death shall be no more, neither shall there be mourning nor crying nor pain any more. (Rev 21: 4)

The Bible tells us that there will be "new heavens and a new earth,"[28] and although we have no way of knowing what specifically this will look like, we do know that this is the eternal reward for those who have remained faithful to God.

> "*We know neither the moment of the consummation* of the earth and of man, nor the way in which the universe will be transformed. The form of this world, distorted by sin, is passing away, and we are taught that God is preparing a new dwelling and a new earth in which righteousness dwells, in which happiness will fill and surpass all the desires of peace arising in the hearts of men."[29] (CCC 1048)

For those who are united to Christ, the end of history is a promise, not a threat. But this brings us to the fourth thing we know about the end of the world. Before this promise of glory can be fulfilled, the Church must endure a time of trial and persecution.

The Last Judgment by Campen.
We should remember that Jesus did not come to condemn the world, but to give us the grace to share in the divine life of the Blessed Trinity.

> Then they will deliver you up to tribulation, and put you to death; and you will be hated by all nations for my name's sake.... And many false prophets will arise and lead many astray. And because wickedness is multiplied, most men's love will grow cold. But he who endures to the end will be saved. (Mt 24: 9-13)

Between the dire predictions of tribulation and false prophets, we might assume that Christ was speaking only to those who are alive at the end of the world. But these words, which were first addressed to the Apostles, are intended for the pilgrim Church in every age. Jesus warned the Apostles—and all of us—about the persecution that comes from faithfully following him. The pilgrim Church on earth has been enduring her time of trial and persecution since the beginning, and with the assistance of the Holy Spirit, she will continue to press on until Christ's glorious return.

ST. JOHN'S VISION OF THE HEAVENLY LITURGY

In addition to what Jesus told his disciples about the end of the world, the final book of the Bible, Revelation, is a prophetic vision of the end times. In Revelation (sometimes called the Apocalypse), we are presented with a confusing and at times terrifying array of visions and symbols: rivers of blood; plagues of locusts; angelic wars; and, of course, strange, demonic beasts.

What these images and symbols portray is the "unveiling" (in Greek, *apokalypsis*) of supernatural realities of the world after the time of Christ. In St. John's vision, we see the ongoing spiritual struggle of the Church against the demonic forces of Satan;[30] we see the solidarity and Communion of Saints and angels in Heaven and on earth;[31] and we see the intimate union shared by Christ and his Bride, the Church, in their glorious marriage feast.[32]

In Revelation, St. John witnesses events that for us are now in the past (the destruction of Jerusalem), as well as events that are still to come (the unveiling of new Heavens and a new earth). But throughout Revelation, his primary focus remains on what is going on eternally in Heaven; the "heavenly liturgy," offered to the Father by Christ with the angels and saints. In this liturgy, Christ is both priest and victim—he wears the robes of the High Priest[33] but also appears as the Lamb, "standing, as though it had been slain."[34]

The Son's whole life was an offering to the Father. Beginning with the Incarnation, his offering reached its ultimate manifestation in the Sacrifice of the Cross, where Jesus was revealed as the new Passover Lamb. In the heavenly liturgy, however, Christ's offering is bloodless. Having already died "once for all,"[35] Christ continually re-presents himself before the Father as the sacrificial Lamb who was slain but is now risen.

> Jesus Christ, the one priest of the new and eternal Covenant, "entered, not into a sanctuary made by human hands...but into heaven itself, now to appear in the presence of God on our behalf."[36] There Christ permanently exercises his priesthood, for he "always lives to make intercession" for "those

St. John the Evangelist on the Island of Patmos, St. John Altarpiece (right wing) by Memling. What these images and symbols portray is the "unveiling" (in Greek, *apokalypsis*) of supernatural realities of the world after the time of Christ.

who draw near to God through him."[37] As "high priest of the good things to come" he is the center and the principal actor of the liturgy that honors the Father in heaven.[38] (CCC 662)

In addition to Christ, the principal actor in this heavenly liturgy, there are others who participate as well. The Book of Revelation shows us that all of Heaven takes part in this liturgy, worshiping God and giving thanks for the salvation they have received through Christ. The angels and the saints join together in offering to God their song of praise:

Holy, holy, holy, is the Lord God Almighty, who was and is and is to come! (Rev 4: 8)

THE HOLY MASS IS A PARTICIPATION IN THE HEAVENLY LITURGY

In examining St. John's description of the heavenly liturgy, we can see many elements of our own liturgy of the Mass: an altar,[39] robed priests,[40] candles,[41] incense,[42] the *Gloria*,[43] readings from Scripture,[44] the "Holy, Holy, Holy,"[45] chalices,[46] and the "Lamb of God."[47] Further, in St. John's vision, the heavenly liturgy reaches its climax in the "marriage supper of the Lamb."

I saw the holy city, new Jerusalem, coming down out of heaven from God, prepared as a bride adorned for her husband; and I heard a great voice from the throne saying, "Behold, the dwelling of God is with men. He will dwell with them, and they shall be his people." (Rev 21: 2-3)

Pope Benedict XVI Celebrates the Eucharist in Brazil. The Sacrifice of the Mass is the same Sacrifice offered by Christ to the Father in Heaven, a bloodless re-presentation of Jesus' Sacrifice on the Cross.

The Mass is where the pilgrim Church shares in fullest communion with Christ—it is the "marriage supper" between Christ and his Bride. Through Jesus' Real Presence in the Eucharist, the dwelling of God is already with men. The Mass is therefore a foreshadowing of the eternal marriage supper that is celebrated in the heavenly liturgy.

"In the earthly liturgy we share in a foretaste of that heavenly liturgy which is celebrated in the Holy City of Jerusalem toward which we journey as pilgrims, where Christ is sitting at the right hand of God, Minister of the sanctuary and of the true tabernacle."[48] (CCC 1090)

Nevertheless, the Mass is not merely a foreshadowing or a preview of coming attractions. What St. John shows us in the Book of Revelation is that our worship on earth is the same as the worship in Heaven. The Mass is not an imitation but an actual participation in the one heavenly liturgy. "It is in this eternal liturgy that the Spirit and the Church enable us to participate whenever we celebrate the mystery of salvation in the Sacraments."[49]

In the Mass, we receive into our midst the presence of Christ crucified and risen, the Lamb "standing, as though it had been slain." The Sacrifice of the Mass is the same Sacrifice offered by Christ to the Father in Heaven, a bloodless re-presentation of Jesus' Sacrifice on the Cross. Although human eyes are unable to perceive it, when we are at Mass, we are really in Heaven, standing before Christ the Eternal High Priest with all the angels and saints.

You have come to Mount Zion and to the city of the living God, the heavenly Jerusalem, and to innumerable angels in festal gathering, and to the assembly of the firstborn who are enrolled in heaven...and to Jesus, the mediator of a new covenant, and to the sprinkled blood that speaks more graciously than the blood of Abel. (Heb 12: 22-24)

United to Christ in the Eucharist, the pilgrim Church on earth already shares in the glory of Heaven, even as we anticipate the final manifestation of that glory on the Last Day. Until that time, Christ remains veiled under the sacramental appearance of bread and wine, reminding us that it is he, the Bread of Life, who nourishes and strengthens us as we continue along our pilgrim journey toward Heaven.

Christ Pantocrator and the Last Judgment, Mosaic in the Baptistry of St. John in Florence.
The saved are shown leaving their tombs in joy at Christ's right hand, and the damned are shown facing their punishments at Christ's left hand.

THE LAST THINGS

For all this, the Church can more easily be described as the divinely instituted institution that seeks the salvation of all souls. The surest way to die a happy death is to live a good Christian life. At death, the soul leaves the body and is judged immediately by God (the Particular Judgment); the possibility of merit or conversion ceases. The soul will immediately go to Heaven, Hell, or Purgatory as deserved.

> Death puts an end to human life as the time open to either accepting or rejecting the divine grace manifested in Christ.[50] The New Testament speaks of judgment primarily in its aspect of the final encounter with Christ in his second coming, but also repeatedly affirms that each will be rewarded immediately after death in accordance with his works and faith. The parable of the poor man Lazarus and the words of Christ on the cross to the good thief, as well as other New Testament texts speak of a final destiny of the soul—a destiny which can be different for some and for others.[51]

> Each man receives his eternal retribution in his immortal soul at the very moment of his death, in a particular judgment that refers his life to Christ: either entrance into the blessedness of heaven—through a purification[52] or immediately,[53]—or immediate and everlasting damnation.[54]

> At the evening of life, we shall be judged on our love.[55] (CCC 1021-1022)

PARTICULAR JUDGMENT

The New Testament speaks of the judgment mainly from the perspective of a final meeting with Christ when he comes again. But we also find in many places within Sacred Scripture references to the retribution immediately after each one's death as a consequence of one's faith and deeds.

Thus, we know with the certainty of faith that each man, after dying, receives—in his immortal soul—his eternal retribution in a *Particular Judgment*. He immediately refers his life to Christ, going through a period of purification, directly to his definitive state in Heaven, or to eternal condemnation.

This passage to the definitive state would not be possible without a previous judgment, where each person's fate is clearly and summarily decided before the judgment seat of Christ, so that each one may receive reward or punishment, according to what he has done in the body.

The Particular Judgment is an act by which God makes the soul see with all clarity. God communicates this act to the soul, which cannot dispute it. By this act, the soul understands in some way its state of either union with or separation from God. It is a light that comes from God and will lead either to the soul's union with God—immediately or through Purgatory—or to its definitive damnation.

PURGATORY

Purgatory is a state of purification from venial sins so that souls achieve the purity necessary to enter the joy of Heaven.[56] These souls must suffer the inability to see God completely and be freed from attachment to creatures. These souls are in a state of grace, a part of the Communion of Saints, but have unrepented venial sins or owe reparation for confessed sins. Purgatory is not an eternal state (which would contradict the Bible), but will only last until the General Judgment at the end of the world.

Before entering Heaven, every trace of attachment to evil must be eliminated, every imperfection of the soul corrected. Purification must be complete. The Church calls *Purgatory* the final purification of the souls of those who, having died in grace, have not fully paid the punishment for their pardoned mortal sins or their venial sins. This purification is completely different from the punishment of the damned.

> **All who die in God's grace and friendship, but still imperfectly purified, are indeed assured of their eternal salvation; but after death they undergo purification, so as to achieve the holiness necessary to enter the joy of heaven. (CCC 1030)**

The term *Purgatory* does not indicate a place but a condition of existence. The separated souls, being spirits, do not properly occupy a *place*. In common language, however, Purgatory is often called a place for these souls.

St. Francis Rescuing Souls from Purgatory.
Purgatory is not another form of Hell but the antechamber of Heaven.

The souls in Purgatory are not farther from God than we are on earth. Unlike us, they are completely sure of beholding God in the future. What constitutes their punishment is the delay in seeing him.

WHY PRAY FOR THE DEAD?

Purgatory is the state in which the soul is purified of the effects of sin after death. From the earliest days, the Church has spoken of a state of purification that happens after death, and the Book of Revelation tells us that "nothing unclean shell enter" Heaven.[57]

The doctrine of Purgatory goes back to the Old Testament. The Second Book of Maccabees 12: 39-45 tells the story of Judas Maccabeus finding pagan amulets on the bodies of dead Jewish soldiers—a sign that they had sinned grievously in practicing idolatry.

Judas "took up a collection, man by man... and sent it to Jerusalem to provide for a sin offering....Therefore he made atonement for the dead, that they might be delivered from their sin." The passage concludes: "It was a holy and pious thought."

Jews in Jesus' time prayed for the dead, and today this traditional Jewish practice is continued in the praying of the *Kaddish*, prayers to reduce the time spent in Gehenna for those who have died.

Why pray for the dead? If they are in Heaven, they do not need prayers. If they are in Hell, prayers will not do them any good. So there must be a state where our prayers do some good. This state is called Purgatory.

St. Paul, for his part, taught that Christians who sin "will be saved, but only as it were through fire."[58] That metaphorical "fire" is the purification of Purgatory. Pope Benedict XVI has speculated that perhaps the fire "which both burns and saves is Christ himself, the Judge and Savior."

> The encounter with him is the decisive act of judgment. Before his gaze all falsehood melts away. This encounter with him, as it burns us, transforms and frees us, allowing us to become truly ourselves. All that we build during our lives can prove to be mere straw, pure bluster, and it collapses. Yet in the pain of this encounter, when the impurity and sickness of our lives become evident to us, there lies salvation. His gaze, the touch of his heart heals us through an undeniably painful transformation "as through fire." But it is a blessed pain, in which the holy power of his love sears through us like a flame, enabling us to become totally ourselves and thus totally of God. In this way the interrelation between justice and grace also becomes clear: the way we live our lives is not immaterial, but our defilement does not stain us for ever if we have at least continued to reach out towards Christ, towards truth and towards love. (*Spe Salvi,* 47)

This is certainly how the early Christians read the Gospels. In the late second century, the North African Christian, Tertullian, spoke of Purgatory, as did his countryman St. Cyprian in the third century. At the same time, we find the doctrine in the writings of Origen in Egypt. St. Augustine's mother, St. Monica, also urged him to pray for her after she died.

This traditional teaching of the Church was confirmed at the Second Ecumenical Council of Lyons in 1274 and later by the Ecumenical Councils of Florence (1439) and Trent (1563). And it is confirmed in our own time by the *Catechism of the Catholic Church*.[59]

Christian symbols on an early fourth-century tombstone from the catacomb of St. Domitilla. Catacombs were underground tunnels dug by Christians to serve as burial places, shrines, and places of worship during the first centuries after Christ.

Therefore, in Purgatory, there is joy and pain at the same time. There is pain because the souls that are retained there long for the vision of God and are prevented from reaching it. Their desire to be with the Lord is no longer weakened by material occupations and realities. The souls of Purgatory are not interested in created goods any more but only in the Lord of all creation, the only good that is capable of satisfying them. Besides, their desire to possess God is extremely intense because they know that they are destined to eternal happiness. But they cannot enjoy God until they totally expiate their faults and the punishment of their sins. They also know perfectly that the blame is exclusively theirs. They could have entered Heaven earlier if, while still on earth, they had avoided venial sin, striven to do the will of God, and accepted with joy the trials and sufferings of life, which are a preparation for Heaven.

However, there is also joy in Purgatory because the souls that are retained there know that they are destined for eternal happiness in paradise. Purgatory is not another form of Hell but the antechamber of Heaven.

Praying for the Holy Souls

The Holy Souls in Purgatory are consoled by the angels. They are helped by our prayers and suffrages of the Church and the prayers of the Virgin and the saints.

Prayers for the dead have always been considered a *pious duty* and as a work of mercy. It is a requirement of *charity* since we have to will the good of others. It is an obligation of *piety* toward members of the same natural or supernatural family. And it is also an obligation of *justice* since some souls may be detained in Purgatory partly through our fault because of our sins of commission or omission.

Hell by Memling.
The souls in Hell died unrepentant of mortal sin or refused the love and mercy of God to the end.

Among the different ways of helping the souls of Purgatory, the most important is the Sacrifice of the Mass. On All Soul's Day, all the priests of the Church offer Mass for the souls in Purgatory. On many other occasions, the Mass may be applied for that intention as well. The application of indulgences for the dead is a common practice, as well as giving alms in their memory or offering up sacrifices and penance on their behalf.

It is also good to remember that, by virtue of the Communion of Saints, the souls in Purgatory can help us greatly with their intercession. The Church does not invoke them in the liturgy, but the custom of invoking them privately is widespread in the Church. This Christian practice has never been forbidden. On the contrary, some prayers asking for their help have even been enriched with indulgences.

HELL

We cannot be united to God unless we freely choose to love him. We cannot love God if we sin grievously against him, our neighbor, or our own selves. "He who does not love abides in death. Anyone who hates his brother is a murderer, and you know that no murderer has eternal life abiding in him."[60] To die in mortal sin, without repentance and without seeking refuge in the compassionate love of God, implies remaining separated from God forever because of our own free choice.

Hell is eternal self-exclusion from communion with God and the blessed in Heaven. The souls in Hell died unrepentant of mortal sin and refused the love and mercy of God to the end. Jesus spoke often of Hell as "fire" and "darkness" where there will be "weeping and gnashing of teeth" as condemned souls are tormented by "the worm that dies not." The souls of Hell continually thirst for God while hating him.

> The teaching of the Church affirms the existence of hell and its eternity. Immediately after death the souls of those who die in a state of mortal sin descend into hell, where they suffer the punishments of hell, "eternal fire."[61] The chief punishment of hell is eternal separation from God, in whom alone man can possess the life and happiness for which he was created and for which he longs. (CCC 1035)

HEAVEN

Heaven is the state of everlasting life in which we see God, become like him in glory, and enjoy eternal happiness. All souls in Heaven are in the light of glory and have an immediate vision of God. They have made up for their sins either on earth or in Purgatory. Jesus speaks of various degrees ("mansions") of happiness in his kingdom according to the various degrees of love and friendship with God through cooperation with his grace. While these are different, each person receives the full measure of happiness he or she can desire—like jars of different sizes each filled to the brim.

> This perfect life with the Most Holy Trinity—this communion of life and love with the Trinity, with the Virgin Mary, the angels and all the blessed—is called "heaven." Heaven is the ultimate end and fulfillment of the deepest human longings, the state of supreme, definitive happiness. (CCC 1024)

Coronation of the Virgin by Lippi.
The essential happiness of Heaven consists in the immediate vision of God, of creatures in God, and in the infinite joy of their vision.

This mystery of blessed communion with God and all who are in Christ is beyond all understanding and description. Scripture speaks of it in images: life, light, peace, wedding feast, wine of the kingdom, the Father's house, the heavenly Jerusalem, paradise: "no eye has seen, nor ear heard, nor the heart of man conceived, what God has prepared for those who love him."[62] (CCC 1027)

The essential happiness of Heaven consists in the immediate vision of God, of creatures in God, and in the infinite joy of their vision. But God's mercy is so great, and he is so generous, that he has wanted his chosen ones to find happiness in the legitimate created goods that man seeks.

Aside from the vision of God, "the full and perfect satisfying of every desire," eternal life consists in "the happy society of all the blessed, and this society will be especially delightful. Since each one will possess all good together with the blessed, and they will love one another as themselves, they will rejoice in the other's good as their own. It will also happen that, as the pleasure and enjoyment of one increases, so will it be for all."[63]

Being with Jesus Christ, the Blessed Virgin, the angels, and the saints is part of the glory, which consists in the "clear and distinct knowledge which each one [of the blessed] shall have of the singular and exalted dignity of his companions [in glory]."[64] Meeting those whom we loved while on earth will cause a special joy.

This joy and happiness is completed as other souls enter Heaven, as loved ones still on earth progress in their spiritual life, and as one's apostolic efforts and sufferings endured in the service of God bear fruit with the passage of time. It is finally crowned after the Last Judgment with the glorification of one's own body.

The Trinity in Glory by Titian.
Being with Jesus Christ, the Blessed Virgin, the angels, and the saints is part of the glory that is Heaven.

The *Catechism* teaches that this mystery of blessed communion with God and with all those who are in Christ surpasses all understanding or representation. "No eye has seen, no ear heard, nor the heart of man conceived what God has prepared for those who love him."[65] "The faithful should be deeply impressed that the happiness of the saints is full to overflowing of all those pleasures which can be enjoyed or even desired in this life, whether they regard the powers of the mind or of the perfection of the body."[66]

THE *PAROUSIA*

The Second Coming of the Lord is also known as the *Parousia*, a Greek word meaning "apparition" or "presence." At the *Parousia*, Christ will appear in power and majesty as judge and establish his kingdom—which was inaugurated at the Incarnation—in all its fullness.

At the General Judgment, God's majesty, wisdom, justice, and mercy will shine forth for all to see as Jesus Christ's final victory on earth. We will see why God sometimes allows the good to suffer and the wicked to prosper. We will also see all the good and bad effects of humans' actions. Souls will be reunited to their now immortal bodies in the resurrection. At this point Jesus will tell the good to come into the Kingdom of Heaven while sending the wicked "into the eternal fire prepared for the devil and his angels."[67]

The Saints
PILLARS OF THE CHURCH

St. Michael the Archangel
"DEFEND US IN BATTLE"

Although there are hundreds of references to angels in the Bible, St. Michael the Archangel is one of only three angels who is ever identified by name (the others are the archangels St. Gabriel and St. Raphael). The Church in Heaven includes all those deceased human beings who received salvation in Christ as well as those angels who resisted the temptation to fall away from God. Therefore, the angels in Heaven are hailed as saints, intercessors, and exemplary members of the Church.

Within Scripture, the most dramatic depiction of St. Michael is found in the Revelation to St. John, where we see him leading the holy angels in battle against the Devil.

> War arose in heaven, Michael and his angels fighting against the dragon; and the dragon and his angels fought, but they were defeated and there was no longer any place for them in heaven. And the great dragon was thrown down, that ancient serpent, who is called the Devil and Satan, the deceiver of the whole world. (Rev 12: 7-9)

As leader of the angelic armies, St. Michael has often been invoked by the Church as her protector against the opposition of the Devil. In 1886, Pope Leo XIII wrote a prayer to St. Michael and encouraged all members of the pilgrim Church on earth to ask for his supernatural assistance and defense:

> *St. Michael the Archangel, defend us in battle; be our protection against the wickedness and snares of the Devil. May God rebuke him, we humbly pray. And do you, O prince of the heavenly host, by the power of God, thrust into Hell Satan and all the evil spirits who prowl about the world for the ruin of souls. Amen.*

St. Michael the Archangel, pray for us.

Jesus Goes Up Alone onto a Mountain to Pray (detail) by Tissot.
The Second Coming of the Lord is also known as the *Parousia*, a Greek word meaning "apparition" or "presence."

From the viewpoint of salvation history, the *Parousia* marks the definitive triumph of Christ over sin and death. This triumph was manifested in Christ's Resurrection and Ascension and can be shared through sanctifying grace. But it will be fully manifested only at the end of the world. The *Parousia* is the culmination of the history of salvation. The plans of God will reach complete fulfillment in a renewed universe inhabited by glorious bodies.

The Church Triumphant will reach her perfection and plenitude at the final moment of history, when Christ shall come in power and majesty to judge the world and to communicate all his saving power to the elect through the resurrection of their bodies and the total renovation of the world.

> The Last Judgment will come when Christ returns in glory. Only the Father knows the day and the hour; only he determines the moment of its coming. Then through his Son Jesus Christ he will pronounce the final word on all history. We shall know the ultimate meaning of the whole work of creation and of the entire economy of salvation and understand the marvelous ways by which his Providence led everything towards its final end. The Last Judgment will reveal that God's justice triumphs over all the injustices committed by his creatures and that God's love is stronger than death.[68] (CCC 1040)

> At the end of time, the Kingdom of God will come in its fullness. After the universal judgment, the righteous will reign for ever with Christ, glorified in body and soul. The universe itself will be renewed:

> > "The Church...will receive her perfection only in the glory of heaven, when will come the time of the renewal of all things. At that time, together with the human race, the universe itself, which is so closely related to man and which attains its destiny through him, will be perfectly re-established in Christ."[69] (CCC 1042)

The Resurrection of Christ by Tintoretto.
The Church reflects the nature of her founder, Jesus Christ, who in his Incarnation united his divine nature to human nature, and who is, therefore, truly God and truly man.

CONCLUSION

We were not made for this earth, but for Heaven. Living in the fallen world, separated from our Creator, we are pilgrims in this life making our way back to Christ. The Church on earth is on this journey toward Heaven, and with the example of the saints, who have already completed this journey, she continuously points to our heavenly reward. If the heavenly Church is our final goal, the Church on earth can be seen as the sure path to guide our journey.

But the earthly Church is more than just the means to an end because she is already in communion with Christ. This communion is real, but it is not yet perfect, which is why the Church on earth continues on her pilgrimage.

The Church also reflects the nature of her founder, Jesus Christ, who in his Incarnation united his divine nature to human nature, and who is, therefore, truly God and truly man. In a like manner, the Church is both present in history through her human members, and at the same time transcends history. In communion with Christ, who sits at the right hand of the Father in Heaven, she is in the world but not of it.

In a letter to his fellow Christians in the first century, St. Ignatius of Antioch wrote, "Wherever Jesus Christ is, there is the Catholic Church." [70] This means that the Church is first and foremost a Mystical Body, present on earth, in Purgatory, and in Heaven.

So while we seek communion with God in this life and enjoy now the Communion of Saints, we do so always with our hearts set on that perfect communion we hope to enjoy with him in the next life as we look forward always, in the words of the Apostles' Creed, to "the forgiveness of sins, the resurrection of the body, and life everlasting. Amen."

VOCABULARY

APOCALYPSE
From the Greek word meaning "to uncover or unveil," another name for the Book of Revelation attributed to St. John while on the island of Patmos. This prophetic work foretells the final victory of Christ and his Church.

CANONIZATION
The Church's official process by which she declares someone a saint.

CHARISM
A specific gift or grace of the Holy Spirit that directly or indirectly benefits the Church. It is given in order to help a person live out the Christian life or serve the common good in building up the Church.

CHURCH MILITANT
The members of the Church on earth, part of the Communion of Saints.

CHURCH SUFFERING
The members of the Church in Purgatory; part of the Communion of Saints.

CHURCH TRIUMPHANT
The members of the Church in Heaven; part of the Communion of Saints.

COMMUNION OF SAINTS
The unity in Christ of all the redeemed, those on earth and those who have died: the Church Triumphant, the Church Militant, and the Church Suffering. It is professed in the Apostles' Creed, where it has also been interpreted to refer to unity in the "holy things," especially the unity of faith and charity achieved through participation in the Eucharist.

ECUMENICAL COUNCIL
From the Greek *oikoumene*, meaning "the whole world." A formal synod of bishops (sometimes with other ecclesiastics) from the whole inhabited world convened to define doctrine, regulate the Christian life, or apply discipline in the Church. The First Ecumenical Council was held in Nicæa AD 325.

HEAVEN
The eternal state of supreme and definitive happiness with God; communion of life and love with the Trinity and all the blessed.

HEAVENLY LITURGY
The worship of God in Heaven by the angels and saints, led by Christ the High Priest, who re-presents the sacrificial offering of himself to the Father, thus renewing the work of our redemption.

HELL
The eternal state of definitive self-exclusion from communion with God.

HOLY SOULS
Refers to the souls in Purgatory being purified in anticipation of entering Heaven. We can pray on their behalf to ease their suffering and hasten their journey to Heaven.

INTERCESSORY PRAYERS
Any prayers on behalf of another person. We intercede for others when we pray for them; the saints in Heaven and the Holy Souls in Purgatory intercede for us when they pray for us. We can pray to the saints and to the Blessed Virgin Mary asking their intercession before God on our behalf.

LAST JUDGMENT
The judgment on the living and the dead at the second coming of Christ, at which time those who died before the second coming and have gone through the Particular Judgment will have their bodies reunited with their souls.

LAST THINGS
Usually refers to death, judgment, Heaven, and Hell; a longer list would include Purgatory and the resurrection of the body.

MARTYR
Greek for "witness." A witness to the truth of the Faith in which a Christian endures even death for Christ.

VOCABULARY Continued

MASS
Also called the Eucharist or Lord's Supper. This name is derived from the Latin dismissal of the faithful, "*Ite, missa est.*" The principal sacramental celebration of the Church, established by Jesus at the Last Supper, in which the mystery of salvation through participation in the sacrificial death and glorious resurrection of Christ is renewed and accomplished.

PAROUSIA
Greek term for the second coming of Christ, who will come for the Final Judgment at the end of time.

PARTICULAR JUDGMENT
The judgment of those who have died or will die before the second coming of Christ. This judgment takes place immediately after death and is confirmed by the eventual Last Judgment.

PURGATORY
A state of final purification after death and before entrance into Heaven for those who died in God's friendship but were only imperfectly purified; a final cleansing of human imperfection before one is able to enter the joy of Heaven.

SACRAMENT
An efficacious sign of grace, instituted by Christ and entrusted to the Church, by which divine life is dispensed to a Christian through the work of the Holy Spirit. There are Seven Sacraments.

SAINT
A member of the Church—the Mystical Body of Christ—on earth, in Purgatory, or in Heaven. The Church may officially declare a member of the Church in Heaven to be a saint by canonization, adding him or her to the calendar and promoting his or her public veneration.

VICAR OF CHRIST
From the Latin "*vicarius*," meaning "in the person of." It emphasizes the role of the Pope as a representative of Christ himself.

The Charity of St. Elizabeth of Hungary (detail) by Leighton.
Born a princess, St. Elizabeth (1207-1231) was married at the age of fourteen, widowed at twenty, relinquished her wealth to the poor, built hospitals, and became a symbol of Christian charity in Germany and elsewhere after her death at the age of twenty-four. She was canonized by Pope Gregory IX in 1235.

STUDY QUESTIONS

1. Identify the three different "states" of the Communion of Saints.

2. What is an *indulgence*? Are indulgences still useful today? How does one receive an indulgence?

3. What does the word saint mean? What can the saints in Heaven do for us today?

4. Why should we seek the intercession of the saints?

5. What is the "great cloud of witnesses" that the Letter to the Hebrews talks about (Heb 12:1)?

6. What three elements are involved in the veneration of saints?

7. According to Jesus, who is the only person who knows when the end of the world will take place?

8. What is St. John's primary focus throughout the Book of Revelation?

9. What will happen on the Last Day?

10. The talk of the end of the world can be scary. As Christians, should we be worried about the end of the world?

11. Explain how the Book of Revelation is St. John's vision of the *heavenly liturgy*.

12. What does the Mass we celebrate today foreshadow?

13. Explain: By celebrating the Mass on earth, we participate in the one heavenly liturgy.

14. What are the *last things*?

15. What is the *Particular Judgment*? How does it differ from the *Last Judgment*?

16. Describe Purgatory. Is it a place of joy or of pain? Explain your answer.

17. Does it do any good to pray for the dead?

18. What three virtues oblige us to pray for the dead?

19. What is the best way to help the Holy Souls in Purgatory?

20. How does a person end up in Hell?

21. If God is so good, loving, and merciful, then why does anyone end up in Hell?

22. What is Heaven like?

23. Will we recognize people whom we knew here on earth?

24. What is the *Parousia*?

25. What is the surest way for a member of the faithful to be guided on the path to Heaven?

Martyrdom of St. Stephen by Vasari. St. Stephen, the first Christian martyr, died by stoning ca. 35. "But he, full of the Holy Spirit, gazed into heaven and saw the glory of God, and Jesus standing at the right hand of God; and he said, 'Behold, I see the heavens opened, and the Son of man standing at the right hand of God.'" (Acts 7:55-56)

PRACTICAL EXERCISES

1. In the Lord's Prayer, which we recite every time we go to Mass, we pray, "Thy kingdom come." Why does the Church pray for the final coming of Christ in glory? In what ways do we already participate in heavenly glory as members of the Church on earth?

2. Imagine you are having a discussion with a friend who asks why she should pray; after all, she says, God is omniscient and knows everything she needs and desires. How would you respond? The same friend then responds by asking why she should pray to the saints; after all, she says, it is Christ who intercedes with his Father (1 Tm 2:5). How would you respond to this?

3. Imagine what Heaven must be like, an endless existence of complete happiness such has never been experienced on earth; imagine also what Hell must be like, an eternal and overwhelming pain and regret for having rejected God. When we consider the contrasting destinies of those who are in Heaven and those who are in Hell, we have to wonder: Why would anyone commit a serious sin and risk losing his or her salvation?

Disputation on the Trinity by Andrea del Sarto.
The saints represented are (kneeling in front) St. Sebastian and St. Mary Magdelene;
(standing) St. Augustine, St. Lawrence, St. Peter Martyr, and St. Francis.

FROM THE CATECHISM

961 The term "communion of saints" refers also to the communion of "holy persons" (*sancti*) in Christ who "died for all," so that what each one does or suffers in and for Christ bears fruit for all.

1026 By his death and Resurrection, Jesus Christ has "opened" heaven to us. The life of the blessed consists in the full and perfect possession of the fruits of the redemption accomplished by Christ. He makes partners in his heavenly glorification those who have believed in him and remained faithful to his will. Heaven is the blessed community of all who are perfectly incorporated into Christ.

1029 In the glory of heaven the blessed continue joyfully to fulfill God's will in relation to other men and to all creation. Already they reign with Christ; with him "they shall reign for ever and ever."[71]

1035 The teaching of the Church affirms the existence of hell and its eternity. Immediately after death the souls of those who die in a state of mortal sin descend into hell, where they suffer the punishments of hell, "eternal fire."[72] The chief punishment of hell is eternal separation from God, in whom alone man can possess the life and happiness for which he was created and for which he longs.

1037 God predestines no one to go to hell;[73] for this, a willful turning away from God (a mortal sin) is necessary, and persistence in it until the end. In the Eucharistic liturgy and in the daily prayers of her faithful, the Church implores the mercy of God, who does not want "any to perish, but all to come to repentance":[74] "Father, accept this offering from your whole family. Grant us your peace in this life, save us from final damnation, and count us among those you have chosen."[75]

1472 To understand this doctrine and practice of the Church, it is necessary to understand that sin has a *double consequence*. Grave sin deprives us of communion with God and therefore makes us incapable of eternal life, the privation of which is called the "eternal punishment" of sin. On the other hand every sin, even venial, entails an unhealthy attachment to creatures, which must be purified either here on earth, or after death in the state called Purgatory. This purification frees one from what is called the "temporal punishment" of sin. These two punishments must not be conceived of as a kind of vengeance inflicted by God from without, but as following from the very nature of sin. A conversion which proceeds from a fervent charity can attain the complete purification of the sinner in such a way that no punishment would remain.[76]

1475 In the communion of saints, "a perennial link of charity exists between the faithful who have already reached their heavenly home, those who are expiating their sins in Purgatory and those who are still pilgrims on earth. Between them there is, too, an abundant exchange of all good things."[77] In this wonderful exchange, the holiness of one profits others, well beyond the harm that the sin of one could cause others. Thus recourse to the communion of saints lets the contrite sinner be more promptly and efficaciously purified of the punishments for sin.

2796 When the Church prays "our Father who art in heaven," she is professing that we are the People of God, already seated "with him in the heavenly places in Christ Jesus" and "hidden with Christ in God;"[78] yet at the same time, "here indeed we groan, and long to put on our heavenly dwelling."[79]

Pope Bl. John Paul II and Bl. Teresa of Calcutta.
"In the glory of heaven the blessed continue joyfully to fulfill God's will
in relation to other men and to all creation. Already they reign with Christ;
with him 'they shall reign for ever and ever.'" (CCC 1029)

ENDNOTES - CHAPTER SEVEN

1. Nicetas, *Expl. Symb.* 10: PL 52: 871B.
2. *Catechism of St. Pius X*, no. 149; cf. CCC 954-955.
3. Paul VI, Apostolic Constitution, *Indulgentiarum Doctrina*, Norm 1.
4. *Indulgentiarum Doctrina*, Norm 2; cf. Norm 3.
5. CIC, can. 994, 84; cf. Council of Trent (1551): DS 1712-1713; (1563): 1820.
6. Gal 6: 2.
7. Ex 32: 30-32; Nm 14: 23.
8. Cf. Job 1: 5.
9. CCC 1498, 1471, 1478.
10. Cf. *LG* 40, 48-51.
11. Bl. John Paul II, *CL* 16, 3.
12. *CL* 17, 3.
13. *LG* 50.
14. DS 1821; *LG* 50.
15. Cf. Lk 7: 7.
16. Cf. 1 Jn 4: 16.
17. Cf. 2 Pt 1: 4.
18. Lk 23: 34.
19. Mt 5: 44.
20. Gal 6: 2.
21. Cf. 1 Cor 11: 1.
22. Rev 5: 8; cf. Rev 8: 3-4.
23. Rev 6: 9-10.
24. Heb 12: 1.
25. *LG* 49; cf. 1 Tm 2: 5.
26. St. Dominic, dying, to his brothers.
27. St. Therese of Lisieux, *The Final Conversations*, tr. John Clarke (Washington: ICS, 1977), 102.
28. 2 Pt 3: 13.

29. *GS* 39 § 1.
30. Rev 12: 17.
31. Rev 7: 3; 19: 10.
32. Rev 19: 7.
33. Rev 1: 13.
34. Rev 5: 6.
35. 1 Pt 3: 18.
36. Heb 9: 24.
37. Heb 7: 25.
38. Heb 9: 11; cf. Rev 4: 6-11.
39. Rev 8: 3.
40. Rev 4: 4.
41. Rev 1: 12.
42. Rev 5: 8.
43. Rev 15: 3-4.
44. Rev 1: 3.
45. Rev 4: 8.
46. Rev 16.
47. Rev 5: 6.
48. *SC* 8; cf. *LG* 50.
49. CCC 1139
50. Cf. 2 Tm 1: 9-10.
51. Cf. Lk 16: 22; 23: 43; Mt 16: 26; 2 Cor 5: 8; Phil 1: 23; Heb 9: 27; 12: 23.
52. Cf. Council of Lyons II (1274): DS 857-858; Council of Florence (1439): DS 1304-1306; Council of Trent (1563): DS 1820.
53. Cf. Benedict XII, *Benedictus Deus* (1336): DS 1000-1001; John XXII, *Ne super his* (1334): DS 990.
54. Cf. Benedict XII, *Benedictus Deus* (1336): DS 1002.
55. St. John of the Cross, *Dichos* 64.
56. Cf. CCC 1030-1032.

57. Cf. Rev 21: 27.
58. 1 Cor 3: 15.
59. Cf. CCC 1030-1032.
60. 1 Jn 3: 14-15.
61. Cf. DS 76, 409, 411, 801, 858, 1002, 1351, 1575; Paul VI, *CPG* § 12.
62. 1 Cor 2: 9.
63. *The Catechetical Instructions of St. Thomas Aquinas*, pp. 74-76.
64. *Catechism of the Council of Trent*, 1.12.8; cf. CCC 1024.
65. 1 Cor 2: 9; cf. CCC 1027.
66. *Catechism of the Council of Trent*, 1.12.12.
67. Mt 25: 41.
68. Cf. Sg 8: 6.
69. *LG* 48; cf. Acts 3: 21; Eph 1: 10; Col 1: 20; 2 Pt 3: 10-13.
70. St. Ignatius, *Letter to the Smyrnæans*, 8.
71. Rev 22: 5; cf. Mt 25: 21, 23.
72. Cf. DS 76, 409, 411, 801, 858, 1002, 1351, 1575; Paul VI, *CPG* § 12.
73. Cf. Council of Orange II (529): DS 397; Council of Trent (1547): 1567.
74. 2 Pt 3: 9.
75. Roman Missal, EP I (Roman Canon) 88.
76. CIC, can. 994, 84; cf. Council of Trent (1551): DS 1712-1713; (1563): 1820.
77. *Indulgentiarum Doctrina*, 5.
78. Eph 2: 6; Col 3: 3.
79. 2 Cor 5: 2; cf. Phil 3: 20; Heb 13: 14.

Mary, Mother of the Church and Our Mother

Mary cares for us with maternal charity and intercedes with her Son to aid us in the quest for perfection through his manifold graces.

The Church
CHAPTER 8

Mary, Mother of the Church and Our Mother

ishing in His supreme goodness and wisdom to effect the redemption of the world, "when the fullness of time came, God sent His Son, born of a woman...that we might receive the adoption of sons" (Gal 4, 4-5). "He for us men, and for our salvation, came down from heaven, and was incarnate by the Holy Spirit from the Virgin Mary."[1] This divine mystery of salvation is revealed to us and continued in the Church, which the Lord established as His body. Joined to Christ the Head and in the unity of fellowship with all His saints, the faithful must in the first place reverence the memory "of the glorious ever Virgin Mary, Mother of our God and Lord Jesus Christ."[2]

The Virgin Mary, who at the message of the angel received the Word of God in her heart and in her body and gave Life to the world, is acknowledged and honored as being truly the Mother of God and Mother of the Redeemer. Redeemed by reason of the merits of her Son and united to Him by a close and indissoluble tie, she is endowed with the high office and dignity of being the Mother of the Son of God, by which account she is also the beloved daughter of the Father and the temple of the Holy Spirit. Because of this gift of sublime grace she far surpasses all creatures, both in heaven and on earth. At the same time, however, because she belongs to the offspring of Adam she is one with all those who are to be saved. She is "the mother of the members of Christ...having cooperated by charity that faithful might be born in the Church, who are members of that Head."[3] Wherefore she is hailed as a pre-eminent and singular member of the Church, and as its type and excellent exemplar in faith and charity. The Catholic Church, taught by the Holy Spirit, honors her with filial affection and piety as a most beloved mother. (*Lumen Gentium*, 52-53)

In this chapter, we will consider the singular woman who carried and gave birth to our Savior, the Son of God. She is the Mother of God and our mother, the Mother of the Church. She is the supreme manifestation of the love, holiness, and faithful obedience that characterizes the one Church established by her Son. The Blessed Virgin Mary is also the perfect realization of the Church, "the image and beginning of the Church as it is to be perfected in the world to come."[4] Above all other avenues, the person of Mary enables us to understand and come to love the mystery of the Church.

> After speaking of the Church, her origin, mission, and destiny, we can find no better way to conclude than by looking to Mary. In her we contemplate what the Church already is in her mystery on her own "pilgrimage of faith," and what she will be in the homeland at the end of her journey. (CCC 972)

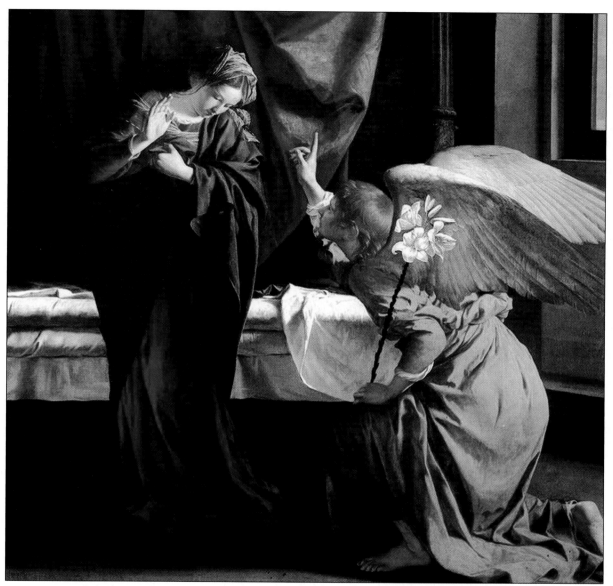

Annunciation by Gentileschi. Mary is the supreme manifestation of the love, holiness, and faithful obedience that characterizes the one Church established by her Son.

IN THIS CHAPTER, WE WILL ADDRESS SEVERAL QUESTIONS:

✢ What is the role of Mary in the Church?

✢ What is the Immaculate Conception?

✢ How can Mary be the Mother of God?

✢ In what way is Mary the Mother of the Church?

✢ What is the Assumption?

✢ What is the role of Mary in the spiritual life of Christians?

MARY IN GOD'S PLAN OF SALVATION

God chose the Blessed Virgin Mary from all eternity to be the Mother of the Redeemer, his Son, Jesus Christ. God's plan of salvation began to unfold in the Old Testament, immediately following the Original Sin committed by Adam and Eve. It is here that we have our first glimpse of Mary, Mother of Christ.

> **I will put enmity between you and the woman, and between your seed and her seed; he shall bruise your head, and you shall bruise his heel. (Gn 3: 15)**

In the New Testament, we encounter this "woman" promised by God in the Book of Genesis. In St. John's Gospel, we hear Christ referring to the "woman" at the wedding at Cana,[5] as he is beginning his redemptive mission, and again at the foot of the Cross,[6] as he is completing this mission. Finally, in the Book of Revelation, St. John describes the "woman," who is "clothed with the sun, with the moon under her feet, and on her head a crown of twelve stars."[7] Just as the story of salvation history began with three characters—Adam, Eve, and the serpent—it shall end with Christ (the New Adam), Mary (the New Eve), and Satan, who is defeated by the Cross.

MOTHER OF GOD

> **At the announcement that she would give birth to "the Son of the Most High.". . . Mary responded with the obedience of faith, certain that "with God nothing will be impossible": "Behold, I am the handmaid of the Lord; let it be [done] to me according to your word."[8] Thus, giving her consent to God's word, Mary becomes the mother of Jesus. (CCC 494)**

The Gospels refer to the Blessed Virgin Mary as the Mother of Jesus and "the mother of my Lord."[9] The custom of calling Mary the "Mother of God" began in the East, and St. Ambrose was the first to use the title in the West.

We can call Mary the Mother of God because her Son, Jesus Christ, is the Second Person of the Blessed Trinity, God the Son. Through Mary, Jesus takes his human nature. However, we do not speak of motherhood in relation to nature, but in relation to a person, and Jesus is a Person with two natures, human and divine. Since the Person to whom she gave birth is God, she is rightly called the Mother of God.

From all eternity, God had planned that the salvation of man be joined to the cooperation of Mary in accepting her role as Mother of Jesus Christ. The grace that Mary received in her Immaculate Conception was

CHURCH DOGMAS ABOUT MARY

Since the time of the Apostles, the Church has always recognized the importance of Mary in the Incarnation. The Church has continued to reflect upon the Deposit of Faith entrusted to her by Christ, and the Church has come to an ever-deepening understanding of the person of Mary and the privileges given to her by Christ, her Son. Among the teachings of the Church regarding Mary, there are four solemn doctrinal definitions, or dogmas, that explain certain aspects of her role in the mystery of salvation.

1. **Mary's Divine Motherhood,** defined at the Ecumenical Council of Ephesus AD 431

2. **Mary's Perpetual Virginity,** defined by the Council of the Lateran AD 649

3. **Mary's Immaculate Conception,** defined by Pope Pius IX AD 1854

4. **Mary's Bodily Assumption into Heaven,** defined by Pope Pius XII AD 1950

Eleusa Icon. *Eleusa* (Greek for tenderness or showing mercy) is a type of *Theotokos* icon depicting the Christ child nestled against the cheek of Mary.

given to her by God so that she could faithfully respond to what he was asking of her. Her unique, God-given vocation as Christ's mother is the reason why God gave her this grace and the reason why the Church honors her above all the angels and saints, second only to Christ himself.

From the Church's earliest centuries, the faithful have revered Mary as the Mother of God (recall the term *Theotokos*, "Bearer of God"), following the example of Mary's cousin St. Elizabeth, who at the Visitation refers to Mary as "the mother of my Lord."[10] Our belief in Mary's divine motherhood originates in the mystery of the Incarnation. Although the Son possesses his divine nature from all eternity, through Mary he took his human nature, thus making him both fully human and fully divine.

Mary is truly Jesus' Mother, but as we know, her motherhood is vastly different from any other mother, for she conceived her Son by the consent that she gave to God. Thus, when one of Jesus' listeners cried out, "Blessed is the womb that bore you," Jesus calls our attention not to the fact of Mary's biological motherhood, but to its cause: "Blessed rather are those who hear the word of God and keep it."[11]

While on the surface Jesus' statement might seem like he is downplaying the unique importance of Mary, he is actually giving her the highest compliment. We know that of all people, it is Christ's Mother who hears the word of God and keeps it most perfectly—"Let it be to me according to your word."[12] But Christ is also calling our attention to the fact that the intimate, graced communion he shared with his Blessed Mother went beyond mere biology and is therefore not limited only to her. For although Mary possesses the fullness and perfection of this communion, in a sense, all who hear the word of God and keep it become themselves bearers of the Word.

Just as Mary gave her consent to the Father and so received the Word made flesh within her womb, so too does the Church give her consent to the Father and receive the Word made flesh in the Eucharist. As Pope Bl. John Paul II wrote, "There is a profound analogy between the *Fiat* ["Let it be done"], which Mary said in reply to the angel, and the *Amen* which every believer says when receiving the Body of the Lord."[13] Indeed, by the power of the Holy Spirit, Christ dwells within the Church as once he dwelt within Mary, and therefore both are truly bearers of the Word.

> "This motherhood of Mary in the order of grace continues uninterruptedly from the consent which she loyally gave at the Annunciation and which she sustained without wavering beneath the cross, until the eternal fulfillment of all the elect. Taken up to heaven she did not lay aside this saving office but by her manifold intercession continues to bring us the gifts of eternal salvation....Therefore the Blessed Virgin is invoked in the Church under the titles of Advocate, Helper, Benefactress, and Mediatrix."[14] (CCC 969)

FIAT: THE "YES" OF MARY

[Gabriel] said to [Mary], "The Holy Spirit will come upon you, and the power of the Most High will overshadow you; therefore the child to be born will be called holy, the Son of God...." And Mary said, "Behold, I am the handmaid of the Lord; let it be to me according to your word." (Lk 1:35, 38)

Annunciation (detail) by Fra Angelico.

The realization of this promise of a New Covenant began with the Blessed Virgin Mary. The Annunciation is the first revelation of this beginning. Indeed, at that moment we hear the Virgin of Nazareth respond with the obedience of faith to God's eternal plan for human salvation through the Incarnation of the Word: the Incarnation of God's Son means the fulfillment of the messianic prophecies as well as the dawning of the Church as the People of the New Covenant. Mary is aware of the messianic dimension of the message she receives and of the *yes* she gives in response.

The mystery of the Incarnation encompasses this motherhood of Mary, divinely accomplished by the power of the Holy Spirit. This, then, is the beginning of the New Covenant, in which Christ, as divine Bridegroom, joins humanity to himself and calls it to be his Church, as the universal People of the New Covenant.

At the moment of the Incarnation, Mary as Virgin-Mother becomes a figure of the Church in both her virginal and maternal character. "In the mystery of the church, which is herself rightly called mother and virgin, the Blessed Virgin stands out in eminent and singular fashion as exemplar both of virgin and mother" (*LG* 63).

— Pope Bl. John Paul II, *L'Osservatore Romano*, n. 49, December 9, 1991.

THE IMMACULATE CONCEPTION

Immaculate Conception by Maella.
It was only through the grace of Christ that Mary was immaculately conceived, that she remained sinless throughout her life, and that she was able to give her consent to all that God would ask of her.

According to Church tradition, Mary's parents were Sts. Joachim and Ann. She was descended through the line of David from the tribe of Judah. Among the precursors of Mary in the Old Testament are Hannah, the mother of Samuel, as well as Deborah, Ruth, Judith, and Esther. These women of God exhibited qualities that Mary possessed to the fullest.

The bulk of the scriptural information we have regarding Mary is in the Gospels of Sts. Matthew and Luke. Mary resided in Nazareth in Galilee. She was betrothed to St. Joseph, but according to the custom, they were not yet living as man and wife. St. Luke relates how the angel Gabriel appeared to her, announcing that she would be the Mother of the Messiah.

And he [Gabriel] came to her and said, "Hail, full of grace, the Lord is with you!" (Lk 1:28)

The Church has always understood this greeting, "full of grace," as a unique Revelation into the nature of Mary, namely, that Christ preserved her from the effects of Original Sin. We know that because of Adam and Eve's disobedience, all mankind is affected by Original Sin, the deprivation of the holiness and communion with God that our first parents originally possessed. For us, it is only through Baptism that Christ restores this graced communion, uniting us to him and giving us his Holy Spirit. For Mary, however, Christ desired that she be fully united to him from the first instant of her human existence.

The most Blessed Virgin Mary was, from the first moment of her conception, by a singular grace and privilege of almighty God and by virtue of the merits of Jesus Christ, Savior of the human race, preserved immune from all stain of original sin.[15] (CCC 491)

In the *Immaculate Conception*, we can see the fullness of salvation that Christ offers to the world. Indeed, the holiness that Christ gives the Church is the same as that which his Blessed Mother received at her conception. Mary is the first and greatest of us who have been chosen by God "before the foundation of the world, that we should be holy and blameless before him."[16]

The Immaculate Conception also reveals our need for God's grace so that we may faithfully

Immaculate Conception by Murillo. We recognize Mary as the *New Eve*.

respond to his call. It was only through the grace of Christ that Mary was immaculately conceived, that she remained sinless throughout her life, and that she was able to give her consent to all that God would ask of her. "In fact, in order for Mary to give the free assent of her faith to the announcement of her vocation, it was necessary that she be wholly borne by God's grace."[17]

Just as sin had entered the world through the disobedience of a man and a woman, so too would sin be destroyed by the obedience of a man and woman: Christ and his Blessed Mother. This is the great twist in the history of man, God's wondrous undoing of our fate through his unbounded love, manifested by the gift of Jesus to mankind. Because of this parallel between our first parents, and Jesus and Mary, we recognize Mary as the *New Eve*, joined by the power of the Holy Spirit to Christ, the New Adam. The marriage of the first Adam and Eve was a sign of God's graced communion with man; the spiritual union of the New Adam and Eve is the perfect realization of that communion. It is this communion that renders Mary holy and immaculate from the moment of her conception, just as it is this communion that renders the Church—the spotless Bride of Christ—holy and immaculate from the moment of her institution.

> **By her complete adherence to the Father's will, to his Son's redemptive work, and to every prompting of the Holy Spirit, the Virgin Mary is the Church's model of faith and charity. Thus she is a "pre-eminent and...wholly unique member of the Church"; indeed, she is the "exemplary realization" (*typus*)[18] of the Church. (CCC 967)**

THE WOMAN OF THE *PROTOEVANGELIUM*

As we saw in earlier chapters, God's first promise of salvation after the Fall—the *Protoevangelium*—speaks not only of the future Messiah, but also of *the woman*, his mother: "I will put enmity between you and the woman, and between your seed and her seed."[19] Although these words were spoken to Eve (and it was from among her descendants that Christ came), they find their ultimate fulfillment in the Blessed Virgin Mary, the New Eve, whose offspring would crush the head of the serpent.

Within the Gospels, we find that Jesus does not address his mother as "mom," "mother," or even "Mary," but rather as "woman."[20] Far from conveying disrespect, Jesus is hailing her as the New Eve, whose obedience helps to restore what the first Eve lost through her disobedience.

Virgin and Child (detail) by Fra Angelico

THE ASSUMPTION OF THE BLESSED VIRGIN MARY

The Immaculate Conception of Mary preserved the Blessed Mother from the effects of the Fall. From the first moment of her conception, Mary was kept free from the spiritual death and decay of Original Sin, and by God's grace she remained sinless throughout her entire life. In addition to remaining free from sin, Mary was free from the inherited punishments of Original Sin. Indeed, tradition holds that Mary was not subjected to the decay of physical death, but rather, as the Church teaches, was assumed, both body and soul, into Heaven at the moment of her death.

> "Finally the Immaculate Virgin, preserved free from all stain of original sin, when the course of her earthly life was finished, was taken up body and soul into heavenly glory, and exalted by the Lord as Queen over all things, so that she might be the more fully conformed to her Son, the Lord of lords and conqueror of sin and death."[21] The Assumption of the Blessed Virgin is a singular participation in her Son's Resurrection and an anticipation of the resurrection of other Christians:
>
>> In giving birth you kept your virginity; in your Dormition you did not leave the world, O Mother of God, but were joined to the source of Life. You conceived the living God and, by your prayers, will deliver our souls from death.[22] (CCC 966)

Just as Mary was the first person to share in the redemption that Christ offered to his Church, so too in her *Assumption* she became the first person to fully share in Christ's Resurrection. (In the East, reference is made to her *Dormition*, or "falling asleep," as in the hymn quoted above.) The entire Church is, in a certain sense, already "risen with Christ" because in the Sacraments we participate in his heavenly glory even as we continue on our earthly pilgrimage. But we know that this spiritual resurrection realized in the Church anticipates a final, bodily resurrection. Mary, however, experienced this bodily resurrection in her Assumption. Because of her unique vocation as the Mother of God, she received in advance what is promised to all of us at the end of history, namely, a resurrected body and entrance into heavenly glory.

Assumption of the Virgin by Gherarducci.

The Feast of the Assumption of Our Lady prompts us to acknowledge the basis for this joyful hope. Yes, we are still pilgrims, but our mother has gone on ahead, where she points to the reward of our efforts. She tells us that we can make it, and, if we are faithful, we will reach home. The Blessed Virgin is not only our model; she is the help of Christians.[23]

The Saints
PILLARS OF THE CHURCH

St. Joseph
"PATRON OF THE UNIVERSAL CHURCH"

St. Joseph was the foster-father of Jesus and the husband of Mary—the head of the Holy Family—and the Church therefore honors him as one of the greatest of all saints. Scripture itself is largely silent about St. Joseph, but what little is said of him in the Gospels of Sts. Matthew and Luke reveals his uniquely important role in God's plan of salvation.

✤ **He is a descendant of David.** St. Joseph was originally from Bethlehem in Judea, the city of David, and it is because of his royal lineage that Jesus was identified as the son of David.

✤ **He is the chaste spouse of the Virgin Mary.** Even though their union was never physically consummated, Mary and St. Joseph were truly and lawfully married. The pure and total love they had for one another was not diminished by their mutual commitment to chastity in continence but was in fact strengthened by it.

✤ **He is a father to Jesus.** Although St. Joseph was not the biological father of Jesus, he nonetheless fulfilled all the normal responsibilities of an earthly father. He named Jesus, provided for him, protected him from the threat of King Herod, and instructed him in both the Law of Moses and the trade of carpentry. Jesus, in turn, was perfectly obedient to St. Joseph, recognizing in him a reflection of his heavenly Father.

✤ **He is a model of holiness.** The Bible describes St. Joseph as a "just man," a title reserved only for the holiest of God's servants. Although he was not preserved free from Original Sin, St. Joseph was given a measure of grace that was proportionate to his vocation as the head of the Holy Family. He was to be Jesus' teacher and guardian, and God therefore led him to holiness, prayerfulness, humility, prudence, and courage to accomplish all that he was called to do. Because of these gifts, St. Joseph is invoked by the faithful as the master of the interior life and a sure guide for all who desire to truly learn how to pray.

Because of his complete obedience to the will of God, St. Joseph was entrusted with God's most precious treasures: the Word made flesh and the Mother of God. But his role as guardian and protector is not limited only to the Holy Family in Nazareth. Indeed, St. Joseph is honored as the patron of the universal Church, protector of the entire Family of God. As Pope Bl. John Paul II stated, "Just as St. Joseph took loving care of Mary and gladly dedicated himself to Jesus Christ's upbringing, he likewise watches over and protects Christ's Mystical Body, that is, the Church, of which the Virgin Mary is the exemplar and model."[24]

St. Joseph, Patron of the Universal Church, pray for us.

THE PERPETUAL VIRGINITY OF MARY

Throughout her two-thousand-year history, the Church has consistently professed her belief in the virginal conception and birth of Jesus Christ. This truth is acknowledged in the Nicene Creed, which is prayed every Sunday during Mass, that Jesus was "born of the *Virgin* Mary." This belief can be found in the Gospels, which give us clear testimony about Mary's virginity at the time of Christ's conception.

> **The angel Gabriel was sent from God to a city of Galilee named Nazareth, to a virgin betrothed to a man whose name was Joseph, of the house of David; and the virgin's name was Mary. (Lk 1: 26-27)**

> **All this took place to fulfill what the Lord had spoken by the prophet: "Behold, a virgin shall conceive and bear a son, and his name shall be called Emmanuel" (which means "God with us").** (Mt 1: 22-23)

Why is the fact of Mary's virginity important to us as Christians? The Virgin Birth of Jesus brings together his two natures. Jesus' physical birth is evidence of his true humanity, and his miraculous conception is evidence of his true divinity. It attests to Jesus' true Father as being God the Father in Heaven. Mary's physical virginity confirms that "that which is conceived in her is of the Holy Spirit."[25] Thus, in reflecting on Mary's virginal motherhood of Christ, the Church has been led to affirm the Perpetual Virginity of Mary, that is, that Mary remained a virgin even after the birth of Jesus: "The Church celebrates Mary as…the 'Ever-virgin.'"[26]

In addition to demonstrating the reality of Jesus' divine nature, Mary's virginity reveals the completeness of her consecration to God. Having received the fullness of divine grace at her Immaculate Conception, Mary offered herself, both body and soul, back to God—"Behold, I am the handmaid of the Lord."[27] Mary's virginal consecration to God, the Father of humanity, also expands her role as Mother. As the betrothed of God, her virginity enables her to not only be the earthly Mother of Christ but also the spiritual Mother of all those who are united to him.

DID JESUS HAVE BROTHERS AND SISTERS?

Objections to the Perpetual Virginity of Mary are sometimes raised from the verses in the Bible that mention the brothers and sisters of Jesus. However, "the Church has always understood these passages as not referring to other children of the Virgin Mary. In fact, James and Joseph, 'brothers of Jesus,' are the sons of another Mary, a disciple of Christ, whom St. Matthew significantly calls 'the other Mary.' They are close relations of Jesus, according to an Old Testament expression."[28]

"Jesus is Mary's only son, but her spiritual motherhood extends to all men whom indeed he came to save: 'The Son whom she brought forth is he whom God placed as the firstborn among many brethren, that is, the faithful in whose generation and formulation she cooperates with a mother's love.'"[29]

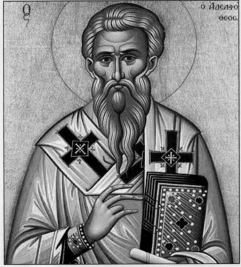

St. James the Less, also known as St. James the Just, was a close relative of Jesus.

MARY, MOTHER OF THE CHURCH

Mary's role in the Church cannot be separated from that of her Son, for it is through her "*yes*" to the Father that the Church came into being. Like the Church, she embarked on a pilgrimage of faith. She joined her suffering completely to that of Jesus and consented to his suffering and Death. Her support of the Church continued in her life of prayer after his Ascension.

Coronation of the Virgin by Veneziano. Mary's role in the Church cannot be separated from that of her Son.

> Predestined from eternity by that decree of divine providence which determined the incarnation of the Word to be the Mother of God, the Blessed Virgin was in this earth the virgin Mother of the Redeemer, and above all others and in a singular way the generous associate and humble handmaid of the Lord. She conceived, brought forth and nourished Christ. She presented Him to the Father in the temple, and was united with Him by compassion as He died on the Cross. In this singular way she cooperated by her obedience, faith, hope and burning charity in the work of the Saviour in giving back supernatural life to souls. Wherefore she is our mother in the order of grace.[30]

Just as Eve was formed from the side of Adam, the Church, the pure and spotless bride of Christ, was formed from the side of Christ as he offered himself as a sacrifice on the Cross.

> *There flowed from his side water and blood.* Beloved, do not pass over this mystery without thought; it has yet another hidden meaning, which I will explain to you. I said that water and blood symbolized baptism and the holy eucharist. From these two sacraments the Church is born: from baptism, "the cleansing water that gives rebirth and renewal through the Holy Spirit," and from the holy eucharist. Since the symbols of baptism and the Eucharist flowed from his side, it was from his side that Christ fashioned the Church, as he had fashioned Eve from the side of Adam.[31]

The Blood and water flowing from the side of Christ on the Cross represent the Sacraments of Baptism and the Eucharist from which the Church is formed. The Church is the Mystical Body of Christ, and, as Mary is the Mother of Christ, she is also the Mother of the Church and Mother of all who are in communion with her Son.

> Thus we find ourselves at the very center of the fulfillment of the promise contained in the Proto-gospel: the "seed of the woman...will crush the head of the serpent" (cf. Gn. 3:15). By his redemptive death Jesus Christ conquers the evil of sin and death at its very roots. It is significant that, as he speaks to his mother from the Cross, he calls her "woman" and says to her: "Woman, behold your son!" Moreover, he had addressed her by the same term at Cana too (cf. Jn. 2:4).[32]

As Jesus was dying on the Cross, he looked at Mary and St. John and said, "Woman, behold your son!" Here again, we hear of the "woman" mentioned in the *Protoevangelium*, when God had promised our first parents that a Redeemer—the Son of the woman—would "crush the head" of the serpent. This is the "woman" to whom Christ spoke at the wedding of Cana, at the beginning of his salvific ministry that would lead to the Cross.

Then he said to the disciple, "Behold your mother!" With these words, Jesus indicated that Mary was to be the mother of St. John and the mother of all who would be united in his Mystical Body, the Church.

> The words uttered by Jesus from the Cross signify that the motherhood of her who bore Christ finds a "new" continuation in the Church and through the Church, symbolized and represented by

"BEHOLD, YOUR MOTHER!"

What Our Lord Saw from the Cross by Tissot.

Through her consent to the will of God at the Annunciation, the Blessed Virgin Mary became the Virgin-Mother of Jesus. Although this new form of motherhood was without the physical pain of labor, it was not without deep spiritual agony. As St. Simeon had foretold at the time of Jesus' Presentation in the Temple, "This child is set for fall and rising of many in Israel...and a sword will pierce through your own soul also."[33]

It is at the Cross that we see Mary experiencing this agony most fully. She remained with Christ until the end, giving her consent to the Father's will and witnessing her only beloved Son tortured and put to Death as part of the Father's plan. But here we also see the ultimate fruitfulness of her consent, for at the Cross Christ gives her as a Mother to all the faithful.

> When Jesus saw his mother, and the disciple whom he loved standing near, he said to his mother, "Woman, behold, your son!" Then he said to the disciple, "Behold, your mother!" (Jn 19: 26-27)

Here, Christ again hails his Mother as "woman," the New Eve. Just as the first Eve became the "mother of all living,"[34] so too did Mary, the New Eve, become the Mother of all who have received new life in Christ.

John. In this way, she who as the one "full of grace" was brought into the mystery of Christ in order to be his Mother and thus the Holy Mother of God, through the Church remains in that mystery as "the woman" spoken of by the Book of Genesis (3: 15) at the beginning and by the Apocalypse (12: 1) at the end of the history of salvation. In accordance with the eternal plan of Providence, Mary's divine motherhood is to be poured out upon the Church, as indicated by statements of Tradition, according to which Mary's "motherhood" of the Church is the reflection and extension of her motherhood of the Son of God.[35]

We have, then, in Mary a new form of motherhood—a supernatural, virginal motherhood that is accomplished by the power of the Holy Spirit. She is the Mother of Christ, and she is also the Mother of the members of Christ's Body, the Church. It is through Mary's consent to God's Word that Christ came into the world, and it is therefore through her consent that each of us has been given the opportunity to receive new life in him. In this way, Mary is mother to the Family of God.

As we have seen, the Church, too, is a mother. By the power of the Holy Spirit, given at Pentecost, the Church has been made to share in this new form of motherhood that is most perfectly realized in Mary. "The Church indeed, contemplating her hidden sanctity, imitating her charity, and faithfully fulfilling the Father's will, by receiving the word of God in faith becomes herself a mother."[36]

MARY, HELP OF CHRISTIANS

St. Roch Asking the Virgin Mary to Heal Victims of the Plague (detail) by David.

Since Mary is truly the Mother of Christ and Mother of the Church, her concern is for all her children united in Christ. Unlike a human mother, Mary will never lose patience with her children or reject them, no matter how wrongly they act. Her union with Jesus in holiness is so complete that she loves with a truly everlasting love.

This profound truth means that we can have a close and intimate relationship with Mary, one which can surpass all human understanding. We can sense this closeness in our hearts by saying the *Memorare* or *Hail Holy Queen* prayers when we are alone.

Mary is the Advocate who sees God face to face, bringing our petitions to him, because she is always truly and totally in Jesus' presence. We are able to establish a personal relationship with Mary through prayer. One way we can do this is by acquiring the habit of praying the Rosary, a mini-Gospel of the main events of the life of our Lord and our Lady, on a daily basis. It will not only bring us closer to Mary but will bring a greater understanding of the major events of Jesus' life.

Coronation of the Virgin by Veronese.
By looking at Mary, we see not only what the Church is right now but also what the Church will be for all eternity.

QUEEN OF HEAVEN

In the Book of Revelation, we find a striking description of Mary's heavenly enthronement as Queen of Heaven and Earth.

> **A great portent appeared in heaven, a woman clothed with the sun, with the moon under her feet, and on her head a crown of twelve stars....She brought forth a male child, one who is to rule all the nations. (Rev 12:1, 5)**

We can see in this image of the "woman clothed with the sun" the fullness of glory that Christ has bestowed upon his Blessed Mother. It is this same glory that awaits the Church at the end of time, for Mary's glory is nothing less than the manifestation of the graced communion that the Father offers all of us in Christ. Thus, Mary is more than just a type or foreshadowing of the Church; she is her archetype, the perfect model on which the Church is patterned.

By looking at Mary, we see not only what the Church is right now but also what the Church will be for all eternity. She is a holy and immaculate virgin, the bearer of the Word, called to give spiritual rebirth and nourishment to us whom Christ has chosen. The Church is not simply an organization, but a person, a mother in whom we are united as one Family of God.

In Mary, the Church has already entered into the fullness of heavenly glory, even as she labors here on earth to bring forth new sons and daughters of the Father. She is opposed at all times by the Devil, the "ancient serpent," who strives to overcome the Church as once he overcame Eve. But even in the face of persecution, the pilgrim Church on earth presses on in hope, for she knows that, with Christ, her victory is assured. As Christ has shown us, it is only through the suffering of love that we are able to enter into that glory which marks the completion of God's plan for our communion with him—when we, too, will be enthroned in Heaven.

CONCLUSION

Because of her life and cooperation with the special graces of God and because of her unique relationship with the Blessed Trinity, the Blessed Virgin Mary is entitled to special veneration. This honor is not the same as the worship offered to God; nonetheless, it is greater than the veneration offered to other saints.

Many people have noted that Mary speaks only twice in the New Testament. This reminds us that her life was one of deeds, one of service to her family, where she sought the will of God. Her life was not easy, but Mary did the chores associated with motherhood with humility and grace. She sought neither fame nor riches but only wished to do the will of her Son. Her example points to the fact that personal sanctity can be found in every life lived in service to others. In today's world, many people prefer fame and fortune to service of Jesus and his Church, in stark contrast to Mary who never sought anything for herself. Fame and fortune may come, but all are called to fulfill their everyday duties without regard to life's fleeting, human rewards.

The human perfection of the Blessed Mother should motivate everyone to imitation of her. Although no human being can duplicate her perfection, everyone can imitate her virtue to a great extent through cooperation with God's grace. Mary cares for us with maternal charity and intercedes with her Son to aid us in the quest for perfection through his manifold graces. As the good mother she is, she awaits our calls for her assistance and brings them personally to her beloved Son.

> After speaking of the Church, her origin, mission, and destiny, we can find no better way to conclude than by looking to Mary. In her we contemplate what the Church already is in her mystery on her own "pilgrimage of faith," and what she will be in the homeland at the end of her journey. There, "in the glory of the Most Holy and Undivided Trinity," "in the communion of all the saints,"[37] the Church is awaited by the one she venerates as Mother of her Lord and as her own mother.
>
> > In the meantime the Mother of Jesus, in the glory which she possesses in body and soul in heaven, is the image and beginning of the Church as it is to be perfected in the world to come. Likewise she shines forth on earth until the day of the Lord shall come, a sign of certain hope and comfort to the pilgrim People of God.[38] (CCC 972)

The Lamentation of Christ by Van Dyck
Mary's example points to the fact that personal sanctity can be found in every life lived in service to others.

The Granduca Madonna by Raphael.
Although no human being can duplicate Mary's perfection, everyone can imitate her virtue to a great extent through cooperation with God's grace.

LITANY OF LORETO

V. Lord, have mercy on us.

R. Christ, have mercy on us.

Lord, have mercy on us. Christ, hear us.

Christ, graciously hear us.

God, the Father of Heaven, have mercy on us.

God the Son, Redeemer of the world, have mercy on us.

God the Holy Spirit, have mercy on us.

Holy Trinity, one God, have mercy on us.

Holy Mary, pray for us.

Holy Mother of God, pray for us.

Holy Virgin of virgins, pray for us.

Mother of Christ, pray for us.

Mother of the Church, pray for us.

Mother of Divine Grace, pray for us.

Mother most pure, pray for us.

Mother most chaste, pray for us.

Mother inviolate, pray for us.

Mother undefiled, pray for us.

Mother most amiable, pray for us.

Mother most admirable, pray for us.

Mother of Good Counsel, pray for us.

Mother of Our Creator, pray for us.

Mother of Our Savior, pray for us.

Virgin most prudent, pray for us.

Virgin most venerable, pray for us.

Virgin most renowned, pray for us.

Virgin most powerful, pray for us.

Virgin most merciful, pray for us.

Virgin most faithful, pray for us.

Mirror of Justice, pray for us.

Seat of Wisdom, pray for us.

Cause of Our Joy, pray for us.

Spiritual Vessel, pray for us.

Vessel of Honor, pray for us.

Singular Vessel of Devotion, pray for us.

Mystical Rose, pray for us.

Tower of David, pray for us.

Tower of Ivory, pray for us.

House of Gold, pray for us.

Ark of the Covenant, pray for us.

Gate of Heaven, pray for us.

Morning star, pray for us.

Health of the Sick, pray for us.

Refuge of Sinners, pray for us.

Comforter of the Afflicted, pray for us.

Help of Christians, pray for us.

Queen of Angels, pray for us.

Queen of Patriarchs, pray for us.

Queen of Prophets, pray for us.

Queen of Apostles, pray for us.

Queen of Martyrs, pray for us.

Queen of Confessors, pray for us.

Queen of Virgins, pray for us.

Queen of All Saints, pray for us.

Queen Conceived without Original Sin, pray for us.

Queen Assumed into Heaven, pray for us.

Queen of the Most Holy Rosary, pray for us.

Queen of the Family, pray for us.

Queen of Peace, pray for us.

Lamb of God, who takes away the sins of the world, Spare us, O Lord.

Lamb of God, who takes away the sins of the world, graciously hear us, O Lord.

Lamb of God, who takes away the sins of the world, have mercy on us.

Pray for us, O holy Mother of God.

That we may be made worthy of the promises of Christ.

Let us Pray

Grant, we beseech Thee, O Lord God, that we thy servants may enjoy perpetual health of mind and body, and by the glorious intercession of Blessed Mary, Ever Virgin, may we be freed from present sorrow, and rejoice in eternal happiness. Through Christ our Lord. Amen.

SUPPLEMENTARY READING

1. The Magnificat of Our Lady

In the Eucharist the Church is completely united to Christ and his sacrifice, and makes her own the spirit of Mary. This truth can be understood more deeply by *re-reading the Magnificat* in a Eucharistic key. The Eucharist, like the Canticle of Mary, is first and foremost praise and thanksgiving. When Mary exclaims: "My soul magnifies the Lord and my spirit rejoices in God my Saviour," she already bears Jesus in her womb. She praises God "through" Jesus, but she also praises him "in" Jesus and "with" Jesus. This is itself the true "Eucharistic attitude."

At the same time Mary recalls the wonders worked by God in salvation history in fulfilment of the promise once made to the fathers (cf. Lk 1: 55), and proclaims the wonder that surpasses them all, the redemptive Incarnation. Lastly, the *Magnificat* reflects the eschatological tension of the Eucharist. Every time the Son of God comes again to us in the "poverty" of the sacramental signs of bread and wine, the seeds of that new history wherein the mighty are "put down from their thrones" and "those of low degree are exalted" (cf. Lk 1: 52), take root in the world. Mary sings of the "new Heavens" and the "new earth" which find in the Eucharist their anticipation and in some sense their programme and plan. The *Magnificat* expresses Mary's spirituality, and there is nothing greater than this spirituality for helping us to experience the mystery of the Eucharist. The Eucharist has been given to us so that our life, like that of Mary, may become completely a *Magnificat*!

— Pope Bl. John Paul II, *Ecclesia de Eucharistia*, 58

2. Mary, Mediatrix of All Grace

There is but one Mediator as we know from the words of the Apostle, "for there is one God and one mediator of God and men, the man Christ Jesus, who gave himself a redemption for all." (1 Tm 2, 5-6) The maternal duty of Mary toward men in no wise obscures or diminishes this unique mediation of Christ, but rather shows His power. For all the salvific influence of the Blessed Virgin on men originates, not from some inner necessity, but from the divine pleasure. It flows forth from the superabundance of the merits of Christ, rests on His mediation, depends entirely on it and draws all its power from it. In no way does it impede, but rather does it foster the immediate union of the faithful with Christ.

Predestined from eternity by that decree of divine providence which determined the Incarnation of the Word to be the Mother of God, the Blessed Virgin was in this earth the virgin Mother of the Redeemer, and above all others and in a singular way the generous associate and humble Handmaid of the Lord. She conceived, brought forth and nourished Christ. She presented Him to the Father in the temple, and was united with Him by compassion as He died on the Cross. In this singular way she cooperated by her obedience, faith, hope and burning charity in the work of the Saviour in giving back supernatural life to souls. Wherefore she is our mother in the order of grace.

This maternity of Mary in the order of grace began with the consent which she gave in faith at the Annunciation and which she sustained without wavering beneath the cross, and lasts until the eternal fulfillment of all the elect. Taken up to Heaven she did not lay aside this salvific duty, but by her constant intercession continued to bring us the gifts of eternal salvation.[39] By her maternal charity, she cares for the brethren of her Son, who still journey on earth surrounded by dangers and difficulties, until they are led into the happiness of their true home. Therefore the Blessed Virgin is invoked by the Church under the titles of Advocate, Auxiliatrix, Adjutrix, and Mediatrix.[40] This, however, is to be so understood that it neither takes away from nor adds anything to the dignity and efficaciousness of Christ the one Mediator.[41]

— *Lumen Gentium*, 60-62

VOCABULARY

ASSUMPTION
The dogma that recognizes the Blessed Virgin Mary's singular participation in her Son's Resurrection by which she was taken up body and soul into heavenly glory when the course of her earthly life was finished.

DOGMA
A revealed teaching of Christ defined to its fullest extent by the authority of the Church's Magisterium. The faithful are obliged to believe the truths of dogmas as defined by the Magisterium.

DORMITION
The "falling asleep" of the Blessed Virgin Mary. This term, used primarily in the East, refers to the end of her earthly life when she was assumed into Heaven. *See also* Assumption.

FIAT
Mary's response of consent at the Annunciation; a Latin word meaning "let it be done."

IMMACULATE CONCEPTION
In light of God's free choice of Mary from all eternity to be the Mother of his Son, this dogma was defined by Pope Bl. Pius IX in 1854. From the moment of her conception, Mary—by a singular grace of God and by virtue of the merits of Jesus Christ—was preserved from all stain of Original Sin.

PERPETUAL VIRGINITY
The dogma that recognizes Mary's virginity before, during, and after the conception and Birth of Jesus Christ.

THEOTOKOS
Greek for "Bearer of God," often translated "Mother of God." Used since the early centuries of the Church, this title of the Blessed Virgin Mary was defended by the Ecumenical Council of Ephesus (431).

VIRGIN BIRTH
The conception of Jesus in the womb of the Virgin Mary solely by the power of the Holy Spirit. The Church teaches not only that Mary conceived and gave birth to Jesus as a virgin, but also that she remained a virgin her entire life. *See also* Perpetual Virginity.

The Virgin and Child Enthroned among Angels and Saints by Gozzoli.
On the left St. Zenobius and St. John the Baptist are shown standing near the kneeling
St. Jerome. On the right stand St. Peter and St. Dominic while the kneeling figure is St. Francis.

STUDY QUESTIONS

1. What are the four Marian dogmas solemnly defined by the Church?

2. When does Mary's cousin St. Elizabeth call her the "mother of my Lord"?

3. According to Pope Bl. John Paul II, to what is Mary's *Fiat* analogous?

4. What does the Church teach about Mary's conception?

5. What was necessary in order for Mary to give consent to all that God would ask of her?

6. What does the Assumption teach us about Mary?

7. Within the Bible, when do we first encounter the Blessed Virgin Mary?

8. From what two effects of the Fall is Mary preserved by Jesus Christ?

9. Why is the fact of Mary's Perpetual Virginity important to the Church?

10. According to the *Catechism of the Catholic Church*, how does the Church bring forth new children?

11. Explain the meaning of the Marian title *Mother of the Church*.

12. When did Christ give Mary to us as the Mother of all the faithful?

13. What does it mean that Mary is the "archetype" of the Church?

PRACTICAL EXERCISES

1. At the moment of her conception (the Immaculate Conception), God gave the Blessed Virgin Mary the fullness of grace so that she could faithfully respond to all that he would ask of her. Why did Mary need God's grace in order to remain sinless throughout her life? Do you think it is possible to avoid sin and be virtuous without the help of God's grace? Discuss.

2. Research the apparitions of the Blessed Virgin Mary to St. Bernadette at Lourdes, France, in 1858. The local parish priest doubted Bernadette's story for a very long time but had a complete conversion after, at his request, Bernadette succeeded in getting the "Lady in White" to reveal who she was. What did the Lady tell Bernadette, and why was this significant to the parish priest?

3. The argument is often made—even by Christians who believe that Mary was a virgin before and at the time of the birth of her Son—that the Blessed Virgin Mary likely did not remain a virgin after the Birth of Christ. What does this argument take away from the figure of Mary? If she were not perpetually a virgin, how would that have changed her relationship with the People of God?

4. The Blessed Virgin Mary is the Mother of the Church, but she is also a perfect image of the Church. Explain how the image of Mary informs our understanding of the Church both on earth and in Heaven.

FROM THE CATECHISM

484 The Annunciation to Mary inaugurates "the fullness of time,"[42] the time of the fulfillment of God's promises and preparations. Mary was invited to conceive him in whom the "whole fullness of deity" would dwell "bodily."[43] The divine response to her question, "How can this be, since I know not man?" was given by the power of the Spirit: "The Holy Spirit will come upon you."[44]

487 What the Catholic faith believes about Mary is based on what it believes about Christ, and what it teaches about Mary illumines in turn its faith in Christ.

488 "God sent forth his Son," but to prepare a body for him,[45] he wanted the free co-operation of a creature. For this, from all eternity God chose for the mother of his Son a daughter of Israel, a young Jewish woman of Nazareth in Galilee, "a virgin betrothed to a man whose name was Joseph, of the house of David; and the virgin's name was Mary":[46]

> The Father of mercies willed that the Incarnation should be preceded by assent on the part of the predestined mother, so that just as a woman had a share in the coming of death, so also should a woman contribute to the coming of life.[47]

489 Throughout the Old Covenant the mission of many holy women *prepared* for that of Mary. At the very beginning there was Eve; despite her disobedience, she receives the promise of a posterity that will be victorious over the evil one, as well as the promise that she will be the mother of all the living.[48] By virtue of this promise, Sarah conceives a son in spite of her old age.[49] Against all human expectation God chooses those who were considered powerless and weak to show forth his faithfulness to his promises: Hannah, the mother of Samuel; Deborah; Ruth; Judith and Esther; and many other women.[50] Mary "stands out among the poor and humble of the Lord, who confidently hope for and receive salvation from him. After a long period of waiting the times are fulfilled in her, the exalted Daughter of Sion, and the new plan of salvation is established."[51]

491 Through the centuries the Church has become ever more aware that Mary, "full of grace" through God,[52] was redeemed from the moment of her conception. That is what the dogma of the Immaculate Conception confesses, as Pope Pius IX proclaimed in 1854:

> The most Blessed Virgin Mary was, from the first moment of her conception, by a singular grace and privilege of almighty God and by virtue of the merits of Jesus Christ, Savior of the human race, preserved immune from all stain of original sin.[53]

495 Called in the Gospels "the mother of Jesus," Mary is acclaimed by Elizabeth, at the prompting of the Spirit and even before the birth of her son, as "the mother of my Lord."[54] In fact, the One whom she conceived as man by the Holy Spirit, who truly became her Son according to the flesh, was none other than the Father's eternal Son, the second person of the Holy Trinity. Hence the Church confesses that Mary is truly "Mother of God" (*Theotokos*).[55]

496 From the first formulations of her faith, the Church has confessed that Jesus was conceived solely by the power of the Holy Spirit in the womb of the Virgin Mary, affirming also the corporeal aspect of this event: Jesus was conceived "by the Holy Spirit without human seed."[56] The Fathers see in the virginal conception the sign that it truly was the Son of God who came in a humanity like our own. Thus St. Ignatius of Antioch at the beginning of the second century says:

> You are firmly convinced about our Lord, who is truly of the race of David according to the flesh, Son of God according to the will and power of God, truly born of a virgin...he was truly nailed to a tree for us in his flesh under Pontius Pilate...he truly suffered, as he is also truly risen.[57]

FROM THE CATECHISM Continued

499 The deepening of faith in the virginal motherhood led the Church to confess Mary's real and perpetual virginity even in the act of giving birth to the Son of God made man.[58] In fact, Christ's birth "did not diminish his mother's virginal integrity but sanctified it."[59] And so the liturgy of the Church celebrates Mary as *Aeiparthenos*, the "Ever-virgin."[60]

507 At once virgin and mother, Mary is the symbol and the most perfect realization of the Church: "the Church indeed...by receiving the word of God in faith becomes herself a mother. By preaching and Baptism she brings forth sons, who are conceived by the Holy Spirit and born of God, to a new and immortal life. She herself is a virgin, who keeps in its entirety and purity the faith she pledged to her spouse."[61]

ENDNOTES - CHAPTER EIGHT

1. *Credo in Missa Romana: Symbolum Constantinopolitanum: Mansi* 3, 566. Cf. *Conc. Ephesinum*, ibid. 4, 1130 (*necnon* ibid. 2, 665; 4, 1071); *Conc. Chalcedonense*, ibid. 7, 111-116; *Con. Constantinopolitanum* II, ibid. 9, 375-396.
2. *Canon Missae Romanae*.
3. St. Augustine, De Sancta Virginitate, 6: PL 40, 399.
4. *LG* 68.
5. Jn 2: 4.
6. Jn 19: 26-27.
7. Rev 12: 1.
8. Lk 1: 28-38; cf. Rom 1: 5.
9. Lk 1: 43.
10. Ibid.
11. Lk 11: 27-28.
12. Lk 1: 38.
13. *Ecclesia de Eucharistia*, 55.
14. *LG* 62.
15. Pius IX, *Ineffabilis Deus* (1854): DS 2803.
16. Eph 1: 4.
17. CCC 490.
18. *LG* 53; 63.
19. Gn 3: 15.
20. Jn 2: 4; 19: 26.
21. *LG* 59; cf. Pius XII, *Munificentissimus Deus* (1950): DS 3903; cf. Rev 19: 16.
22. Byzantine Liturgy, *Troparion*, Feast of the Dormition, August 15.
23. CPB 177.

24. *Redemptoris Custos*, 1.
25. Mt 1: 20.
26. CCC 499.
27. Lk 1: 38.
28. CCC 500.
29. CCC 501.
30. *LG* 61.
31. St. John Chrysostom, *Catecheses* 3, 13-19.
32. *Redemptoris Mater*, 24; *LG* 55.
33. Lk 2: 34-35.
34. Gn 3: 20.
35. *Redemptoris Mater*, 24; cf. St. Leo the Great, *Tractatus 26, de Natale Domini*, 2: CCL 138, 126.
36. *LG* 64.
37. *LG* 69.
38. *LG* 68; cf. 2 Pt 3: 10.
39. Cf. Kleutgen, *Textus Reformatus de Mysterio Verbi Incarnatii* IV: Mansi 53, 290; cf. St. Andrew Cret., *In Nat. Mariae, Sermo* 4: PG 97, 865 A. – St. Germanus Constantinop., *In Annunt. Deiparae*: PG 98, 321 BC; *In Dorm. Deiparae*, III: col. 361 D. St. John of Damascus, *In Dorm. B. V. Mariae*, Hom. 1, 8: PG 96, 712 BC-713 A.
40. Cfr. Leo XIII, Encyclical *Adiutricem Populi*, Sept. 5, 1895: ASS 15 (1895-96), p. 303. – St. Pius X, Encyclical *Ad Diem Illum*, Febr. 2, 1904: *Acta*, I, p. 154 – Denz. 1978 A (3370). Pius XI, Encyclical *Miserentissimus*, May 8, 1928: AAS 20 (1928) p. 178. Pius XII, *Nuntius Radioph.*, May 8, 1946: AAS 38 (1946) p. 266.

41. St. Ambrose, *Epist.* 63: PL 16, 1218.
42. Gal 4: 4.
43. Col 2: 9.
44. Lk 1: 34-35 (Gk.).
45. Gal 4: 4; Heb 10: 5.
46. Lk 1: 26-27.
47. *LG* 56; cf. *LG* 61.
48. Cf. Gn 3: 15, 20.
49. Cf. Gn 18: 10-14; 21: 1-2.
50. Cf. 1 Cor 1: 17; 1 Sm 1.
51. *LG* 55.
52. Lk 1: 28.
53. Pius IX, *Ineffabilis Deus* (1854): DS 2803.
54. Lk 1: 43; Jn 2: 1; 19: 25; cf. Mt 13: 55; et al.
55. Council of Ephesus (431): DS 251.
56. Council of the Lateran (649): DS 503; cf. DS 10-64.
57. St. Ignatius of Antioch, *Ad Smyrn* 1-2: Apostolic Fathers, ed. J. B. Lightfoot (London: Macmillan, 1889), II/2, 289-293; SCh 10, 154-156; cf. Rom 1: 3; Jn 1: 13.
58. Cf. DS 291, 294, 427, 442, 503, 571, 1880.
59. *LG* 57.
60. Cf. *LG* 52.
61. *LG* 64; cf. 63.

ART AND PHOTO CREDITS

Cover

Second Vatican Council, St. Peter's Basilica, Vatican; Archivo Oronoz

Front Pages

iii   *See* Cover Credit
iv   *Commission to St. Peter*, Illumination from the *Pericopes of Henry II*, ca. 1002-1012; Bayerische Staatsbibliothek, Munich, Germany
viii   *Washing of the Feet*, Giovanni Agostino da Lodi; Gallerie dell'Accademia, Venice, Italy
x   *God the Father with Four Angels and the Dove of the Holy Spirit*, Giovanni Francesco da Rimini; Brooklyn Museum, New York

Chapter 1

1   *Separation of the Earth from the Waters* (detail), Michelangelo; Sistine Chapel, Vatican
3   *Holy Trinity* (detail), Hendrick van Balen; Sint-Jacobskerk, Antwerp, Belgium
4   *God Creating the Sun, the Moon and the Stars in the Firmament*, Jan Brueghel II; Private Collection
5   *Paradise*, Lucas Cranach the Elder; Kunsthistorisches Museum, Vienna, Austria
6   *God Presents Eve to Adam* (detail from *Triptych of Garden of Earthly Delights*), Hieronymus Bosch; Museo del Prado, Madrid, Spain
7   *St. Irenæus of Lyons*; AG Archives
8   *God Resting After Creation*, Byzantine Mosaic; Cathedral of Monreale, Sicily, Italy
9   *Adam and Eve's Life of Toil*, Panel from *Grabow Altarpiece*, Master Bertram; Kunsthalle, Hamburg, Germany
10   *The Dove Returns to Noah*, James Tissot; The Jewish Museum, New York, New York
11   *The Departure of Abraham*, Joseph Molnar; Hungarian National Gallery, Budapest, Hungary
12   *The Sacrifice of Isaac*, Caravaggio; Galleria degli Uffizi, Florence, Italy
13   (left) *Isaac Bears the Wood for His Sacrifice*, James Tissot; The Jewish Museum, New York, New York;
     (right) *The Ascent to Calvary* (detail), Tintoretto; Scuola Grande di San Rocco, Venice, Italy
14   *Moses Before the Burning Bush*, Domenico Feti; Kunsthistorisches Museum, Vienna, Austria
15   *The Signs on the Door*, James Tissot; The Jewish Museum, New York, New York
16   *The Plague of Lice, the Plague of Frogs, the Plague on Livestock, the Plague of Flies*; Illustration from *The Golden Haggadah*, Scenes from Exodus, folio 12v, MS 27210, The British Library, London, England
17   *Departure of the Israelites*, David Roberts; Birmingham Museum and Art Gallery, Birmingham, England
18   *The Israelites' Camp and Wilderness Temple at Mount Sinai*, French School, eighteenth century; Private Collection
19   *Joshua Passing the River Jordan with the Ark of the Covenant*, Benjamin West; Art Gallery of New South Wales, Sydney, Australia
20   *Saul Is Anointed King By Samuel*, Michiel van der Borch; Illumination from Maerlant's "Rhimebible" of Utrecht, MMW 10B, Museum Meermanno Westreenianum, The Hague, Netherlands
21   *Anointing of David*, Felix-Joseph Barrias; Musee du Petit-Palais, Paris, France
22   *King David Playing the Zither*, Andrea Celesti; Private Collection
24   *The Idolatry of Solomon*, Sebastiano Conca; Museo del Prado, Madrid, Spain; Archivo Oronoz
25   *Moses*, Henry Schile; Library of Congress Prints and Photographs Division, Washington, D.C.
26   *The First Commandment*, Lucas Cranach the Elder; Lutherhalle, Wittenberg, Germany
27   *The Water Rushing From the Rock*, Raphael; Raphael's Loggia, Palazzi Pontifici, Vatican
31   *Madonna and Child with the Lamb of God*, Cesare da Sesto; Museo Poldi Pezzoli, Milan, Italy
33   *Abraham and the Three Angels*, James Tissot; The Jewish Museum, New York, New York

Chapter 2

35   *The Last Supper*, Carl H. Bloch; Frederiksborg Palace Chapel, Denmark
37   *The Miraculous Draught of Fishes*, Jacopo Bassano; National Gallery of Art, Washington, D.C.
38   *The Sermon of the Beatitudes* (detail), James Tissot; Brooklyn Museum, New York
39   *St. Augustine* (detail), Joos Van Wassenhove; Musée du Louvre, Paris, France
40   *Incarnation of Jesus*, Piero di Cosimo; Galleria degli Uffizi, Florence, Italy
41   *The Adoration of the Magi*, Quentin Massys; Metropolitan Museum of Art, New York, New York
43   *The Sower*, James Tissot; Brooklyn Museum, New York
44   *Christ Healing the Sick* (*Le Christ Guerissant un Malade*), Mathieu Ignace van Brée; Private Collection
45   *The Last Supper*, Sassetta; Pinacoteca Nazionale, Siena, Italy
47   *The Emmaus Disciples*, Abraham Bloemaert; Musées Royaux des Beaux-Arts, Brussels, Belgium
48   *Communion of the Apostles* (detail), Luca Signorelli; Museo Diocesano, Cortona, Italy
49   *Lamentation*, Andrea Solario; National Gallery of Art, Washington, D.C.
50   *The Resurrection of Christ*, Paolo Veronese; Gemäldegalerie, Dresden, Germany
51   *The Ascension*, James Tissot; Brooklyn Museum, New York

ART AND PHOTO CREDITS

ART AND PHOTO CREDITS

Chapter 4

107 *St. Peter's Basilica*, "Good Shepherd" Sunday Mass, May 7, 2006; ©L'Osservatore Romano

109 *St. Paul of the Cross Church*, Park Ridge, Illinois; Julie Koenig, photographer

110 *First Communion*, Wojciech Dubis, photographer; Midwest Theological Forum Archives

111 *St. Peter's Square, Canonization of St. Josemaria Escriva*; Wojciech Dubis, photographer; Midwest Theological Forum Archives

112 *The Last Supper* (detail), Simon Vouet; Palazzo Apostolico, Loreto, Italy

113 *Pope Benedict XVI Celebrates Mass*, November 5, 2009; ©L'Osservatore Romano

115 *St. Peter's Basilica, Ordination of Twenty-nine Deacons by Pope Benedict XVI*, April 27, 2008; ©L'Osservatore Romano

116 *St. Peter Enthroned with Saints*, Cima da Conegliano; Pinacoteca di Brera, Milan, Italy

119 *Pontifical Swiss Guard*, Wojciech Dubis, photographer; Midwest Theological Forum Archives

120 *The Martyrdom of St. Ignatius*; Midwest Theological Forum Archives

121 (top left) *St. Louis Cathedral*; Archdiocese of New Orleans, Louisiana, 2004; Rafal Konieczny, photographer
(bottom right) *Bishop's Chair*; Basilica of St. John Lateran, Rome, Italy; Ernie Bello, photographer

122 *Second Vatican Council*, St. Peter's Basilica, Vatican; Archivo Oronoz

123 *Pope Benedict XVI Ordains Twenty-two Men to the Priesthood*, St. Peter's Basilica, April 29, 2007; ©L'Osservatore Romano

124 *St. Mary of the Angels Church*, Chicago, Illinois; Julie Koenig, photographer

125 *Christ Handing the Keys to St. Peter* (detail), Pietro Perugino; Sistine Chapel, Vatican

127 *St. John on Patmos*, Berto di Giovanni; Galleria Nazionale dell'Umbria, Perugia, Italy

128 *Immaculate Conception*, Peter Paul Rubens; Museo del Prado, Madrid, Spain

129 *St. Augustine*; Midwest Theological Forum Archives

131 *Pope John Paul II in Ireland*, 1979; ©L'Osservatore Romano

132 *Pope Benedict XVI at the Aida Refugee Camp*, May 13, 2009, Holy Land Visit; ©L'Osservatore Romano

133 *The Last Sermon of Our Lord*, James Tissot; Brooklyn Museum, New York

134 *Pope St. Clement Adoring the Trinity*, Giovanni Battista Tiepolo; Alte Pinakothek, Munich, Germany

136 *Pope Benedict XVI at the Western Wall of Jerusalem*, May 12, 2009, Holy Land Visit; ©L'Osservatore Romano

140 *St. Jerome as a Scholar*, El Greco; Metropolitan Museum of Art, New York

142 *Papal Bull: Humanæ Salutis*; Vatican Document Archives

143 *Statue of St. Peter*, Arnolfo di Cambio; St. Peter's Basilica, Vatican

Chapter 5

145 *Adoration of the Trinity*, Vicente López y Portaña; Private Collection

146 *St. Peter's Basilica and Square, the Canonization of St. Josemaria Escriva*; Wojciech Dubis, photographer; Midwest Theological Forum Archives

147 *The Voice from on High*, James Tissot; Brooklyn Museum, New York

148 *Christ Handing the Keys to St. Peter* (detail), Master of the Legend of the Holy Prior; Wallraf-Richartz Museum, Cologne, Germany

149 *The Savior*, Juan de Juanes; Museo del Prado, Madrid, Spain; Archivo Oronoz

150 *Pope St. Leo the Great*; Mosaic, Papal Basilica of St. Paul Outside the Walls, Rome, Italy

151 *The Council of Nicæa*; Church of San Martino, Rome, Italy; Archivo Oronoz

152 *Pope Benedict XVI visits an agricultural area in Guaratinguetá, São Paulo, Brazil*; Valter Campanato/ABr, photographer

153 *Baptism of Christ*, Piero della Francesca; National Gallery, London, England

154 *St. Basil the Great and St. Athanasius*, Alonso Sanchez Coello; Royal Monastery of St. Lawrence of Escorial, Madrid, Spain; Archivo Oronoz

155 *Emperor Theodosius Exiling Nestorius*; Fresco, sixteenth century church, Cyprus; AG Archives

156 *Martin Luther Nailing His Ninety-Five Theses to the Wittenburg Church Door*, Hugo Vogel; Archiv Für Kunst und Geschichte, Berlin, Germany

157 *Pope Paul VI meets with Patriarch Athenagoras I*; Archivo Oronoz

158 (top right) *Pope John Paul II in Athens*, 2001; AG Archives
(bottom left) *Pope Benedict XVI at Memorial Ceremonies at the Auschwitz-Birkenau Concentration Camp*, 2006; Archive of the Chancellery of the President of the Republic of Poland, Lech Kaczyński

159 *St. Augustine and St. Monica*, Ary Scheffer; Musée du Louvre, Paris, France

160 *The Pentecost*, Unknown French Goldsmith (active 1150-60 in Meuse Valley); Metropolitan Museum of Art, New York

161 *The Resurrected Christ*, Salvator Rosa; Musée Condé, Chantilly, France

162 *St. Cyril of Jerusalem*, Icon; Orthodox Church in America, www.oca.org

ART AND PHOTO CREDITS

163 *Early Church Fathers*, Icon; Midwest Theological Forum Archives
165 *Appearance While the Apostles Are at Table*, Duccio; Museo dell'Opera del Duomo, Siena, Italy
166 *Pope Benedict XVI Ordains a New Bishop, Mons. Giorgio Corbellini*, 2009; ©L'Osservatore Romano
167 *Crucifixion*, Titian; Museo Civico, Ancona, Italy
173 *The Black Madonna of Czestochowa*, Icon; Jasna Góra Monastery, Czestochowa, Poland

Chapter 6

177 *Last Communion of St. Lucy*, Giovanni Battista Tiepolo; Santi Apostoli, Venice, Italy
178 *Christ Carrying the Cross*, Luis de Morales; Museo del Pariarca, Valencia, Spain
179 *The Baptism of Christ* (detail), Jean Baptiste Camille Corot; Church of St. Nicolas-du-Chardonnet, Paris, France
180 *St. Peter Enthroned*, Guido di Graziano; Pinacoteca Nazionale di Siena, Italy
181 *Christ Handing the Keys to St. Peter*, Peter Paul Rubens; AG Archives
182 *St. Peter's Square, Canonization of St. Josemaria Escriva*; Wojciech Dubis, photographer; Midwest Theological Forum Archives
183 *The Fall of Jericho* (detail), Jean Fouquet; From the French Translation of the work of Flavius Josephus; Bibliotheque Nationale, Paris, France
184 *Midtown*, Chicago, Illinois; Julie Koenig, photographer
185 *Jesus Preaching on the Mount* (detail), Gustave Doré; Private Collection
186 *St. Gianna Beretta Molla* with Pierluigi, November 1957; www.saintgianna.org
187 The *Ecce Agnus Dei* during the Mass; celebrated by Fr. Mark Borkowski, St. Josaphat Catholic Church, Detroit, Michigan; Darth Malus, photographer
189 *Good Friday Liturgy—Intercessory Prayers*, Cistercian Monks; Abbey Heiligenkreuz, Austria; Melchior, photographer
190 *St. Mary of the Angels Church*, Chicago, Illinois; Julie Koenig, photographer
191 *Sacrament of Baptism*, Wojciech Dubis, photographer; Midwest Theological Forum Archives
192 *The Miracle of the Loaves and Fishes*, James Tissot; Brooklyn Museum, New York
193 *St. Paul of the Cross Church*, Park Ridge, Illinois; Julie Koenig, photographer
194 *The Disciples of Jesus Baptize*, James Tissot; Brooklyn Museum, New York
195 (top right) *Baptism of Christ* (detail), Pietro Perugino; Sistine Chapel, Vatican
    (bottom left) *The Baptism of the Neophytes* (detail), Masaccio; Cappella Brancacci, Santa Maria del Carmine, Florence, Italy
197 *Sacrament of Confirmation*, St. Paul the Apostle Catholic Church; Midwest Theological Forum Archives
198 *Pentecost*, Duccio; Museo dell'Opera del Duomo, Siena, Italy
199 *The Last Supper* (detail), Giovanni Battista Tiepolo; Musée du Louvre, Paris, France
200 *Adoration of the Lamb* (detail), *The Ghent Altarpiece*, (central panel, lower tier), Jan Van Eyck; Cathedral of St. Bavo, Ghent, Belgium
201 *The Last Supper*, Juan de Juanes; Museo del Prado, Madrid, Spain; Archivo Oronoz
202 *Supper at Emmaus* (detail), Hendrick Terbrugghen; Schloss Sanssouci, Berlin
203 *The Liturgy of the Eucharist*, St. Mary of the Angels Church, Chicago, Illinois; Julie Koenig, photographer
204 *St. John Nepomucene*, Stained Glass; St. Stanislaus Catholic Church, Warsaw, North Dakota; Stephanie Walker, photographer; AG Archives
205 *Cain and Abel*, Titian; Santa Maria della Salute, Venice, Italy
206 *Christ Healing the Sick*, Benjamin West; Tate Gallery, London, England
207 *Seven Sacraments Altarpiece; Right Wing* (detail), Rogier van der Weyden; Koninklijk Museum voor Schone Kunsten, Antwerp
208 *Sacrament of Holy Orders*, Ordination to the Priesthood; Photo courtesy of Fr. Marty Miller; Midwest Theological Forum Archives
209 *Sacrament of Matrimony*, Wojciech Dubis, photographer; Midwest Theological Forum Archives
210 *The Marriage of the Virgin* (detail), Raphael; Pinacoteca di Brera, Milan
211 *Pope John Paul II Kneels in Prayer at the Vatican*; ©L'Osservatore Romano
212 *The Lord's Prayer*, James Tissot; Brooklyn Museum, New York
213 *Prayers of Devotion*, Wojciech Dubis, photographer; Midwest Theological Forum Archives
214 *St. Jerome*, Pietro Perugino; Galleria Nazionale dell'Umbria, Perugia, Italy
215 *World Youth Day, Palm Sunday*, April 5, 2009, St. Peter's Square; ©L'Osservatore Romano
216 *Scenes from the Life of St. Francis* (detail), Scene 7, Benozzo Gozzoli; Apsidal chapel, San Francesco, Montefalco, Italy
217 *Pope John Paul II in Assisi, Italy*, 2002; ©L'Osservatore Romano
219 *St. Josemaria Escriva*; Midwest Theological Forum Archives
220 *St. Thomas More*, Peter Paul Rubens; Prado Museum, Madrid, Spain; Archivo Oronoz
221 *Catholic High School Students Volunteering at a Nutrition Center*; Julie Koenig, photographer
223 *St. Rose of Lima*, Carlo Dolci; Palazzo Pitti, Florence, Italy
224 *St. Benedict* (detail), Fra Angelico; Museo di San Marco, Florence, Italy
225 *St. Mary of the Angels Church*, Chicago, Illinois; Julie Koenig, photographer

ART AND PHOTO CREDITS

228 *St. Dominic and His Friars Fed by Angels* (detail), Giovanni Antonio Sogliani; Convent of San Marco, Florence, Italy

229 *Family at Mass*; Design Pics, Stock Image

236 *Station of the Cross, No. 7: Jesus Falls the Second Time*; Sts. Peter and Paul Church, Naperville, Illinois; Julie Koenig, photographer;

239 *Crucifixion*, Andrea da Firenze; Pinacoteca, Vatican

Chapter 7

241 *The Incarnation with Six Saints*, Fra Bartolomeo; Musée du Louvre, Paris, France

242 *Our Lord Jesus Christ* (detail), James Tissot; Brooklyn Museum, New York

243 *Virgin and Child with Saints*, Boccaccio Boccaccino; Gallerie dell'Accademia, Venice, Italy

244 *Madonna with Angels and Saints, The Maesta* (front central panel), Duccio; Museo dell'Opera del Duomo, Siena, Italy

245 *St. John Chrysostom Statue*, St. Patrick's Cathedral, New York City; Dr. Swan, photographer

246 *St. Vincent de Paul Helping the Plague-Ridden*, Antoine Ansiaux; Musee de l'Assistance Publique, Hopitaux de Paris, France

247 *Virgin and Child in Glory with Saints*, Giovanni Battista Carlone; Private Collection

248 *St. Therese of Lisieux*; Midwest Theological Forum Archives

249 *St. Paul Preaching in Athens* (detail), Raphael; Victoria and Albert Museum, London, England

250 *Last Judgment*, Michelangelo; Sistine Chapel, Vatican

251 *The Last Judgment*, Jacob van Campen; St. Joriskerk, Amersfoort, Netherlands

252 *St. John the Evangelist on the Island of Patmos, St. John Altarpiece* (right wing), Hans Memling; Memlingmuseum, Sint-Janshospitaal, Bruges, Belgium

253 *Pope Benedict XVI Celebrates Mass,* Canonization of Friar Galvão, May 11, 2007, São Paulo, Brazil; Agência Brasil, Fabio Pozzebom/ABr

254 *Christ Pantocrator and the Last Judgment*, Mosaic; Baptistry of St. John, Florence, Italy

255 *St. Francis Rescuing Souls from Purgatory*; Native American, ca. 1805-1850, New Mexico; Brooklyn Museum, New York

256 *Tombstone in the Catacomb of St. Domitilla*; *The Oxford Illustrated History of Christianity*, John McManners, Editor, 1990

257 *Hell*, panel from the *Triptych of Earthly Vanity and Divine Salvation*, Hans Memling; Musée des Beaux-Arts, Strasbourg, France

258 *Coronation of the Virgin*, Fra Filippo Lippi; Duomo, Spoleto, Italy

259 *The Trinity in Glory*, Titian; Museo del Prado, Madrid, Spain

260 *The Archangel St. Michael* (detail), Jaume Huguet; Museu Nacional d'Art de Catalunya, Barcelona, Spain

261 *Jesus Goes Up Alone onto a Mountain to Pray* (detail), James Tissot; Brooklyn Museum, New York

262 *The Resurrection of Christ*, Tintoretto; Scuola Grande di San Rocco, Venice, Italy

264 *The Charity of St. Elizabeth of Hungary* (detail), Edmund Blair Leighton; Private Collection

265 *Martyrdom of St. Stephen*, Giorgio Vasari; Pinacoteca, Vatican

266 *Disputation on the Trinity*, Andrea del Sarto; Galleria Palatina (Palazzo Pitti), Florence, Italy

268 *Pope John Paul II and Bl. Teresa of Calcutta*; ©L'Osservatore Romano

Chapter 8

269 *Madonna in the Forest*, Fra Filippo Lippi; Staatliche Museen, Berlin, Germany

271 *Annunciation*, Orazio Gentileschi; Galleria Sabauda, Turin, Italy

273 *Eleusa*, Icon, seventeenth century; Historic Museum, Sanok, Poland

274 *Annunciation* (detail), Fra Angelico; Museo Diocesano, Cortona, Italy

275 *Immaculate Conception*, Mariano Salvador de Maella; Museo del Prado, Madrid, Spain

276 *Immaculate Conception*, Bartolomé Esteban Murillo; Museo del Prado, Madrid, Spain

277 *Virgin and Child* (detail), *San Pietro Martire Triptych*, Fra Angelico; Museo di San Marco, Florence, Italy

278 *Assumption of the Virgin*, Don Silvestro dei Gherarducci; Pinacoteca, Vatican

279 *St. Joseph with the Infant Jesus* (detail), Guido Reni; The Hermitage, St. Petersburg, Russia

280 *St. James the Less*, Icon; AG Archives

281 *Coronation of the Virgin*, Paolo Veneziano; National Gallery of Art, Washington, D.C.

282 *What Our Lord Saw from the Cross*, James Tissot; Brooklyn Museum, New York

283 *St. Roch Asking the Virgin Mary to Heal Victims of the Plague* (detail), Jacques-Louis David; Musée des Beaux-Arts, Marseille, France

284 *Coronation of the Virgin*, Paolo Veronese; San Sebastiano, Venice, Italy

285 *The Lamentation of Christ*, Sir Anthony Van Dyck; Koninklijk Museum voor Schone Kunsten, Antwerp, Belgium

286 *The Madonna del Granduca*, Raphael; Galleria Palatina (Palazzo Pitti), Florence, Italy

289 *The Virgin and Child Enthroned among Angels and Saints*, Benozzo Gozzoli; The National Gallery, London, England

INDEX

INDEX